Making Amends for Historic Wrongs

Making Amends for Historic Wrongs

Reparative Justice and the Problem of the Past

MAYO MORAN

Professor of Law and Irving & Rosalie Abella Chair in Justice & Equality, Faculty of Law, University of Toronto, Toronto, ON, Canada

OXFORD
UNIVERSITY PRESS

OXFORD
UNIVERSITY PRESS

Oxford University Press is a department of the University of Oxford. It furthers the University's objective of excellence in research, scholarship, and education by publishing worldwide. Oxford is a registered trade mark of Oxford University Press in the UK and in certain other countries.

Published in the United States of America by Oxford University Press
198 Madison Avenue, New York, NY 10016, United States of America.

Library of Congress Cataloging-in-Publication Data
Names: Moran, Mayo author
Title: Making amends for historic wrongs : reparative justice and the problem of the past / Mayo Moran.
Description: New York : Oxford University Press, 2025. |
Includes bibliographical references and index.
Identifiers: LCCN 2025038692 (print) | LCCN 2025038693 (ebook) |
ISBN 9780190927264 hardback | ISBN 9780190927288 epub | ISBN 9780190927271 updf |
ISBN 9780190927295 online
Subjects: LCSH: Reparations for historical injustices | Reparation (Criminal justice) | LCGFT: Law materials
Classification: LCC KZ6785 .M67 2026 (print) | LCC KZ6785 (ebook) |
DDC 347/.077—dc23/eng/20250820
LC record available at https://lccn.loc.gov/2025038692
LC ebook record available at https://lccn.loc.gov/2025038693

DOI: 10.1093/9780190927295.001.0001

Printed by Lightning Source, Inc., United States of America

The manufacturer's authorized representative in the EU for product safety is Oxford University Press España S.A. of Parque Empresarial San Fernando de Henares, Avenida de Castilla, 2 – 28830 Madrid (www.oup.es/en or product.safety@oup.com). OUP España S.A. also acts as importer into Spain of products made by the manufacturer.

For Karen

Contents

Acknowledgments

The person who most deserves my gratitude for this book is someone I can no longer thank—my dear University of Toronto law faculty colleague and soul mate, Karen Knop. She died suddenly in 2022, and I was not able to properly thank her for encouraging me to keep writing despite the administrative jobs that took up so much of my time. Karen was an outstanding interlocutor. I talked through the early stages of this project with her, and she was the one who pressed me to connect with Jamie Berezin at Oxford University Press. Without her constant interest, unfailing support, and brilliant insights, this book would not have happened, and it breaks my heart that I cannot tell her that now.

I have also benefited greatly from ever interesting and challenging conversations with my other outstanding colleagues at the University of Toronto Faculty of Law, beginning with my doctoral supervisor, Ernie Weinrib, and committee members Arthur Ripstein, and Bruce Chapman, all of who have remained sources of wisdom and inspiration. Among my many other wonderful colleagues, I am especially grateful for the support and insight of David Dyzenhaus. It was during our early collaborations on the Chinese Canadian Head Tax case that I first started to think about the shifting understanding of the past, and I have been fortunate to have had a continuing conversation about many of these topics with David in the years since then.

My work on Canada's groundbreaking residential schools processes also profoundly shaped my thinking about historic injustice. I want to acknowledge my colleagues who work on those issues, especially John Borrows, Kent Roach, and Douglas Sanderson. As I discuss in the text, the residential schools processes—imperfect though they are—would never have happened without the courageous and wise leadership of former National Chief of the Assembly of First Nations, Phil Fontaine. Working alongside the Honorable Frank Iacobucci, they created a new model for addressing historic wrongs. It is courage like that of Phil Fontaine and so many other survivors that has been the driving force of our changing view of old wrongs. My approach to historic injustice was also profoundly shaped by my experience as Chair of the Residential Schools Oversight Committee, and I learned a great deal from the many people involved in that process, from the Chief Adjudicators Dan Ish and Dan Shapiro, to the Honorable Warren Winkler, to the members of the Oversight Committee, the staff, and especially the survivors.

I have been fortunate throughout this work to have had generous support from the University of Toronto law school, and I am especially grateful to Dean Jutta Brunnée who, on top of everything else, helped me refine the title of my book. Two years ago, I was honored to be awarded the inaugural Irving and Rosalie Abella Chair in Justice and Equality and am deeply grateful to the law school, the supporters of the chair, and especially to the amazing Rosie and Itchie who have been friends and sources of inspiration for much of my thinking about rectifying injustice. I am also grateful for the support that the project received early on from the Social Sciences and Humanities Research Council. The President's Impact Award and the Carolyn Tuohy Public Policy Award from the University of Toronto, as well as Trinity College, provided important support for the final stages of this project.

My colleagues and collaborators on the Restitution Dialogues— Alexander Herman, Leora Bilsky and Jennifer Orange—have also helped to shape my approach to these issues. Early versions of some of this work benefited greatly from the input at presentations, especially at the Minerva Centre for Human Rights, the University of Helsinki and Bonn University. Among many others, my conversations with Leora Bilsky and Matthias Weller have been particularly important. Similarly, I am grateful to the reviewers and editors at the *University of Toronto Law Journal* and the *Georgetown Journal of Gender and the Law* for the refinement of earlier versions of some parts of this work. I also especially benefited from the suggestions of one of the anonymous reviewers for OUP who was very helpful and encouraged me to look at the restitution side of the issues as well.

I am also indebted to the work of many outstanding research assistants from the University of Toronto Faculty of Law who assisted with various parts of the work. I owe a special debt of gratitude to Kate Mitchell whose assistance was invaluable in the final year of writing and manuscript preparation. At Trinity College, I was fortunate to benefit from the support of Cera Maugey who was especially helpful with technology. I am also grateful for the support and guidance I received from OUP, beginning with Jamie Berezin and finishing with Brian Stone and Cassidy Schumm.

I have to reserve a special note of gratitude for the outstanding support of Judith Lavin. She was my executive assistant and right-hand woman through all of my years as dean of the Faculty of Law and then as provost of Trinity College. Judith always carved time out of my busy schedule for me to write, assisted with coordinating research assistants and most importantly relieved me of as much of the administrative burden as possible so that I was able to find time to think and write, despite my demanding schedule. She was a joy to work with, and I could not have done it without her.

My friends and family have also been unfailingly supportive, especially over the last year when my demanding writing schedule often necessitated forgoing other adventures. I am especially grateful to my husband Stuart Payne and my son, Aidan Cunningham. Their keen interest and constant encouragement ensured I got this project across the line and gave us all a reason to celebrate.

1
How the Past Came Back to Haunt Us

Introduction

Something is going on with the past. Not too long ago, complaints about what happened in the past were dismissed with statements like 'let sleeping dogs lie' or 'forgive and forget' or 'time heals all wounds' Conventional wisdom told us that whatever terrible events happened in the past, we should try to ignore them and move on. Only by putting things behind us would we be able to heal. Law too was unmoved by old grievances. Courts waved away survivors of assault, rape, torture, and theft, telling them it was just too late. But that has changed. The problems of our past are coming back to haunt us, and many of them now count among the most pressing contemporary challenges.

We have always known that history was replete with terrible events. Since Thucydides at least, war and violence have formed much of the raw material that historians pore over. His modern counterparts too often focus on terrible events like the Holocaust, racial violence, slavery, genocide, and colonialism. Our interest in the troubling events of the past is not new—what is new is how we understand those events. Until recently, they were horrific or terrible. But now they are not just wrong, they are *wrongs*. They have, in short, become injustices, and, as such, they demand repair. Institutions large and small are being confronted with their pasts and face complex reckonings with what their forebearers did or did not do. They struggle to find ways to make amends.

From the Holocaust to child sexual abuse to colonialism, from wartime atrocities to slavery, demands to rectify old wrongs pose unsettling modern challenges. Nearly two decades ago while tracing what was then called the residential schools litigation, it became apparent to me that our approach to the past was undergoing a larger shift. At that time, as I discuss in the following chapters, it was possible to see the early elements of our rethinking of historic wrongs. But the idea that there could actually be responsibility to make amends for old wrongs was generally seen as far-fetched and was met with constant objections and often derision. And there was at most a trickle of redress activity. However, over the past two decades, the activity surrounding historic wrongs has become so vast that it cannot be effectively captured. But a few recent examples will help to illustrate what a pressing current issue the problematic past has become.

Making Amends for Historic Wrongs. Mayo Moran, Oxford University Press. © Mayo Moran 2025.
DOI: 10.1093/9780190927295.003.0001

A Snapshot of How the Past Is Coming Back to Haunt Us

There is nothing new about the pursuit of justice after atrocity. In the aftermath of mass violence and abuse, survivors typically sought rectification, amassing evidence and pleading their cases to political leaders and sometimes even to courts. But they almost always failed. Political leaders were largely unmoved by their pleas, and courts pointed to numerous barriers and told them to go away. The survivors certainly did not give up, but they did endure a long period when the hope of achieving any sense of justice seemed very dim indeed. However, beginning in the late 1980s, that ground started to shift. In the following chapters, we will explore just how that happened, but here are a few current examples that give a sense of how much the attitude to old wrongs has changed.

The Holocaust, which has had such a dramatic effect on how we understand old wrongs, is a fitting place to begin. While there were some reparations in the aftermath of World War II and in the 1990s, for many survivors there was very little progress. Those who sought return of stolen belongings, for example, were almost always thwarted. Families who did manage to track down their belongings were typically told that they were out of time or that the current holder of the property had some kind of protection. Many of them struggled for decades through the tangle of processes, jurisdictions, and rules that kept their property beyond their reach. Most of them failed.

But after many decades of inertia, the tide has discernibly turned in favor of return. Even just a very few of the developments since 2020 illustrate this shift. In 2023, France passed a new restitution law that enabled public entities to return property stolen during the Holocaust.[1] Museums across that country, including the Louvre, have been prompted to identify art whose provenance is suspect. In 2024, California also passed a law that makes it easier for victims of persecution to recover stolen property despite the passage of time.[2] At the same time, specialized bodies to consider Holocaust restitution are being revamped—as Germany's was in 2024 and Holland's was shortly before that. In 2025, other jurisdictions such as Switzerland and Flanders have finally fulfilled decades-old commitments to create specialized bodies to tackle Nazi-looted art.[3] Courts and

[1] Projet de loi relatif à la restitution des biens culturels ayant fait l'objet de spoliations dans le contexte des persécutions antisémites perpétrées entre 1933 et 1945, dépôt le mercredi 19 avril 2023 (Fr.).

[2] *See Governor Newsom Signs Legislation to Help Holocaust Survivors Recover Art Stolen by the Nazis*, GOVERNOR OF CALIFORNIA (Sept. 16, 2024), https://www.gov.ca.gov/2024/09/16/governor-newsom-signs-legislation-to-help-holocaust-survivors-recover-art-stolen-by-the-nazis/.

[3] *See Flanders to Tackle Art Looted by Nazis with Expert Group and Restitution Commission*, BELGA (May 2, 2025), https://www.belganewsagency.eu/flanders-to-tackle-art-looted-by-nazis-with-expert-group-and-restitution-commission; *Swiss Parliament Approves CHF987.9 Million Cultural Budget After Resolving Looted Art Dispute*, ARTDEPENDENCE MAGAZINE (Mar. 20, 2025), https://www.artdependence.com/articles/swiss-parliament-approves-chf9879-million-cultural-budget-after-resolving-looted-art-dispute/.

other bodies are also showing themselves to be far more supportive of return. In 2024, the Dutch restitutions committee ruled in favor of the return of Matisse's painting *Odalisque* to the heirs of Albert Stern whose family was decimated in the Holocaust. In 2025, the Supreme Court of the United States ordered reconsideration of a Jewish heir's claim to a Pissarro painting that the family had been trying to get back since 1999. Nearly eighty years after the end of the Holocaust, long-standing efforts to get back at least some of what was stolen were finally seeing some success.

This new willingness to rectify even very old wrongful takings is not limited to the Holocaust. The approach to colonial-era belongings has undergone what is perhaps an even more dramatic shift, as cases like the Benin Bronzes illustrate. Thousands of these treasures were stolen during a violent 1897 British raid on Benin City and eventually made their way into leading museums and private collections around the world. Although Nigeria had been seeking return since at least the 1930s, there was no movement even well into the twenty-first century. However more than 120 years after the takings, returns began to happen. In 2021, Aberdeen University and Jesus College Cambridge returned two pieces and started a surge of other restitution activity that extended to German and American museums, including the Smithsonian. In 2022, France gave back to Benin items that had been looted by French soldiers.[4] Early in 2025, the Netherlands indicated that it would return nearly 120 Benin Bronzes from Dutch museums, the largest return to date.[5]

This recent surge in efforts to make amends for old wrongs also extends well beyond the restitution of stolen belongings. Those who suffered violent personal injuries, most of them many decades old, are also finally seeing efforts to make amends. The sad example of child sexual abuse is a graphic illustration of the difference in how we now approach old injuries. Not so long ago, courts were quick to dismiss even the most grievous abuse, saying time had run out. In the 1990s, adult survivors of childhood incest trying to sue their abusers were told by both the English courts and the European Court of Human Rights that they had waited too long to complain.[6] That case was not an outlier. In Australia, a court similarly dismissed a child sexual abuse claim for "unreasonable delay," on the grounds that it would prejudice the defendant, even though he had already been convicted of eighteen counts of sexual offences against multiple children.[7]

[4] *See* Joshua Surtees, *"They Fill Me with Emotion"... Benin Celebrates the Return of Its Looted Treasure*, The Guardian (Feb. 22, 2022).

[5] *See The Netherlands Returns 119 Stolen Sculptures to Nigeria*, Al Jazeera (June 21, 2025).

[6] Stubbings v. Webb [1993] AC 498; Stubbings & Others v. United Kingdom, App. Nos. 22083/93 & 22095/93, [1996] ECHR 44.

[7] *See* Ben Mathews, *Limitation Periods and Child Sexual Abuse Cases: Law, Psychology, Time and Justice* 11 T.L.J. Lexis 15, 20–22 (2003).

But like old claims for return of stolen property, the approach to historic child sexual abuse has undergone a dramatic change.

Laws concerning child sexual abuse have changed so much that in many places there is no longer any time limit for such actions. As a result, institutions that were once able to shield behind limitations periods and other protections have found themselves face to face with what are often terrible histories. Until a few decades ago, the Catholic Church avoided almost all claims of abuse by arguing that survivors were out of time. But a 2025 Georgetown University report revealed how much that had changed—Catholic dioceses in the United States alone had paid over $5 billion to settle tens of thousands of historic abuse cases, a pattern repeated all over the world.[8]

The Catholic Church is not alone. An explosive 2024 Church of England report concluded that the Church had covered up rampant sexual abuse for decades, including the violent saga of the most prolific abuser in the Church's history, who abused as many as 130 boys. That report prompted the resignation of the Archbishop of Canterbury, the first such resignation in 1,000 years, and also cast a cloud of suspicion over one of his predecessors.[9] In 2025, the Church announced that a further seven clergy members would be disciplined, including a bishop.[10] In another telling example of how much the approach has changed, in 2024, the Council of Europe voted in favor of a package of measures that included an investigation, an official apology, and reparations payments to European survivors of child abuse in state or religious institutions.[11]

Courts too are now more willing to address old wrongs that had languished for decades. Again, a few recent examples illustrate the broader shift in attitude. After decades of survivor advocacy, in mid-2024, Japan's highest court awarded compensation to those who had been involuntarily sterilized decades before. Among other holdings, the court ruled that the statute of limitations could not be applied to forced sterilization claims.[12] Late in that same year, a Belgian court awarded compensation to five mixed-race women who Belgium had removed from their Congolese mothers between 1948 and 1953 in colonial Congo and

[8] *See* Aleja Hertzler-McCain, *More than $5 Billion Spent on Catholic Sexual Abuse Allegations, New Report Finds*, NCR (Jan. 17, 2025).

[9] *See* Harriet Sherwood, *Justin Welby Was too "Overwhelmed" by Scale of Abuse in C of E to Take Action*, The Guardian (Mar. 29, 2025); Harriet Sherwood, *George Carey Among Clergy Who Could Face Life Ban over John Smyth Abuse Case*, The Guardian (Feb. 25, 2025); Harriet Sherwood, *C of E Covered Up Attacked by Serial Abuse John Smyth, Review Finds*, The Guardian (Nov. 7, 2024).

[10] *See Seven Clergy to Face Disciplinary Action*, BBC News (June 5, 2025).

[11] *See Child Abuse: Council of Europe Wants to Compensate Victims*, Protect Children (Mar. 18, 2024), https://www.suojellaanlapsia.fi/en/post/child-abuse-council-of-europe-wants-to-compensate-victims.

[12] *See* Kelly Ng & Chika Nakayama, *Japan Top Court Says Forced Sterilisation Unconstitutional*, BBC News (July 3, 2024).

sent to a Catholic mission school.[13] Though just a small sliver of judicial activity addressing historic wrongs, cases like these illustrate the dramatic change in attitude toward old injuries.

The attitude toward old racial violence including slavery has also undergone a significant shift. Former slaves have been pursuing redress since well before 1916, the year they brought their first class action against the United States. Despite the loss there, they continued their quest for decades, with little progress. But here too things have changed, especially in the wake of the 2020 murder of George Floyd. A 2023 cover of *Time Magazine* proclaimed "Slavery Reparations are Coming."[14] Around the same time, both the Dutch king and prime minister apologized for their country's involvement in slavery and declared 2023–2024 slavery memorial year. In California, the United States' first state Task Force on Reparations for Slavery was struck, and it released its groundbreaking report in 2023.[15] The governor formally apologized in 2024, amid many other apologies across the nation and around the world. Reparations efforts were also springing up on a more local level, such as the 2024 Palm Springs' settlement with former residents of a largely Black neighborhood destroyed in the 1960s in what was called "a city-engineered holocaust."[16] In 2025, Namibia marked its first day of remembrance of the genocidal violence inflicted by Germany in the early years of the twentieth century. This happened as the two countries tried to finalize an agreement in which Germany would make amends.[17]

Transitional justice style bodies and task forces like California's are also increasingly being used to address the wrongs of the past, not in transitional regimes but in stable democracies. In 2020, Belgium made history as the first European country to strike a Truth and Reconciliation Commission. Norway struck a similar body to address its relationship with the Sami people, and it released its report in 2023.[18] Cities, universities, and other institutions across many jurisdictions also began to employ such bodies to explore their troubling histories, especially with slavery and colonialism. In 2025, France's President Macron announced the creation of a joint commission with Haiti to examine the countries' shared past. The announcement was made on the bicentennial of

[13] *See* Jennifer Rankin, *Belgium Found Guilty of Crimes Against Humanity in Colonial Congo*, The Guardian (Dec. 2, 2024).

[14] *See* Janell Ross, *Inside Barbados' Historic Push for Slavery Reparations*, Time (July 6, 2023).

[15] California Task Force to Study and Develop Reparation Proposals for African Americans, Final Report (2023).

[16] Audra D.S. Burch, *Their Palm Springs Neighbourhood Burned More than 50 Years Ago. They Want Compensation*, The New York Times (May 21, 2024).

[17] *See* Natasha Booty, *Namibia Marks Colonial Genocide as Reparations Hang in the Balance*, BBC News (May 28, 2025).

[18] *See* John Last, *Norway Truth Commission Details Country's Dark History of Assimilation*, CBC News (June 2, 2023).

Haiti's 1825 Agreement to pay France reparations following Haiti's revolution against slavery.[19]

This new sense that old injustices require some effort to make amends is also apparent in some purely symbolic, but nonetheless telling, developments. The movement to posthumously pardon those wrongly convicted is one example. In 2021, Virginia's governor posthumously pardoned seven young Black men who were executed in 1951 for the rape of a white woman. Although the consequences could not be undone, Governor Northam said that this was about "righting wrongs."[20] In June 2025, the British Library also made symbolic amends for an old injustice when it reinstated Oscar Wilde's library reader pass, 130 years after it was revoked following his conviction for gross indecency.[21] The library said it wanted to acknowledge the injustice of Wilde's treatment. Also in June 2025, French politicians unanimously supported a "symbolic effort to promote Alfred Dreyfus, the Jewish French Army Captain, to brigadier general."[22] They noted that he was accused of treason and then condemned, imprisoned, and exiled because he was Jewish. This posthumous promotion, said former Prime Minister Gabriel Attal, would "constitute an act of reparation."[23]

Though these are but a few illustrations of the changed approach to historic wrongs, they give a sense of the profound shift that has taken place. The confidence that old wounds would heal over time was unsettled by cases as diverse as those involving the Holocaust, child abuse, and injuries springing from war and colonialism. The voices of survivors began to displace the conviction that grievous old harms would fade away. Many of the events of our past started to look like they were more than just terrible—they looked like injustices. And that meant that they could not simply be ignored, but instead demanded repair. So across a very wide array of different issues in many different places, there was a growing sense that those responsible for old wrongs must make an effort to set things right. The significance of this re-understanding of our past is also seen in the strength of some of the backlash it has prompted. In the United States in particular, memorials that were renamed to address concerns about slavery are being renamed again to reassert a rosier read of history. But for the purposes of the discussion here, the salient fact is that the meaning of the past and its

[19] *See* Natricia Duncan, *Macron Announces Joint Commission with Haiti Amid Calls for Reparations*, The Guardian (Apr. 17, 2025).

[20] *See* Jonathan Franklin, *These 7 Black Men Were Executed for an Alleged Rape. Now, They Have Been Pardoned*, National Public Radio (Aug. 31, 2021).

[21] *See* Dalya Alberge, *British Library to Reinstate Oscar Wilde's Reader Card 130 Years After It Was Revoked*, The Guardian (June 13, 2025).

[22] *See* Ashifa Kassam, *France Finally Acts to Deliver Justice in Infamous Dreyfus Case*, The Guardian (June 2, 2025).

[23] *Id.*

significance as a matter of justice is now at the forefront of public debate, even when that significance is being disputed.

How Did This Happen?

This snapshot of just a very few of the current developments in the reckoning with historic wrongs prompts the question of how this remarkable shift happened. Telling that story is a central task of this book, but here let me sketch an overview of the plot. The reshaping of our attitude to old wrongs really begins with a constellation of events in the late 1980s and early 1990s. This was a period of change characterized by several interconnected developments in the political landscape, as well as in law and human rights. Together they would provide the foundation for the resurgence of the venerable principle of reparative justice, which played a critical role in prompting a larger reckoning.

After the fall of the Berlin Wall, the shift in global politics led to renewed efforts to respond to some of the harms of the Holocaust and World War II. In the immediate aftermath of that war, Nuremberg famously introduced the transformative possibility of justice as a response to atrocity. By expanding the options beyond vengeance and amnesia, those trials began to alter both how we understood the past and what we thought we could do about it. But not until the late 1980s and early 1990s did this dimension of Nuremberg really come to the fore as a number of regimes emerged from authoritarian rule and sought to establish democratic and rights-respecting orders. The rise of what came to be called "transitional justice" brought together elements that would turn out to be important in reshaping the broader approach to historic wrongs.

To help meet the challenges of regime change, transitional justice turned its gaze on past wrongs, particularly the kind of massive human rights abuses that characterized oppressive regimes like apartheid South Africa, Argentina, and former Eastern Bloc countries. And as it did so, it expanded the range of justice responses in a critical way. Although Nuremberg-style criminal prosecutions continued to play a role, the truth commission emerged as an important addition to the responses to atrocity. Unlike criminal trials, these bodies looked not only backward but also forward. But they were different in other ways as well. For the first time, they brought the voices of survivors to the fore. In place of the old injunction to 'forgive and forget' truth commissions began to valorize remembering. The truth commission shifted the focus in another important sense too. It looked beyond individual perpetrators. By focusing on the institutionalized nature of massive human rights abuses, truth commissions highlighted the issue of accountability for widely shared wrongs.

While the Nuremberg model was being reworked in the context of regime change, human rights-oriented advocates across a range of non-transitional legal systems were identifying similar challenges. This included feminists who were expressing frustration with the limitations of criminal law and its failure to protect fundamental human rights, especially bodily integrity. In a parallel to transitional justice, advocates for women and other marginalized groups pointed to how criminal law's focus on the individual missed something vitally important in cases where there was an institutional dimension to the wrongdoing. They also worried about how the criminal model treated victims—given only a marginal role in the process and left remediless at the end of it. These limitations provided an impetus to think creatively about how to develop a more effective means of vindicating fundamental rights violations. What they turned to was the civil action of private law. The venerable idea of reparative justice was having the first stirrings of new life.

Alongside the feminist advocates who were looking to harness the power of private law, a closely allied movement was exploring the possibility that they might adapt international law's concept of reparations to help secure redress for issues like historic violence and racism. That movement saw early success when apologies and compensation were extended to citizens of Japanese origin who had been interned during World War II. Inspired by successes like these, advocates started to craft a new type of claim that was anchored in private law, but that drew in the kind of human rights norms found in constitutional and international law. These "reparations-style" claims began to surface in the domestic legal systems of non-transitional regimes. Most of them were for wrongs that were not only massive but also old.

The most significant of these were the Holocaust cases filed in the late 1990s. With the reunification of Germany, there was renewed interest in addressing some of the neglected legacies of the Holocaust. Lawyers for survivors and descendants launched a series of reparations-style civil suits in US courts against private corporations, beginning with Swiss banks and soon followed by German corporations that had used slave and forced labor. The multibillion-dollar settlements that resulted included compensation for over two million survivors and funding for projects associated with history and human rights. They stunned the legal world and fueled a much larger engagement with history's most grievous wrongs.

This Holocaust reparations litigation was transformative. It showed that the most extreme state-sponsored crimes could, among other things, generate individual and collective redress. In addition to focusing on the plight of survivors, they also shifted attention away from individual wrongdoing and toward the important but long ignored dimension of institutional responsibility. And by bringing claims for redress of old wrongs outside of the context of regime change, they helped to spur a much broader interest in rectifying historic wrongs. The leverage of private law was critical to this strategy. Nuremberg had given credence to the idea that some of the terrible events of the past were more than just wrong, they were injustices. But its reliance on criminal law left the state in control. By contrast, because it deployed the civil action, the Holocaust reparations litigation placed the means of securing justice in the hands of survivors. It also showed that private law pressure could yield both compensation for decades-old harms as well as more transformative remedies. In this way, the Holocaust litigation illuminated the broader promise of the reparative form of justice that animated private law. And inspired in part by those historic settlements, advocates began to examine how a similar approach might help to address other terrible old wrongs such as abuse, torture, violence, and slavery.

Yet, for all of this apparent promise, reparations-style actions for historic wrongs faced formidable barriers. Because the Holocaust cases had settled, they sidestepped many of them. But what looked like insuperable obstacles remained in the way of other efforts to redress historic wrongs. However, as it turned out, another set of changes was afoot that would dismantle many of those barriers and help to give reparative justice new purchase on the wrongs of the past. During the same period that transitional justice was developing and the new civil action was on the rise, the terrible events of what eventually became known as the Catholic Church sexual abuse crisis were starting to unfold. In the mid-1980s, investigative journalists started to expose stories of rampant child sexual abuse and well-orchestrated church cover-ups. Gradually, brave survivors and their families broke the code of silence and began to bring legal actions against the Church for child sexual abuse. The changes in the law wrought by those claims and their fallout would open up responsibility for past wrongs on a scale that would have been unimaginable only a short time before.

In the early days, individuals contemplating bringing a sex abuse claim against the Church faced daunting challenges. The impact of child sexual abuse, especially when committed by trusted individuals like clergy, was such that it took decades before most survivors could bring themselves to come forward. But that meant that virtually all of their claims were barred because limitations rules precluded actions that were more than a few years old. Even when claimants managed to address these obstacles, the Church could shield itself because as a charity it had immunity. On top of this, the more powerful the Church was in a jurisdiction, the more likely it was to benefit from additional protections as well as other more political forms of insulation. And even if it were possible to overcome these barriers, courts were reluctant to hold an institution liable for an individual employee's criminal act such as sexual abuse. There were also more pragmatic challenges like obtaining evidence and financing litigation against a legally sophisticated, well-funded transnational entity like the Catholic Church.

Despite these hurdles, cases against the Catholic Church for historic sexual abuse did begin to move forward, and some of the barriers eventually started to erode. Across jurisdictions, those cases began to make it clear that the Church had systematically protected abusers, thereby perpetuating the horrific damage they were able to inflict upon children. As the Church showed itself to be similarly ruthless in defending against survivors, courts started to question many of their protections, and limitations periods began to fall. The uncovering of what the Pennsylvania Grand Jury referred to as the Church's "playbook" for child sexual abuse claims confirmed the troubling idea that not only an individual—but sometimes also an institution—could be at fault. Courts started to question charitable immunity. The revelation that so much of the wrongdoing actually was institutional also began to create more openness to holding those institutions themselves liable. Together these changes were beginning to reconfigure private law to give it new leverage—leverage that others were increasingly looking to in their own quests to rectify old wrongs.

Most survivors of old wrongs, however, did not begin by launching legal claims. They asked politicians for acknowledgment, for apologies, and sometimes for redress. But for decades and sometimes longer, those pleas had fallen on deaf ears. Yet, in the shifting political environment of the late 1980s, this too began to change. The landmark redress programs for the wartime internment of citizens of Japanese origin showed that there was hope for survivors of old wrongs and inspired others. But most other efforts to secure redress for historic abuse and violence faltered, particularly when it came to individual redress. That is why survivors of old wrongs began to look to law.

While historic injustice cases remain legally challenging, the force of the arguments in favor of repair gave some of these claims surprising power. And as some cases that seemed improbable began to see success, other old wrongs also started to come under scrutiny. The cascading effect of these developments across jurisdictions and institutions, often prompted by journalists and propelled by terrible events like the murder of George Floyd or the discovery of unmarked graves of Indigenous children, resulted in a surge of encounters with historic wrongs.

Canada's Indian Residential Schools Settlement was a critical development, not only because of how early it occurred but also because its transformative ambitions illustrated the potential reach of reparative justice and made it a model for others. The settlement addressed egregious abuses of Indigenous children in residential schools that were, for a century and a half, run by churches and the federal government. It began with a flood of private law claims and ended in a $6 billion settlement that included two multibillion-dollar individual reparations programs and the first truth commission in an established democracy. The settlement showed that survivors of decades-old institutional abuse could secure substantial redress. But beyond this, its use of the truth commission drew transitional justice thinking into private law actions for redress of a vast historic wrong well outside of regime change. This approach, it started to seem, could be relevant to a much wider array of injustices, many of them in stable regimes. The dramatic settlement changed the landscape and encouraged survivors of eugenics, sexual abuse, and other grievous old rights violations to think that it was not too late to pursue justice. Moreover, by taking aim at colonial policy itself, it pointed to how reparative justice could engage an even more ambitious category of old wrongs.

One such category involved actions that inflicted serious harm but that were legal when they were committed. It had always been assumed that legally authorized acts could not give rise to liability—an obstacle that had special relevance for issues like eugenics. While the Holocaust did cast a dark shadow over the practice, eugenics remained a challenging redress context. Eugenic sterilization was mandated by law, undertaken by governments, enforced by the state, and even found constitutional in an infamous opinion of the Supreme Court of the United States. Nonetheless, many decades after the struggle for redress began, even here there was movement. Beginning in Sweden and then moving across jurisdictions, survivors of eugenics gradually started to see some success. Investigative journalists played a key role in bringing this issue to the fore, just as they did in the Catholic Church cases. And because the practice was so transnational, developments in one jurisdiction prompted new scrutiny and pressure in others, as provinces, states, and countries from Europe to Canada to Japan to the United States began to apologize and to extend redress to survivors.

Similar dynamics also started to create movement on other issues that had languished for many decades. Like legalized wrongs, wartime injuries were also challenging for redress. Responsibility for wartime violence was typically a matter of state-to-state negotiation and, as the early Holocaust reparations programs showed, survivors were typically not high on the agenda. Moreover, because war is replete with violence, even the most egregious injuries had not normally been thought to give rise to redress. This was especially true of the wartime sexual violence so often inflicted on women. Survivors of Japan's wartime military sexual slavery, euphemistically referred to as 'comfort women' epitomize the long struggle for justice in the context of war. After many decades and when very few survivors were left, there was a significant upsurge of activity. While the issue continues to defy resolution, the few remaining elderly survivors continue their efforts backed by a large movement and commemorated by "Peace Statues" all over the world.

Dramatic issues like these started to prompt a re-understanding of the past as the terrain not just of terrible events but also of *injustices*. Much of this was due to survivors and advocates who worked hard to capture the legal nature of the wrong and the imperative of correction. For injuries to the person, like those above, they fashioned reparations-style claims based on reparative justice's insistence that the wrongdoer repair the harm they did. But reparation was not the only legal idea that was being redeployed to tackle grievous old wrongs. Alongside it, another doctrine was being reshaped to address a closely connected set of issues involving stolen property. That doctrine was restitution.

The most powerful early application of this new kind of restitution claim also had roots in the Holocaust, especially the looted art cases that sought to address Nazi plunder. Based on the demand to return something wrongfully taken, claims like these began to breathe new life into the rather arcane principle of restitution. Though there were numerous earlier attempts to retrieve stolen property, a critically important development came in form of the Holocaust litigation of the 1990s referred to above. In the Swiss banks claim, restitution was the basis for demanding the return of Nazi-era assets that persecuted Jews had been encouraged to deposit in Switzerland's banks but had never been able to retrieve despite decades of trying. A settlement returned almost $720 million to over 18,000 Holocaust victims and heirs—it was restitution on an unprecedented scale.

These cases and their dramatic effects helped to inspire what has been termed a "restitution revolution."[24] Like their counterparts working on reparations claims, restitution advocates put pressure on the technical and procedural elements that had kept the doctrine within narrow parameters. As it was liberated from those confines, there was greater scope for the underlying principle—the original owner's right to the return of that which was wrongfully taken. *Portrait of Wally* by Egon Schiele made headlines when a *New York Times* report led the Manhattan District Attorney to prevent its return to Austria. The complicated legal proceedings took a decade, but finally returned the painting to the heirs of the woman who had been forced to sell it many decades before. *Woman in Gold* also followed a tortuous journey before it was returned. Similar examples from all over the world kept making headlines.

Holocaust restitution also began to turn new attention to colonial belongings. That issue leapt into prominence when France's President Macron commissioned a report on the material legacy of French colonialism in Africa. The report's emphasis on restitution as a moral imperative set off shock waves across Europe's former colonial powers and in settler societies. It sparked a series of initiatives focused on return of wrongly taken belongings. This gathered speed as museums, galleries, auction houses, universities, and others began to initiate their own processes to examine their collections, something that often led them to engage in restitution. Old claims that had languished for decades—sometimes

[24] Bénédicte Savoy, *The Restitution Revolution Begins*, The Art Newspaper (Feb. 16, 2018).

even centuries—suddenly began to see movement. From the sagas of works like the *Woman in Gold*, the Benin Bronzes, and even the Parthenon Marbles, to Indigenous and colonial-era belongings held in institutions all over the world, the landscape of restitution has dramatically changed.

As the demand to redress old wrongs has become increasingly powerful, it has also begun to engage a wider array of issues. Cases such as those involving Catholic Church abuse, residential schools, eugenics, and stolen belongings all recast those claims more forcefully in the language of injustice. By using the leverage of reparative justice—and reshaping its venerable legal principles like reparation and restitution—advocates pressed against the barriers that had kept old injustices outside of the range of liability. But many of those claims did more than this. They also connected discrete wrongs like abuse or looting to wider issues such as discrimination, dehumanization, and genocide. In this way, the reach of reparative justice into the past also began to force a reckoning with much larger old wrongs like colonialism and slavery. And while the remedies for issues of this scale and antiquity inevitably differ, even wrongs as vast as these are increasingly understood as injustices that demand some kind of repair.

Canada's residential schools redress efforts are noteworthy on this larger issue as well because they form such a sustained encounter between the demands of reparative justice and the legacy of colonialism. As the residential schools issues continued to unfold, courts, legislators, and institutions became far more responsive to the idea of atoning for colonial-era actions that once seemed far beyond a duty to repair. The 2023 "Band Reparations" settlement is a striking example. It cast the colonial-era law and policy as the legal wrong and extended funding to Indigenous bands for the reinvigoration of the very languages and cultures that the state had once made its policy to destroy.

Colonial violence was also at the center of another groundbreaking case of redress for historic wrongs. Mau Mau survivors of torture during the 1950s uprising in Kenya surprised observers when they convinced an English court to issue two important rulings in their favor over five decades after the events occurred. As part of that saga, historians found themselves in the spotlight, and colonial-era archives were forced open. The archival materials ended up being central to an unprecedented £20 million settlement that included individual compensation to thousands of survivors of colonial-era violence, a government statement of regret, and a memorial in Kenya. As cases like these began to see some success, it amplified the pressure in other even more difficult cases of historic wrongs. And across many examples, the 2020 public murder of George Floyd increased both the scrutiny and the demands to reckon with the legacy of colonialism.

Germany's ongoing efforts to address its colonial legacy in Namibia serve as an example. More than 70,000 were murdered in what is considered the first genocide of the twentieth century. With concentration camps and chilling "scientific" experiments, it is often seen as a training ground for the Holocaust. After decades of denial, in the late 1990s, Germany began making efforts to respond. Over the decades, this has included a series of statements of regret and two attempts by survivors to sue Germany in US courts. Germany finally issued a formal apology, and as of the end of 2024, an agreement that includes $1.5 billion is reportedly in the works. Restitution is also playing a role here as German institutions are returning cultural belongings to Africa as one part of atoning for their own colonial legacies.

Germany is not alone. Other former colonial powers face similar pressures, and following 2020 particularly, countries began to issue formal apologies both for their larger colonial legacies and for particular events. Cities and other institutions did so too, and they sometimes began their own examinations of history. As noted, Belgium made history with its commission on the colonial past, though it later imploded. France's president announced a joint effort to study their history with Algeria—which also faced difficulties—as well as the 2025 joint commission on Haiti. Some, like the Netherlands, also set up reparations funds. Each such step also inevitably increased the pressure on others.

Former colonies have also stepped up their advocacy. Over ten years ago, the Caribbean nations developed a plan for reparatory justice that has served as a touchstone ever since. Though it contains familiar elements like apology and repatriation of cultural belongings, it also focuses on larger structural remedies. And while there has not been significant movement on these large-scale responses, the question of how to repair some of the injustices of colonialism is now a live one that both former powers and former colonies are grappling with. The same is true of the closely connected issue of slavery. Like colonialism, not too long ago, most would have seen the terrible injustices of slavery as simply "too big to remedy."

Despite the more than century long push for reparations for slavery, until recently there had not been many gains. However, the ground has dramatically shifted. While we are not approaching anything like true reparations, the steps that have been taken would have been unimaginable only a few years ago. Former colonial powers are also coming under pressure on the issue of slavery—pressure that extends beyond government and to institutions and individuals. Former slave-holding families have formed a network. They are pressing governments to respond, and some descendants have apologized and made reparations. Universities have formed networks to study and find ways to atone for their involvement in slavery. Businesses and churches are also engaged in similar activity.

Redress activity has also picked up significantly in the United States, where the legacy of chattel slavery has been the subject of reparations debates at least since abolition. Despite early failures, advocates were inspired to reignite their efforts by developments like the Holocaust restitution cases, the South African Truth and Reconciliation Commission, and redress for Japanese-American internment. They pressed for a commission to examine slavery and launched reparations actions in US courts. While these actions did not bear fruit, 2020 brought a whole new level of attention and urgency to this issue. Institutions large and small, from universities to cities to states, began to grapple with their legacies. Apologies have multiplied, and reparative efforts have gotten underway. Multiple task forces and similar bodies have been struck, the most important of which is California's Task Force on Reparations for Slavery, which issued its final report in 2023. Although some of its recommendations, particularly those focused on individual reparations, were met with skepticism, other measures such as targeted housing and education support for descendants of slaves are currently under consideration.

As this suggests, the demand that even very old wrongs must be righted is making itself felt not only in courts but well beyond, in the political realm and directly in institutions. The ability of survivors to use the reparative justice pressure of private law has turned out to be a pivotal factor in this, since it often provided the leverage necessary to motivate reluctant institutions. But the reckoning with our past has extended beyond this. Even former colonial powers and those who benefited from slavery are coming under a new kind of pressure to make amends, and many of them are taking steps that would have been unthinkable only a few years ago. And although the terrain remains uncertain in these especially challenging examples, the very fact of their reframing as questions of justice and the efforts to make some progress on redress is testimony to the magnitude of the change in how we understand the wrongs of the past.

What Should We Do About It?

This shift in how we understand the terrible events of the past has changed the sense of what we need to do about them. The fact that so many are now seen as injustices means that they demand some effort at repair. But how do we right wrongs and repair injuries that are so enduring and life-altering? The encounter with old wrongs is making itself felt in institutions large and small, from churches to museums and galleries to auction houses, universities, cities, and states. The past has become not only a legal problem but also a very political issue. While it is inspiring backlash especially in the United States with the re-election of President Trump, that should not obscure the fact that at the same time, at many levels, and in many institutions, there are ongoing efforts to respond to the felt imperative to make amends for we know we did wrong.

This makes it timely to consider how those seeking answers can best respond. But if we begin by looking at what has happened so far, there seem to be at least as many negative lessons as positive ones. And unfortunately, many of those negative lessons revolve around lawyers. There is an irony in this because without the commitment of dedicated lawyers, who often work for years without pay, historic wrongs would not have garnered their current attention. Yet, while the lawyers who are tireless advocates for forgotten survivors do appear as heroic figures, a closer look reveals that lawyers all too often also appear in more villainous roles.

From the institutional abuse cases to colonial violence to reparations for racial discrimination and slavery, historic injustice cases contain many examples of self-serving lawyers who exploit vulnerable survivors for their own benefit. Claims for redress of historic wrongs are replete with lawyers who target vulnerable survivors and undermine the processes designed to help healing. Redress schemes struggle with lawyer misconduct, spending inordinate time and scarce resources trying to protect survivors from self-dealing and fraud. And unfortunately, the courts and regulators who are supposed to ensure that lawyers act in the public interest frequently offer little in the way of assistance. Nonetheless, as redress schemes and other programs have multiplied, there are also positive lessons that can be drawn about how to curb such misconduct while retaining the benefit that good legal counsel undoubtedly offers survivors.

The problems with lawyers, however, are not limited to the obvious self-interest of the greedy members of the profession. Outside of the parties, lawyers are the most important other players in issues of redress for historic wrongs. This means that inside institutions, lawyers are typically extremely influential, not only on legal matters but also on broader approach and strategy. If the greedy lawyers are driven by excessive self-interest, institutional lawyers are too often blinded by excessive institutional protectiveness. They make morally suspect arguments, pursue strategies that reflect poorly on their clients, and damage the chances of resolution because of aggressive litigation postures. The result is that they frequently end up undermining the larger interests of the institutions that they serve. Here too there are lessons to be learned both on the part of institutions, especially those that regulate lawyers, as well as on the part of legal education.

Fortunately, there are also many positive lessons to take from the efforts to make amends for old wrongs. If the most important negative lesson warns of too much reliance on lawyers, the most striking positive lesson focuses on the benefits of engagement with survivors and descendants. Across many different examples, it is clear that the sooner in the process they are involved, the better the outcome is likely to be. Similarly, the more extensively they can be involved, the smoother the path to resolution. The burgeoning field of examples has many illustrations of what a significant difference this can make.

Understanding what matters most to survivors and framing responses accordingly dramatically enhances the likelihood of positive resolution. Institutions and governments tend to focus on financial issues, but for most survivors, other elements may hold much more significance—the question of who pays compensation, for example, may be as important as how much compensation is paid. Similarly, the question of who delivers an apology or acknowledgment and how survivors are engaged in that process has a profound impact on its chances of success. Without engaging with survivors directly, institutions have a poor chance of getting it right on elements like these. By contrast, it is clear that those institutions that have connected with survivors early on and focused on places where it was possible to make some progress have established much more positive relationships, which in turn enhanced the likelihood of a better outcome.

In most historic injustice matters, non-monetary issues like acknowledgment, apology, and commemoration are key objectives for survivors and are often critical to resolution. The nature of the issues is also such that there is often a link in these cases between reparations claims and restitution, and this can be helpful in fashioning responses. When Germany returned skulls to Namibia, it was one small step toward atoning for its genocidal behavior more than a century before. Similarly, when Holland returned its large collection of Benin Bronzes, it was part of making amends for its troubling colonial history. In many other cases too, the two kinds of reparative justice claims are deeply linked in ways that can make either a negative or a positive difference to the prospect of resolution. And since these issues are ultimately about the importance of establishing relations of respect, every act is deeply symbolic and its significance weighty.

For this reason especially, ceremony matters and can play an especially profound role in the process of making amends. A thoughtful ceremony of return developed in collaboration with survivors and communities can show atonement and form part of building a relationship of respect. There are moving examples of this, such as the "rematriation" of a totem pole from the National Museum of Scotland to the Nisga'a nation in British Columbia.[25] The importance of marking the moment is also evident in how the British Library chose to restore Oscar Wilde's library pass—it planned a ceremony that included the launch of a book about Wilde's life and the presentation of Wilde's new card to his grandson.[26] Similarly, at the beginning of an event for the survivors of the abusive Magdalene Laundries, the people of Dublin poured into the streets to

[25] *See* Mark Brown, *Totem Pole Begins "Rematriation" from Edinburgh to Nisga'a Nation in Canada*, The Guardian (Aug. 28, 2023).
[26] *See* Alberge, *supra* note 21.

welcome them, carrying signs that said "We honour you," and "Welcome home." The impact was profound for survivors and for the community that needed to find a way to express its atonement. Symbolism and ceremony can in this way form a critical means of acknowledgment and commemoration, both of which matter deeply di to survivors and to the institution seeking to make amends.

Some Terminology

The issues that are the subject of this exploration are often described using a great deal of different terminology, much of it employed in varied or even conflicting ways. In part, this is because many of these issues have attracted very broad attention, much of it from beyond the academy. That is why some of the writers on these subjects use more philosophical and technical terminology, while others use the language in a more general way. Because I am aiming at a broader account, I purposely try to use accessible language and to avoid technical terms. Similarly, to make the discussion easier to follow, I use some terms such as redress and reparations relatively interchangeably, as they are often used in the literature, even though it may be technically possible to draw distinctions between them. Where it is necessary for clarity or to my argument, I specify in more detail exactly what the term refers to.

As will be apparent, the idea of reparative justice is central to my argument here. I use the term in its classical sense to refer to the case where justice demands that the wrongdoer repair the harmful consequences of their wrong. Reparative justice in its simplest form therefore connects the one who inflicted the wrong and the one who suffered its consequences. In her Aquinas Lecture, *What Is Reparative Justice*, Margaret Urban Walker stresses the same elements when she notes that at the heart of this ancient and basic form of justice is the "idea of reparation—of amends owed for wrongs and wrongful harms."[27] This is a concept of justice "between parties," in the sense that it demands that the one responsible for wrongdoing repair their unjustly inflicted harms or restore that which they wrongly took. It serves as the animating principle of much of tort law and the law of restitution, both of which are central to the discussion in this book. Tort theorists such as Ernest Weinrib often use the similar term "corrective justice" to describe this idea of justice that underlies private law.[28] Although there is considerable overlap in meaning, I prefer the term reparative because repair is a more capacious idea in contrast with the narrower idea of correction. Given the kinds of wrongs that this book discusses and the transformative aims of those

[27] Margaret Urban Walker, What Is Reparative Justice? 9 (2010).
[28] *See* Ernest Weinrib, The Idea of Private Law (2012).

who seek justice, repair seems more apt here than correction. While the term reparative justice has not been very common until recently, it is now increasingly turned to in the context of mass human rights violations where sometimes the term "reparatory justice" is used instead. Though those discussions often dovetail with my analysis here, on occasion they do invoke a broader and more diffuse obligation of repair in contrast with my emphasis here, which for the most part focuses more sharply on the wrongdoer's obligation of repair.

Although I attempt to avoid technicalities, I do want to briefly note some distinctions that are relevant to this discussion. First, there is an important distinction between reparative justice—that is what justice demands in the way of repair as between parties—and retributive justice, in which the retribution or punishment is exacted by the state, as in criminal law. So too would I distinguish reparative justice from distributive justice, in which goods are allocated according to some criterion of distribution, such as for example, pensions to those above a certain age. Distributive justice arguments are often significant in the context of very vast old wrongs like colonialism and slavery because of how particular wrongs such as forced labor intersect with and are compounded by distributive issues like discrimination. For that reason, as we will see, distributive justice remedies are often suggested as more apt in such cases. The third form of justice often referred to and sometimes used interchangeably with reparative justice is restorative justice. Here too, I see a distinction. Although restorative justice has come to have a wide and even unwieldy meaning, its primary field of application is in the criminal law context where it stresses the importance of re-integration of the offender into the community. While these other forms of justice may well have a role to play in the reckoning with historic wrongs, the emphasis in my argument here is on how the turn to reparative justice arguments have served as a vital catalyst in reshaping our engagement with the past.

Beyond the forms of justice at work in this discussion, there are also several other terms that are worth briefly noting. I often use the term redress to refer to efforts to undo or repair the relevant harm to individuals. This is the term commonly used in the literature, and here as well, to refer to individual compensation. But it also often extends to broader elements of repair, especially apology, acknowledgment, commemoration, and the like. Reparations also has a wide range of meanings in the literature and is discussed in more detail in the following chapters. It is often used as a synonym for redress, and like redress, ranges in meaning from individual compensation for grievous harm through to other elements such as apologies and commemoration. The term is also sometimes used to mean reparations programs, especially in the context of vast wrongs. Typically, this use includes a broader array of remedies, some of which are more structural, although many also involve an element of individual compensation. As discussed in the body of this work, whatever term is used, it is the issue of individual compensation for old wrongs that is typically the most controversial. Because of the range of meanings for both redress and reparations, in the more detailed discussion in the chapters below, I clarify the salient elements where they are especially significant to the discussion.

The term restitution is simpler, referring as it does to the return of wrongly taken value. In most of the cases discussed here, it involves personal property or belongings, though it is by no means confined to these types of property. Restitution is based on what justice demands as between parties and hence is also an expression of reparative justice. In the paradigmatic cases of historic wrongs like the ones discussed in the chapters below, it generally requires the return of the wrongly taken property to the party from whom it was taken. However, restitution can also apply to cases of unpaid wages for work and hence is one way of articulating the justice reasoning behind claims for compensation for slavery and slave labor. In many of the cases like these, there are deep interconnections between redress for personal injury and restitution for stolen labor. Holocaust and colonial-looted belongings are the most well-known among many examples.

A Caveat and a Clarification

The caveat—writing this book made me uneasy. I wanted to tell a story about how the past has emerged as a daunting contemporary problem. But because this account aims to be general and not particular to an historic wrong, or even to a category of historic wrongs, it requires touching very lightly on many terrible old events. In every case I discuss, and many beyond, there is a rich and detailed literature that explores the nuances that I cannot go into here. These accounts are interesting and valuable, but I wanted to do something different—I wanted to tell an overarching story about our shifting sense of old wrongs writ large. In order to trace how that broader attitude has shifted, it was essential to keep the discussion of examples at a very high, and sometimes perhaps even superficial, level. I am uneasy as I do so because there is so much that I cannot touch upon and because all of the examples that I cover would benefit from more attention than a more general discussion of this kind allows. For those interested, I highly recommend exploring the literature that exists on the illustrations I discuss. I only hope that this more overarching account that I present here adds something to our understanding of how the past came back to haunt us and encourages us to think more deeply about what we can do about such a striking development.

The clarification—the issues that I discuss in this book are extremely topical, and so it is not surprising that almost everyone I spoke to about it had strong views about them. It was not uncommon for people to question why those of us around today should have to pay for the errors of those who went before us. There was often hostility both to the idea of individual reparations and also to delving into what happened long ago. Interestingly, however many of these general reactions were quite different than the reactions to specific instances of redress for issues like childhood sexual abuse and other institutional abuse, involuntary sterilization, sexual slavery, and stolen property. Most of the strongest concern was reserved for those claims that were furthest away from living individuals and from specific tangible injuries like sexual abuse or torture or theft. In the chapters below, I discuss some of the complications of applying a purely reparative justice account to vast old wrongs like colonialism and slavery and note how many of the proposed solutions, even when they use the language of reparations, often invoke remedies that are closer to distributive justice.

Interesting as these questions about whether we bear responsibility for historic wrongs are, they are not my subject here. There are many thoughtful accounts of what, if anything, we owe in light of what our ancestors did. There are illuminating discussions of what those who were harmed are entitled to and how far any such entitlements extend. The focus of this book is different—it is not about what should happen but rather about what has happened. It is the story of how our approach to old wrongs has changed. As the examples discussed throughout this book illustrate, many things that were done in the past are now seen very differently, and many of the things that were done in our name now seem to us to be wrong. As we have come face to face with the grievous events of the past and also with the harm that they still occasion, something has shifted. Instead of seeing them as simply wrong, we now see them as *wrongs,* in other words as injustices. Along with this uncomfortable sense has come the view that we need to do something about some of those events—to find ways to atone or make amends. In this sense, reparative justice has forced an encounter with the wrongs of the past and has prompted us to think we need to respond. This is an effort to trace how that happened and how we might, in the face of it, achieve some measure of justice.

2

Confluences: A Brief History of Reparations

Introduction

There has been a dramatic shift in how we approach the wrongs of the past. Not too long ago, the view was that wrongs—even terrible ones—faded over time. But that has changed. Many grave old injuries—decades or sometimes even centuries old—have come to be understood as injustices. That has resulted in demands to redress an increasing array of past wrongs. The past, in that sense, has become a very contemporary problem. How did that come to be? Our task here is to begin to answer this question by tracing the larger currents that started to give shape to a new kind of claim. These claims were a kind of hybrid that brought together private and public law in a unique way, and they eventually began to describe their novel ambitions using the language of reparations. In this way, the law—and particularly private law—began to press open the doors of past wrongdoing that had so long been firmly shut.

Viewed in retrospect, the 1980s and 1990s was a remarkable period. From the perspective of interest in historic wrongs, it was characterized by a number of different but related developments. Together they provided the strands that were eventually woven together into a new idea of reparations, one that was responsive to the quest to address grievous old wrongs. This went hand in hand with an emerging conviction that it was necessary to come to terms with the past. The result was a surge of demands to redress old wrongs.

The Old Past: Vengeance and Amnesia

Violence and injury have always formed part of human history. That is not new. But what has changed is our attitude toward it. Vengeance is likely our most venerable response to violence. An ancient example is found in Aeschylus's *The Oresteia*—its murderous plot driven by the relentless logic of vengeance. The downward spiral abates only at the end of the final play, *The Eumenides*, when justice holds out the possibility of an end to the cycle of revenge.[1]

[1] Aeschylus, The Oresteia (Ted Hughes trans., Farrar, Straus and Giroux 1999); Aiskhylos, Sophokles & Euripides, An Oresteia: Agamemnon by Aiskhylos; Elektra by Sophokles; Orestes by Euripides (Anne Carson trans., Farrar, Straus and Giroux 2010).

Making Amends for Historic Wrongs. Mayo Moran, Oxford University Press. © Mayo Moran 2025.
DOI: 10.1093/9780190927295.003.0002

Over a thousand years later, Shakespeare's king in *Henry V* invoked revenge and retaliation as his justification for the murder of defenseless prisoners. In more recent times, the Allies famously considered vengeance as a possible response to the horrors of the Holocaust—an option that at various times received support, not just from Stalin but also from Churchill and Roosevelt (among others). Sadly, vengeance as a response to violence endures—the Rwandan genocide is a horrifying but by no means isolated contemporary example.

The dangerous nature of the spiraling violence that Aeschylus chronicles in *The Oresteia* helped to prompt the other common response to atrocity—"collective amnesia" or suppressing the memories of past violence in order to move forward. As Harald Wydra writes:

> Ever since Greek antiquity, forgetting has been by far the most dominant response of communities to acts of atrocity and violence (Meier 2010). From the re-establishment of democracy in Athens in 403 BC to the *perpetua oblivio* included in the Peace of Westphalia in 1648, and from the re-establishment of the monarchy in England to the return of the Bourbons to the throne of France in 1816, amnesty and oblivion have been essential to overcome atrocities and violence.[2]

Sometimes the act of forgetting has been strikingly deliberate. When King Henry IV of France issued the Edict of Nantes in 1598 to bring an end to devastating religious wars, he "declared" official amnesia and expressed it in law:

> That the memory of all things passed on the one part and the other, since the beginning of the month of *March*, 1585, until our coming to the Crown, and also during the other precedent troubles, and the occasion of the same, shall remain extinguished and suppressed, as thing that had never been.[3] (emphasis in the original)

As this suggests, forgetting the past involved everything from the passive idea of letting it fade away to active suppression. In the wake of the horrors of vengeance, collective amnesia held out the promise of a way forward that avoided

[2] Harald Wydra, Politics and the Sacred 157 (2015).

[3] The Huguenot Connection: The Edict of Nantes, Its Revocation, and Early French Migration to South Carolina 88 (Richard M. Golden ed., 1988), cited in Mihai Stelian Rusu, *Transitional Politics of Memory: Political Strategies of Managing the Past in Post-communist Romania*, 69 Eur.-Asia Stud. 1257, 1257–79 (2017).

more annihilation. And for this reason, the idea of putting the past behind us has often seemed to afford the only peaceful path forward.

When the world began to contemplate a post-Holocaust order as the end of World War II drew nigh, vengeance and amnesia may therefore have seemed to exhaust the range of possibilities. As at the end of *The Oresteia*, however, a new path started to appear.

Nuremberg and the Holocaust

Into the stark choice between vengeance and amnesia, Nuremberg introduced a transformative alternative—justice. For this reason, among many others, the trials at Nuremberg worked a dramatic shift both in how we understood the past and in what we thought we could do about it. The International Military Tribunal at Nuremberg made it possible to consider legal accountability for atrocity. Of course, use of the legal process to hold war aggressors accountable was not entirely new.[4] In the aftermath of World War I, putting the Kaiser on trial was discussed, in part as a means of vindicating international morality.[5] That, however, was a spectacular failure. Despite all of its flaws, the same could not be said of the International Military Tribunal at Nuremberg.

Among its other powerful effects, Nuremberg represented a rejection of the paradigm of pure vengeance. As World War II came to a close, a dramatic decision was made—the institutions of law would determine the fate even of the Nazi regime's worst perpetrators. In place of revenge, Nuremberg chose criminal justice, thereby adding a new and important possibility to the range of responses to mass violence. Exploring the full meaning of Nuremberg is obviously beyond our scope here. But whatever else they did, those trials expanded the range of options for responding to past violence, introducing legal justice (very partial though it undoubtedly was) into the complicated terrain of war and atrocity. As a result of Nuremberg, a new and more expansive view of accountability began to take shape. And this shift was not just in the law itself, but also in the legal and moral imagination.

The introduction of the vocabulary of justice into the context of violence and war was certainly not a foregone conclusion. The old idea of vengeance has always held appeal. Perhaps it is not surprising that at the Tehran Conference in 1943 Stalin advocated shooting 50,000–100,000 Germans.[6] With hindsight of

[4] *See* Gary Jonathan Bass, Stay the hand of Vengeance: The politics of War Crimes Tribunals 1–146 (2000); Martha Minow, Between Vengeance and Forgiveness: Facing History After Genocide and Mass Violence (1998).

[5] Bass, *supra* note 4. See especially Chapter 3: Leipzig on the "crashing failure" of that effort to hold Germans accountable for aggression and other war crimes. *Id.* at 58–105.

[6] *See id.* at 147.

history, it is easy to demonize Stalin, but he was not alone. The idea of a legal response to such horrific state crimes was novel and contentious, even amongst the Allied nations.[7] Many of the Allies questioned the legality of the trials,[8] with perhaps the most striking critique coming from the Chief Justice Harlan Fiske Stone of the US Supreme Court. He famously described the work of his erstwhile Supreme Court colleague, Nuremberg's United States Prosecutor Robert Jackson, as a "high-grade lynching."[9] Within the American administration, some hard liners such as Henri Morgenthau shared Stalin's view that the key perpetrators should simply be executed. On the opposing side were those in favor of "legalism," who insisted that trials were more consistent with American ideals of justice and fair procedures.[10] Britain too initially favored execution of top Nazis, but eventually sided with the legalist approach that had gained ascendancy in the United States.[11] The alternative to the International Military Tribunal, as Michael Marrus notes, was not some alternative judicial procedure, it was "swift execution"—vengeance in its classic form.[12] Morgenthau, for example, "had no patience for plodding legalism" and believed that a swift and terrible response was more appropriate for mass atrocity.[13] The American public, and for that matter the British public, agreed with him.[14] Nonetheless, legalism won out.[15] A new model for dealing with mass violence began to take shape—it involved accountability, though certainly a very partial version of it. For Nuremberg, of course, accountability took the form of criminal law.

The debates surrounding the establishment of the International Military Tribunal at Nuremberg associated a number of important goals with criminal prosecutions. These included establishing the truth, educating, promoting a shared understanding of the past, and re-establishing morality and the rule of law in the wake of mass violence and atrocity. This was famously captured by Robert Jackson's opening statement at the 1945 trial of Nazi leadership:

[7] *See* Donald Bloxham, Genocide on Trial: War Crime Trials and the Formation of Holocaust History and Memory vii (2001).

[8] *See* Michael R. Marrus, *International Law: The Nuremberg Trial: Fifty Years After*, 66 Am. Scholar 563 (1997); Bass, *supra* note 4, at 147–205.

[9] Bass, *supra* note 4, at 25, quoting Alpheus Thomas Mason, Harlan Fiske Stone: Pillar of the Law (1956).

[10] For an excellent history of the trials, see Marrus, *supra* note 8. *See also* Judith N. Shklar, Legalism: Law, Morals, and Political Trials 63 (1964); Bass, *supra* note 4, at 147–205. For a critique contemporaneous with the trials, see Charles E. Wyzanski, *Nuremberg: A Fair Trial? A Dangerous Precedent*, The Atlantic, Apr. 1946, at 66.

[11] *See* Bass, *supra* note 4, at 147–49.

[12] Marrus, *supra* note 8, at 564.

[13] Bass, *supra* note 4, at 152.

[14] *See id.* at 160–61, 181–84.

[15] *See id.* at 168–73, 184–91. *See also* Michael Bazyler, Holocaust, Genocide, and the Law: A Quest for Justice in a Post-Holocaust World 69–72 (2016).

> That four great nations, flushed with victory and stung with injury stay the hand of vengeance and voluntarily submit their captive enemies to the judgment of the law is one of the most significant tributes that Power has ever paid to Reason.[16]

And despite the limitations of those trials and the critiques, many of which are powerful and legitimate, Nuremberg did represent a paradigm shift away from the idea that the sovereign was immune from external accountability.[17] The notion, as Gary Bass has put it, that a civilized and fair trial was preferable to arbitrary vengeance put a new and important option on the table.[18] It also gave rise to the idea that history would be pored over, put on trial, examined, and cross-examined and that law had an important role in that enterprise. Legalism had won a major victory even if, as Bass notes, it is easy to "forget that the margin was razor-thin."[19]

For that reason, Nuremberg can be understood as helping to give birth to the idea that even the most egregious wrongs of the past could be understood as, among other things, legal wrongs or injustices. There was an aptness in this. A striking feature of the Holocaust was the fact that it was in very large measure created by law. As Michael Bazyler observes, it was "*legalized* barbarism . . . that made the massive killings of the Holocaust possible" (emphasis in the original).[20] The groundwork for murder, he argues, "was established almost entirely within the legal framework of German law."[21] Given the central role of law in perpetrating the atrocities, it was fitting and important that law was chosen as the mode of response. The world needed to re-establish moral order in the wake of such atrocity, but law too needed redemption. The International Military Tribunal at Nuremberg thus began an important change in our notion of the past and expanded the sense of the work that law could do—forging a new connection between past atrocity and legal justice. If law could enact atrocity, as it did in the hands of the Nazis, Nuremberg also showed its reflexive capacity, its ability to question itself. So despite the controversies and complexities of its legacy, Nuremberg changed the conversation and helped to shape the surge of interest in past wrongs that we see today.

The Holocaust also played a central role in starting to displace the idea that past wrongs recede over time. Both the history of the Holocaust and its legacy

[16] Robert H. Jackson, The Case Against the Nazi War Criminals: Opening Statement for the United States of America and Other Documents 3 (1946), cited in Bass, *supra* note 4, at 147.
[17] *See generally* Bass, *supra* note 4, at 147–205.
[18] *Id.* at 147–205.
[19] *Id.* at 204.
[20] Bazyler, *supra* note 15, at xxiv–xxv.
[21] *Id.* at xxv.

challenged that orthodox view of the past. As Holocaust historian Omer Bartov put it:

> There are episodes in history whose centrality can only be recognized from a chronological distance. The mass of inexplicable, often horrifying details is endowed with sense and meaning only retrospectively, after it has passed. Gradually such events come to cast a shadow over all that had previously seemed of greater significance, reaching backward and forward, until they finally touch our normal lives, reminding us with ever growing urgency that we are the survivors of cataclysms and catastrophes that we never experienced. The Holocaust is such an event.[22]

The memory of the Holocaust, in this sense, also opened up the remembering of other genocides. Whereas once it was amnesia and forgetting that seemed to afford a path forward, coming out of the Holocaust it seemed that only through remembering would we avoid repeating the horrors of history. And so the language of "Never Again" began to be invoked by others who also sought reckonings for mass violence.[23] The Holocaust and Nuremberg in this sense provided not only a model but also an inspiration for others who had suffered at the hands of history. In it they saw important parallels and began to seek their own forms of reckoning.

The trials at Nuremberg also drew a link between reckoning and records. Bass notes that one argument in favor of trying the Kaiser after World War I was the fact that there would be "for all time a record of German brutality."[24] The argument in favor of recording brutality gained new importance in the aftermath of the Holocaust. In addition to providing powerful expression of the idea that both the norms and the processes of justice could extend to reach the greatest atrocities, the Nuremberg trials also created a new and vast archive devoted to mass violence. There was certainly powerful symbolism in that—the publicity of the trials explicitly displaced the possibility of amnesia and its dangerous counterpart, repetition. But it was more than that. By their very nature, the trials—both in the documents they generated and in the public record—created new, powerful and public resources for probing the wrongs of the past.

Among their other powerful effects, the fact that the public recording and the documentary procedures of the criminal trial directed themselves to the

[22] Omer Bartov, Germany's War and the Holocaust: Disputed Histories 192 (2003), quoted in Bazyler, *supra* note 15, at xx.

[23] *See* Bazyler *supra* note 15, at xxii; John Torpey, Making Whole What has been Smashed: On Reparation Politics 37–41 (2006).

[24] Bass, *supra* note 4, at 302.

horrors of organized mass violence gave rise to new kinds of records, as well as to a shifting relation between law and history. This growing interest in historical archives—both in exploring and mining them but also in creating them—was another powerful legacy of Nuremberg. This in turn helped to generate an increased interest in other historic wrongdoing, alongside a growing impetus to examine history. In this sense, creating records of the past began to emerge as a new kind of imperative that found the early seeds of its existence in the Nuremberg trials. Marrus puts the "cultural effect" of Nuremberg in the following way:

> Nuremberg has had an important place, first, by having brought forward an extraordinarily vast body of documentation—"evidence far exceeding that previously presented to any tribunal in history," as Sir Hartley Shawcross pointed out. More than many of the organizers even hoped, Nuremberg was a voice for history—in the form of thousands of documents on the Third Reich assembled by the court and released for the scrutiny of historians and writers with every possible viewpoint.[25]

One result was that law began to emerge as a tool to pry open the annals of history—a powerful feature of the law that has been critical in shaping the approach to other past wrongs.[26] And because they rendered visible that which had been hidden, records assumed new importance in efforts to respond to old wrongs. So much so that, as we shall see, the unearthing of records and the creation of archives are now such common objectives of efforts to respond to past wrongs that they often function as their own kind of redress.[27]

In this sense then, Nuremberg was a powerful force in expanding available responses to atrocity and beginning to reshape the relationship between law and history. At the same time, it had critical limitations. As the world faced dramatic change in the 1980s, and as demands to address the past became more widespread and more insistent, some of these would prove especially troubling.

[25] Marrus, *supra* note 8, at 569–70.

[26] Technology has made archives increasing accessible. Harvard Law School, for example, holds over one million pages of the original Nuremberg trial records and in the late 1990s, it began digitizing these records so that they could be provided on an open access basis for anyone. *See* Harvard Law School Nuremberg Trials Project, http://nuremberg.law.harvard.edu/intro (last visited Dec. 3, 2024).

[27] Survivors often seek the opening or creation of archives—such as in the slave labor, Swiss gold, and residential schools cases discussed below.

Transitional Justice and the Expansion of Responses to Past Wrongs

The strengths and weakness of the International Military Tribunal at Nuremberg have rightly received a great deal of attention. As demands to confront mass wrongdoing were on the rise, it was Nuremberg's reliance on a criminal law model of accountability that came to the fore. In pursuing legal accountability for the Holocaust, it was of course not surprising that the architects of the International Military Tribunal would have reached for its most powerful manifestation—criminal law. This would turn out to play a central role in the development of international criminal law. But the confrontation with mass wrongs would also reveal some of that model's most serious limitations.

With the advent of what Samuel Huntington called the "Third Wave" of democratization that began in the 1980s,[28] these limitations loomed large. Given its penal sanctions, it was natural that the criminal model would focus on the culpability of individual wrongdoers.[29] Its ability to respond effectively to massive state-sponsored wrongs had already been questioned in the aftermath of the Holocaust, not least by Hannah Arendt who highlighted the challenges of using highly individualized concepts of criminal responsibility to address "administrative massacres organized by the state apparatus."[30] The criminal law model of accountability was inapt in another sense too—its focus was not on the victims. They had no role in the criminal law process and the restoration it aimed at was not theirs:

> The wrongdoer is brought to justice because his act has disturbed and gravely endangered the community as a whole, and not because, as in civil suits, damage has been done to individuals who are entitled to reparation. The reparation effected in criminal cases is of an altogether different nature; it is the body politic itself that stands in need of being "repaired," and it is the general

[28] Samuel P. Huntington, The Third Wave: Democratization in the Late Twentieth Century (1991).

[29] However, it is worth noting that the further the charges strayed from the terrain of classical criminal wrong, the more controversial they were. For a discussion of the controversy over criminalizing aggression, see Tom Dannenbaum, *Why Have We Criminalized Aggressive War*, 126 YALE L.J. 1242, 1254–86 (2017).

[30] Hannah Arendt, Eichmann in Jerusalem: A Report on the Banality of Evil 302 (Penguin Books 2006) (1963). *See also* Leora Bilsky, The Holocaust, Corporations and the Law: Unfinished Business 8–9 (2017) [hereinafter The Holocaust, Corporations and the Law] (noting that the victims were nearly absent from Nuremberg—the prosecution relied instead on documentary evidence and the testimony of the perpetrators); Leora Bilsky, *Hannah Arendt's Judgement of Bureaucracy*, Law Explorer (Nov. 1, 2015), https://lawexplores.com/hannah-arendts-judgement-of-bureaucracy/.

> public order that has been thrown out of gear and must be restored, as it were. It is, in other words, the law, not the plaintiff, that must prevail.[31]

Given the role of law in promulgating the Nazi atrocities, as we have noted, the law did indeed need repair. But with the punishment of individual perpetrators as the singular focus of the criminal model, there was no space for the victims of atrocity. The Eichmann trial attempted to correct their absence from Nuremberg by making their voices heard. Still, the fact that the survivors of violence seemed entirely beside the point began to emerge as another critical limitation of the Nuremberg approach.

A related worry was emerging in countries undergoing the transitions to democracy that accompanied the end of the Cold War. Criminal law accountability was undeniably powerful, but it looked backward, eschewed regard for the future, and missed the institutional dimension of atrocity. During the 1980s and 1990s, in countries from Argentina and elsewhere in Latin America, to the former Eastern Bloc countries in Europe to South Africa, there was a widespread move away from authoritarian regimes and toward democracy. In the midst of this rapid and widespread regime change, it started to seem that an alternative or perhaps a complement to the Nuremberg model was necessary. The field of transitional justice was born, and with it, interest in addressing past wrongs took a great leap forward.

The term transitional justice emerged in the early 1990s to describe human rights–focused activity designed to address the transition to democracy.[32] While the study of transitions was not new,[33] the novelty of "transitional justice" was found in its insistence that the imperatives of justice mattered even in the context of regime change. This in turn subtly reinforced the idea that official actions, even those long past, could be understood as "wrongs" that demanded redress. In 1988, activists, journalists, and theorists gathered in Aspen to consider the justice issues in their rapidly changing world. Among other questions, they pondered whether there was an obligation to punish human rights violations and whether states had an obligation to establish the truth about past human rights violations.[34]

[31] Arendt, *supra* note 30, at 273.

[32] *See* Paige Arthur, *How "Transitions" Reshaped Human Rights: A Conceptual History of Transitional Justice*, 31 Hum. Rts. Q. 321, 327–31 (2009); Ruti Teitel, *Transitional Jurisprudence: The Role of Law in Political Transformations*, 106 Yale L.J. 2009 (1996); Ruti G. Teitel, Transitional Justice 84–92 (2000).

[33] *See* Jon Elster, Closing the Books: Transitional Justice in Historical Perspective (2004).

[34] *Id.* at 352.

The punishment of human rights violations was a familiar issue from Nuremberg, though it remained controversial and complex.[35] But where the Aspen Conference changed the conversation about past wrongs was in its exploration of other mechanisms for responding to mass violence beyond criminal law. Lawrence Weschler, writing for *The New Yorker*, noted how "the same two imperatives seem to rise to the fore—the intertwined demands for [criminal] justice and for truth."[36] More gatherings followed, including the important 1994 South African conference "Dealing with the Past." The creation of the International Center for Transitional Justice in 2001 brought new prominence to the field, which it describes as follows:

> Transitional justice is a response to systematic or widespread violations of human rights. It seeks recognition for the victims and to promote possibilities for peace, reconciliation and democracy. Transitional justice is not a special kind of justice but justice adapted to societies transforming themselves after a period of pervasive human rights abuse.[37]

Alongside these developments, the central tools of transitional justice—truth commissions, prosecutions, and reparations or restitution programs—also took shape. Much of the ongoing work focuses on comprehensively addressing past injustice by also incorporating commemoration, apologies, institutional reform, and educational initiatives.[38] In 2011, the United Nations appointed its first Special Rapporteur on the promotion of truth, justice, reparation, and guarantees of non-recurrence.[39]

As the Aspen Conference had foreshadowed, the increasing concern with just transitions started to strain the Nuremberg-inspired idea that criminal law was always the best tool to address mass state-sponsored wrongs. Criminal prosecution certainly continued to be important, but its limited conception of responsibility simply could not meet the broader needs of transitional justice. In the search for mechanisms that embodied broader notions of accountability, understanding the past became an important imperative, and the truth commission started to emerge as a central institution of transitional justice. Unlike criminal

[35] For a seminal work on this complex issue, see Diane F. Orentlicher, *Settling Accounts: The Duty to Prosecute Human Rights Violations of a Previous Regime*, 100 Yale L.J. 2537 (1991).
[36] Arthur, *supra* note 32, at 353, quoting Lawrence Weschler, *Afterword*, *in* State Crimes: Punishment or Pardon—Papers and Report of the Conference, November 4–6, 1988, Wye Center, Maryland 89, 90, 92 (Justice and Society Program of The Aspen Institute 1989).
[37] International Center for Transitional Justice, *What Is Transitional Justice?* (2008), https://legal.un.org/avl/pdf/ls/Van-Zyl_RecReading1_.pdf [hereinafter ICTJ, *What Is Transitional Justice?*].
[38] *See e.g.* ICTJ, https://www.ictj.org/how-we-work (last visited Dec. 3, 2024).
[39] *Special Rapporteur on Truth, Justice and Reparation*, United Nations Office of the High Commissioner for Human Rights, https://www.ohchr.org/en/special-procedures/sr-truth-justice-reparation-and-non-recurrence (last visited Dec. 3, 2024).

law, most truth commissions looked both backward and forward—"truth" was about understanding and documenting the past; "reconciliation" and "non-recurrence" were about the future. They attempted to find a path, as Martha Minow put it, "between too much memory and too much forgetting."[40] Along two very different but related dimensions, the truth commission widened the lens of accountability.

The first such widening responded to the Arendtian worry about the uneasy fit between the criminal trial and the bureaucratized nature of mass violence.[41] By looking beyond the activities of individual perpetrators and attempting to understand the institutional dimension of widespread violence, the truth commission helped to fill out criminal law's limited picture of responsibility. The framing of such commissions and their rules of procedure and evidence gave them a latitude that the criminal law model understandably lacks. Even beyond this, truth commissions are often explicitly asked to probe the role played by the powerful institutions of society—the police, the military, the judicial system, government, business, or the church—in human rights violations. The groundbreaking Argentinian National Commission on the Disappearance of Persons, for example, expressly focused on examining the role of the military in the disappearances.[42] In South Africa, the Truth and Reconciliation Commission held specific institutional hearings about the legal profession and the judges. After German reunification in 1989, two commissions of inquiry focused on the role of the former East German government in perpetrating human rights abuses. Their mandates specifically referred to the assessment of the roles of prominent institutions, including not only government but churches, other organizations, and many other dimensions of society.[43]

In addition to highlighting the institutional dimension of massive wrongdoing, the truth commission also brought the victim clearly into view for the first time. In sharp contrast with Nuremberg, the first-person narrative of the victims began to gain prominence with the arrival of transitional justice. The mandate of South Africa's important Truth and Reconciliation Commission explicitly included "allowing victims the opportunity to tell their story."[44] Over 21,000 survivors gave testimony, and 2,000 spoke at public hearings that were

[40] MINOW, *supra* note 4, at 4.

[41] See ARENDT, *supra* note 30.

[42] See COMISIÓN NACIONAL SOBRE LA DESAPARICIÓN DE PERSONAS, NUNCA MÁS (1984).

[43] *Germany: Law Creating the Commission of Inquiry on Working Through the History and Consequences of the SED Dictatorship—Act No. 12/2597 (May 14, 1992), in* 3 TRANSITIONAL JUSTICE: HOW EMERGING DEMOCRACIES RECKON WITH FORMER REGIMES 216, 216–19 (Neil J. Kritz ed., 1995).

[44] Katherine Beaty Chiste, *The Origins of Modern Restorative Justice: Five Examples from the English-Speaking World*, 46 U.B.C. L.REV. 33, 53 (2013). For more detail, *see* SOUTH AFRICAN TRUTH AND RECONCILIATION COMMISSION, https://www.justice.gov.za/trc/report/ (last visited Dec. 3, 2024).

widely broadcasted. This focus on the voices of survivors inspired others, including Canada's Truth and Reconciliation Commission, which was similarly mandated "to receive statements and documents from former students, their families, community and all other interested participants" and to recognize "the unique experiences" of all former students.[45] Many thousands took up this opportunity, and the Truth and Reconciliation Commission published a volume called *The Survivors Speak*.[46] This "victim-centered approach" was a dramatic departure from the Nuremberg model, drawing as it did on survivors as the "primary sources of information for truth commissions."[47] This focus also began to spur interest in the role of other survivor-centered elements, especially commemoration and apology.

As the wrongs of institutions and the voices of survivors gained prominence, the range of responses to wrongs also expanded. The shift in gaze from Nuremberg's focus on the wrongdoer to transitional justice's concern with the survivor gave new prominence to the idea of repairing the wrong. The more that truth commissions, study projects, and archival work focused on the suffering of the victims, the more it seemed necessary to respond in some significant way to their individual injuries. And the fact that the truth commissions were simultaneously exploring a wider understanding of who was responsible for those wrongs also brought a new possible class of institutional defendants into the picture. This prompted work on how to rectify wrongs, perhaps the most significant of which—and certainly the most controversial—was the increasing interest in material reparations as a necessary part of any response to atrocity.[48]

The Center for Transitional Justice captured this emerging sense, noting that reparations "acknowledge and repair the causes and consequences of human rights violations" and all victims have a right to reparation.[49] Reconciliation after atrocity, many have noted, requires a credibility that only the implementation of a tangible economic and social program can provide.[50] In the transitional justice

[45] TRUTH AND RECONCILIATION COMMISSION OF CANADA, THE SURVIVORS SPEAK: A REPORT OF THE TRUTH AND RECONCILIATION COMMISSION OF CANADA 1 (2015).

[46] *Id.*

[47] INTERNATIONAL CENTER FOR TRANSITIONAL JUSTICE, TRUTH SEEKING: ELEMENTS OF CREATING AN EFFECTIVE TRUTH COMMISSION 11 (2013).

[48] *See generally* THE HANDBOOK ON REPARATIONS, (Pablo de Greiff ed., 2006); TORPEY, *supra* note 23, at 42–77; Luke Moffett, *Transitional Justice and Reparations: Remedying the Past?*, *in* RESEARCH HANDBOOK ON TRANSITIONAL JUSTICE 377 (Cheryl Lawther et al. eds., 2017); Debra Satz, *Countering the Wrongs of the Past: The Role of Compensation*, *in* TRANSITIONAL JUSTICE 129 (Melissa S. Williams et al. eds., 2020) (and sources cited therein).

[49] *Reparations*, INTERNATIONAL CENTER FOR TRANSITIONAL JUSTICE, https://www.ictj.org/reparations#:~:text = ICTJ%20helps%20victims%20articulate%20their,designing%20and%20implementing%20reparations%20programs (last visited Dec. 3, 2024).

[50] Sampie Terreblanche, *Dealing with Systematic Economic Injustice*, *in* LOOKING BACK, REACHING FORWARD: REFLECTIONS ON THE TRUTH AND RECONCILIATION COMMISSION OF SOUTH AFRICA 265, 265–76 (Charles Villa-Vicencio & Wilhelm Verwoerd eds., 2000); PRISCILLA HAYNER, UNSPEAKABLE TRUTHS: CONFRONTING STATE TERROR AND ATROCITY (2001).

context, reparation is generally understood broadly to encompass a range of efforts to restore the survivor as far as possible to the pre-wrong condition. This could include return of especially personally significant property—for instance, restitution of artwork or the family home. But it also includes individual financial compensation aimed at undoing at least some of the effects of catastrophic wrongdoing.[51] For victims, reparations are often "the most tangible manifestation" of the seriousness of efforts to remedy their harms, yet ironically they are also often the weakest element.[52] In the context of the South African Truth and Reconciliation Commission, for example, the Reparations and Rehabilitations Committee was tasked with making recommendations regarding "the granting of reparation to victims" or "other measures aimed at rehabilitating and restoring the human and civil dignity of victims."[53] Their eventual recommendations acknowledged the critical symbolic effect of material reparations—the nation's way of "saying sorry."[54] This in turn reflected the fact that reparative justice and its commitment to repairing past wrongs were starting to become an integral part of the lexicon of transitional justice.

Beyond serving as the institutional expression of this new and broader form of accountability, the truth commission also had a larger cultural effect. It did more than just give legitimacy to the duty to remember, it also gave a powerful means by which to accomplish it. The old 'time heals' approach was giving way to a new conviction that remembering, not forgetting, was the only way to come to terms with the past.[55] Whereas once moving on required memory be suppressed, transitional justice promoted the opposite—it should be explored, acknowledged, and commemorated. What some commentators have referred to as the "memory boom" was born.[56] A whole new vocabulary emerged—the "politics of memory"

[51] *See generally* de Greiff, *supra* note 48. As he discusses, the reparations element was in a sense late to the game of transitional justice, and he describes the record on implementing reparations as "dismal." *Id.* at 466.

[52] *See* Pablo de Greiff, *Introduction—Repairing the Past: Compensation for Victims of Human Rights Violations, in* THE HANDBOOK OF REPARATIONS, *supra* note 48, at 1, 2.

[53] Promotion of National Unity and Reconciliation Act 34 of 1995, § 4(f) (S. Afr.).

[54] *See* 5 TRUTH AND RECONCILIATION COMMISSION OF SOUTH AFRICA, FINAL REPORT 170–95 (1998) (outlining the Reparation and Rehabilitation Policy). The recommendations of the Reparation and Rehabilitation Committee have been the subject of ongoing controversy because of the lack of implementation. *See e.g.* Brandon Hamber, *Repairing the Irreparable: Dealing with Double-Binds of Making Reparations for Crimes of the Past*, 5 ETHNICITY & HEALTH 215 (2000); Adam Yates, *Justice Delayed: The TRC Recommendations 20 Years Later*, DAILY MAVERICK (S. Afr., Sept. 5, 2018).

[55] Martha Minow expressed this attitudinal shift when she stated that "[c]losure is not possible." Minow, *supra* note 4, at 5.

[56] *See* Peter J. Verovšek, *Collective Memory, Politics, and the Influence of the Past: The Politics of Memory as a Research Paradigm*, 4 POL., GROUPS & IDENTITIES 529 (2016). For a good overview of prior work, see THE POLITICS OF MEMORY AND DEMOCRATIZATION (Alexandra Barahona De Brito et al. eds., 2001). *See also* MEMORY, TRAUMA AND WORLD POLITICS: REFLECTIONS ON THE RELATIONSHIP BETWEEN PAST AND PRESENT (Duncan Bell ed., 2006); MEMORY, POLITICS AND IDENTITY: HAUNTED HISTORY (Cillian McGrattan ed., 2013); ZHENG WANG, MEMORY POLITICS, IDENTITY AND CONFLICT: HISTORICAL MEMORY AS A VARIABLE (2017); Sarah Kenyon Lischer,

became a term of art and frequent references to "collective memory" started to appear.[57] *The New Yorker*, *The Economist*, and *Psychology Today*, as well as a vast new academic literature started to tackle the issue of collective memory in its many manifestations and, with it, the sudden prevalence of the past.[58] Academic programs, courses, and book series were devoted to issues such as collective memory, memory studies, and transitional justice.[59] Columbia University, for instance, hosts a platform called the Historical Dialogues, Justice, and Memory Network, which explores "issues relating to historical dialogues, historical and transitional justice, and public and social memory."[60] And so, alongside the rise in transitional justice came a very different attitude to history, one that valorized re-examining trauma and that prompted a deep interest in exploring the wrongs of the past.

The truth commission was the most important institutional expression of this new interest in uncovering the troubling truths about the past. But what should follow in its wake? This became a critical question for transitional justice and inspired a range of responses that focused on acknowledgment. Among the most important of these was the apology, which began to occupy an important role in holistic transitional justice programs.[61] As the International Center for Transitional Justice report on the subject notes, when properly crafted, apologies can play a critical role in serving as a "public acknowledgement that human rights violations were committed in the past, that they caused serious and often

Narrative Atrocity: Genocide Memorials, Dark Tourism, and the Politics of Memory, 45 Rev. Int'l Stud. 805 (2019); The Politics of Memory in Chile: From Pinochet to Bachelet (Cath Collins et al. eds., 2022); Handbook on the Politics of Memory (Maria Mälksoo ed., 2023); Remembering Mass Atrocities: Perspective on Memory Struggles and Cultural Representations in Africa (Mphathisi Ndlovu et al. eds., 2024).

[57] For an illustration, see Rusu, *supra* note 3, at 1274, 1277.

[58] *See* Charlemagne, *The Politics of Memory*, The Economist (Apr. 9, 2016); Jane Kramer, *Letter from Germany: The Politics of Memory*, The New Yorker (Aug. 14, 1995); Sam Osherson, *How the Politics of Memory Affects Us All*, Psychology Today (Apr. 16, 2015). These are but a few examples of what has become a vast literature exploring the politics of memory, collective memory, and related concepts. For an overview, see Verovšek, *supra* note 56; Stiina Löytömäki, Law and the Politics of Memory: Confronting the Past (2014).

[59] *See e.g. Book Series: Memory Politics and Transitional Justice*, Palgrave MacMillan, https://www.palgrave.com/gp/series/14807 (last visited Dec. 3, 2024); *Memory Studies and the Politics of Memory*, University of Nottingham, https://www.nottingham.ac.uk/research/groups/memory-studies-and-the-politics-of-memory/index.aspx (last visited Dec. 3, 2024); *Politics of Memory in Global Context*, Columbia University, https://cgt.columbia.edu/research/memory/ (last visited Dec. 3, 2024); *MSc Politics and International Relations*, SOAS University of London, https://www.soas.ac.uk/study/find-course/msc-politics-and-international-relations (last visited Dec. 3, 2024).

[60] *Historical Dialogues, Justice and Memory Network*, Columbia University Institute for the Study of Human Rights, https://historicaldialogues.org/about/mission-statement/ (last visited Dec. 3, 2024).

[61] *See* Teitel, Transitional Justice, *supra* note 32; Elster, *supra* note 33.

irreparable harm to victims, and that the state, group, or individual apologising is accepting some or all of the responsibility for what happened."[62]

Alongside apologies and often hand in hand with them, the issue of commemoration also gained prominence in discussions of transitional justice:

> Victims of human rights abuses cannot forget, and states have a duty to preserve the historical memory of periods of violence and repression. In this regard, architectural memorials, museums, and commemorative activities are indispensable educational initiatives that establish a public record and serve as a bastion against denial and recurrence.[63]

Material commemoration has thus become a prominent element of transitional justice programs, and truth commissions often recommend memorialization activities.[64] The museum has assumed an especially important role in commemoration, as exemplified by the many Holocaust museums, Chile's Museum of Memory and Human Rights, and many other examples.[65] In the African Union's Draft Framework for Transitional Justice, one of the first steps in the implementation plan is a human rights memorial at the African Union Compound to commemorate the Rwandan genocide.[66] Days of remembrance, such as for the Holocaust and Northern Ireland's National Day of Commemoration, are another common form of commemoration.[67]

[62] International Center for Transitional Justice, Reparative Justice—More Than Words: Apologies as a Form of Reparation 1 (2015).

[63] *Truth and Memory*, International Center for Transitional Justice, https://www.ictj.org/our-work/transitional-justice-issues/truth-and-memory (last visited Dec. 3, 2024).

[64] This has been the case in Chile, Guatemala, South Africa, and Sierra Leone, for example. *See* Judy Barsalou and Victoria Baxter, United States Institute of Peace, The Urge to Remember: The Role of Memorials in Social Reconstruction and Transitional Justice (2017), cited in Laia Balcells et al., *Do Museums Promote Reconciliation? A Field Experiment on Transitional Justice* (Feb. 16, 2018), http://web.isanet.org/Web/Conferences/San%20Francisco%202018-s/Archive/d263dc13-0674-4cd5-8c6a-724cb3d2de69.pdf.

[65] There is a broad literature on the role of museums in transitional justice. For some examples, see Brandon Hamber, *Museums, Nostalgia, and Dreaming of Never Again*, 18 Peace & Conflict 268 (2012); Duncan Light & Craig Young, *Public Memory, Commemoration, and Transitional Justice: Reconfiguring the Past in Public Space*, *in* Post-Communist Transitional Justice: Lessons from Twenty-Five Years of Experience 233 (Lavinia Stan & Nadya Nedelsky eds., 2015); Johanna Mannergren Selimovic, *The Stuff from the Siege: Transitional Justice and the Power of Everyday Objects in Museums*, 16 Int'l J. Transitional Just. 220 (2022); Eduardo Briceño-Florez & Kathryn Eccles, *Museums as Platforms of Resistance: The Use of Technology in Memory, Transitional Justice and Peacebuilding*, 74 Museum Int'l 82 (2022).

[66] *What Is the Role of Truth Commissioners in the Peace Processes in Africa?*, International Center for Transitional Justice (Apr. 18, 2016), https://www.ictj.org/news/african-union-kofi-annan-ictj-truth-commissions-peace.

[67] *See* Yael Daniele, *Healing Aspects of Reparations and Reparative Justice for Victims of Crimes Against Humanity*, *in* Reparations for Victims of Crimes Against Humanity: The Healing Role of Reparations 7, 16–17 (Jo-Anne W. Wemmers ed., 2014). *See e.g. National Day for Truth and Reconciliation*, Government of Canada (Nov. 22, 2024), https://www.canada.ca/en/canadian-heritage/campaigns/national-day-truth-reconciliation.html; *International Day of*

This focus on remembering and understanding also spurred new interest in studying the past more deeply, often with a special emphasis on the creation of archives. The dramatically titled "Atrocity's Archives" is an example of the emphasis that transitional justice programs place on archives. A collaborative project between the Stasi Records Office in Berlin, the Faculty of Law at Oxford, and swisspeace in Bern, it aims at a better understanding of the role of archives in the aftermath of conflict and violence, as well as guidance on best practices.[68] Transitional justice brought a new kind of interest in what we teach about the past and how we do so. For example, the International Center for Transitional Justice has a major research project that aims to illuminate "how transitional justice can shape the reform of education systems by ensuring programs are sensitive to the legacies of the past."[69] And as transitional justice has grown as a field, we have seen the development of organizations devoted to educating in the wake of atrocity. An example is found in Facing Our History, Shaping Our Future, which has helped to develop post-transition education projects in contexts as diverse as South Africa, Rwanda, and Northern Ireland.[70]

One result of the rapid growth of interest in transitional justice was that its impact began to reach beyond its original context of regime change. By expanding the understanding of accountability, encouraging examination of past wrongs, and shifting emphasis to those who suffered, transitional justice provided the foundation for a deeper and more critical engagement with history even where there was no abrupt official break with the past. Its insistence on understanding and addressing past wrongs prompted a broader interest in reckonings, especially from those who had suffered at history's hands in long-standing democracies. As it turned out, seemingly unrelated developments taking place in stable democracies helped to provide some of the critical tools that would help to force such reckonings beyond the transitional context.

Commemoration in Memory of the Victims of the Holocaust, UNESCO, https://www.unesco.org/en/days/holocaust-remembrance (last visited Feb. 16, 2025); Marc Raboy, *Memory, Truth, and Justice as Argentina Honours the Victims of State Terrorism*, Oxford University Press Blog (Mar. 24, 2022), https://blog.oup.com/2022/03/memory-truth-and-justice-as-argentina-honours-the-victims-of-state-terrorism/.

[68] *See Atrocity's Archives: The Role of Archives in Transitional Justice*, University of Oxford, https://www.law.ox.ac.uk/role-archives-transitional-justice (last visited Dec. 3, 2024).

[69] *Transitional Justice, Education, and Peacebuilding*, International Center for Transitional Justice, https://www.ictj.org/our-work/research/education-peacebuilding (last visited Dec. 3, 2024).

[70] *See* Tricia Logan & Karen Murphy, *Reflections on Education and Transitional Justice: Notes from the Field*, 53 Comp. Educ. 483 (2017).

The Turn to Civil Remedies

While transitional justice thinkers were questioning the primacy of the Nuremberg model of criminal accountability, human rights-oriented advocates in many domestic legal systems were identifying related challenges. Frustrated with the limitations of criminal law, they started to look for new ways to protect the most fundamental human rights—especially bodily integrity. Domestic human rights advocates for women and other marginalized groups pointed to the individual focus of the criminal model as a challenge, particularly in situations where there was an institutional dimension to the wrongdoing. They also worried about how the criminal model largely left the victim out of the picture. These limitations provided an impetus to think creatively about how to find more effective means of vindicating fundamental rights violations in stable democracies. What they turned to was private law's civil remedy.

The 1980s was a period of dramatic political and legal change, not just transnationally but also in stable democracies. The burgeoning civil justice movement—beginning with the tragic *Tarasoff* case—was a critical element of this.[71] Poddar, a student at the University of California at Berkeley, became obsessed with a fellow student, Tatiana Tarasoff. When she rejected his advances, he became depressed. During a session with a university psychiatrist, Poddar said that he intended to kill Tarasoff. He was briefly committed, but then released. Sadly, no one was warned and Poddar carried out his plan. He was criminally convicted, but her family, infuriated with the institutional complicity in their daughter's death, sued the University of California and the doctor. In a groundbreaking opinion, the Supreme Court of California found that a mental health professional has a duty not only to a patient but also to individuals who are specifically threatened by a patient. *Tarasoff* highlighted the inability of criminal law to capture the institutional dimension of wrongdoing and the failure to protect women in particular. It also inspired others who began to see civil justice as an alternative to criminal law.

Then in 1980, Yale Law School professor Owen Fiss published an important article on the rise of civil remedies for human rights violations.[72] In an intriguing parallel to transitional justice, Fiss pointed to the shift toward civil justice as a necessary supplement to the criminal model because the traditional legal system was poorly equipped to address human rights violations committed by bureaucratic organizations, both state and private. The growth of large bureaucracies and organizations made it especially important, he argued, to recognize group liability including through civil remedies and class action lawsuits.

[71] Tarasoff v. Regents of Univ. of California, 17 Cal. 3d 425 (1976).
[72] Owen M. Fiss, *The Forms of Justice*, 93 Harv. L. Rev. 1 (1979).

In the same year that Fiss's groundbreaking article came out, another very different landmark civil remedies case shook the legal establishment. In *Filartiga v. Pena-Irala*, the United States Court of Appeals for the Second Circuit held that a little used piece of legislation from 1789, the Alien Tort Statute, enabled American courts to hear civil actions for torture committed elsewhere. Two Paraguayan citizens had invoked the Alien Tort Statute to sue a Paraguayan police official who had tortured and killed their relative in Paraguay. The district court had dismissed the claim for lack of subject matter jurisdiction, but the Second Circuit reversed.[73] Judge Kaufman found that the reference to a "violation of the law of nations" in the Alien Tort Statute encompassed evolving notions of customary international law.[74] That law specified that all individuals, regardless of their nationality, possess a fundamental human right to be free from "deliberate torture perpetrated under color of official authority."[75] On remand, the district judge awarded the two Paraguayan citizens a default judgment against the Paraguayan police chief of nearly $10.4 million in compensatory and punitive damages.[76] Between *Tarasoff* and *Filartiga*, the idea that civil remedies could be used to redress fundamental violations of human rights was starting to take hold of the domestic legal imagination.

In the following decades, enormous energy and creativity were devoted to exploring the potential of civil remedies to address some of the limitations of traditional legal responsibility. Feminist advocates were particularly influential. Disillusioned with how female victims of male violence fared in criminal law, they turned to tort law and their work helped to inspire others who saw promise in the civil justice model.[77] This was especially important in the United States where the rise of civil remedies for "constitutional torts"[78] and especially for "mass torts"[79] dramatically expanded their role in human rights violations. Sexual violence was one of the most important areas for the exploration of civil remedies. Across a wide range of jurisdictions, victims of sexual violence and

[73] Filartiga v. Pena-Irala, 630 F.2d 876 (2d Cir. 1980).

[74] *Id.* at 881.

[75] *Id.* at 878.

[76] Filartiga v. Pena-Irala, 577 F. Supp. 860 (E.D.N.Y. 1984).

[77] *See e.g.* Leslie Bender, *A Lawyer's Primer on Feminist Theory and Tort*, 38 J. LEGAL EDUC. 3 (1988); Leslie Bender, *Overview of Feminist Torts Scholarship*, 78 CORNELL L. REV. 575 (1993); Adrian Howe, *The Problem of Privatized Injuries: Feminist Strategies for Litigation*, 10 STUD L. POL. & SOC'Y 119 (1990); Adrian Howe, *The Problem of Privatized Injuries: Feminist Strategies for Litigation*, *in* AT THE BOUNDARIES OF LAW: FEMINISM AND LEGAL THEORY 148 (Martha Albertson Fineman & Nancy Sweet Thomadsen eds., 1991).

[78] *See* Christina B. Whitman, *Government Responsibility for Constitutional Torts*, 85 MICH. L. REV. 225 (1986); Michael Wells, *The Past and the Future of Constitutional Torts: From Statutory Interpretation to Common Law Rules*, 19 CONN. L. REV. 53 (1986); Michael Wells, *Constitutional Torts, Common Law Torts, and Due Process of Law*, 72 CHI.-KENT L. REV. 617 (1997); John C. Jeffries, *Disaggregating Constitutional Torts*, 110 YALE L.J. 259 (2000).

[79] *See e.g.* Elizabeth J. Cabraser, *Human Rights Violations as Mass Torts: Compensation as a Proxy for Justice in the United States Civil Litigation System*, 57 VAND. L. REV. 2211 (2004).

incest also started to sue civilly. Beginning in the 1980s, advocates began to file civil suits against the perpetrators of sexual violence, particularly in cases involving familial abuse or incest.[80] In a groundbreaking Canadian case, Karen Marciano sued her father for childhood sexual abuse. Although the limitations period had long expired, the Supreme Court of Canada reshaped the limitations regime for sexual abuse survivors and began a dramatic shift across jurisdictions for survivors of childhood sexual abuse.[81]

By the 1990s, following the lead of *Tarasoff*, survivors were also beginning to direct their attention to the institutions that enabled the abuse. The sexual abuse crisis in the Catholic Church was, as discussed below, especially important in opening up institutional responsibility for sexual violence and other violations. Related developments were occurring across jurisdictions. In Canada, a rape victim successfully sued the Toronto Police Service for failing to warn her of a serial rapist, despite the fact that they had identified her as a likely victim.[82] Novel civil actions also started to target other violations of fundamental rights. A woman who had been wrongly sterilized under Alberta's eugenics program sued the province and was awarded $740,780 in damages.[83] In England, the family of the last victim of the Yorkshire Ripper sued the police, and while they did not prevail, it did signal the beginning of a turn to civil remedies for fundamental rights violations.[84] Novel civil actions were also on the rise in Australia where survivors of childhood sexual abuse began suing both the perpetrators and the institutions that made the abuse possible. Though Australian courts tended to be rather unsympathetic to these early claims, often ruling that the claimants were out of time,[85] institutions started to feel a new and different kind

[80] *See* Jocelyn B. Lamm, *Easing Access to the Courts for Incest Victims: Toward an Equitable Application of the Delayed Discovery Rule*, 100 YALE L.J. 2189 (1991); Camille W. Cook & Pamela Kirkwood Millsaps, *Redressing Wrongs of the Blamelessly Ignorant Survivor of Incest*, 26 U. RICH. L. REV. 1 (1991); Meredith Felise Sopher, *"The Best Of All Possible Worlds": Balancing Victims' and Defendants' Rights in the Child Sexual Abuse Case*, 63 FORDHAM L. REV. 633 (1994); Joyce McConnell, *Incest as Conundrum: Judicial Discourse on Private Wrong and Public Harm*, 1 TEX. J. WOMEN & L. 143 (1992).

[81] M.(K.). v. M.(H.), [1992] 3 S.C.R. 6 (Can.).

[82] Doe v. Metropolitan Toronto (Municipality) Commissioners of Police (1998), 39 O.R. (3d) 487, 1998 CanLII 14826 (Can. Ont. Gen. Div.).

[83] Muir v. Alberta (1998), 132 D.L.R. (4th) 695, 1996 CanLII 7287 (Can. Alta. K.B.), as discussed in more detail below in Chapter 4.

[84] *Hill* was followed by the controversial *Osman* in which the family of a murder victim killed by a known stalker sued the police: Osman v. United Kingdom, [1998] ECHR 101. The European Court of Human Rights overruled English courts and held that police could be liable for failure to protect likely targets of foreseeable criminal harm, though on the facts it found no liability. The issue has continued to be complex. *See* Gordon Anthony, *Public Authority Liability in the United Kingdom: A Common Law Perspective*, *in* TORT LIABILITY OF PUBLIC AUTHORITIES IN EUROPEAN LAWS 80 (Giacinto della Cananea & Roberto Caranta eds., 2020).

[85] *See* discussion in ROYAL COMMISSION INTO INSTITUTIONAL RESPONSES TO CHILD SEXUAL ABUSE, REDRESS AND CIVIL LITIGATION REPORT 435–43 (2015).

of pressure. The litigation was a critical catalyst for Australia's important Royal Commission into Institutional Responses to Child Sexual Abuse.

Though this is but a very brief overview, it does serve to highlight several striking features of this turn to civil remedies. To begin with, it is significant that much of it was occurring at the same time serious transitional justice efforts were underway. But second and more fundamentally, it seems noteworthy that so much of the thinking in both undertakings was focused on how to expand beyond the constrained criminal law model of responsibility. Civil justice advocates certainly had many pragmatic reasons to prefer the civil to the criminal domain, including greater control for the complainant and a more plaintiff-friendly burden of proof, as well as a superior array of remedies. But there were also deeper currents at work. These ambitious new civil actions were beginning to stretch the underlying concept of legal responsibility, pressing for an expanded understanding of the duty to repair wrongs or reparative justice. As we shall see, this turned out to play a very significant role in giving rise to the new pressure to redress historic wrongs.

Reparations Reborn

As transitional justice was taking hold in the transnational sphere and the new more ambitious use of civil remedies was on the rise in a number of domestic jurisdictions, an idea important to what would become the problem of the past was migrating from the transnational to the domestic arena. The idea was reparations.

The term is a venerable one that takes its meaning from "repair" and in that sense often refers generically to compensation for (wrongful) injury. However, the meaning of reparations has changed in telling ways over the past few decades. Traditionally, reparations were primarily understood as part of the post-conflict framework of relations between nations and referred to payments the losing state was obligated to pay the victor for damages arising out of war.[86] The most widely known example is the controversial multibillion-dollar reparations payments imposed on post-war Germany as part of the Treaty of Versailles.[87]

However, this understanding began to shift in the aftermath of World War II. Unlike its predecessors, the post-war German reparations program was not limited to interstate compensation but also extended to individuals. This

[86] *See* Ariel Colonomos & Andrea Armstrong, *German Reparations to the Jews After World War II: A Turning Point in the History of Reparations*, *in* The Handbook of Reparations, *supra* note 51, at 390, 390–91.

[87] *See id. See also* Richard Falk, *Reparations, International Law, and Global Justice: A New Frontier*, *in* The Handbook of Reparations, *supra* note 51, at 478, 486.

larger "duty of moral and material reparations" was justified by West Germany's Chancellor on the ground that "unspeakable crimes were committed in the name of the German people."[88] As this suggested, the logic of reparations was shifting away from victory and defeat to an emphasis on moral culpability and an associated duty to repair. The West German reparations program included payments to Israel and individuals. Distributed through both pre-existing Jewish organizations and the Conference on Jewish Material Claims Against Germany, more than half a million victims of Nazi persecution received over $86 billion between 1945 and 2018, and the number continues to grow, despite dwindling numbers of survivors.[89] In addition to its scale, the post-war German program also marked the first time that a state had compensated its own citizens alongside those of the enemy.[90] In that sense, it helped to establish a new reparations model that moved away from the traditional interstate meaning and toward a more individualized understanding. In the transitional justice context, it was that individualized understanding that began to come to the fore.

Though reparations developed more slowly than other features of transitional justice, the conferences in Aspen, Salzberg, and South Africa all called attention to the importance of reparations for victims of gross violations of human rights.[91] This concern was a critical impetus for transitional justice's repurposing of the idea of reparations but with a more individualized focus. In the transitional justice context, the term reparations began to be used to refer to individualized measures such as material compensation for victims of human rights violations and accompanying symbolic measures such as apologies and commemoration.[92] While criminal prosecutions were "against perpetrators," this emerging form of reparations was "on behalf of victims."[93] What has been called the "incipient normative revolution of the 1990s" was characterized in large measure by a newfound concern with "rectifying harm previously done to individuals and groups."[94] In the important *The Handbook on Reparations*, Pablo de Greiff stressed this orientation, as evidenced by the title of his introduction, "Repairing the Past: Compensation for Victims of Human Rights Violations."[95] And as the

[88] Colonomos & Armstrong, *supra* note 86, at 393, citing CHRISTIAN PROSS, PAYING FOR THE PAST: THE STRUGGLE OVER REPARATIONS FOR THE SURVIVING VICTIMS OF THE NAZI TERROR 22 (1998).

[89] Gideon Taylor, *Where Morality Meets Money*, *in* HOLOCAUST RESTITUTION: PERSPECTIVES ON THE LITIGATION AND ITS LEGACY 163, 163 (Michael J. Bazyler & Roger P. Alford eds., 2006); *Justice for Uncompensated Survivors Today (JUST) Act Report*, U.S. DEPARTMENT OF STATE (March 2020), https://www.state.gov/reports/just-act-report-to-congress/germany/.

[90] *See* Lily Rothman, *"I Felt Elated." Holocaust Survivors Make Gains in Latest Negotiations with German Government*, TIME (July 12, 2017).

[91] *See* Arthur, *supra* note 32, at 325–29; STATE CRIMES: PUNISHMENT OR PARDON, *supra* note 36.

[92] *See* de Greiff, *supra* note 48, at 452–53.

[93] de Greiff, *supra* note 48, at 2.

[94] Falk, *supra* note 87, at 479.

[95] *See* de Greiff, *supra* note 48, at 1.

idea of reparations individualized and began to focus more sharply on compensation for fundamental human rights violations, it was also beginning to take a form that had salience far beyond the transitional justice context and that linked up quite naturally with the interest in novel civil actions in the domestic legal arena.

At the same time that these transitional justice developments were underway, non-transitional regimes were also witnessing the beginnings of a revival of a much older debate about reparations in the United States. The question of reparations for American chattel slavery was not new. It had been raised immediately after the Civil War in the form of the well-known suggestion that "forty acres and a mule" would be one possible way to compensate freed slaves for their unpaid labor. Though that effort came to an end with the short-lived period of Reconstruction, this was only the beginning of efforts to secure reparations. The first slavery reparations lawsuit, *Johnson v. McAdoo*, was brought in 1915. Frustrated after decades of fruitless advocacy, freed slaves sued the United States for $68,000,000, pointing to the fact that the cotton taxed by the government was produced by their "involuntary servitude."[96] The Court of Appeals denied their claim, saying that the government was immune, and the Supreme Court agreed.[97] But efforts to secure reparations for slavery continued. Dr. Martin Luther King and others often raised reparations as an issue during the civil rights struggle, though they did not meet with success. Then in 1973, Yale Law School tax law professor Boris Bittker stunned the academic world with the publication of his book, *The Case for Black Reparations*, which concluded that reparations was not a far-fetched idea.[98]

These developments laid the foundation for the modern reparations movement that got underway in earnest in the United States at about the same time that the key transitional justice conferences were taking place internationally. In 1987, Mari Matsuda published *Looking to the Bottom: Critical Legal Studies and Reparations*, which is viewed as one of the key texts in the resurgence of modern reparations.[99] Around the same time, the first serious non-transitional reparations success, the Civil Liberties Act of 1988, extended individual compensation and a presidential apology to Japanese-Americans interned during World

[96] Johnson v. McAdoo, 45 App. D.C. 440 (1916), *aff'd*, 244 U.S. 643 (1917); Miranda Booker Perry, *No Pensions for Ex-Slaves: How Federal Agencies Suppressed Movement to Aid Freedpeople*, 42:2 Prologue Magazine (2010). For a discussion of the case, *see* John G. Browning, *"Seeking the Fruits of Their Labors": The Story of* Johnson v. McAdoo, *The First Major Reparations Case*, 11 J. Race, Gender, and Ethnicity 1 (2022).

[97] *Id.*

[98] Boris Bittker, The Case for Black Reparations (1973).

[99] Mari J. Matsuda, *Looking to the Bottom: Critical Legal Studies and Reparations*, 22 Harv. C.R.-C.L. L. Rev. 323 (1987). *See also* Alfred L. Brophy, *Reparations Talk: Reparations for Slavery and the Tort Law Analogy*, 24 B.C. Third World L.J. 81, 82 (2004); Charles J. Ogletree, Jr., *Repairing the Past: New Efforts in the Reparations Debate in America*, 38 Harv. C.R.-C.L. L. Rev. 279, 283 (2003).

War II.[100] Canada followed suit with its own reparations program and apology for Japanese-Canadians who were subjected to internment.[101] A burgeoning literature on reparations soon followed, beginning in the United States but quickly expanding far beyond its boundaries.[102] Alongside this expanding literature, cases that could be thought of as reparations-style claims also began to appear in domestic courts. Many of these cases, as it turned out, involved wrongs that were not only massive—they were also old.

Holocaust Litigation

The most significant of these were the Holocaust cases. Though Germany's reparations program was the largest of its kind, it also suffered from some very important gaps. In addition to being geographically limited, it compensated only a fraction of the survivors and did not extend to victims of forced or slave labor.[103] But the fall of the Berlin Wall and the reunification of Germany brought a new interest in addressing some of the neglected legacies of the Holocaust. And when American courts intimated that the Alien Tort Statute might also encompass the wrongs of private actors,[104] those excluded from the post-war reparations programs started to show an interest in the promise of civil actions. They brought a series of suits against private corporations, beginning with Swiss banks and soon followed by a number of other German corporations that had used slave and forced labor. By now, however, among many other difficulties, these claims were at least a half of a century old.

The Swiss banks claims were for dormant accounts. In the 1930s, the Swiss government had enacted laws that ensured banking secrecy. As the Holocaust loomed, these secrecy laws promised safe haven for Jewish assets. As a result, vast sums were deposited in Swiss banks. However, after the war, the very secrecy that had protected the victims of Nazi persecution now prevented their families from getting information about those accounts. Under pressure from

[100] Civil Liberties Act of 1988, Pub. L. No. 100–383, 102 Stat. 903 (1988). For a discussion of the various factors that led to this legislation, *see* Leslie T. Hatamiya, Righting a Wrong: Japanese Americans and the Passage of the Civil Liberties Act of 1988 (1994).

[101] *See* Matthew McRae, *Japanese Canadian Internment and the Struggle for Redress*, Canadian Museum for Human Rights (May 19, 2017), https://humanrights.ca/story/japanese-canadian-internment-and-struggle-redress; Alexandra L. Wood, *Rebuild or Reconcile: American and Canadian Approaches to Redress for World War II Confinement*, 44 Am. Rev. Can. Stud. 347 (2014).

[102] *See* Matsuda, *supra* note 99; Roy Brooks, Atonement and Forgiveness: A New Model for Black Reparations (2004); Torpey, *supra* note 23; Time for Reparations: A Global Perspective (Jacqueline Bhabha et al. eds., 2021).

[103] *See* Bilsky, The Holocaust, Corporations and the Law, *supra* note 30, at 24–25. For a fulsome discussion of the program, *see* Colonomos & Armstrong, *supra* note 86.

[104] *See* Kadic v. Karadzic, 70 F.3d 232 (2d Cir. 1995).

the World Jewish Congress, the United States Senate Banking Committee held hearings on the dormant Swiss accounts in 1996. That same year, lawyers filed the first Holocaust class action suit against Swiss banks, seeking return of the unjustly held property and the associated profits.[105]

The Swiss banks suit was quickly followed by claims against German corporations, including for slave and forced labor. The plaintiffs pointed to international law violations, including war crimes and crimes against humanity, as well as violations of German criminal and civil law including prohibitions on slavery and involuntary servitude.[106] The litigation expanded along the way, including more banks as well as other private corporations. By the time the settlement was reached, the seventeen defendants included the giants of German industry. The CEO of Daimler/Chrysler was the defendants' chief negotiator. The United States Department of State became heavily involved, with Under Secretary of Commerce Stuart Eizenstat leading the complex negotiations in Washington.[107]

The Swiss banks claims were the first to settle, agreeing to the stunning amount of $1.25 billion USD in compensation for five different classes of claims. The banks also agreed to an independent audit headed by former chair of the United States Federal Reserve, Paul Volker (the Volker Committee). And in 1996, the Swiss government established the important Bergier Commission, which researched the spoliation of property in Switzerland during World War II. The work of both of these bodies informed the court-administered settlement.[108] The Swiss banks settlement was distributed to 457,000 claimants living in more than 80 countries. Shortly afterwards, the claims against German corporations settled. A fund of $5 billion USD was created, contributed to jointly by the corporations and the German government. The fund was housed in a foundation named Remembrance, Responsibility and the Future. Eighty percent was set aside to compensate laborers, while the other 20% went to property and insurance claimants as well as to the Future Fund, which commemorated the deceased victims.[109] Among other things, that foundation has paid out 8.7 billion DM to 1,665,000 surviving forced laborers.[110] The foundation also continues to

[105] For an excellent account and analysis, *see* Bilsky, The Holocaust, Corporations and the Law, *supra* note 30.

[106] *See id.* at 38–39.

[107] *See id.*, citing William Z. Slany, *The State Department, Nazi Gold, and the Search for Holocaust Assets, in* Holocaust Restitution, *supra* note 89, at 30; Stuart Eizenstat, Imperfect Justice: Looted Assets, Slave Labor, and the Unfinished Business of World War II (2003).

[108] *See* Bilsky, The Holocaust, Corporations and the Law, *supra* note 30, at 36–38.

[109] *See id.* at 38–40.

[110] *Payment Programme of the Foundation EVZ*, Das Bundesarchiv (last visited Feb. 25, 2025), https://www.bundesarchiv.de/zwangsarbeit/leistungen/direktleistungen/leistungsprogramm/index.html.en.

fund projects associated with history and human rights.[111] In the context of the settlement, German corporations also agreed to set up a historical commission and to open their archives to historians.[112]

This transnational Holocaust litigation was transformative. Among its other effects, it set off a wave of other Holocaust-related litigation across a wide variety of other jurisdictions, some of which is ongoing. This included litigation against the French state-owned railway company (SNCF) for the transport of over 70,000 Jews to concentration camps in Poland. A number of cases were filed both in the United States and in France, and at the same time Congress was considering the Holocaust Rail Justice Act, which would have given federal courts jurisdiction over such cases. All of these efforts foundered. However, as Maryland was considering a multibillion dollar rail contract to the parent company of SNCF, the French government suddenly announced that it would make payments to the deportees.[113] And related redress and other efforts to come to terms with the legacy of the Holocaust continue. At the end of November 2018, the Dutch Government issued an apology for the role of its railways in transporting over a hundred thousand Jews to concentration camps and announced a compensation scheme.[114] There has also been other litigation and threats of litigation related to the legacy of the Holocaust, including concerning unpaid insurance claims and the role of the Vatican Bank.[115] Historical work also continues to explore the wrongdoing including *Nazi Billionaires: The Dark History of Germany's Wealthiest Dynasties*. Published in 2022, it details the Nazi connections of the giants of German industry like BMW and their ongoing failure to come to terms with that legacy.[116]

From the perspective of the problem of the past, the Holocaust reparations litigation was especially pivotal. It was premised on the idea that the most extreme state-sponsored criminal wrongs could (amongst other things) also generate claims to individual redress through domestic civil litigation. In this sense, it redirected attention away from the extraordinary legal mechanisms associated with transitional justice and toward the most garden variety aspect of the domestic legal system—the civil remedy. The Holocaust

[111] For an outline of compensation and current projects, see *What We Support*, STIFTUNG EVZ, https://www.stiftung-evz.de/en/what-we-support/ (last visited Dec. 3, 2024).

[112] *See* BILSKY, THE HOLOCAUST, CORPORATIONS AND THE LAW, *supra* note 30, at 40.

[113] *See* BAZYLER, *supra* note 15, at 165–68; *France Agrees Holocaust SNCF Rail Payout with US*, BBC NEWS (Dec. 5, 2014).

[114] *See* Daniel Boffey, *Dutch Rail to Pay Compensation for Transporting Jews to Nazi Death Camps*, THE GUARDIAN (Nov. 28, 2018).

[115] *See* GERALD POSNER, GOD'S BANKERS: A HISTORY OF MONEY AND POWER AT THE VATICAN 383–94 (2015); *Insurance Claims—ICHEIC*, CONFERENCE ON JEWISH MATERIAL CLAIMS AGAINST GERMANY (Nov. 2007), http://www.claimscon.org/about/history/closed-programs/icheic/.

[116] DAVID DE JONG, NAZI BILLIONAIRES: THE DARK HISTORY OF GERMANY'S WEALTHIEST DYNASTIES (2022).

reparations cases also began to shift attention away from individuals and toward those institutions that had outlived the Nazi era and now carried on business inside Germany and beyond. And by bringing claims for civil redress in the domestic courts of stable regimes against long-standing transnational institutions like IBM and Volkswagen, the Holocaust reparations claims also marked an important departure from the transitional justice paradigm. They created a foothold in non-transitional regimes and in so doing helped to inspire the idea that even stable regimes might be subject to claims for redress of old wrongs.

This new idea of reparations gradually began to take shape. Given its international law lineage, it is perhaps not surprising that reparations was not a common law term of art, nor was it a traditional cause of action in private law. However, the Holocaust cases started to change that by establishing a link between reparations and the domestic private law of non-transitional regimes. The Holocaust claims did have deep links with transitional justice, both in their connection to regime change and in their focus on compensation for the terrible human rights violations of the Nazi and affiliated states. However, they took the legal form of a private law action for damages brought in the domestic courts of a stable non-transitional legal system. This novel melding of the form of an ordinary civil action and the content of historical atrocity represented a distinctive kind of justice claim and the language of reparations emerged as a way to describe it.

In this way, the Holocaust litigation was an important contributor to the rise of a new interest in reparations far beyond the context of regime change. Its emphasis on the idea that grievous violations of fundamental human rights warranted some form of redress and that the domestic civil actions could be adapted to achieve this made it ideally suited to migrating from the transitional justice context into stable democracies. Moreover, for the first time, it brought significant redress to survivors of grievous decades-old wrongs.

Thus it is not surprising that groups that had suffered terrible injustices in stable regimes started to wonder why their own histories would not be subject to similar scrutiny. While they may have applauded the redress to survivors in the Holocaust litigation, they were also prompted to ask why victims of historic injustices in stable regimes should be left without any form of redress. Inspired by the Holocaust reparations litigation and the redress for the war-time internment of citizens of Japanese origin, they began to consider redress for a wide array of serious past wrongs, including slavery, mistreatment of racialized populations, forced sterilization of mentally disabled persons, and institutional abuse. As we shall see, around the globe, domestic political and legal systems started to come under a new kind of pressure as advocates increasingly invoked reparations to voice their demands for justice.

Conclusion

The modern reparations movement got underway in earnest with the confluence of several developments that took place during the rights revolution that began in the late 1980s. As transitional justice was on the rise in regimes emerging from authoritarian rule, a number of domestic legal systems were also beginning to develop a novel kind of civil action focused on redress for violations of fundamental human rights. These elements came together in a powerful way in the Holocaust reparations litigation of the early 1990s, which in turn served as a source of inspiration for many others who sought redress for grievous historic wrongs. That litigation forged a critical link between the important but conceptually distinct developments underway in transitional justice and the tools of domestic private law.

However, the Holocaust movement still remained deeply tied to the transitional justice context. The underlying wrongs were those of the Nazi regime, not of a continuing state and not of the state in which the litigation was filed. While this transnational element complicated the claims in a number of ways, it also enabled the claims to avoid doctrinal impediments may have doomed them right from the start. The fact that the claims were anchored to the Holocaust context, where the wrongdoing was so apparent and so extreme, also helped to generate the kind of normative force needed to surmount procedural barriers in these kinds of claims. And though the claims remained both legally challenging and controversial, they did provide a powerful example of how civil redress could be employed to respond to vast historic wrongs.

Important though this was, the problematic past would not have been able to assert itself in the way that it has without something more. Reparations claims for past wrongdoing needed to be liberated from their transitional justice beginnings. And while the Holocaust reparations claims provided a new paradigm for those seeking redress for grievous old wrongs, they did so safely, one might say. Because they remained moored to the Holocaust, they operated at some distance from the domestic legal system in which the cases were filed. So although these claims brought reparations home to the domestic legal system of non-transitional states, since the wrongs took place far away, they did so only in one sense of the term. Before reparations for old wrongs could truly take hold in the domestic legal systems of stable democracies, something more was required.

The past has traditionally been insulated from legal scrutiny by an array of rules and doctrines. The most obvious are of course limitations periods, which explicitly bar legal consideration of the past. In addition, many important institutions like governments and churches have traditionally been protected by various forms of immunities. And beyond these barriers, there were also other deeper and much less obvious ways that the past was off-limits. Private law's account of responsibility, which implicitly drew on its more robust criminal law counterpart, also viewed culpability as an essentially individual matter. But this conception turned out to be too limited to capture the important institutional dimension of grievous old wrongs. Until these strictures were loosened, private law would have great difficulty reaching many of the most egregious instances of past injustice. And this loosening occurred, as we shall see, in a rather surprising way.

3
How the Catholic Church Sexual Abuse Crisis Opened Up Private Law

Introduction

While the world was grappling with the legacy of the Holocaust, developments in transitional justice, and the growth of novel civil actions, something else was underway that would turn out to be critical to the problem of the past—the Catholic Church sexual abuse crisis. It came to public attention in the 1980s, which, as we have seen, was a period characterized by an increasing interest in the redemptive role of law. But the domestic legal systems of stable regimes remained insulated from claims for widespread historic wrongs. The Catholic Church sex abuse crisis changed that.

During the 1980s, those seeking redress of old wrongs were noting how transitional justice was bringing a new focus on repairing even very old wrongs. But as yet, there was no domestic law analogue. Civil litigation for historic wrongs looked very unpromising. The procedural barriers were formidable. The passage of time and limitations periods defeated most claims before they even got started. Important institutions like governments and churches were also protected by immunities. And private law was generally hostile to the idea that an institution could be liable for a serious criminal wrong carried out by an individual. The reparations consciousness that was developing in the transitional justice context could not take hold more broadly while civil actions in domestic courts faced those barriers.

However, the growing realization that the Church across time and place had systematically protected abusers, thereby perpetuating the horrific damage they were able to do to children, began to undercut these longstanding barriers to liability. An institution itself, it started to seem, and not simply the most errant within it, could indeed act badly and thus beat fault in the way that the law used to believe was essentially individual. The resulting willingness to revisit charitable immunities along with a deeper shift in institutional liability rules combined with the related opening up of limitations periods to work a profound transformation in the important private law of civil wrongs.

Making Amends for Historic Wrongs. Mayo Moran, Oxford University Press. © Mayo Moran 2025.
DOI: 10.1093/9780190927295.003.0003

A Brief Overview of the Catholic Church Sex Abuse Crisis

At the heart of the Catholic Church sex abuse crisis is human tragedy. The lives of hundreds of thousands of children, perhaps more, were permanently damaged and often destroyed in the process. Their families and the very foundations of communities were shaken as it gradually became apparent that the most trusted of institutions—the Church—was deeply implicated in horrific wrongdoing.[1] The media first uncovered this story of trust, abuse, and betrayal, and continued to play a critical role. The legal story that is the focus here is, however, not so nearly well known.

Paradigm-shifting responsibility cases stand out because of how deeply they connect to the legal system's most fundamental commitments, such as the repair of grievous wrongs.[2] In the Catholic Church sexual abuse cases, these wrongs were profound. They targeted children and often the most vulnerable among them—those without family or protection. The abuse was carried out by clergy, teachers, custodians, and caregivers. The abusers were typically in positions not only of trust but also of moral or spiritual power, and they had the social standing that came with it. Sexual abuse was an act of profound betrayal. In clergy abuse cases like those in the Catholic Church, the terrible harms that such abuse always inflicts were made even worse because the depravity was hidden behind the cloak of virtue. Survivors of childhood sexual abuse are always burdened by guilt, but the circumstances of this crisis ensured that that guilt was especially profound. This is part of the reason why many survivors of child sexual abuse never come forward and why those that do typically take a very long time to report—on average thirty-three years according to Australia's Royal Commission on Institutional Responses to Child Sexual Abuse.[3] So we will never know how many children's lives were damaged or destroyed as part of the Catholic Church sex abuse crisis.

It is clear however that the scale of the wrongs is vast. But attaching reliable numbers to it is extremely difficult, if not impossible. It was decades before most of the abuse started to come to light, in part because it involved child victims

[1] The Catholic Church was by no means the only institution that was implicated in childhood sexual abuse scandals—many others, including other churches, also had their own scandals. But the Catholic Church stands out not only because of the scale of issues but more profoundly because the Church's responses—from its reaction to disclosures right up to its litigation strategies—suggest, as we will see, an institutional ethos that implicates the Church, including at the highest level, in a distinct and troubling way. There are many strong Catholic voices within the Church that have long advocated a different and more responsive path of reform, but to date they have not been able to overcome that institutional ethos.

[2] *See* Mayo Moran, *The Problem of the Past: How Historic Wrongs Became Legal Problems*, 69 U. Toronto L.J. 421 (2019).

[3] Claire Blumer et al., *Child Sex Abuse Royal Commission: Data Reveals Extent of Catholic Allegations*, ABC News (Austl., Feb. 6, 2017).

and acts perpetrated in secret. There were also systematic efforts at almost every level to silence the victims and cover-up the abuse. Many claims—especially early ones—were settled in secret and confidentiality was invariably demanded. Events also took place over a daunting array of jurisdictions. Moreover, despite what we think we already know, more keeps coming to light. All of this makes it impossible to tell the full story. But here is a sketch of the crisis.

The movie *Spotlight* and its depiction of the important role of *The Boston Globe* in exposing the abuse and cover-up in the Boston Archdiocese highlights the much more general fact that investigative journalists were critically important in uncovering the abuse. The crisis is commonly identified as surfacing in the United States in the mid-1980s, following Jason Berry's reporting on the case of Father Gilbert Gauthe. Gauthe was a priest and a voracious predator who for over a decade repeatedly and violently sexually assaulted young boys.[4] He eventually admitted that he had abused more than 300 children over several decades, pled guilty to 34 criminal charges, and was sentenced to 20 years in prison.[5] His abuse started to come to light in 1983 when one of the victims told his father, who reported the abuse to the diocese.[6] The bishop sent Gauthe away for psychological treatment and offered nine families confidential settlements of more than $4 million.[7] One of the families refused to settle and took the case to court. A ten-year-old boy testified in graphic detail, and reporter Jason Berry did a 1985 exposé that brought the issue to public consciousness.[8]

However, it would take another fifteen years and the award-winning investigative journalism of *The Boston Globe* before the crisis really exploded. Beginning in January 2002 and over a series of over 800 articles, the *Globe* systematically laid out how over 70 priests in the diocese had sexually abused children. Equally devastatingly, they detailed that the bishops knew and did nothing to protect the children. That reporting launched new allegations, waves of lawsuits, the opening of records, suspending of priests, and, before the end of the calendar year, the resignation of the cardinal.[9] The Catholic Church sexual abuse crisis was underway and has not abated since.

[4] Madeleine Baran, *It All Began in Lafayette*, MINN. PUB. RADIO (July 21, 2014).

[5] *Id.* Other reports brought to light other serial abusers, including Father John Geoghan, who was accused of abusing 130 people. *See* Rachel Martin, *Abuse Scandal Still Echoes Through Catholic Church*, NATIONAL PUBLIC RADIO (2007).

[6] Baran, *supra* note 4.

[7] *Id.*

[8] Jason Berry, *The Tragedy of Gilbert Gauthe*, TIMES OF ACADIANA (May 23, 1985). *See also* Baran, *supra* note 4.

[9] *See* John Henley, *How the Boston Globe Exposed the Abuse Scandal that Rocked the Catholic Church*, THE GUARDIAN (Apr. 21, 2010); Matt Carroll et al., *Church Allowed Abuse by Priest for Years*, THE BOSTON GLOBE (Jan. 6, 2002).

In the decades since those revelations, the activity has mushroomed such that the most that can be done here is to give some indications of the scale.[10] The "Abuse Tracker" of the watchdog BishopAccountability.org has posted more than 100,000 news articles on the topic since the pivotal year of 2002.[11] It also lists over 100 publicly accused bishops.[12] The number of lawsuits and settlements in the United States is similarly vast, beginning with early cases such as the $85 million settlement in the Boston Archdiocese. Litigation and settlements have exploded since then. In 2024, the Archdiocese of Los Angeles settlement set a new record, bringing its total compensation to survivors of sexual abuse to over $1.5 billion.[13] In early 2025, a Georgetown University report estimated that over $5 billion USD had been spent by US Catholic entities on allegations of the sexual abuse of minors.[14] Over forty Catholic religious organizations have sought bankruptcy protection.[15]

As the crisis has grown, it has begun to generate other legal activity. In 2018, then Pennsylvania Attorney General Josh Shapiro commissioned a grand jury report on the "widespread sexual abuse of children within six dioceses of the Catholic Church in Pennsylvania and the systematic cover-up by senior church officials in Pennsylvania and the Vatican."[16] The two-year investigation resulted in a nearly 900-page report.[17] Like *The Boston Globe* reporting, it set off a new cycle of activity, and in the years since then, more than twenty other investigations into the Catholic Church have been initiated by state attorneys general.[18]

This pattern is echoed elsewhere, and there have now been countless reports from around the world involving the sexual abuse of children at the hands of the Catholic Church. Ireland's announcement that it would set up an inquiry into sexual abuse in religious schools followed a "harrowing" report that was just the

[10] For a more detailed overview and outline of the arguments upon which this chapter draws, see Mayo Moran, *Cardinal Sins: How the Catholic Church Sexual Abuse Crisis Changed Private Law*, 21 Geo. J. Gender & L. 95 (2019).

[11] *Abuse Tracker*, Bishop Accountability, https://www.bishop-accountability.org/category/news-archive/abusetracker/ (last visited Feb. 21, 2025).

[12] *Bishops Accused of Sexual Abuse and Misconduct*, Bishop Accountability, http://www.bishop-accountability.org/bishops/accused/global_list_of_accused_bishops.htm (last visited Feb. 21, 2025).

[13] *See* Richard Winton & Hannah Fry, *L.A. Catholic Church Payouts for Clergy Abuse Top $1.5 Billion with New Record Settlement*, Los Angeles Times (Oct. 16, 2024).

[14] *See* Aleja Hertzler-McCain, *More than $5 Billion Spent on Catholic Sexual Abuse Allegations, New Report Finds*, National Catholic Reporter (Jan. 17, 2025).

[15] *See Catholic Dioceses in Bankruptcy*, PennState Law, https://elibrary.law.psu.edu/bankruptcy/index.5.html (last visited Feb. 21, 2025).

[16] *Pennsylvania Diocese Victims Report*, Pennsylvania Office of the Attorney General, https://www.attorneygeneral.gov/report/ (last visited Feb. 21, 2025).

[17] Office of the Attorney General for the Commonwealth of Pennsylvania, 40th Statewide Investigating Grand Jury Report 1 (2018).

[18] *See* Ruth Graham, *What the Latest Investigations into Catholic Church Sex Abuse Mean*, The New York Times (June 2, 2023).

latest in a long series of horrific revelations and subsequent reports about the abuse of children in Catholic institutions in Ireland.[19] Australia, New Zealand, Canada, and the United Kingdom have also had their own ambitious task forces or commissions focused on child sexual abuse, much of it involving the Catholic Church. In 2021, an independent inquiry in France concluded that more than 200,000 children had been sexually abused by Catholic clergy.[20] An independent commission in Spain echoed this not long afterwards, finding that over 200,000 Spanish children had been sexually abused by Catholic clergy.[21] And other commissions and investigative bodies across a wide array of jurisdictions too numerous to catalog have been struck to investigate the scale and dynamics of child sexual abuse in the Catholic Church.[22] As this happens and more cases of abuse arise, there are also many calls for other independent commissions, including in Latin America.[23] Late in 2024, the Pontifical Commission for the Protection of Minors finally issued its first report, which outlines a number of the ongoing situations, processes, and challenges across the globe, covering Mexico, Belgium, many countries in Africa, and Asia (to name but a few).[24] The report acknowledged that "the Commission has seen Church leaders who have been subjects of past administrative actions and/or inactions that have been the source of additional harm to victims/survivors of sexual abuse."[25]

Given all of this, it is hardly surprising that the abuse crisis began to generate transnational activity as well. In September 2011, a submission was lodged with the International Criminal Court alleging that then-Pope Benedict along with a number of key cardinals had committed crimes against humanity by failing to prevent and punish perpetrators of rape and sexual violence in a "systematic and widespread" concealment that included failure to co-operate with relevant law enforcement agencies.[26] The prosecutor's office decided against charges on the grounds that some of the alleged offences "do not appear to fall

[19] Katy Dartford, *Ireland to Set Up Inquiry into Sexual Abuse at Religious Schools Following "Harrowing" Report*, EuroNews (Apr. 9, 2024).

[20] *See French Clergy Sexually Abuse "Over 200,000 Children" Since 1950*, Al Jazeera (Oct. 5, 2021).

[21] *See* Kathryn Armstrong, *Spanish Church Sexual Abuse Affected 200,000 Children, Commission Finds*, BBC News (Oct. 27, 2023).

[22] *See Reports of Attorneys General, Grand Juries, Individuals, Commissions, and Organizations*, Bishop Accountability, https://www.bishop-accountability.org/AtAGlance/reports.htm (last visited Feb. 21, 2025).

[23] *See* Adalberto Méndez López, *The Time Is Ripe for a Clergy Abuse Inquiry in Latin America*, Al Jazeera (Mar. 29, 2022).

[24] Pontifical Commission for the Protection of Minors, Annual Report on Church Policies and Procedures for Safeguarding (2024).

[25] *Id.* at 13.

[26] *See* Karen McVeigh, *Pope Accused of Crimes Against Humanity by Victims of Sex Abuse*, The Guardian (Sept. 13, 2011). On the viability of this kind of claim in international law, *see* Dermot Groome, *The Church Abuse Scandal: Were Crimes Against Humanity Committed?* 11 Chi. J. Int'l L. 439 (2011).

within the (court's) jurisdiction."[27] However, the United Nations also began to take notice.

In 2014, the United Nations Committee on the Rights of the Child issued a report noting that the Church "has consistently placed the preservation of the reputation of the Church and the protection of the perpetrators above the child's best interests."[28] It also observed that "a code of silence imposed on all members of the clergy under penalty of excommunication" has resulted in cases of sexual abuse rarely being reported.[29] The Committee expressed grave concerns that the policies and practices of the Holy See enabled the abuse to continue and extended impunity to perpetrators. It was in the wake of this international pressure that then Pope Francis set up the Pontifical Commission for the Protection of Minors. However, that body was so plagued with resignations and difficulties that it did not manage to issue its first annual report until late in 2024.[30]

The Holy See also faced more international activity after a spate of allegations in 2018. Among them, the United Nations Committee against Torture agreed to hear the complaint of a woman who was a survivor of Ireland's Magdalene Laundries,[31] and a civil action was filed in US courts that directly implicated the Vatican itself.[32] Claimants also tried to bring actions against the Vatican before the European Court of Human Rights, but they did not meet with success.[33] However, in the wake of many reports of widespread clergy sexual abuse across Latin America, in 2020 the Inter-American Commission on Human Rights held its first hearing on clergy sexual abuse of children.[34] Many other efforts to understand and address the crisis are also underway. For example, spurred on in large measure by the issues across the globe in the Catholic Church, in 2019 the

[27] *See For Now, Vatican Officials Will Not Face Criminal Charges*, SURVIVORS NETWORK OF THOSE ABUSED BY PRIESTS (June 13, 2013), http://www.snapnetwork.org/for_now_vatican_officials_will_not_face_criminal_charges.

[28] Committee on the Rights of the Child, *Concluding Observations on the Second Periodic Report of the Holy See* 5, U.N. Doc. CRC/C/VAT/CO/2 (Feb. 25, 2014).

[29] *Id.* at 10.

[30] Cardinal Pietro Parolin, *Chirograph of His Holiness Pope Francis for the Institution of a Pontifical Commission for the Protection of Minors*, VATICAN (Apr. 21, 2015), http://w2.vatican.va/content/francesco/en/letters/2014/documents/papa-francesco_20140322_chirografo-pontificia-commissione-tutela-minori.html. *See also* Elisabetta Povoledo, *Vatican Issues First Report on Sexual Abuse, to Immediate Criticism*, THE NEW YORK TIMES (Oct. 29, 2024).

[31] *See* Eithne Shortall, *Kerry Woman Elizabeth Coppin Takes Magdalene Laundries Case to UN Committee Against Torture*, THE TIMES (UK, Nov. 4, 2018). In 2023, the majority of the Committee Against Torture concluded that Coppin's human rights had not been breached. Committee Against Torture, *Decision Adopted by the Committee under Article 22 of the Convention, Concerning Communication No. 879/2018*, U.N. Doc. CAT/C/73/D/879/2018 (May 12, 2022).

[32] First Amended Class Action Complaint and Jury Demand, Timothy Lennon et al. v. United States Conference of Catholic Bishops and Holy See, No. 18-cv-2618 (D.D.C. Nov. 13, 2018).

[33] *See* Richard Allen Greene & Kara Fox, *Dismissing Catholic Abuse Victims' Lawsuit, ECHR Rules Vatican Cannot Be Sued by European Courts*, CNN (Oct. 12, 2021).

[34] *See* Inés San Martín, *Inter-American Human Rights Commission to Look into Clerical Sexual Abuse*, CRUX (Dec. 9, 2020).

Economist Intelligence Unit, along with other partners, began issuing a series of reports that evaluate countries on how much they do to protect children against sexual abuse and exploitation.[35]

This is an extremely brief overview of this far-reaching, heavily litigated, and complex transnational set of issues. Although there is too much activity to fully capture, certain things are now abundantly clear. First, and most importantly, many hundreds of thousands of children worldwide (and perhaps more) have been abused by Catholic clergy. It is also clear that the abuse was committed by a very large number of clergy and encompasses those at the highest levels, which includes many bishops as well as cardinals. Something else is clear as well—the Church across time and place has continued, as the United Nations Committee on the Rights of the Child noted over a decade ago, to prioritize the protection of the institution and thereby also of perpetrators above the protection of children. While the issue continues to evolve and the Church has been forced to confront its past in a way that would have been unthinkable only a few decades ago, this essential feature does not appear to have changed. And more than any other feature this is what has driven both the crisis and its broader impact on both the Church and the law. With this backdrop in mind, let us examine how the crisis opened up the law, and particularly private law, to responsibility for historic wrongdoing.

How the Catholic Church Crisis Changed Private Law

Looking at the magnitude of the Catholic Church sex abuse crisis, it is tempting to view it as inevitable. However, when the issues began to surface in the 1980s, the prospect of a crisis that would rock the foundations of the Church would have seemed profoundly unlikely. Survivors certainly had compelling moral and emotional arguments, but legally speaking they faced what looked like insuperable barriers. Other historic injustice claims such as those arising out of the Holocaust also had many of these problems, but the early Catholic Church litigation predated the Swiss banks litigation and the related slave labor cases.[36] Moreover, the political nature of the Holocaust reparations claims and the fact that they were understood from the beginning as mass claims created pressure to settle, which enabled those claims to avoid a direct confrontation with legal impediments. By contrast, the Catholic Church crisis began in a piecemeal

[35] *See Measuring Progress Towards a World Free of Child Sexual Violence*, Out of the Shadows, https://outoftheshadows.eiu.com/wp-content/uploads/2019/01/Out-the-Shadows-Whitepaper.pdf (last visited Feb. 21, 2025).

[36] *See* Chapter 2; Leora Bilsky, Unfinished Business: The Holocaust, Corporations, and the Law: Unfinished Business (2017).

fashion, mainly by individual actions brought in isolation from each other and across many jurisdictions. It took a long time before the disparate actions came to be seen as interconnected events. The isolated individual nature of the initial efforts to get legal redress certainly made it very challenging for plaintiffs. But it also meant that a significant volume of litigation and even decided cases accumulated—a feature that distinguishes the Catholic Church crisis from many other claims for historic wrongs, and which to some degree accounts for its dramatic impact on the shape of the law.

In the early days, individuals contemplating bringing a sex abuse claim against the Church faced daunting challenges. Though there was variation across jurisdictions, in every case they faced one barrier after another.[37] Because of the passage of time, statutes of limitations that barred actions considered old were the threshold challenge. But the Catholic Church also had special legal protections including charitable immunity and sometimes also sovereign immunity arising out of the status of the Vatican in international law. Moreover, the more powerful the Church was in a jurisdiction, the more likely it was to benefit from additional special legal protections alongside other more political forms of insulation.[38] And even if it were possible to overcome these procedural barriers, other more substantive doctrines also made private law inhospitable terrain. Narrow institutional liability rules ensured that early civil sexual abuse claims were very unlikely to succeed. Add to this the pragmatic issues such as the difficulty of obtaining evidence, the challenges of child witnesses, and the unlikelihood of corroboration, and one can wonder how these cases ever managed to gain any traction. And this of course was compounded by other challenges, from emotional issues right through to the daunting financial ones associated with bringing a suit against a legally sophisticated, well-funded transnational entity.

Despite these many hurdles, some Church sex abuse cases did begin to move forward. They initially proceeded under the radar—individual cases rarely subject to academic commentary and not generally conceived of as having broader salience. However, a significant amount of legal reasoning and judicial

[37] For a discussion of the challenges faced by potential claimants, *see* LAW COUNCIL OF AUSTRALIA, SUBMISSION TO THE ROYAL COMMISSION INTO INSTITUTIONAL RESPONSES TO CHILD SEXUAL ABUSE (2014).

[38] For instance, the Irish state deferred to Church authorities when complaints were made directly to a government department. *See* CAROLE HOLOHAN, AMNESTY INTERNATIONAL IRELAND, IN PLAIN SIGHT: RESPONDING TO THE FERNS, RYAN, MURPHY AND CLOYNE REPORTS 31 (2011). In Australia, the Ellis doctrine precluded the Church from being held vicariously liable for the sexual abuse committed against minors by Catholic priests. *See* Andrew Morrison, *The* Ellis *Defence: How the Catholic Church Evades Liability*, 124 PRECEDENT 15 (2014). Several priests who have been convicted of sexual abuse in the United States have been able to take refuge in South America, where the Church and its officials are shielded by the rigorous and inflexible application of limitations periods. *See* Will Carless, *South America Has Become a Safe Haven for the Catholic Church's Alleged Child Molesters*, AGENCE FRANCE-PRESS (July 30, 2016).

precedent began to accumulate. Though there were many more defeats for survivors than victories, some of the barriers did begin to erode. And while the trans-jurisdictional nature of the Church—and its vast resources—posed many problems for plaintiffs, it also began to spur a transnational advocacy movement. Critical media coverage and technological changes that facilitated information sharing meant that progress (or for that matter defeat) in one jurisdiction began to have ramifications for how matters developed elsewhere. As the barriers started to weaken, the historic sexual abuse actions against both the direct perpetrators and the Church itself slowly became legally plausible.

Limitations Periods

Limitations periods are undoubtedly the most challenging threshold problem for any claim involving historic wrongdoing. This was certainly true for the sexual abuse claims against the Catholic Church. Statutes of limitations reflect the law's preference for settling disputes quickly and require that if someone wants to sue for a wrongful injury, then they must do so relatively quickly, usually within a few years.[39] This 'time's up' approach created an almost insurmountable hurdle for clergy sexual abuse claims. The wrongs occurred in secret and were long hidden, and it was typically decades before sexual abuse victims could bring themselves to make a claim.[40] An Australian Catholic Bishops Conference study of cases involving the sexual abuse of minors found that the limitation period had expired in 96.77% of them.[41] The Australian Royal Commission into Institutional Responses to Child Sexual Abuse later confirmed this, finding that it took an average of thirty-three years for a survivor to come forward.[42] Because statutes of limitations were "an overwhelming source of dismissal" in child sexual abuse claims, they effectively immunized the Church from liability.[43] This is why limitations periods started to come under such pressure in the Catholic

[39] The basic tort limitation period is six years in the United Kingdom. Limitation Act 1980, c. 58, § 2 (Eng.). It ranges from two to six years in the United States and Canada, depending on where the injury occurred. For a discussion regarding limitations periods across Canada, *see* Elizabeth Adjin-Tettey & Freya Kodar, *Improving the Potential of Tort Law for Redressing Historical Abuse Claims: The Need for a Contextualized Approach to the Limitation Defence*, 42 Ottawa L. Rev. 95, 100 (2010). For an overview of limitations periods in each state, *see* Matthiesen, Wickert & Lehrer, S.C., Statutes of limitations for all 50 states (2019), https://www.mwl-law.com/wp-content/uploads/2013/03/statute-of-limitations-for-all-50-states.pdf.

[40] *See* Timothy D. Lytton, Holding Bishops Accountable 60 (2008).

[41] *See* Kieran Tapsell, *"Catastrophic Institutional Failure" Can be Fixed*, National Catholic Reporter (Jan. 9, 2018).

[42] *See* Blumer et al., *supra* note 3. *See also* Royal Commission into Institutional Responses to Child Sexual Abuse, Redress and Civil Litigation Report 457 (2015).

[43] Lytton, *supra* note 40, at 60. *See also* Royal Commission into Institutional Responses to Child Sexual Abuse, *supra* note 42, at 434–59.

Church litigation and also why the resulting impact on the traditional 'time's up' approach has been so profound. Since many developments got underway in the United States, that is where we will begin.

Revelation and Reform

A pivotal moment in the Catholic Church sex abuse crisis came, as noted above, with the reporting coming out of Lafayette. The terrible revelations there and in Boston put child sexual abuse on the radar and began to attract attention to the problems posed by limitations periods. As the crisis unfolded, liberalizing limitations periods became a major law reform initiative. A research institute dedicated to limitations reform for child sexual abuse victims, named after a young man who died while bringing a criminal case against a Philadelphia priest, tracks reform beginning in 2002—not coincidentally the year that *The Boston Globe* story broke.[44] The early law reform efforts focused on extending the period of time or "tolling" for those under the age of majority so that the period would not have expired before they became old enough to sue. While there were some earlier reform efforts, the intense reform activity began in the early 2000s after *The Boston Globe* reporting.[45] In contrast with when the Lafayette scandal broke, nearly every state now suspends the statute of limitations for minors.[46]

The next swath of law reform efforts focused on creating "revival windows"—laws that gave survivors a chance to sue by allowing them to bring previously time-barred claims while the window was open or until they reached a certain age.[47] New York made news shortly after the 2018 Pennsylvania Grand Jury report when it finally passed the Child Victims Act, which allows child victims to

[44] Child Sex Abuse Statute of limitations Reform: The Sean P. McIlmail Statutes of Limitations Research Institute at Child USA, https://childusa.org/sol/ (last visited Feb. 21, 2025). The institute is named in honor of a young man who died of an overdose while trying to bring a case against Philadelphia priest Father Brennan to justice. According to a 2005 Grand Jury report, the archdiocese was made aware of inappropriate or suspicious behavior by Brennan with more than twenty boys from four different parishes, but the cardinal either ignored the reports or transferred Brennan to an "unsuspecting parish." Brennan was removed from active service in 2005. *See* Alex Rose, *Former Priest Accused of Sexual Abuse Gets Five Years Probation*, Delco Times (Apr. 1, 2022). In 2022, he was convicted of lying to the FBI. *See Former Catholic Priest Sentenced for Making False Statements in Connection with Church Abuse Investigation*, United States Attorney's Office for the Eastern District of Pennsylvania (Mar. 31, 2022), https://www.justice.gov/usao-edpa/pr/former-catholic-priest-sentenced-making-false-statements-connection-church-sex-abuse.

[45] *See* Jeffrey Pruzan, *Abuse, Mediation and the Catholic Church: How Enforcing and Improving Existing Statutes Will Help Victims Recover*, 13 Cardozo J. Conflict Resol. 593, 603–7 (2012); Marci A. Hamilton et al., Child USA, History of U.S. Child Sex Abuse Statutes of Limitation Reform from 2002 to 2020 (2021).

[46] *Child Sexual Abuse: Civil Statutes of Limitations*, National Conference of State Legislatures (Nov. 29, 2023), https://www.ncsl.org/human-services/state-civil-statutes-of-limitations-in-child-sexual-abuse-cases.

[47] Child Sex Abuse Statute of limitations Reform, *supra* note 44.

sue their abuser until the age of fifty-five. By 2025, thirty-three states and territories had revival windows or revival age limit laws, with more scheduled to open.[48]

As terrible stories continued to make headlines—many involving the Catholic Church crisis—some jurisdictions went further, completely eliminating limitations defenses in child sexual abuse cases.[49] Baltimore is a striking example. Less than a week after the release of a report on the Baltimore Archdiocese documenting decades of "staggering" sexual abuse and cover-ups, the governor of Baltimore signed a law ending all limitations periods for child sexual abuse.[50] In 2022, President Biden signed The Eliminating Limits to Justice for Child Sex Abuse Victims Act, which abolished federal time limits for child sexual abuse.[51] By mid-2024, nineteen states, the federal government, and two territories had eliminated the statute of limitation for civil actions for child sexual abuse.[52]

While events in the United States were certainly important, the unfolding of the Catholic Church crisis has played a key role in rethinking limitations periods across many jurisdictions. An example is found in Canada. In 1989 in the Canadian province of Newfoundland, a small local paper published a story outlining decades of sexual abuse and church and government cover-ups at the Catholic Church's Mount Cashel Orphanage.[53] That reporting and the public inquiry that followed unleashed a flood of claims against the Catholic Church, the government, and other defendants, bringing the issue of child sexual abuse to national consciousness. Fueled in part by the increased awareness and related advocacy, in 1992 the Supreme Court of Canada issued an important decision that called the limitations defense into question in the context of familial sexual abuse.[54] Following that decision and an influential report into institutional child abuse prompted in part by the Mount Cashel scandal, Canadian provinces began to amend their limitations legislation to avoid prejudicing victims of childhood sex abuse.[55] All

[48] *Id.*

[49] Legislators in Alaska, Maine, and Utah have enacted statutory reforms that allow victims of child sexual abuse to bring a civil action against perpetrators at any time. *See Child Sexual Abuse: Civil Statutes of Limitations*, *supra* note 46.

[50] *See* Lea Skene et al., *Report Details "Staggering" Church Sex Abuse in Maryland*, Associated Press (Apr. 5, 2023); Brian Witte, *Maryland's Highest Court Upholds Ending Statute of Limitations on Child Sex Abuse Lawsuits*, National Catholic Reporter (Feb. 4, 2025).

[51] *See* Chloe Folmar, *Biden Signs Bill Eliminating Civil Statute of Limitations for Sex Abuse Victims*, The Hill (Sept. 17, 2022).

[52] *2024 SOL Tracker*, ChildUSA, https://childusa.org/2024sol/ (last visited Feb. 22, 2025).

[53] *See* Philip Lee, *Mount Cashel, and the Redemptive Power of Pulling Stories from the Darkness*, CBC News (Apr. 17, 2016).

[54] M.(K.) v. M.(H)., [1992] 3 S.C.R. 6 (Can.).

[55] Law Commission of Canada, Restoring Dignity: Responding to Child Abuse in Canadian Institutions (2000).

provinces in Canada have now abolished time limits on civil actions for sexual assault.[56]

In Australia and New Zealand as well, the Catholic Church crisis has prompted liberalization of limitations rules. Revelations about the Catholic Church were a key catalyst for the creation of the Australian Royal Commission into Institutional Responses to Child Sexual Abuse, and many of the hearings focused specifically on the Catholic Church, detailing thousands of allegations of abuse against the Church.[57] In September 2015, the Royal Commission issued its *Redress and Civil Litigation Report*.[58] It recommended removing all limitation periods for child sexual abuse in an institutional context, with retrospective effect.[59] All states and territories have now removed limitations periods with both prospective and retrospective effect.[60]

There were parallel developments elsewhere. In 2017, Scotland reformed its limitations regime specifically as it applied to childhood sexual abuse, abolishing the three-year limitation rule (with retrospective effect for most child abuse), bringing it into line with Canada, Australia, and many jurisdictions in the United States. Multiple public child abuse scandals in the Scottish Catholic Church were unfolding during the lead up to this reform. In 2013, when the Church was already grappling with several other historical abuse scandals, Cardinal Keith O'Brien—the Archbishop of St. Andrew's and Edinburgh and the United Kingdom's most senior Catholic—was accused of decades of sexual misconduct.[61] O'Brien resigned shortly thereafter, and the Church commissioned an independent report into childhood sexual abuse.[62] That report detailed decades of child abuse by Catholic priests and cover-up by the Church hierarchy.[63] Its publication in mid-2015 prompted commentators to call on the government to "order a full public inquiry into the extent of the abuse and force the Catholic

[56] *See* Sarah Boesveld, *Ontario and Nova Scotia Loosening Rules on Sex Abuse Cases, Making It Easier for Victims to Sue Their Attackers*, The National Post (Can., Apr. 7, 2015); Dean Bennett, *Alberta to End Time Limit on Civil Suits Around Sexual or Domestic Violence*, Edmonton Journal (Mar. 7, 2017). In 2021, Prince Edward Island became the final jurisdiction to eliminate limitation periods for sexual abuse cases. *See* An Act to Amend the Statute of Limitations, S.P.E.I. 2021, c. 44.

[57] *See* Philippa McDonald & Riley Stuart, *Royal Commission into Child Sexual Abuse: 1,880 Alleged Perpetrators Identified in Catholic Church*, ABC News (Austl., Feb. 6, 2017).

[58] Royal Commission into Institutional Responses to Child Sexual Abuse, *supra* note 42.

[59] *Id.* at 434–59.

[60] *See* Ben Mathews & Elizabeth Dallaston, *Reform of Civil Statutes of Limitations for Child Sexual Abuse Claims: Seismic Change and Ongoing Challenges*, 43 U. N.S.W. L.J. 386 (2020).

[61] *See* Catherine Deveney, *UK's Top Cardinal Accused of "Inappropriate Acts" by Priests*, The Guardian (Feb. 23, 2013); Severin Carrell, *Catholic Church in Scotland Asks Forgiveness from Child Abuse Victims*, The Guardian (Aug. 18, 2015); Mark Tran, *Pope Francis Accepts Scottish Cardinal Keith O'Brien's Resignation*, The Guardian (Mar. 20, 2015).

[62] *See* Severin Carrell & Sam Jones, *Cardinal Keith O'Brien Resigns Amid Claims of Inappropriate Behaviour*, The Guardian (Feb. 25, 2013).

[63] *See* Kevin McKenna, *The Catholic Church Must Think Upon Its Sins*, The Guardian (Sept. 6, 2015).

church to begin to pay proper compensation," and in October 2015, the Scottish Child Abuse Inquiry was established.[64] Its first investigation involved a notorious orphanage run by the Catholic order, the Daughters of Charity of St. Vincent de Paul. Scotland's abolition of limitations periods in 2017 played out against this backdrop of repeated revelations about the Catholic Church and related survivor advocacy, both of which brought new attention and concern to the issue of child sexual abuse and the devastating impact of limitations periods on those seeking redress.

Around the same time, limitations periods were also a source of concern in England and Wales, and the Catholic Church sex abuse crisis was once again a dominant feature in the discussion. For several decades, the English law of limitations for sexual abuse had been a source of concern and uncertainty, much of it coming out of litigation involving the Catholic Church.[65] Following a public sexual abuse scandal involving entertainer Jimmy Savile,[66] the United Kingdom government struck the Independent Inquiry into Child Sexual Abuse. One of the Inquiry's investigation reports was on the Roman Catholic Church.[67] Like a number of the other reports, it highlighted the limitations period problem for sexual abuse survivors.[68] The Inquiry's interim report identified limitations reform as an important issue and noted that other jurisdictions including Scotland had abolished limitations for child abuse.[69] In 2019, the *Accountability and Reparations Investigation Report* recommended further exploration of limitation reform to make it easier for survivors to bring claims.[70] One of its case studies focused on litigation arising out of abuse and cover-ups at two Catholic run institutions. The report pointed to the role of limitations periods in that thirteen-year saga, something that was an issue for survivors across institutions.[71] A consultation on limitations followed, and early in 2025, the limitations period was removed for child sexual abuse, bringing the United Kingdom in line

[64] *Id.*

[65] A. v. Hoare et al., [2008] UKHL 6. *See also* G.H. v. The Catholic Child Welfare Society (Diocese of Middlesbrough) & Ors., [2016] EWHC 3337 (Q.B.); Archbishop Bowen & Anor. v. J.L., [2017] EWCA Civ 82.

[66] *See Profile: Jimmy Savile*, BBC News (Oct. 2, 2023).

[67] It said that the Church's "moral purpose was betrayed over decades by those in the Church who perpetrated this abuse and those who turned a blind eye to it." The well-being of children, it observed, was neglected "in favour of protecting its reputation." The Inquiry especially drew attention to the Church's slow responses to previous reports, the failures of leadership, and the Holy See's "lack of cooperation" with the Inquiry, something which they said "passes understanding." *See* Independent Inquiry into Child Sexual Abuse, The Roman Catholic Church Investigation Report v–ix (Nov. 2020).

[68] *Id.* at 122.

[69] Independent Inquiry into Child Sexual Abuse, Interim Report of the Independent Inquiry into Child Sexual Abuse 55–57 (2018).

[70] Independent Inquiry into Child Sexual Abuse, Accountability and Reparations Investigation Report 104 (2019).

[71] *Id.* at 17–19.

with Scotland, Australia, Canada, many US states, and other jurisdictions, and marking another dramatic departure from the situation before the child sexual abuse crisis erupted.[72]

Limitation periods reform is also on the radar in Ireland, where the Catholic Church is a dominant institution and where there has been wave after wave of issues involving the sexual abuse of children at the hands of the Church. In the early 1990s, the issue surfaced in the case of Father Brendan Smyth, who eventually admitted to molesting hundreds of children over a forty-year period in Dublin, Belfast, and the United States.[73] When it became clear that the Church—including the Cardinal—had repeatedly been alerted but simply moved him and that the Irish Attorney General had protected him from facing charges in Northern Ireland, there was public outrage and civil actions were launched against the Catholic Church.[74] Eventually Smyth pleaded guilty to over a hundred counts of sexual abuse and died in prison in 1997. In 1999, the government publicly apologized, established the Laffroy Commission, and set up a compensation scheme. It also enacted a one-year suspension of limitations periods for victims of clergy sexual abuse, which led to another flood of claims.[75] While Ireland generally remains restrictive, the 2024 allegations of widespread child sexual abuse in schools runs by religious orders—the vast majority of them Catholic—are renewing pressure on limitations reform.[76]

The Church's Responses to Limitations Reform

Although this is only a very partial picture of the many developments in the law of limitations in some of the most active jurisdictions over the last few decades, it is clear that it is a dramatically different world for the survivor of child sexual abuse than it was when Jason Berry broke the Lafayette story in the mid-1980s.

[72] Press Release, *New Reforms to Support Victims of Child Sexual Abuse*, GOVERNMENT OF THE UNITED KINGDOM (Feb. 5, 2025), https://www.gov.uk/government/news/new-reforms-to-support-victims-of-child-sexual-abuse.

[73] *See* LYTTON, *supra* note 40, at 194.

[74] *Id. See also Fr. Brendan Smyth: A Timeline*, THE IRISH TIMES (June 22, 2015); Liam Collins, *Brendan Smyth's Evil Deeds Can Never Be Forgotten*, THE IRISH INDEPENDENT (July 22, 2017). In 2010, Cardinal Seán Brady, the Roman Catholic Archbishop of Armagh, faced pressure to resign after admitting that in 1975, he witnessed two teenage boys sign oaths of silence after testifying in a Church inquiry against Smyth. *See* Simon Caldwell & Nick Pisa, *Leader of Roman Catholic Church in Ireland Urged to Quit over Abuse Victims' Silence Vow*, DAILY MAIL (U.K., Mar. 15, 2010).

[75] See generally James Gallen, *Historical Abuse and the Statute of Limitations*, 39 STAT. L. REV. 103 (2016) (discussing Statute of Limitations [Amendment] Act 2000, s. 2 [Ir.]).

[76] *See* Fiachra Gallagher, *"Their Childhood Stopped the Day the Abuse Started": Almost 2,400 Allegations of Abuse in Religious Run-Schools*, THE IRISH TIMES (Sept. 3, 2024); Mary Carolan, *Amending Law on Time Limits Could Assist Victims Seeking Redress over Child Abuse in Schools, Says Solicitor*, THE IRISH TIMES (Sept. 7, 2024).

And while no one catalyst alone accounts for the erosion of limitations periods, the Catholic Church sex abuse crisis is striking for the magnitude of its impact. By 2010, even the Vatican had modified the limitations periods in its own disciplinary processes as a result of the abuse cases.[77]

However, as advocates were working to liberalize limitations laws for child sexual abuse, it also started to become apparent that the Catholic Church was their key opponent. This attracted critical scrutiny, and commentators started to inquire into the Church's use of resources.[78] *The Guardian* put it bluntly: "[t]he US Catholic church has poured millions of dollars over the past decade into opposing accountability measures for victims of clergy sex abuse, according to state lobbying disclosures."[79] That reporting revealed that in a number of jurisdictions the Church had paid millions of dollars to lobbyists, including for "issues associated with timelines for commencing certain civil actions related to sex offenses."[80] The Church's efforts to stop limitations reform activity increased with the Pennsylvania Grand Jury Report, which among other things recommended such reform. In 2019, a law firm investigation revealed that the Church had spent more than $10.6 million in the northeastern United States alone trying to defeat legislative efforts to liberalize limitation periods for victims of child sexual abuse, with over $5 million spent just in Pennsylvania.[81] The Church's lobbying was widely publicized and drew condemnation, particularly in light of the fact that it coincided with Pope Francis's extraordinary summit aimed at preventing child sexual abuse.[82]

The dramatic revelations of 2018 prompted even more significant change, confirming the depth of the connection between limitations reform and the Catholic Church sex abuse scandal. For many, the Pennsylvania Grand Jury Report removed the "benefit of the doubt" once enjoyed by bishops and the

[77] *See* John Allen Jr., *Vatican Revises Church Law on Abuse Cases*, National Catholic Reporter (July 15, 2010).

[78] *See* Marci A. Hamilton, *The Catholic Bishops Lobby Against Legislation to Protect Children*, Verdict (Apr. 19, 2012); Stephanie Ebbert, *Legislature Postpones Extending Statue of Limitations for Child Sex Abuse*, The Boston Globe (Aug. 2, 2012); James T. O'Reilly & Margaret S.P. Chalmers, The Clergy Sex Abuse Crisis and the Legal Responses 66–68 (2014); *Bill Extending Statute of Limitations for Sexual Abuse Fails to Pass PA. House*, the Times Herald (Pa., Sept. 23, 2021); Alexis Linkletter, *California is Removing the Statute of Limitations for Rape*, VICE (Oct. 3, 2016); Catholic Whistleblowers Steering Committee, *Statutes of Limitations Regarding Clergy Sexual Abuse of Minors*, Catholic Whistleblowers (Sept. 23, 2014), http://www.catholicwhistleblowers.com/whistleblower-essays/statutes-of-limitations-regarding-clergy-sexual-abuse-of-minors.

[79] George Joseph, *US Catholic Church Has Spent Millions Fighting Clergy Sex Abuse Accountability*, The Guardian (May 12, 2016).

[80] *Id.*

[81] Williams Cedar et al., *Church Influencing State: How the Catholic Church Spent Millions Against Survivors of Clergy Abuse* (2019), https://www.williamscedar.com/wp-content/uploads/2020/09/ChurchInfluencingStateCatholic.pdf.

[82] *See* Laura Benshoff, *Catholic Church Lobbying Costs Spiked in Pa. as Statute of Limitations Debate Rages*, PennLive (June 11, 2019).

Church.[83] New York exemplifies this. In that state, the powerful policy arm of the Church led by Cardinal Dolan reportedly paid lobbying firms millions to work against limitations reform for sex offenses.[84] And for years, New York was among the most restrictive regimes in the country, giving survivors only until their twenty-third birthday to initiate civil or criminal cases. The proposed solution—the Child Victims Act, which extended the age to fifty-five for civil cases, to twenty-eight for felony criminal cases, and created a one-year "look-back" period—remained stuck for over a decade.

In 2017, the Church again vigorously opposed the bill, which once again failed.[85] However, after the revelations of 2018, Governor Cuomo pledged support and pointed to the Catholic Church as the obstacle. Cardinal Dolan then published an opinion piece arguing that the act "pilloried" the Church and ignored its positive efforts.[86] In the furor that followed, a Catholic spokesperson tried to clarify the Cardinal's words.[87] Governor Cuomo showed evidence that the Church had opposed the act for years.[88] The Church eventually dropped its opposition.[89] For some, however, Cardinal Dolan simply proved yet again that the Church "didn't get it" and would never take the necessary steps without legal pressure.[90] Finally, with control of the state senate passing to Democrats, the Child Victims Act became law in the last days of January 2019.[91]

The Church's efforts to prevent liberalizing limitations periods for child sexual abuse do not, however, end when they fail to defeat reform in the legislature. Even where liberalizing reforms have been passed, the Church has actively challenged them either in court on the grounds of retroactivity or by lobbying for a gubernatorial veto, often despite withering internal and external criticism. Connecticut is an illustration. Until the 1990s, its traditional limitations rules meant that

[83] David Crary, *States Move to Ease Restrictions on Child Sex-Abuse Lawsuits*, Associated Press (Jan. 23, 2019).

[84] *See* Kenneth Lovett, *Catholic Church Spent $2M on Major N.Y. Lobbying Firms to Block Child-Sex Law Reform*, New York Daily news (April 8, 2018).

[85] Michael O'Keefe, *Timothy Cardinal Dolan Ripped for Delaying Talk on Child Sex Abuse*, New York Daily news (Apr. 8, 2018).

[86] Cardinal Timothy Dolan, *Speed Aid to Abuse Survivors: The Child Victims Act Should Build on the Success of Catholic Church Compensation Funds*, New York Daily news (Dec. 31, 2018).

[87] *See* Corky Siemaszko, *Catholic Cardinal Says Any New NY Law for Abuse Victims Should Avoid "Breaking" the Church*, NBC News (Jan. 2, 2019).

[88] *See* Carl Campanile, *Cuomo Calls Out Church for Opposing Child Victims Act in Feud with Dolan*, The New York Post (Jan. 29, 2019). *See also* Cardinal Timothy Dolan, *Why Are Cuomo, Democrats Alienating Catholics?* The New York Post (Jan. 28, 2019).

[89] *See* Augusta Anthony, *New York Passes Child Victims Act, Allowing Child Sex Abuse Survivors to Sue Their Abusers*, CNN (Jan. 28, 2019), https://www.cnn.com/2019/01/28/us/new-york-child-victims-act/index.html.

[90] *See* Marci A. Hamilton, *Cardinal Timothy Dolan Proves Once Again the Church Will Never Reform Itself Without the Law and Civil Society Behind It*, Verdict (Jan. 18, 2019).

[91] *See* Marci A. Hamilton, *Miracles in Child Sex Abuse Statutes of Limitation Reform: Three of the Worst States Are Stepping Up*, Verdict (Mar. 1, 2018); Anthony, *supra* note 89.

survivors had to file lawsuits within two years of turning eighteen.[92] In 1991, they enacted reforms to allow survivors to bring claims until they were thirty-five.[93] After a rash of claims against the Roman Catholic Diocese of Bridgeport, in 2002 lawmakers again extended the age limit, giving potential plaintiffs until age forty-eight to file claims.[94] When this legislation was being considered, the archbishop and bishops wrote to priests, "instructing them to urge their parishioners to oppose the bill" because of its financial consequences.[95] Despite this, the legislation passed and survivors launched countless successful claims against the Church, with an estimated value in the tens of millions of dollars.[96]

The Archdiocese of Hartford then brought a constitutional challenge to the limitations reform. The case involved Reverand Ivan Ferguson, who was found to have repeatedly assaulted thirteen-year-old schoolboy "Jacob Doe." Ferguson had been assigned to lead Jacob's school even though he had admitted to the archbishop that he had sexually abused children while at his previous school. In 2002, when the statute of limitations on civil lawsuits in sex abuse cases was extended, Jacob Doe sued the archdiocese. A jury found in his favor and ordered the archdiocese to pay Doe $1 million.[97] But the Church challenged that award, arguing that it was unconstitutional to extend the statute of limitations retroactively. A scathing editorial noted the contrast with Pope Francis's words and referred to "the Archdiocese of Hartford's un-Christlike attempt to stomp on the legislatively granted rights of child sex abuse victims."[98] The Supreme Court of Connecticut rejected the challenge and unanimously upheld the legislation and the award to Doe.[99] The Church's decision to expend its resources challenging the legislation was the subject of considerable criticism, and the archdiocese issued a statement after the decision was handed down.[100]

[92] Conn. Gen. Stat. § 52-577d (1986). Also see Doe v. Hartford Roman Cath. Diocesan Corp., 317 Conn. 357, 416–28 (2015), for a discussion regarding the public policy rationales motivating the legislative reform in 1991.

[93] Conn. Gen. Stat. § 52-577d (amended 1991). *See* Roberts v. Caton, 224 Conn. 483 (1993).

[94] Conn. Gen. Stat. § 52-577d (amended 2002) (applying retroactively). *See* Dave Altimari, *Church to Seek Reversal of Law That Extended Time Abuse Accusers May Sue*, Hartford Courant (Sept. 21, 2014). This legislation was amended once again in 2019, giving survivors until age fifty-one to bring a claim.

[95] Editorial, *Archdiocese of Hartford at Odds with Pope Francis' Words on Money, Sex Abuse*, Middletown Press (Sept. 27, 2014).

[96] *See* Christian Nolan, *Catholic Church Tries to Stave Off Priest Abuse Lawsuits*, Connecticut Law Tribune (Sept. 19, 2014).

[97] *See* Doe v. Hartford Roman Catholic Diocesan Corp., 317 Conn. 357 (2015).

[98] Editorial, *Archdiocese of Hartford at Odds with Pope Francis' Words*, *supra* note 95.

[99] *See* Daniel Tepfer, *Supreme Court Upholds Rights of Abuse Victims*, Connecticut Post (June 26, 2015).

[100] *See* Dave Collins, *Connecticut Court Upholds $1m Verdict in Priest Abuse Case*, The Boston Globe (June 26, 2015); Editorial, *Archdiocese of Hartford at Odds with Pope Francis' Words*, *supra* note 95.

The Church has also gone beyond constitutional challenges, and in the face of widespread limitations, reform introduced two new strategies to avoid liability that will be discussed later. The first is often called a "permanent stay." Across jurisdictions Church lawyers are arguing that, even where limitations periods have been removed, the death of a perpetrator requires a permanent stay of all actions because of the interests of a fair trial. The Catholic Church tried this argument in Canada and lost before the Supreme Court in 2019.[101] They continued to press this argument elsewhere, including the High Court of Australia, where they again lost in 2023.[102]

The second technique involves seeking bankruptcy, even where vast church assets remain.[103] This undercuts limitations reform because once the diocese files for bankruptcy, no one can file claims for abuses that happened before that date, even if the statute of limitations has been retroactively extended. This "end-all strategy for the Catholic Church"[104] was used by the Archdiocese of Portland, Oregon in 2004. Despite its estimated half a billion dollars in assets, it filed for bankruptcy protection on the eve of civil trials that alleged failure to remove a priest accused of abusing more than fifty boys.[105] Multiple California dioceses also filed for bankruptcy after California passed 2019 limitations reform that opened a three-year revival window, and survivors again pointed to the Church's assets.[106] The Archdiocese of New Orleans filed for bankruptcy in 2020, and after five years of litigation and the church paying over $41 million in legal fees for the bankruptcy proceedings, the judge is threatening to dismiss the case for lack of progress.[107] As of 2025, over forty US Catholic dioceses and religious orders have filed for bankruptcy protection, along with thirty-seven dioceses and three religious orders. Other organizations soon followed the Church's lead, including the Boy Scouts and gymnastics organizations. Elsewhere too, including in the multidecade saga involving the Mount Cashel Orphanage in the Canadian province of Newfoundland, bankruptcy is used as the Church's new liability avoidance tactic because of how it defeats limitations reform.[108] As a result, and in

[101] L'Oratoire Saint-Joseph du Mont-Royal v. J.J., 2019 SCC 35 (Can.).

[102] G.L.J. v. The Trustees of the Roman Catholic Church for the Diocese of Lismore, [2023] HCA 32 (Austl.).

[103] *See* Marci A. Hamilton & Bridget Brainard, *Rethinking Chapter 11 for Mass Child Sexual Abuse Claims: Shifting the Focus from Debtor Institutions to the Victims*, 30 J. BANKR. L. & PRAC. 1 (2021). See also the Mount Cashel litigation.

[104] Joshua Bowling, *Why So Many Catholic Dioceses File for Bankruptcy*, SOJOURNERS (Feb. 13, 2025).

[105] *See* Hamilton & Brainard, *supra* note 103, at 4.

[106] *See* Robin Buller, *Catholic Dioceses Are Declaring Bankruptcy. Abuse Survivors Say It's a "Way to Silence" Them*, THE GUARDIAN (Nov. 21, 2023).

[107] *See* David Hammer, *New Orleans Catholic Diocese Ordered to Defend Bankruptcy Case from Dismissal*, THE GUARDIAN (Apr. 29, 2025).

[108] *See* Kevin Clarke, *After 35 Years, a Final Settlement Reached in the Mount Cashel Orphanage Sex Abuse Cases*, AMERICA MAGAZINE (July 11, 2014).

another cycle of law reform and circumvention, efforts are underway to make the bankruptcy process fairer for sexual abuse victims in the face of what is now recognized as "the 'disturbing trend' of organizations facing liability over sex abuse seeking refuge in bankruptcy court."[109]

The Emergence of Institutional Liability

At first blush, limitations changes may seem to be the most significant legal legacy of the Catholic Church sex abuse crisis. Those changes played a vital role in weakening once powerful temporal barriers and making historic wrongs legally accessible as never before. But the most profound change that the Catholic Church crisis had on the law may be the opening up of institutional liability rules. From cementing the decline of immunities to the more fundamental reworking of the underlying theory of responsibility, the Catholic Church sex abuse crisis also played a very important role in changing the rules that govern when institutions could be legally liable. While this would not have happened without the liberalization of limitations periods, these broader changes had even more profound reverberations both in law and beyond.

The rise of institutional liability is one of the most important transformations in contemporary private law. The increasing exposure of institutions to tort liability in particular has wrought shifts both in the law and in institutions themselves, shifts that have enormous implications that include the past but that extend far beyond it.[110] In addition to barriers such as limitations periods, tort law also used to be replete with protections that turned on the nature of the actor or defendant. These took the form of immunities that protected publicly oriented institutions such as charities, churches, and governments from legal liability. Alongside such immunities were weaker but still powerful institution-specific protections such as the public policy exceptions to the duty of care and special damages rules. Beyond this—and more profoundly—substantive rules also restricted the range of actors and acts to which liability could attach.

On both the procedural and the substantive dimensions, the Catholic Church crisis played a pivotal role in changing this picture. Not only was it instrumental in solidifying the elimination of institution-specific immunities, it also helped to transform the underlying understanding of liability. The emergence of the general duty of care in negligence in the early twentieth century began a new and

[109] Soma Biswas, *Bankruptcy Bill Would Weaken Protections for Organizations Facing Abuse Claims*, Deborah Ross (Apr. 18, 2024), https://ross.house.gov/2024/4/bankruptcy-bill-would-weaken-protections-for-organizations-facing-sex-abuse-claims.

[110] *See* Mayo Moran, *Reshaping Responsibility: The Emerging Private Law of Institutional Wrongs*, *in* Private Law and Power 263 (Kit Barker et al. eds., 2017).

serious engagement between private law and the idea of wrong. But private law had scanty resources for this undertaking, and so it is perhaps not surprising that it looked to refashion criminal law's more well-developed account of culpability. While responsibility for wrongs could sometimes be shifted to or shared with the institutions associated with the individual actors, those were seen as extraordinary cases. Wrongdoing was essentially understood as a matter of individual personal responsibility. The idea of an institutional wrongdoer did not sit easily with such a view. The Catholic Church sex abuse crisis changed that.

The picture that gradually emerged from the crisis was deeply unsettling. It started to become clear that the problems were not primarily a matter of mishaps and mistakes, of carelessness and confusion, of lack of coordination, though certainly those elements were present. Instead, it suggested something far more troubling—a consistent, well-coordinated, well-financed, and powerful institution operating with ruthless self-interest. From the initial toleration of the abuse, to the well-organized cover-ups, to the aggressive litigation and lobbying strategies designed to protect the Church at all costs—the crisis started to challenge the traditional individual view of responsibility and wrongdoing. The Pennsylvania Grand Jury Report encapsulated this troubling dimension of the crisis when it outlined the Church's playbook for sexual abuse cases. Of course, most of those involved with the Church were not bad. But a shocking idea started to suggest itself—that at least in this matter to some degree the institutional ethos of the Church itself was.

While many institutions and indeed many churches had their own child abuse issues, it started to become apparent that there was a distinct dimension to the Catholic Church crisis. The Church itself, at all levels, actively and repeatedly covered up cases of egregious known child abuse, allowing abusers within their ranks to carry on abusing yet more children from their positions of profound trust and sometimes from positions of great power. Equally important, the Church was quick to use its power and resources to suppress abuse claims, and it did not hesitate to rely on any available means to defeat claims and shield assets. It counted on being able to separate its legal tactics from all else that it did and was. But the Church that benefited from special legal protections extended to agents of public good could not relentlessly pursue its own institutional interest at the expense of those it injured as children without casting its special status into doubt. As commentators started to notice troubling patterns, the special institutional immunities that might have protected the Church were called into question.

When the tactics of the Catholic Church started to come to light in these cases, the implications of a powerful global institution acting with such clear strategic intent also began to prompt reconsideration of the old personalized understanding of responsibility. Traditionally, courts were reluctant to attribute liability in the absence of fault to an institution when someone in its employ carried out a crime. This was especially the case when individuals were pursuing their own malign purposes, such as sexual crimes. But the way that the Catholic Church handled cases of sexual abuse of children radically undermined this view. If such a trusted religious institution was willing to repeatedly put children at continued risk in order to cover-up the Church's role in egregious crimes against them and to then do everything possible to defeat their claims for redress, perhaps the idea of institutional liability for the criminal acts of employees was not so untenable. As events unfolded, institutional liability started to seem important and even necessary.

The Catholic Church sex abuse crisis in this way started to erode the idea that wrongdoing was essentially personal. In its place, a broader and more complex conception of responsibility began to emerge—a conception that was far more open to the idea of institutional wrongs. This had special significance in historic injustice cases in part because institutions have a 'shelf life' that extends far beyond the natural limits of human life. So even for acts anchored in the deep past, there will often be a defendant to pursue—a government or agency, a church, a corporation, and so on. This is true even when the individual wrongdoers may be dead, as is often the case by the time that child abuse survivors contemplate legal action. Institutions are also more likely to be able to compensate survivors for the harm they suffered. Once again, the Catholic Church cases are illustrative since very few of the individual defendants even were they alive would have had the resources to compensate the survivors for the terrible harms they suffered.

But there are also deeper reasons why institutional liability matters. Some claims involve wrongdoing that is systemic in nature—the Holocaust, the residential schools system, the eugenics movement, slavery, and the Catholic Church sex abuse crisis, to name but a few examples. Such wrongs are not and cannot be carried out simply by individuals. The fact that they involve many individuals carrying out similar, coordinated, or related wrongs points toward an institutional dimension to such wrongs. Often such wrongs take the form of explicit policy or even law, as in the Holocaust and eugenics cases, the residential schools cases, and slavery. In most cases, it is also a matter of concerted institutional action and institutional ethos—the Catholic Church's approach to the sex abuse claims is an illustration of this. In such contexts, the old unitary and personal view of responsibility inevitably falls short. Even attempting to aggregate individual wrongs—impossible though it likely is in cases such as these—would almost certainly miss the larger and more troubling narrative of collective malfeasance. Ultimately, this is the most important reason behind the shift toward a broader conception of responsibility capable of capturing the institutional dimension of such wrongs. The emergence of that broader conception can be traced back in significant measure to the distinctive institutional cast of so many of the Catholic Church sex abuse cases. And reshaping the conception of responsibility in order to capture this form of wrongdoing turned out to implicate both the institutional immunities as well as the deeper background institutional liability rules.

Immunities

The Catholic Church, like so many of the institutions threatened with liability for widespread historic wrongs, traditionally benefited not just from limitations protection but also from institution-specific blanket protections or immunities. For churches, this took the form of charitable immunity, while governments and public agencies found protection in Crown or sovereign immunity, and foreign governments in foreign sovereign immunity. In the case of the Catholic Church, its unique relationship to the Holy See meant that for at least some purposes, it was in the unusual position of being protected by both charitable and sovereign immunity. And importantly, so long as these immunities were in place, even lifting the limitations bar would not have enabled private law to reach the wrongdoing in the Catholic Church sex abuse cases. However, many of the relevant institution-specific immunities have also been weakened or entirely removed.[111] Here too the Catholic Church sex abuse crisis played a major role—accelerating the waning power of immunities until they no longer cast their protective cloak over church activities. The litigiousness of the Church and its willingness to rely on what has been described as a largely discredited doctrine to protect itself even in the context of egregious child sex abuse claims helped to drive the final 'nail in the coffin' of the doctrine. It is a sad irony that the Church's willingness to do anything to defend itself hastened the elimination of any remaining elements of the special protections it had once enjoyed.

An illustration of how the Church's reliance on charitable immunity to shield itself in child abuse cases helped to ensure the demise of the doctrine can be found in *Schultz v. Roman Catholic Archdiocese*.[112] In that case, the Supreme Court of New Jersey found that the Church was immune from liability for clergy sexual abuse. The victim was a young boy who attended a school owned by the archdiocese and participated in a parish-sponsored Boy Scout troop. Robert Coakley, a Franciscan brother, was both a teacher and scoutmaster. He forced sexual contact on the boy at camp and then continued the abuse at school. Though Coakley threatened the boy, he eventually told his parents. Tragically,

[111] *See also* O'Reilly & Chalmers, *supra* note 78, at 161, citing Matthew Cobb, *A Strange Distinction: Charitable Immunity and Clergy Sexual Abuse*, 62 Me. L. Rev. 703 (2010).

[112] Schultz v. Roman Cath. Archdiocese, 95 N.J. 530, 536 (1984).

despite medical and psychological care, the boy committed suicide. His parents brought an action against the archdiocese, which responded with a claim of charitable immunity. A majority of the court reluctantly held that the immunity did protect the Church. It explicitly stated that it was only ruling on legal responsibility and flagged the issue of moral responsibility, suggesting that the legislature consider abolition. The powerful dissent rebuked the Church for invoking charitable immunity to protect itself in a case involving "[t]he sexual exploitation of an innocent child by a perverted employee" and referred to the "tragic and evil setting" and the "heinous character of the conduct" as the kind of factors that totally negate the application of the doctrine.[113] Eventually New Jersey amended the legislation to explicitly exclude from immunity the very situation that *Schultz* involved—sexual offences against minors.[114] Ironically, as in other examples that we have seen, the Church's decision to invoke immunity even in a case like this helped to cement the demise of that "discredited doctrine."

The Church's aggressive reliance on immunity in troubling cases like *Schultz* resulted in more and more jurisdictions repealing the doctrine. Moreover, even where it remained in place, courts began to show their displeasure with the Catholic Church's willingness to invoke it to defend themselves against childhood sexual abuse cases. As a result, here too they began to narrow the scope of the doctrine. In *Picher v. Roman Catholic Bishop of Portland*, the Maine Supreme Court held that the traditional doctrine of charitable immunity did not apply to intentional torts.[115] Picher, who was abused as a child, brought an action against Melville, a priest in the Diocese of Portland, as well as against the Bishop of Portland. He was awarded over $4.2 million dollars against Melville on the basis of assault, battery, and other torts. Picher also alleged that the bishop knew that Melville had sexually abused another child before he was assigned to Picher's parish but failed to report it to law enforcement officials. The bishop moved for summary judgment on the basis that the Church was protected by charitable immunity. The lower court held that the Church was protected by immunity, but the Maine Supreme Court overturned that ruling. The majority described charitable immunity as a "discredited doctrine" that had been largely abrogated in most other states and found that even where some elements of such immunity were intact, it was never intended to and did not extend to intentional actions, such as fraudulent concealment and child abuse.[116]

The cumulative result is that, as *Picher* points out, the vast majority of jurisdictions in the United States no longer recognize charitable immunity as a defense to tort

[113] *Id.* at 552.
[114] N.J. Stat Ann. § 2A:53A-7.4 (West 2006).
[115] Picher v. Roman Cath. Bishop of Portland, 974 A.2d 286 (Me. 2009).
[116] *Id.* at 291–98.

claims.[117] Despite this, some states responded to judicial refusals to grant charitable immunity by legislatively enacting limits on damages. Thus, for example, in both New Jersey and Massachusetts, the legislature imposed limits on the amount that a plaintiff could recover from a charitable entity. In the case of Massachusetts, it limited recovery to $20,000 for claims relating to charitable activities but placed no restrictions on damages that resulted from a charitable organization's commercial endeavors.[118] However, even in such cases, the magnitude of the wrongdoing in some of the Catholic Church litigation has led courts to refuse to extend protections for intentional torts.[119] Moreover, perhaps uneasy with some of the consequences of invoking the doctrine, the Church has sometimes resorted to settlement in amount far above the cap rather than risk the further possible damage associated with invoking immunity.[120]

A similar relationship between the Catholic Church sex abuse crisis and the diminishing salience of charitable immunity is also apparent in other jurisdictions. In Canada, church immunity became an issue in the Mount Cashel sex abuse scandal. The Christian Brothers decided to wind up their charitable corporation in order to compensate the victims whose claims were estimated to be $36 million. However, the Brothers argued that two British Columbia schools owned by them and worth approximately $38.5 million should not be sold to satisfy the claims.[121] Without the schools, their assets amounted to only $4 million. In an attempt to shield the schools, the Brothers invoked a number of grounds, including charitable immunity. The Chambers Judge held that there was no doctrine of charitable immunity, but he accepted the Brothers' argument that the schools were protected by a special purpose trust. On appeal, the Ontario Court of Appeal affirmed the unavailability of charitable immunity and rejected the special purpose trust exemption. The court noted that the Church's approach would leave their assets "woefully short" of what they owed to survivors and quoted Madam Justice McLachlin on this outcome:

> The suggestion that the victim must remain remediless for the greater good smacks of crass and unsubstantiated utilitarianism. Indeed, it is far from clear to me that the "net" good produced by non-profit institutions justifies the price placed on the individual victim, nor that this is a fair way for society to order its resources.[122]

[117] *Id. See also* Cobb, *supra* note 111, at 707, citing American Law Institute, Restatement (Second) of Torts § 895E (1979).
[118] O'Reilly & Chalmers, *supra* note 78, at 161.
[119] *Id.*
[120] *Id.*
[121] Christian Brothers of Ireland in Canada (Re) (2000), 47 O.R. (3d) 674, 2000 CanLII 5712 (Can. Ont. C.A.).
[122] *Id.* ¶ 84. *See also* Rowland v. Vancouver College Ltd., 2001 BCCA 527 (Can.).

The Court of Appeal's bluntness highlights the fact that the Church's legal strategy risks more than simple legal defeat—it also risks moral damage to the institution and often results in further erosion of the very protections invoked in their defense. Despite this judicial censure, the Christian Brothers appealed to the Supreme Court of Canada, which denied leave to appeal.[123]

Unfortunately, these examples are not isolated, again suggesting a much wider institutional strategy at work. While in the early days of the crisis the Church tended to try to quietly settle cases, as numbers began to mount it adopted a 'no holds barred' litigation strategy, going so far as to countersue victims and their families, accusing them of negligence for trusting Catholic priests.[124] Under oath at the Australian Royal Commission into Institutional Responses to Child Sexual Abuse, even the Church itself conceded that some of its tactics were unfair "from a Christian point of view."[125] This aggressive legal strategy has also backfired for the Church. As we have already noted, the openness of the legal forum, combined with the Church's willingness to raise any possible defense no matter how troubling or unpalatable, brought the Church's tactics into public view in a way that it almost certainly did not anticipate.

Another example can be found in the Church's efforts to get around the demise of charitable immunity by invoking the "special purpose trust." While the Church often invokes this defense, courts and commentators are critical of what they see as a "tactic" to avoid compensating abuse victims. In the Mount Cashel case above, the court's strong confirmation that charitable immunity was not available was almost certainly affected by the Church's willingness to forward its alternative special purpose trust argument that the court was so critical of. Similar Church tactics have drawn criticism elsewhere including in Ireland. When the Sisters of Mercy transferred €412 million to a trust in order to avoid compensating survivors of the Magdalene Laundries, it generated more than criticism—it also resulted in calls to rethink the historic protections and benefits the Church received from the state.[126] Similarly, in Australia, the Catholic Church was notorious for using the "*Ellis* defence" to shield church assets from

[123] Christian Brothers of Ireland in Canada (Re), 2000 CarswellOnt 4334 (Can. S.C.C.).

[124] *See* Michael Powell & Lois Romano, *Roman Catholic Church Shifts Legal Strategy; Aggressive Litigation Replaces Quiet Settlements*, THE WASHINGTON POST (May 13, 2002).

[125] Thomas Oriti, *George Pell Tells Sex Abuse Royal Commission Case Against John Ellis Was Unfair "From a Christian Point of View,"* ABC NEWS (Austl., Mar. 26, 2014).

[126] *See* Máiréad Enright, *Abuse Redress, Property and the Catholic Church in Ireland*, HUMAN RIGHTS IN IRELAND (Nov. 4, 2013), https://web.archive.org/web/20170917215625/http://humanrights.ie/law-culture-and-religion/abuse-redress-property-and-the-catholic-church-in-ireland/; Joe Little, *Priest Says Abuse Scandal "Almost Fatally Destroyed" Catholic Church*, R.T.E. (Feb. 9, 2017), https://www.rte.ie/news/analysis-and-comment/2017/0208/851235-church-clerical-abuse/. On the role of the Church in the Irish state, see especially HOLOHAN, *supra* note 38.

sexual abuse claims.[127] The Church's continued reliance on what was perceived to be an unjust and immoral "loophole" led to public criticism and numerous calls for legislative abolition both by the Victoria Inquiry and by the Australian Royal Commission.[128] In 2015, Victoria became the first jurisdiction in Australia to introduce legislation to abolish the defense, and other jurisdictions have followed suit.[129]

The Church's decision to aggressively litigate child sexual abuse cases has also led to other legal changes that ended up creating yet more challenges for them. Such tactics ended up calling attention to the Church's single-minded focus on protecting its assets, which in turn attracted public criticism and judicial censure. Courts and legislators became more inclined to close off the Church's remaining liability-evading routes as well as to reconsider other special treatment the Church receives. The Sydney Archdiocese is an example. When it was asked to provide property valuations to Australia's Royal Commission, it used historic acquisition costs. The Commission challenged this, noting that, along with the Church's exclusion of the value of schools and local parishes, it certainly meant that the archdiocese was understating its true wealth.[130] Subsequent investigations have suggested a vast gulf between what the Church reported to the Royal Commission and the true value of its assets. This in turn has led to calls for elimination of many other forms of special privileges the Church enjoys, including extremely valuable benefits such as its tax-exempt status.[131]

Examples like this suggest that the Church's 'no holds barred' approach has come at a very high price. Churches have had the benefit of special legal protections like immunities because they have been seen as different from ordinary legal actors by virtue of their pursuit of public rather than private good. While the Church is entitled to protect itself including behaving like any other aggressive legal actor, it does so at a cost. Not only does this approach damage the reputation of the Church, but as the demise of charitable immunity shows, its repeated demonstration of the priority it places on self-preservation fatally undermines the very reason that it benefited from so many legal protections in the first place.

In addition to the shield of charitable immunity, the Catholic Church is in a unique position by virtue of its relationship to the Holy See. Because of this,

[127] *See* Patsy McGarry, *Clerical Sex Abuse Scandal Has Led to Few Convictions*, The Irish Times (Aug. 26, 2016); Melissa Davey, *Victoria to Abolish "Ellis Defence" That Protects Church Assets from Abuse Victim Claims*, The Guardian (Mar. 6, 2018).

[128] *See* Desmond Cahill & Peter Wilkinson, Centre for Global Research, Child Sexual Abuse in the Catholic Church: An Interpretive Review of the Literature and Public Inquiry Reports (2017).

[129] *See* Mathews & Dallaston, *supra* note 60, at 394–95.

[130] *See* Royce Millar, et al., *Catholic Church's Massive Wealth Revealed*, The Sydney Morning Herald (Austl., Feb. 12, 2018).

[131] Royce Millar et al., *Catholic Inc.: What the Church Is Really Worth*, The Age (Feb. 12, 2018).

alone among churches it has another defense at its disposal—foreign sovereign immunity. The Church often invoked this immunity and until recently it too proved powerful.[132] However, as with the other immunities and protections, the Church's willingness to use foreign sovereign immunity to protect itself from the claims of child sexual abuse victims also began to erode that benefit. *Doe v. Holy See* illustrates this. This case involved a priest named Ronan who began abusing boys in the mid-1950s in Ireland. He was transferred to Chicago, where he admitted to abusing more boys before being transferred to a parish in Portland, Oregon, where he was accused of abusing the plaintiff Doe. In addition to suing the Archbishop of Portland and others, Doe sued the Holy See based on both vicarious and direct liability.

The claim against the Holy See was considered a long shot, and the Holy See did claim immunity. However, the Ninth Circuit Court of Appeals rejected the idea that the Holy See was entirely immune from civil suit. It carved out an exception for tortious acts committed within the scope of employment.[133] And *Doe* was the second child sexual abuse case in 2009 in which the Holy See was "thwarted trying to preserve its sovereign immunity."[134] As one commentator has noted, the documented willingness of Catholic Church entities to use bankruptcy, asset-shifting, and other tactics to avoid paying claims has likely played a role in the judicial willingness to shift liability to the Holy See by limiting sovereign immunity.[135] The Church did seek to overturn *Doe* at the Supreme Court of the United States, but the court denied certiorari.[136] The resultant narrowing of foreign sovereign immunity represented yet another significant step toward institutional accountability, and here too the Catholic Church sexual abuse crisis and the Church's response to it was a catalyst for profound legal change.

Reshaping Institutional Responsibility

So as we have seen, one legacy of the Catholic Church sex abuse crisis was the gradual erosion of most of the procedural barriers that had once protected the Church. And as the crisis unfolded, the Church's willingness, even when confronted with devastating child abuse, to continue to defend itself at any cost, only accelerated this process. But the aggressive defense tactics did more than

[132] O'Bryan v. Holy See, 556 F.3d 361 (6th Cir. 2009). *See also* Robert J. Wheeler, *The Shifting Relationship Between Law and Ministry*, 22 New Theological Rev. 46, 49 (2009).

[133] Doe v. Holy See, 557 F.3d 1066, 1081 (9th Cir. 2009).

[134] Edan Burkett, *Victory for Clergy Sexual Abuse Victims: The Ninth Circuit Strips the Holy See of Foreign Sovereign Immunity in Doe v. Holy See*, 2010 BYU L. Rev. 35, 44 (2010), citing O'Bryan v. Holy See, 556 F.3d 361 (6th Cir. 2009).

[135] *See* Burkett, *supra* note 134.

[136] *See* Julie Bolcer, *Supreme Court Rejects Vatican Appeal*, Advocate (June 29, 2010).

this. The troubling continuity between how the Church first handled the information about child abuse and then subsequently litigated those cases started to suggest that an important element of the wrongdoing was deeply institutional. This in turn prompted re-examination of the underlying conception of responsibility—in this context, institutional liability started to seem both apt and necessary.

However, even once procedural obstacles were set aside, the path to institutional liability remained far from straightforward. As noted above, traditionally the law imagined wrongs as intentional individual acts: the underlying conception of responsibility was by disposition discrete, personal, and unitary. The less a claim looked like this, the less likely it was to succeed. But clergy sexual abuse claims typically involved institutional as well as individual actions and did not easily fit into this traditional view. However here too the Catholic Church crisis has had a role in the move toward a more complex picture of responsibility. The growing willingness to countenance multiple overlapping duties gradually reshaped liability rules to make them more able to capture institutional responsibility. In the process, liability opened up in a new and very different way.

Vicarious liability is the most important institutional liability doctrine. It enables responsibility for a wrong done by institution's employee to be passed on to the institution itself even if it was not at fault. But because it was a strict form of liability, courts narrowly circumscribed the operation of this doctrine. The more egregious the wrong, the more likely it was to be seen as a purely individual act and the less likely to engage the vicarious liability of the institution. This was a significant hurdle for claimants in the Catholic Church cases given that they began with individual criminal acts of sexual assault.

This was compounded by the fact that the direct perpetrator had often died by the time the case was brought, leaving child abuse survivors without remedies. In 1999, the English Court of Appeal confirmed that a school council was not vicariously liable for the acts of a teacher who sexually accosted a student with mental disabilities during a school field trip.[137] The court reasoned that the sexual tort was the teacher's independent act, outside the scope of his authority, and as such it could not be attributed to the employer. But this approach was about to undergo a process of dramatic change, and here too the Catholic Church cases played a pivotal role.

To see why this matters, it is useful to note the deeply institutional nature of what went wrong in the Catholic Church sex abuse cases. *Doe v. Holy See*, discussed above, illustrates the complex nature of so many of the Catholic Church claims:

[137] S.T. v. North Yorkshire City Council, [1998] EWCA (Civ) 1208 (Eng.).

> Doe alleged that the Archdiocese and the Order were vicariously liable for Ronan's abuse of Doe, and that the Chicago Bishop and the Order were negligent in failing to warn the Archdiocese and Doe of Ronan's propensities. Doe also alleged that the Holy See was vicariously liable for Ronan's abuse of Doe and for the negligent actions of the Archdiocese, the Order, and the Chicago Bishop, and that the Holy See was itself negligent in its retention and supervision of Ronan and in failing to warn of his propensities.[138]

In John Doe's case, Father Ronan had died in 1992. Thus, in the absence of institutional liability, the injured plaintiff is very likely to be left without any remedy.

While resources are one reason that the institution is critical in claims like these, it is not the most important reason. In *Doe* as in so many of the Catholic Church sex abuse cases, the institution was well aware of the propensities of the perpetrator—Ronan admitted to abusing multiple boys in Ireland and then in Chicago before being moved to Portland where he abused Doe. The Church hierarchy, including the Bishop of Chicago, knew that Ronan was a sexual predator yet they moved him to another diocese and placed him in charge of children. They did not warn anyone of the danger. And this pattern was repeated in countless cases across many jurisdictions. This made it hard to see the Church's actions as the result of errant individuals here and there. It began to look like a policy—a reflection of an ethos about what most mattered to the Church. In this sense, cases like Doe's made it clear that in addition to the egregious personal wrongs committed by Ronan, the Church itself as an institution was also deeply implicated in wrongdoing. Yet under traditional liability rules, Doe could only claim against Ronan.

However, when Doe claimed damages against the Church based in part on vicarious liability, the Ninth Circuit Court of Appeal rejected the Church's argument that it could not be responsible for the criminal act of its employee. It ruled that an employer could be liable even for an employee's criminal act where the employment was "a necessary precursor" to the criminal act and where that act was "a direct outgrowth" conduct that was within the scope of employment.[139] It found that Doe's allegations met this standard because he "came to know Ronan as his priest, counselor and spiritual adviser" and because Ronan used his "position of authority" to "engage in harmful sexual contact upon" Doe in "several places including the monastery and surrounding areas" in Portland, Oregon.[140] Under such circumstances, the court concluded, the Church could not claim that it had no responsibility for the priest's acts. As this illustrates, the traditional

[138] Doe v. Holy See, 557 F.3d 1066, 1071 (9th Cir. 2009).
[139] *Id.* at 1082, citing Fearing v. Butcher, 977 P.2d 1163, 1168 (Or. 1999).
[140] Doe v. Holy See, 557 F.3d 1066, 1083 (9th Cir. 2009).

rules that had long protected the Church began to shift as courts started to look more closely into what went so wrong in these terrible child sexual abuse cases.

Another illustration is found in Canada. In a case involving a residential treatment facility for children, the Supreme Court had also rejected the traditional exclusion of criminal conduct and held that, under certain circumstances, employers could indeed be vicariously liable for sexual assaults committed by employees.[141] A few years later, the Supreme Court was faced with a case involving Father Bennett, who had sexually abused dozens of boys in St. George's diocese in Newfoundland. Though the abuse was reported to successive bishops of the diocese, they did nothing to stop the abuse. Thirty-six victims of Father Bennett eventually sued him, St. George's, various bishops, and the Catholic Church. The trial judge found Bennett directly liable and St. George's and the bishop vicariously liable.[142] Before the Supreme Court, St. George's relied on the traditional argument that it could not be liable because Bennett's actions violated the norms of the Church and the charitable nature of the diocese's activities. Though a majority of the Court of Appeal had accepted this, the Supreme Court unanimously rejected it. The court noted the close relationship between St. George's and Bennett, the fact that St. George's substantially enhanced the risk that led to the wrongs, and the fact that it provided Bennett both with great power in relation to vulnerable victims and with the opportunity to abuse that power. Vicarious liability, it concluded, was justified in such circumstances.[143]

A similar erosion of the protection of traditional vicarious liability rules is apparent more broadly. Australia's Royal Commission brought to light the Church's legal tactics and in particular its perceived abuse of a number of defenses.[144] The Commission's *Redress and Civil Litigation Report* made

[141] Bazley v. Curry, [1999] 2 S.C.R. 534 (Can.).

[142] John Doe v. Bennett, 2004 SCC 17 (Can.).

[143] The emergence of what is commonly called a "non-delegable duty" is arguably also another effect of the crisis. *See* Moran, *Reshaping Responsibility*, *supra* note 110. In my view, such a duty is best understood as having a conceptual connection to fiduciary duties and hence more apt in matters like institutional child abuse. The primary focus of traditional vicarious liability is on the relationship between the wrongdoer and the institution. In contrast, in most institutional abuse cases, the relationship between the institution and the victim is at least equally salient. It is the victim's vulnerability to harm along with the institution's undertaking of responsibility that grounds the enhanced (fiduciary-like) duty that the institution has to protect them—hence, the non-delegability. The relationship to the wrongdoer of course matters, but that is because of the institution's ability to control the situation and potentially avoid the harm. On my reading, the idea of non-delegability is a way (admittedly rather inelegant) of capturing the primacy and strength of this kind of duty differs from duties owed to arms-length parties that are capable of taking care of themselves. In the latter cases, vicarious liability is the more apt frame of reference.

[144] As one commentator summarized it, "[t]he Catholic Church's words ring hollow in light of merciless legal tactics." Paul Kennedy, *The Catholic Church's Words Ring Hollow in Light of Merciless Legal Tactics*, ABC NEWS (Austl., Aug. 5, 2017). *See also* Catherine Armitage, *Church Threatening Sex Abuse Victims with Court: Solicitor*, THE SYDNEY MORNING HERALD (Austl., Sept. 7, 2013); Barney Zwartz, *Headed to Court, Cardinal Pell Is No Stranger to Controversy*, NATIONAL CATHOLIC REPORTER (July 24, 2017); Paul Kennedy & Conor Duffy, *Flaws in Church's Protocol*, ABC LATELINE (Austl., July 15, 2008).

several recommendations that were directly responsive to the Church's "unnecessarily adversarial responses to claims."[145] These included not only removing limitations periods and the *Ellis* defence but also reforming vicarious liability and related doctrines.[146] Among other things, the report recommended that legislatures change the law to make institutions liable for child sexual abuse by any person associated with the institution. States in Australia have responded legislatively, closing many of the defenses on which the Church had traditionally relied and which had been the subject of enormous criticism.

As jurisdictions began to adopt a more survivor-focused approach to vicarious liability, the Church began to invoke a second line of defense—it insisted that vicarious liability could never apply to priest–church relationships. In *Doe v. Bennett*, above, the Church also made this argument, insisting that vicarious liability did not apply to the priest–church relationships because the priest was not an employee. However, the Supreme Court of Canada rejected this as well, finding that the diocese of St. George's was vicariously liable for the acts of its priests, noting that their relationship was "sufficiently close relationship" and "akin to an employment relationship."[147]

In the United Kingdom as well the Church began to argue that the unique nature of the relationship between priest and bishop precluded the application of vicarious liability. But in *J.G.E. v. The Trustees of the Portsmouth Roman Catholic Diocesan Trust*, the English Court of Appeal disagreed, finding that although there was no contract of service between a priest and the bishop, that relationship was so close in character to the employer/employee relationship that it could fairly be said to be "akin to employment"[148] with the consequence that "it is just and fair to hold the employer vicariously liable."[149] Shortly thereafter, in a case involving the Christian Brothers, the Supreme Court of the United Kingdom confirmed this, noting that "vicarious liability is on the move" and specifically referencing cases of childhood sexual abuse, often implicating priests and religious orders.[150] Lord Phillips went on to conclude in no uncertain terms that the Christian Brothers Institute was vicariously liable for abuse committed by its members.[151] The exact parameters of this expanded doctrine of institutional

[145] Simon Thomsen, *Here Is the Shocking Opening Address to the Royal Commission About Child Abuse in the Catholic Church*, Business Insider Australia (Feb. 6, 2017), http://web.archive.org/web/20170208180635/https://www.businessinsider.com.au/here-is-the-shocking-opening-address-to-the-royal-commission-about-child-abuse-in-the-catholic-church-2017-2.

[146] *See* Helen Davidson, *Child Sexual Abuse Royal Commission Delivers Final Report—As It Happened*, The Guardian (Dec. 15, 2017).

[147] John Doe v. Bennett, 2004 SCC 17, ¶ 27 (Can.).

[148] JGE v. Portsmouth Roman Cath. Diocesan Trust, [2012] EWCA (Civ) 938 (Eng.).

[149] *Id.* ¶ 73.

[150] The Catholic Child Welfare Society and others (Appellants) v. Various Claimants (FC) and The Institute of the Brothers of the Christian Schools and others (Respondents), [2012] UKSC 56, ¶ 19.

[151] *Id.* ¶ 94.

responsibility continue to be the subject of considerable litigation. Once again, much of that litigation involves the Catholic Church.[152]

In this way, a more complex picture of responsibility began to emerge. Unlike the old unitary view, it implicitly accepted the notion that injury could be occasioned by multiple wrongdoers, engaging in different kinds of wrongs or, in the case of vicarious liability, perhaps no wrongs at all. The Catholic Church crisis was bringing to light terrible cases where a complex set of acts—some criminal, some intentional, some negligent, and some without provable fault—worked together to inflict life-altering injuries on children. Moreover, as events unfolded, it became apparent that there was a consistent pattern of behavior at every level within the Catholic Church. It may have seemed to the Church that it was good strategy to fight every possible issue in court, but it resulted in the gradual accumulation of a robust record of public judgments documenting and often condemning the behavior of the Church.

The greater openness to institutional liability in this context was certainly borne in part by a desire to compensate survivors, but it was more profound than that. A growing body of public evidence revealed how the Church approached child sexual abuse, and it was a deeply troubling picture. It brought to light the existence of a shared institutional mindset—an ethos about what really mattered—that was consistently expressed through the actions of many different actors at many different levels within the Church. It also became increasingly clear that it implicated the Church itself at the highest levels. Certainly, individuals could cause grievous harm, but it was becoming apparent that so too could an institution. To its shame and to its detriment, the Catholic Church sex abuse crisis made that abundantly clear.

Conclusion

When issues concerning the sexual abuse of children by Catholic clergy started to come to public attention in the early 1980s, the world was in flux and the events that eventually became part of that crisis were part of the foment. These were the early days of increasing rights-consciousness and a related optimism about the power of law to secure and vindicate those rights. As survivors of child sexual abuse began to turn to the courts, the Church responded with increasingly

[152] The High Court of Australia released a controversial ruling late in 2024 overturning a lower court and finding that an assistant parish priest who sexually abused a five-year-old was not "in a strict legal sense" an employee of the diocese that was therefore not liable. *See* Bird v. DP (a pseudonym), [2024] HCA 41, ¶ 27 (Austl.). The ruling prompted calls for more law reform of liability rules. *See* Christopher Knaus, *High Court Rules Catholic Church Not Liable for Child Abuse by Priest It Didn't Directly Employ*, The Guardian (Nov. 13, 2024).

aggressive defensive tactics. Perhaps this is not surprising—it would have been hard for the Church to fathom that the very tactics that had so long protected them were about to backfire in a spectacular fashion. But now over the several decades of litigation that began in the 1980s, the Catholic Church has paid out many billions of dollars to survivors for its role in their sexual abuse. In that ongoing process, the Church has been profoundly changed. But so too has the law.

The law has traditionally been somewhat skeptical about the idea that collectives such as institutions could be understood as sufficiently culpable to be legally responsible for grievous wrongs. However, that is no longer the case. While a shift like this certainly cannot be attributed to any one factor, among the various causes the Catholic Church sex abuse scandal holds a place of prominence. The rise of the general duty in negligence certainly started to implicate corporate and institutional defendants in a new way. However, responsibility did not come home to institutions in a more profound sense until the law began to shift its approach to procedural hurdles such as limitations and immunities. The Catholic Church sex abuse crisis was an important catalyst in this shift. But the closer the law came to serious wrongdoing, the more likely it was to hang on to the idea of individual responsibility. Here too the Catholic Church crisis played a critical role in bringing liability much closer to the institution. The unfolding of the crisis and the Church's handling of it eroded the belief that serious wrongdoing was essentially personal. It became clear that an institution could be culpable in a deeper sense of the term. In this, the role of the Catholic Church crisis was especially important. It is a sad irony that the strength of the Church's commitment to self-preservation turned out to be instrumental in bringing about the very catastrophes it was so determined to avoid.

4
Redress for Institutionalized Human Rights Abuse

Is it possible that the antonym of "forgetting" is not "remembering," but justice?[1]

Introduction

The elements that would lead to rise of interest in historic injustice were beginning to come together. The Holocaust reparations model was a critical source of inspiration for the neglected victims of history's wrongs. But there was more to it than that. The fact that those actions were launched in US courts drew an implicit link between transitional justice and problems of historic injustice in non-transitional legal regimes. In so doing, they raised the difficult question, "why them and not us"? In the legal realm, the most obvious response was found in the procedural and substantive rules that confined private law responsibility. But as we have seen, under the enormous strain of the Catholic Church sexual abuse crisis, that was changing. In the face of those terrible cases, it was hard to sustain the idea that time heals all wounds. Increasingly, neither procedural barriers associated with the passage of time nor traditional immunities offered the complete protection they once did. And as private law began to open up, so too did the prospect of a concept of responsibility more responsive to the growing demands to make amends for historic wrongs.

Although law turned out to be very important to the rise of responsibility for old injustices, it was rarely the first choice of survivors. Most of them instead began by reaching out to politicians, hoping for recognition and sometimes for redress. While the political sphere had typically been unresponsive, in the shifting environment of the late 1980s that too began to change. Survivors of historic wrongs started to feel new hope, and some did see success after many decades of inertia. The landmark apologies and redress programs for the wartime internment of North American citizens of Japanese origin showed that

[1] Yosef Hayim Yerushalmi, Zakhor: Jewish History and Jewish Memory 117 (1996).

Making Amends for Historic Wrongs. Mayo Moran, Oxford University Press. © Mayo Moran 2025.
DOI: 10.1093/9780190927295.003.0004

there was hope for survivors of old wrongs and inspired others.[2] Rosewood was a rare example of another successful political redress effort. In 1923, that small African American town in Florida was burned to the ground by a group of white people after a white woman claimed she had been raped by an African American man. At least eight African Americans were also murdered. Here too investigative journalism was critical. After decades of silence, Gary Moore's reporting got nationwide attention. As a result, in 1994—more than seventy years after the massacre—Florida passed House Bill 591. Although it did not use the term reparations, it set up a commission to study the events, provided up to $150,000 in individual compensation to survivors of the massacre, created a fund to compensate descendants of those who lost property, and established college scholarships for the descendants of the victims.[3] Rosewood was a notable success—the first reparations program for African Americans—but it was not the harbinger of broader change. While there were numerous other political efforts to make amends for historic racial violence, most faltered particularly when it came to individual reparations.[4] As we shall see, it would take decades, and another horrific public murder of an African American man, before much success was found in the political arena.

But the legal landscape was shifting and that meant that another powerful instrument—law—was suggesting itself to survivors of historic wrongs. The result was that across a wide array of cases, there was new interest in litigating the wrongs of the past and increasing pressure to make amends. Historic injustice cases certainly remained legally challenging. But like the Catholic Church litigation, the arguments in favor of repair had considerable power. That power sometimes even proved sufficient to erode the many legal barriers these novel claims faced. Moreover, once raised, some of these claims also proved surprisingly difficult to counter, setting in motion dynamics of their own. Gradually, cases that had once seemed improbable became legally plausible, and as this happened, other old wrongs also started to come under scrutiny. While now too numerous

[2] The Civil Liberties Act of 1988 provided a formal apology and $20,000 in reparations. That same year, the Japanese Canadian Redress Agreement was signed, including an apology, compensation of $21,000 to survivors, a $12 million community fund, and funding for the creation of the Canadian Race Relations Foundation. *See* Chapter 2.

[3] *See generally* C. Jeanne Bassett, *House Bill 591: Florida Compensates Rosewood Victims and Their Families for a Seventy-One-Year-Old Injury*, 22 Fla St. U. L. Rev. 503 (1994), cited in Martha Minow, *Not Only for Myself: Identity, Politics, and Law*, 75 Or. L. Rev. 647, 679 (1996); Robert Samuels, *After Reparations: How a Scholarship Helped—and Didn't Help—Descendants of Victims of the 1923 Rosewood Racial Massacre*, The Washington Post (Apr. 3, 2020).

[4] Introduced in the US Congress in 1989 by Representative Harry Conyers, House Resolution 40—a reference to the Sherman order that proposed that forty acres of land should be set aside for the families of former slaves—proposes a congressional commission to study the modern legacy of slavery and Jim Crow and make recommendations, including the possibility of reparations. *See* Michela Moscufo, *Reparations Bill Returns to Congress as Trump Leads Charge Against Racial Equity in Government*, NBC News (Feb. 12, 2025).

to catalog in full, let us look at some developments that were especially important in altering the approach to historic injustice.

We begin with a particularly significant example of redress for historic wrongs—Canada's Indian Residential Schools Settlement Agreement. That landmark settlement addressed egregious abuses of Indigenous children in residential schools run by churches and the federal government. It broke new ground in drawing transitional justice thinking into private law actions for redress of a vast historic wrong well outside of the transitional context. In the process, it helped to suggest that this new kind of ambitious redress claim could be relevant to a much wider array of injustices, many of them in stable regimes. The settlement was also important because of how it also simultaneously engaged two of the most important branches of redress for old wrongs. First, it showed that victims of institutionalized human rights abuses could find some measure of justice, a success that helped to change the landscape and encouraged survivors of eugenics, sexual abuse, and other grievous rights violations to pursue redress even after many decades, or longer. Second, by putting colonialism itself on trial, the settlement showed how redress could engage an even more ambitious category of old wrongs. In this chapter we will explore how the quest for redress expanded from cases like the Indian Residential Schools Settlement Agreement to large scale institutionalized human rights abuses like the practice of eugenics and wartime sexual slavery.[5] Later, we will trace how progress on these issues created momentum to make amends for some of the damage caused by the great wrongs of history like colonialism and slavery.

From Tort Law to Transformative Justice: Canada's Indian Residential Schools Settlement Agreement

Canada's residential schools litigation and eventual settlement is a pivotal illustration of how the problem of historic wrongs started to come home to stable democracies, and it has served as both model and inspiration across the globe. That litigation began with individual tort cases and ended in a $6 billion settlement that included an historic apology, two multibillion-dollar individual redress programs, and the first truth and reconciliation commission in an established democracy. It also changed how Canada understood itself and its history.

[5] As others have noted, the term 'military sexual slaves' is more accurate and appropriate, but the term 'comfort women' is the common description of the victims of the Japanese military's sexual slavery system during World War II. I often use the term sexual slavery here, but where I do adopt the conventional term, I mark my concern about it by using scare quotes. *See also* Jimin Kim et al., *Teaching About the Comfort Women During World War II and the Use of Personal Stories of the Victims*, 24 ASIAN LIT. HUMAN. & SOC. SCI. 58 (2019).

While the initial claims shared important similarities with the Catholic Church cases, they were also infused with something else—the broader ambitions of the Holocaust reparations litigation. In this way, the residential schools litigation used the increasing openness of private law to press forward larger claims about historic wrongs—claims that drew broader norms and transitional justice issues into stable legal orders, problematizing their pasts and creating profound difficulties for their major institutions, including law itself.

The residential schools system that was the subject of this litigation was made up of 139 residential schools run by the Canadian government in partnership with various churches.[6] During the nearly 150 years of its operation, at least 150,000 Indigenous children were forcibly taken from their parents and placed in these schools.[7] While education was the stated purpose, mistreatment, malnutrition, cruelty, and sexual abuse were rampant, often committed by persons in positions of authority. Even when someone summoned the courage to make a complaint, most perpetrators were simply moved to new schools where they continued to abuse other children. Physical abuse included everything from malnutrition to severe corporal punishment to putting children in electric chairs. When children spoke their own languages or practiced their own spiritual beliefs, they were punished. Horrifyingly, medical experiments were also conducted on the children.[8] The trauma was exacerbated by the fact that children were purposely isolated from their families, even to the point of separating siblings. Children often died in the residential schools, and frequently their families were not even told. For a long time, silence surrounded the residential school experience. However, this changed due to a significant report of the Royal Commission on Aboriginal Peoples[9] and the leadership of a courageous First Nations leader, National Chief of the Assembly of First Nations Phil Fontaine. And so, beginning in the mid-1990s, survivors started to bring residential school cases to court.

[6] *See* Mayo Moran, *The Role of Reparative Justice in Responding to the Legacy of Indian Residential Schools*, 64 U. Toronto L.J. 529, 531 (2014) [hereinafter Moran, *The Role of Reparative Justice*]. *See also* 1 Truth and Reconciliation Commission of Canada, Final Report of the Truth and Reconciliation Commission of Canada—Canada's Residential Schools: The History, Part I—Origins to 1939 (2015).

[7] Truth and Reconciliation Commission of Canada, The Survivors Speak: A Report of the Truth and Reconciliation Commission of Canada vi (2015).

[8] *See* Ian Mosby, *Administering Colonial Science: Nutrition Research and Human Medical Experimentation in Aboriginal Communities and Residential Schools, 1942–1952*, 46 Soc. His. 145 (2013); Zia Akhtar, *Canadian Genocide and Official Culpability*, 10 Int'l Crim. L. Rev. 111, 116–19 (2010); Noni E. Macdonald, Richard Stanwich, & Andrew Lynk, *Canada's Shameful History of Nutrition Research on Residential School Children: The Need for Strong Medical Ethics in Aboriginal Health Research*, 19 Pediatrics & Child Health 64 (2014).

[9] *See* Royal Commission on Aboriginal Peoples, Report of the Royal Commission on Aboriginal Peoples (1996).

Inspired in part by litigation against the Catholic Church (with which it has considerable overlap since the Catholic Church ran most of the schools), the early residential schools cases were civil claims by multiple survivors of serious sexual and physical abuse. In most cases, the perpetrator had already been criminally convicted. Still, as decades-old civil claims primarily against the institutions that ran the schools, they were extraordinarily legally complex. The plaintiffs faced challenges with limitation periods, immunities, narrow vicarious liability rules, and apportionment of responsibility between churches and government. Defendants probably felt confident of success when the litigation began. But that confidence, as it would turn out, was not warranted. In common with the Catholic Church cases and for related reasons, there was unexpected force on the plaintiff side. The early cases presented courts with horrific claims involving highly credible violations of the most fundamental rights of vulnerable children forcibly taken from their families and entrusted to the care of church and state.

While the claims did face many challenges, they were launched at a time when private law responsibility was beginning to open up as a result of the Catholic Church sexual abuse crisis.[10] Crucially, limitation periods were beginning to lose their all-powerful effect, waning in the courtroom and being reshaped by legislators outraged at the abuse of children at the hands of those who were supposed to care for them. Liability rules were also under pressure, making it increasingly possible to hold institutions responsible for the criminal and other wrongs of individuals in their employ. All of this meant a new kind of legal openness to at least some claims of historic wrongs. The early residential schools litigation picked up on this, and in the mid-1990s, those cases started to come to court. However, these were no ordinary private law cases, even by the challenging standards of the Catholic Church litigation. While the sadly familiar claims of sexual assault of children formed the legal core of most of the early claims, they were also accompanied by other larger and even more unsettling claims directed at systemic wrongs and seeking responses far beyond ordinary civil remedies.

An illustration is found in *Blackwater v. Plint*.[11] It arose out of the infamous Alberni Indian Residential School. After decades of abuse, a dormitory supervisor named Plint was finally found guilty of multiple counts of sexual abuse and sentenced to eleven years in prison. The judge in that criminal trial described the entire residential schools system as "nothing but a form of institutionalized pedophilia."[12] Following the 1996 conviction, twenty-seven former students claimed

[10] *See* Chapters 2 and 3. *See also* Moran, *The Role of Reparative Justice*, *supra* note 6, at 533–40.

[11] Blackwater v. Plint, 2005 SCC 58 (Can.).

[12] R v. Plint, 1995 CarswellBC 1745, ¶ 14 (Can. B.C. Sup. Ct.) (WL). *See also* Leslie Thielen-Wilson, *Troubling the Path to Decolonization: Indian Residential School Case Law, Genocide, and Settler Illegitimacy*, 29 CAN. J. L. & SOC'Y 181 (2014).

damages against the United Church and the Government of Canada for the abuse. In some respects, *Plint* was a relatively "easy" historic injustice case. The criminal trial took many evidentiary questions off the table. Earlier child abuse litigation had also brought helpful changes. Limitation periods were no longer applicable for childhood sexual abuse, and vicarious liability was undergoing a dramatic shift on the very question of an institution's liability for an employee's criminal conduct, including sexual abuse.[13] Without these dramatic changes, *Plint* would have been unthinkable, criminal conviction notwithstanding. But it remained far from simple—the sweeping nature of the underlying claims and the daunting problems they raised only served to highlight the deeper challenges associated with litigating past wrongs.

An illustration can be found in *Plint*'s assessment of damages. Limitations periods were only lifted for sexual abuse. This meant that all of the other claims were time-barred, including physical abuse as well as more complex claims like loss of culture. Anxious to limit its damages, the Government of Canada put forward a defense that the trial judge called "shameful." They argued that Indigenous children were "severely disadvantaged by the negative life-long effects of the simple fact of attending" a residential school, even in the absence of abuse.[14] The judge summarized how both the plaintiffs and the defendants described the residential school experience:

> Leaving aside the sexual assault, the plaintiffs would still have been at [the Alberni Indian Residential School] and they would a) have been living away from their families, communities and culture; b) have been forced to speak English instead of their own Native languages; c) have had to eat food that was vastly different from what they were used to; d) have been subjected to the physical pain and the fear associated with the violence among the children; e) have endured the terror of the gauntlet; f) have been victims of excessive corporal punishment from supervisors and other adults at [the Alberni Indian Residential School]; and g) have been subject to racist discrimination when bussed to public schools.[15]

The government's defense, in other words, was that the damages owed to the plaintiffs should be reduced because most of the harm they suffered actually came, not from sexual assaults, but rather from the whole residential schools

[13] The residential school litigation was certainly on the radar when landmark vicarious liability cases were heard. In Bazley v. Curry, [1999] 2 S.C.R. 534 (Can.), the intervenors included three of the major church entities eventually involved in the Indian Residential Schools litigation, as well as Indian bands and some overlapping counsel.

[14] Blackwater v. Plint, 2001 BCSC 997, ¶ 332.

[15] Blackwater v. Plint, 2001 BCSC 997, ¶ 334.

system. And because of limitations periods and because the system itself was legal, that broader harm could not give rise to damages.[16] The judge reluctantly agreed that this "distasteful" argument did reduce the government's damages.[17] However, this 'bad but legal system' argument was going to prove costly.

By the time that *Plint* reached the Supreme Court of Canada in 2005, these large systemic issues were in the foreground, but this time they appeared not as a defense but as an argument from the plaintiffs that the government had violated its fiduciary duty to the children. At trial, fiduciary duty was read narrowly and rejected, but in the Supreme Court of Canada, Chief Justice McLachlin acknowledged a "broader argument focussing on Aboriginal children collectively."[18] As she described it, that argument alleged that "the system of residential schools robbed Indian children of their communities, culture and support and placed them in environments of abuse."[19] Although she declined to address this claim because it was only raised at the Supreme Court of Canada, the very fact that the government's 'bad but legal system' defense was now being reframed by plaintiffs as a breach of fiduciary duty argument fueled deep concern among defendants. It also inspired other claims that raised these large-scale issues much more directly.

Residential schools cases began to flood in at an alarming rate, outstripping the ability of the courts to deal with them. As the litigation increased, so too did the systemic claims about the damage caused by the residential schools system as a whole. Ironically, the very facts about the system that the government had raised to limit their liability in *Plint*—the forced separation from family; the loss of language, culture, and spirituality; the physical abuse; and the racism—were now being used by plaintiffs to ground the claim that the defendants had breached their fiduciary duty to the children. The courts were also showing themselves more willing to listen. Whatever compensation gains the government might have made with its 'bad but legal system' defense in *Plint* seemed to evaporate.

The more that courts and the public heard about the residential schools system through the litigation, the harder it was to maintain the *Plint* line of

[16] *See id.* ¶ 458 (Can.):

I have earlier pointed to a stark incongruity in this case. The defendants, who were jointly responsible for [the Alberni Indian Residential School], are in complete agreement with the plaintiffs' depiction of their non-sexual abuse mistreatment at [the Alberni Indian Residential School]. By emphasizing the statute barred non-sexual abuse, the defendants seek to minimize the relative impact of the compensable sexual abuse. As distasteful as this may appear it is nonetheless the inevitable result of the Legislature's decision to remove any limitation period for the tort of sexual assault while leaving all other limitation periods unchanged.

[17] As Brenner C.J.S.C. put it, "even the defendants concede" that the plaintiffs were "severely compromised" simply by virtue of being forced to attend the [Alberni Indian Residential School]. Blackwater v. Plint, 2001 BCSC 997, ¶ 336 (Can.).

[18] Blackwater v. Plint, 2005 SCC 58, ¶ 61 (Can.).

[19] *Id.*

defense. The defendant community must have felt uneasy as the very arguments that the government had used to limit damages now began to show up in a much different role in important judgments. For example, when former students of the Mohawk Institute Residential School sought class certification, Justice Goudge of the Ontario Court of Appeal described the essence of their claim as follows:

> Broadly put, their claim is that the School was run in a way that was designed to create an atmosphere of fear, intimidation and brutality. Physical discipline was frequent and excessive. Food, housing and clothing were inadequate. Staff members were unskilled and improperly supervised. Students were cut off from their families. They were forbidden to speak their native languages and were forced to attend and participate in Christian religious activities. It is alleged that the aim of the School was to promote the assimilation of native children. It is said that all students suffered as a result.[20]

The lower courts had rejected these claims. However, the Ontario Court of Appeal disagreed, holding instead that the sweeping claims about the nature of the system did indeed constitute the kind of common basis that warranted certification as a class. This was a long way away from the trial court that had reluctantly accepted the *Plint* 'bad but legal system' defense only a few years earlier. As *Cloud v. Canada* and related claims moved forward, appellate courts began to listen to arguments about the whole residential schools system. Though not tantamount to finding those arguments valid, this was striking, not only because of the vast implications but also because the claims went well beyond damages for acts that were illegal at the time like sexual abuse. Indeed, in *Cloud* most of the alleged wrongful acts were authorized and even required by the positive law of the day.

The increasing judicial willingness to countenance the idea that acts that were once demanded by the law could now be the basis of a claim for wrongful injury was also apparent elsewhere. *Bonaparte v. Canada* is a dramatic example. It was a class action by the children of survivors of residential schools alleging that they had been denied the transmission of their Indigenous culture. The Ontario Court of Appeal described the claims as follows:

> They allege that the residential schools were established to implement a governmental policy, the objective of which was to bring about the eradication of the aboriginal culture, past, present and future. Hence, they submit that it was foreseeable, if not intended by the Crown, that the long-term consequence of

[20] Cloud v. Canada, 73 O.R. 3d 401, 2004 CanLII 45444, ¶ 12 (Can. Ont. C.A.). *See also* Baxter v. Canada (Attorney General), 83 O.R. (3d) 481, 2006 CanLII 41673, ¶¶ 2–3 (Can. Ont. S.C.).

> its actions would deprive not only the primary plaintiffs, but also their generational descendants, of their culture, history and status as a nation. In these circumstances, they submit that the fiduciary obligations arising from the Crown's actions extended not only to the residents of the schools but also to themselves as the members of the next generation.[21]

The motions judge had struck out this claim as disclosing no reasonable cause of action, but the Ontario Court of Appeal again disagreed:

> [T]he very purpose of the Crown's assumption of control over the primary plaintiffs was to strip the Indian children of their culture and identity, thereby removing, as and when they became adults, their ability "to pass on to succeeding generations the spiritual, cultural and behavioural bases of their people." Hence, the secondary plaintiffs claim that they were specifically targeted by the governmental policy. They further allege that they were profoundly and adversely affected as a result.[22]

The Court of Appeal held that the claim should proceed, noting the rapid evolution in the law of fiduciary obligations.[23] Along with *Cloud*, this signaled openness to awarding damages for exactly the kind of systemic claims that the trial court in *Plint* had reluctantly accepted as a *defense* only a few years earlier. The scale of such systemic claims was certainly concerning the defendants. But so was the fact that it now seemed that none of the traditional defenses based on statutory authority or public policy was strong enough to immunize actions that, though legal at the time, were now viewed as profoundly wrong. As we saw in the Catholic Church cases, the powerful reparative justice core of the claims was placing ordinary legal rules under pressure, and in the process opening the past up to liability on a scale that would have been unthinkable only a few short years earlier.

Strikingly then, as the litigation developed, the courts seemed increasingly willing to consider liability, even for the very aspects of the system that were intended and authorized by the positive law of the day. For plaintiffs this was vital, since damages would never capture the essential harm of residential schools unless there was a way to address the systemic legalized wrongs. This judicial openness must also have sparked serious concern among the defendants, particularly the federal government. The prospect of liability to *all* residential schools survivors and their descendants far exceeded what anyone would

[21] Bonaparte v. Canada., 64 O.R. 3(d) 1, 2003 CanLII 40016, ¶ 21 (Can. Ont. C.A.).
[22] *Id.* ¶ 35.
[23] *Id.* ¶ 36.

have contemplated only a few years before. Indeed, by 2006, there were approximately 15,000 ongoing claims involving an estimated 79,000 claimants.[24] Along with escalating costs and increasing judicial gridlock, the sheer number and escalating complexity of these claims was a very strong incentive to settle. Another powerful reason was found in the idea that the entire system—however legal it may have been at the time—might now be considered to have been so wrongful that it could ground damages. As it turned out, this idea also affected the shape of the ultimate settlement in a profound and meaningful way.

In the face of mounting numbers and unsettling setbacks in cases like *Cloud* and *Bonaparte*, in 2005, the Canadian government changed course. Prime Minister Paul Martin appointed a former Supreme Court of Canada judge, the Honorable Frank Iacobucci, to lead discussions. Working in partnership with former National Chief Phil Fontaine, they negotiated an agreement that many thought impossible. In May 2006, the Indian Residential Schools Settlement Agreement was signed by over seventy parties.[25] At an estimated value now approaching $6 billion dollars, it was not only Canada's largest class action settlement—it remains perhaps the most comprehensive effort anywhere to respond to a vast historic injustice.[26] It also broke new ground in reparations with two programs of individual compensation. The first extended a Common Experience Payment to every person who attended a residential school.[27] The second awarded individual compensation for serious physical and sexual assaults through an inquisitorial claimant-centered adjudication system called the Independent Assessment Process (IAP).[28] The Agreement also supported commemorative activities, establishing a healing fund and provided for the creation of a national archive. Most importantly, it created a Truth and Reconciliation Commission that issued its final report in 2015. The prime minister also issued an historic apology for the entire Indian Residential Schools system in the House of Commons in 2008.[29]

[24] Baxter v. Canada (Attorney General), 83 O.R. (3d) 481, 2006 CanLII 41673, ¶¶ 4, 13 (Can. Ont. S.C.).

[25] This settlement was approved by the court, subject to some changes. *See id.*

[26] *See generally* Moran, *The Role of Reparative Justice*, *supra* note 6, at 554–65. For a comparison of the Indian Residential School Settlement Agreement with other programs responding to institutional abuse of children, *see* Kathleen Daly, Redressing Institutional Abuse of Children 112–57 (2014).

[27] The deadline to apply for a Common Experience Payment was September 19, 2011. There were 105,530 applications, with 79,309 being paid. The total of CEP payments was over $1.6 billion, and the average payment was $20,000. *See Statistics on the Implementation of the Indian Residential Schools Settlement Agreement*, Government of Canada (Feb. 19, 2019), https://www.rcaanc-cirnac.gc.ca/eng/1315320539682/1571590489978.

[28] There were 38,257 claims made, and the average payment (including legal costs) was $111,265. *Id.*

[29] Gaps in the Agreement led to other litigation and significant settlements. In 2019, the federal government signed a $1.47 billion settlement in the Indian Day Schools class action. *See* McLean v. Canada, 2019 FC 1075 (Can.). In 2023, there was another $2.8 billion settlement for loss of

The residential schools settlement is important for many reasons, but two key features are especially noteworthy for our purposes here. The first concerns the dramatic trajectory of the residential schools cases, which began as tort law claims and ended up with a new model for redress of historic wrongs. This 'transformative justice' model was a complex mix of private law-style damages, including billions in individual reparations payments, alongside elements closer to the transitional justice context, such as apologies, healing programs, commemoration, and most importantly the first national truth commission in an established democracy.[30] The Truth and Reconciliation Commission traveled the country, did extensive research, and held hearings that gave voice to thousands of survivors. Its six-volume final report created a fulsome account of the residential schools system and the broader colonial context, and its ninety-four Calls to Action demanded changes in everything from education to health care to law. The litigation also prompted apologies, created a permanent archive, and led to ongoing research. In the midst of this, Canada began to re-evaluate its self-understanding, something paralleled in many of its key institutions. The profound impact of the litigation and settlement was in large measure a result of how the claims created a new model that demanded more than just individual redress—they also sought to uncover the truth and to have that truth acknowledged, redressed, and commemorated. In so doing, they highlighted the deep connections between emerging issues of historic wrongs in stable regimes and the domain of transitional justice.[31]

This transformative quality connects to a second feature of these cases—courts and the law itself are often awkwardly positioned in redress for historic injustice claims like these. They are pulled between the ordinary deference toward the past and the tension that arises when they are faced with old laws that are profoundly inimical to their core values. In contrast with the Catholic Church claims, the residential schools cases sought damages not only for acts that were legally wrong at the time they were committed but also—and much more controversially—for acts that were actually legal when they were committed. This meant that they exhibited a kind of legal complexity that was not

language, culture, and heritage caused by the residential school system. *See* Tk'emlúps te Secwépemc First Nation v. Canada, 2023 FC 327 (Can.). Ongoing litigation includes a claim brought by the children of survivors for the intergenerational harm suffered. *See* Kathleen Martens, *Class-Action Lawsuit Aims to Compensate Children of Residential School*, APTN News (Feb. 29, 2024).

[30] *See Canada's Truth and Reconciliation Commission*, International Center for Transitional Justice (2008), https://www.ictj.org/sites/default/files/ICTJ-Canada-Truth-Facts-2008-English.pdf ("[a]s the first national truth commission to be created in an established democracy Canada's Truth and Reconciliation Commission is a bold experiment").

[31] *See e.g.* Pablo de Greiff, *Introduction—Repairing the Past: Compensation for Victims of Human Rights Violations*, *in* The Handbook on Reparations 1, 10–12 (Pablo de Greiff ed., 2006) discussing the integrity or coherence of reparations programs.

found in the Catholic Church cases. Because of how the residential schools cases combined the claims for redress of legal wrongs like assault with these deeper systemic claims, they forced courts to confront law's uneasy relationship to its own past. Symbolized by claims for the loss of family, language, and culture, this second category of claim asked courts for compensation for something that not only was not legally wrong at the time but strikingly was intended and often mandated by the law of the day.

When concern about the mounting claims prompted the government to seek resolution through settlement discussions, the nature of the resulting mandate was important. It was not simply to end litigation but to effect a "fair, comprehensive and lasting resolution" and promote "reconciliation and commemoration."[32] This suggested openness to terms that went beyond legal entitlements, something that was critical to addressing the systemic injustices of residential schools. And the settlement that resulted responded not only to those harms occasioned by unlawful acts but also to harms resulting from acts that were lawful at the time. The Common Experience Payment was a vital element of this. While the IAP compensated survivors for acts that were illegal at the time, the Common Experience Payment compensated every person who attended a residential school for the acts that were *legal* at the time—being forcibly removed from family and community and placed in an institution designed to destroy family ties, language, and culture. No amount of money can ever repair the harms that were done by those forced takings of children and by the pain, loss, and cultural eradication that occurred as a result. But it was essential that there was a serious effort at acknowledgment, and hence it was important that the Common Experience Payment amount was not trivial. The Agreement stipulated $10,000 for the first year of attendance at a residential school and $3,000 per year thereafter. More than 105,000 applications were received, and the average payment was $20,457.[33]

In addition to the Common Experience Payment compensation, it was also significant that the prime minister's historic 2008 apology in the House of Commons officially acknowledged for the first time that it was not simply the mistakes of the system that constituted wrongs—it was the very system itself. The idea at the heart of it and, as the courts began to intimate, the laws that put it in place were so flawed that although perhaps formally valid they could not immunize actions that we now acknowledge are profoundly at odds with our core

[32] *Indian Residential Schools Settlement Agreement*, Government of Canada 6 (May 8, 2006), https://www.residentialschoolsettlement.ca/settlement.html.

[33] The agreement allocated $1.9 billion to the program and over $1.6 billion was spent. The remainder was allocated to personal credits that Common Experience Payment recipients and certain family members can redeem at approved educational entities and groups. *Statistics on the Implementation of the Indian Residential Schools Settlement Agreement*, *supra* note 27.

legal values. The Common Experience Payment served as material acknowledgment that all children who were taken from their parents and placed in a residential school were wronged, even if their taking was legal at the time.[34] The larger significance of this was underscored by the fact that a truth and reconciliation commission—the central transitional justice institution—was employed in Canada to address its treatment of its Indigenous population. The normative distance was shrinking between established democracies like Canada and those like South Africa whose 'evil' pasts required some form of reckoning.

The residential schools example in this sense is an especially dramatic illustration of how private law can be deployed to draw in larger and more destabilizing legal arguments, including those like loss of language and culture. While the early residential schools litigation resembled the individual claims in the Catholic Church litigation, as it evolved it began to take on a more transformative character that also had deep connections to the kind of reparations programs found in the transitional justice context. The scale of the settlement, which extended significant individualized reparations for historic wrongs to well over 100,000 survivors, made it even more striking. This scale, alongside the novelty of elements such as the redress schemes, the apology, and the truth commission meant that the residential schools settlement also reverberated much more than ordinary litigation. In this way, the transformative approach of the Residential Schools Agreement helped to shift the discussion around vast old wrongs, inspiring others along the way. It also helped to further erode many of the standard defenses to reparations claims. It was becoming less plausible—and sometimes even damaging, as institutional lawyers were discovering—to invoke the standard defenses such as the 'bad but legal' argument in cases like these.[35] As other victims of grievous old wrongs increasingly asked "why not us?" defendants were finding it more difficult to respond. In this changing context, many survivors of old wrongs began to renew long-standing redress demands, and some of them finally saw much belated progress. Though there are many examples, the eugenics and wartime sexual slavery cases serve to illustrate the broader trend. We will discuss them in turn.

[34] Because the residential schools agreement included several different kinds of redress, it seems to display a fairly high degree of what de Greiff calls "internal coherence," which occurs when the various forms of benefits mutually support each other. See de Greiff, *supra* note 31, at 11. The Common Experience Payment responded to the systemic wrongs done to each child, the Independent Assessment Process to the additional individual wrongs, the apology referred to these wrongs specifically, and the funds for the healing foundation responded to the additional broader needs of survivors.

[35] As discussed in Chapter 7, such cases hold important lessons for institutional lawyers. When institutions come under threat in cases like these, the approach of their lawyers often exacerbates matters, as we saw in the Catholic Church litigation and in the Canadian government's "bad but legal system" defense discussed above.

When Law Goes Wrong: Reparations for Eugenics

Canada's Indian Residential Schools Settlement Agreement brought responsibility for widespread historic wrongs home to stable regimes in a dramatic way and in so doing established a new and ambitious model for setting things right. The fact that this model owed so much to the transitional justice context also highlighted that the problems of the past were no longer comfortably confined to cases of regime change. But the residential schools example also did something else that turned out to be critically important—it showed that there could be redress for injuries inflicted under the authority of law. It had always been assumed that actions that were legal at the time could not give rise to liability or compensation.[36] But as the residential schools litigation went on, courts became more open to the idea that acts like the forced taking of children might now be considered wrongful even though it was legal at the time. And in the Common Experience Payment, the eventual settlement did extend reparations for acts done under the authority of the law, opening up the possibility of redress for a much broader range of historic wrongs. As possibilities like these emerged, many other old redress efforts started to gain new life. Eugenics is a globally important example.

While challenges to eugenics are almost as old as the practice itself, it has always been an especially difficult context for redress. Although the strong link to the Holocaust might seem to bolster the case, that connection may also have had the paradoxical effect of increasing the reluctance to acknowledge eugenics. But there was also another much more legal problem—eugenics was a thoroughly legalized practice. It was mandated by law, undertaken by governments, and enforced by the state. Virginia's Sterilization Act, upheld in the infamous Supreme Court of the United States decision in *Buck v. Bell,* illustrates the depth of the entanglement with the state.[37] That act allowed for individuals to be "sexually sterilized" if found to be "afflicted with hereditary forms of insanity that are recurrent, idiocy, imbecility, feeble-mindedness or epilepsy," and it authorized state officials to perform the operations.[38] Moreover, the entire process was overseen by the courts and was held constitutional by the country's highest court. While the practice has long come under intense criticism, the fact that the

[36] *See* Mayo Moran, *The Problem of the Past: How Historic Wrongs Became Legal Problems*, 69 U. Toronto L. J. 421, 425–26 (2019). For example, in some of the eugenics litigation, only those cases where officials exceeded legal authority gave rise to claims, such as the *Muir* case discussed below. See also the discussion of the difficulties of these issues in Mayo Moran, *Time, Place and Value:* Mack *and the Influence of the* Charter *on Private Law, in* Calling Power to Account: Law, Reparations and the Chinese Canadian Head Tax Case (David Dyzenhaus & Mayo Moran eds., 2005). This has also been a persistent issue with claims about reparations for slavery, discussed in Chapter 6 below.

[37] Buck v. Bell, 274 U.S. 200 (1927).

[38] An Act to Provide for the Sterilization of Inmates of State Institutions in Certain Case, Va. Acts of Assembly ch. 394 (1924) (repealed 1974).

harmful acts were sanctioned by law had always posed formidable challenges for survivors. But even here the shifting approach to historic wrongs began to result in movement many decades after the struggle began.

The early twentieth century saw the rise of involuntary sterilization programs designed to promote 'racial hygiene', often targeting the poor, illiterate, and racialized. While Nazi state may come to mind first, the practice was transnational and was embraced in Europe, North America, Japan, and many other parts of the world.[39] The term eugenics (derived from the Greek word for good origin or good birth) was coined in the 1880s by Charles Darwin's half-cousin, Francis Galton.[40] He argued that selective breeding could produce a "highly-gifted race of men."[41] Public concern that the "genetically undesirable" were breeding at an "alarming rate" led to conferences and seminars designed to spread Galton's theories.[42] The United Kingdom eventually enacted the Mental Deficiency Act of 1913, which resulted in the institutionalization of tens of thousands of people.[43] Eugenics was also embraced with enthusiasm in the United States, where race, not class, was at its center. While the English movement focused on institutionalization and selective breeding, forced sterilization quickly came to dominate the American approach to the elimination of "undesirable traits."[44]

In 1907, Indiana became the first state to enact sterilization legislation.[45] Harry Laughlin's Model Eugenical Sterilization Law was much admired, and by 1931, twenty-eight other states had followed suit.[46] Laughlin's model code provided for the involuntary sterilization of the "socially inadequate," including those who were "feebleminded, insane, criminalistic, epileptic, inebriate, diseased, blind, deaf; deformed; and dependent" as well as "orphans, ne'er-do-wells, tramps, the homeless and paupers."[47] By 1924, over 3,000 people had been

[39] *See* Philippa Levine & Alison Bashford, *Introduction: Eugenics and the Modern World*, *in* The Oxford Handbook of the History of Eugenics 1, 10 (Alison Bashford & Philippa Levine eds., 2012).

[40] *See* Francis Galton, Inquiries into Human Faculty and Its Development 17 (1883).

[41] Francis Galton, Hereditary Genius: An Inquiry into Its Laws and Consequences 1 (1869).

[42] *See* Clyde Chitty, The Origins of the Eugenics Movement 38 (2007), cited in Eugenics Archive, http://eugenicsarchive.ca/discover/connections/51722216eed5c6000000000b (last visited Dec. 16, 2024).

[43] Mental Deficiency Act 1913, 3 & 4 Geo. 5, c. 28 (Eng.); Mathew Thomson, Regenerating England: Science, Medicine and Culture in Inter-War Britain 235 (2000); Eugenics Archive, https://www.eugenicsarchive.ca/timeline?id=517145a4eed5c60000000004 (last visited Dec. 19, 2024).

[44] *See generally* Teryn Bouche & Laura Rivard, *America's Hidden History: The Eugenics Movement*, Scitable by Nature Education (Sept. 18, 2014), https://www.nature.com/scitable/forums/genetics-generation/america-s-hidden-history-the-eugenics-movement-123919444.

[45] Acts of the Indiana General Assembly, H. 364, ch. 215 (1907).

[46] See Bouche & Rivard, supra note 44, citing Paul Lombardo, *Eugenic Sterilization Laws*, Eugenics Archive, http://www.eugenicsarchive.org/html/eugenics/essay8text.html (last visited Dec. 16, 2024); Edwin Black, War Against the Weak: Eugenics and America's Campaign to Create a Master Race (2004).

[47] Lombardo, *supra* note 46.

sterilized in the United States, with the vast majority in California.[48] In that same year, Virginia passed sterilization legislation and selected Carrie Buck as the first person to sterilize.[49] When that test case came before the Supreme Court in 1927, Justice Oliver Wendell Holmes—later heralded as the great protector of liberty—enthusiastically endorsed eugenics, famously proclaiming that "[t]hree generations of imbeciles are enough."[50] This was despite evidence that showed that Carrie Buck was not "feeble-minded" and was pregnant out of wedlock only because she had been raped by the friend of her foster parent.[51] But Justice Holmes's views were not idiosyncratic. More than thirty states embraced eugenics, and it is estimated that there were more than 60,000 eugenic sterilizations in the United States alone.[52]

Negative eugenics, that is discouraging the procreation of those deemed undesirable, was also catching on elsewhere. In the same year that *Buck v. Bell* was decided, the Canadian province of Alberta introduced its Sexual Sterilization Act.[53] Following Alberta's lead, British Columbia enacted legislation.[54] Eugenics was also on the rise in Europe. Denmark was quite possibly the first European country to introduce sterilization legislation, which it did in 1929. However, as the world now knows, eugenics was about to escalate to a whole new level.

Shortly after Hitler became chancellor in 1933, Germany passed its Law for the Prevention of Hereditarily Diseased Offspring.[55] Inspired by Laughlin's model, it authorized compulsory sterilization of those with genetic disorders.[56] "Race hygiene" (Rassenhygiene) was aggressively implemented. As the 1930s wore on, interest shifted to "eugenicide." In 1939, Hitler authorized "Action T4," a program of "euthanasia" involving the killing of those who were ill, disabled, emotionally

[48] *Id. See also* Black, *supra* note 46; ADAM COHEN, IMBECILES: THE SUPREME COURT, AMERICAN EUGENICS, AND THE STERILIZATION OF CARRIE BUCK (2016).

[49] *See* COHEN, *supra* note 48.

[50] Buck v. Bell, 274 U.S. 200 (1927).

[51] *See* COHEN, *supra* note 48.

[52] *See* Alexandra Minna Stern, *Eugenics, Sterilization, and Historical Memory in the United States*, SCIELO BRAZIL (Dec. 2016), http://www.scielo.br/scielo.php?script = sci_arttext&pid = S0104-59702016000900195.

[53] The Sexual Sterilization Act, S.A. 1928, c. 37 (Can. Alta.) (repealed in 1972). It was broadened a number of times, including in 1942 by which time the Alberta government was aware of the Nazi program.

[54] *See* An Act Respecting Sexual Sterilization, S.B.C. 1933, c. 59 (Can. B.C.) (repealed in 1973). *See also* Carolyn Strange & Jennifer A. Stephen, *Eugenics in Canada: A Checkered History, 1850s–1990s*, *in* THE OXFORD HANDBOOK OF THE HISTORY OF EUGENICS, *supra* note 39, at 523, 531.

[55] Gesetz zur Verhütung erbkranken Nachwuchses vom 14. Juli 1933 [Law for the Prevention of Hereditarily Diseased Offspring], July 14, 1933, RGBl. I S. 529 (Ger.).

[56] Both the Rockefeller and the Carnegie Foundation funded collaborations between American and German eugenicists. Californian eugenicists published and distributed pamphlets designed specifically for German scientists, and California provided the model for the German eugenics program. *Mein Kampf* makes it clear that Hitler admired American eugenics laws. The admiration was a two-way street—American eugenicists invited German scientists to their conferences and complained that the Germans were "beating us at our own game" even as Germany embarked on what was to become a sinister program of eugenics. *See* BLACK, *supra* note 46.

distraught, or elderly.[57] On a visit in 1940, an American eugenicist admired how the Nazi regime was "weeding out the worst strains in the Germanic stock in a scientific and truly humanitarian way."[58] Other American eugenicists agreed, noting, "[w]hile we were pussy-footing around . . . the Germans were calling a spade a spade."[59] Up to 250,000 people are estimated to have been killed as part of Action T4, which is considered a precursor to the Holocaust.[60] By the end of the Nazi regime, over 400,000 people were also sterilized.[61]

Yet revelations about the Nazi practices at the end of the war did not spell the end of eugenics. It was not until the 1970s that attitudes began to shift as advocates worked for the repeal of eugenics legislation, as well as for recognition and redress.[62] California was home to almost one-third of the involuntary sterilizations in the United States. Many were Latina women who were sterilized after signing forms in English that they did not understand. Most did not know what had happened until they later realized that they could not have children. In 1975, the "Madrigal Ten" brought a case against the hospital that sterilized them, arguing that there was no informed consent and that the practice targeted Latinas. In 1978, the court rejected their claim, finding that the issues were not deliberate policy but were rather the result of misunderstandings and communication breakdowns.[63] Advocates continued to seek redress for eugenics, but their

[57] T4 killing centers murdered disabled children and adults and others deemed to be unsuitable or non-contributors. Most of this killing took place in hospitals, some by starvation, some by gassing, some by lethal injection. The German psychiatric community was deeply involved, including through a new bureaucracy staffed by physicians with a mandate to kill anyone "deemed to have a 'life unworthy of living.'" *See* Michael Berenbaum, *The T4 Program*, ENCYCLOPEDIA BRITANNICA, https://www.britannica.com/event/T4-Program (last accessed Dec. 16, 2024).

[58] Stefan Kühl, THE NAZI CONNECTION: EUGENICS, AMERICAN RACISM, AND GERMAN NATIONAL SOCIALISM 62 (2002).

[59] *See* BLACK, *supra* note 46.

[60] *See* SUZANNE E. EVANS, FORGOTTEN CRIMES: THE HOLOCAUST AND PEOPLE WITH DISABILITIES 67 (2004) ("at least 70,000 and perhaps as many as 250,000 people with disabilities had been murdered in the six T4 killing centers"); *Adolf Hitler enacts Action T-4*, EUGENICS ARCHIVE, https://www.eugenicsarchive.ca/timeline?id=517305eaeed5c60000000029 (last visited Dec. 16, 2024).

[61] LAWRENCE A. ZEIDMAN, BRAIN SCIENCE UNDER THE SWASTIKA: ETHICAL VIOLATIONS, RESISTANCE, AND VICTIMIZATION OF NEUROSCIENTISTS IN NAZI GERMANY 327 (2020); BLACK, *supra* note 46.

[62] The reparations regimes established in Germany in the aftermath of World War II excluded victims of involuntary sterilization. *See* Ariel Colonomos & Andrea Armstrong, *German Reparations to the Jews After World War II: A Turning Point in the History of Reparations*, *in* THE HANDBOOK ON REPARATIONS 390, 406–8 (Pablo de Greiff ed., 2006). Survivors' efforts to be recognized as victims of Nazi persecution and to have the law annulled had very limited success. And while Germany did provide some compensation to involuntary sterilization victims, it was on the basis of hardship, not recognition of wrongdoing. The law was never formally abolished, though in 2006, the Bundestag passed a declaration that the 1933 Nazi sterilization law had never in fact been constitutionally valid. *See* Ächtung des Gesetzes zur Verhütung erbkranken Nachwuchses vom 14. Juli 1933, DEUTSCHER BUNDESTAG: DRUCKSACHE [BT] 16/3811 (2006) (Ger.).

[63] Maya Manian, *The Story of Madrigal v. Quilligan: Coerced Sterilization of Mexican-American Women*, *in* REPRODUCTIVE RIGHTS AND JUSTICE STORIES (Melissa Murray et al. eds., 2019). Nonetheless, in the wake of the case, California changed its law.

efforts often foundered in part because of the deep involvement of the state and its laws.

However, just as other survivors of historic wrongs began to press their causes anew, redress for eugenics was also on the cusp of change. The Canadian province of Alberta had had an especially aggressive eugenics program. In 1959, it had sterilized a woman named Leilani Muir. In the early 1990s, she brought a civil action against Alberta. By the time of trial, the government had accepted that it owed her compensation because she had never been properly tested. In 1996, in what was perhaps the first successful eugenics lawsuit, Muir was awarded a total of over $740,780.[64] When hundreds of other claims flooded in, the government attempted to force a settlement by introducing a bill that would limit claims against the province and prevent challenges under *The Canadian Charter of Rights and Freedoms*.[65] In the furor that followed, it eventually apologized and paid out more than $140,000,000 to settle more than 880 claims, with individual damages capped at $150,000.[66] The case was reported around the world.[67] An award-winning 1996 film called *The Sterilization of Leilani Muir* received global attention.[68] Around this same time, historians and authors elsewhere were also beginning to turn their attention to this shameful and ignored part of history.[69] After decades, the legacy of eugenics was starting to receive serious attention.

Around the same time that news of the victory in *Muir* was spreading, there were important developments in Sweden. While all four Nordic countries had adopted eugenics legislation in the 1930s, Sweden stood out. It sterilized more people than any other European state except Nazi Germany, over 60,000 people deemed "mentally defective."[70] Survivors had been struggling for recognition

[64] Muir v. Alberta, 132 D.L.R. (4th) 695, 1996 CanLII 7287 (Can. Alt. K.B.).

[65] *See Several Hundred Legal Actions Initiated Against Alberta,* Eugenics Archive, http://eugenicsarchive.ca/discover/connections/51731db3eed5c6000000003e (last accessed Dec. 16, 2024).

[66] *See id*; *News Release*, Government of Alberta (Nov. 2, 1999), https://www.alberta.ca/release.cfm?xID = 8353.

[67] *See e.g.* Emily Buchanan, *Playing God with People's Lives*, The Guardian Weekly (Mar. 23, 1997); *Sterilised in Alberta: Forced-Sterilization Victims Bring Lawsuits Against the Province*, 341 The Economist 82 (Nov. 9, 1996); Associated Press, *Alberta's Sterilizations Trigger Surge of Lawsuits: The Canadian Province Sterilized more than 2,800 People from 1928 to 1972*, Orlando Sentinel A5 (Dec. 26, 1996).

[68] It won awards at the 1997 Huesca International Film Festival in Lake Tahoe, Nevada, and the Western Psychological Association Film Festival in Seattle, Washington.

[69] *See e.g.* East Lansing, Eugenics and the Welfare State: Sterilization Policy in Denmark, Sweden, Norway, and Finland (1996); Mathew Thomson, The Problem of Mental Deficiency: Eugenics, Democracy, and Social Policy in Britain c. 1870–1959 (1998); Elof Axel Carlson, The Unfit: The History of a Bad Idea (2001); Black, *supra* note 46; Harry Bruinius, Better for All the World: The Secret History of Forced Sterilization and America's Quest for Racial Purity (2006); Cohen, *supra* note 48.

[70] *See Here, of All Places*, The Economist (Aug. 30, 1997); Declan Butler, *Eugenics Scandal Reveals Silence of Swedish Scientists*, Nature (Sept. 4, 1997); Dean E. Murphy, *A Victim of Sweden's Pursuit of Perfection*, Los Angeles Times (Sept. 2, 1997); *Sweden Admits to Racial Purification*, The Independent (Aug. 25, 1997).

and redress since the early 1980s with little to show for it.[71] But in 1997, a series of hard-hitting articles published in Swedish newspaper *Dagens Nyheter* broke the story open.[72] In response, the government set up a state commission to investigate the practice and to recommend reparations. Approximately 3,000 survivors each received 175,000 kronor, making Sweden one of the first states to voluntarily extend reparations to survivors of eugenics.[73]

Like *Muir*, the Swedish developments were covered internationally. As one commentator put it, the articles that "set off a furor in Sweden that reverberated elsewhere in the world."[74] *Radio Free Europe* pointed out that Sweden borrowed its model from the United States and bluntly noted that its "sterilization program has plenty of company" across Europe.[75] Historians and academics began delving more deeply into the global links and the gaze inevitably turned back to the United States.[76] Of particular importance was the state of Virginia, home to *Buck v. Bell* and second only to California in the number of sterilizations. In May 2002, on the seventy-fifth anniversary of *Buck v. Bell*, Governor Warner issued the first American apology for eugenics.[77] In a ceremony that honored Carrie Buck, he formally apologized saying it "was a shameful effort in which state government never should have been involved."[78] Some of the reporting on his apology explicitly referred to Alberta's apology and compensation for victims of sterilization.[79]

As with other problems of the past, investigative journalism played a critical role, both in uncovering troubling histories and also in helping to ensure that developments in one place created pressure elsewhere. North Carolina also had an aggressive program that sterilized an estimated 7,600 people and continued well into the 1970s. The American Civil Liberties Union launched a lawsuit in 1984, but it failed.[80] However, in 2002—the same year as Virginia's apology—*The*

[71] *See* Claire Armstrong, *Thousands of Women Sterilised in Sweden Without* Consent, 315 BMJ 563 (1997).

[72] *See* Dan Balz, *Sweden Sterilized Thousands of "Useless" Citizens for Decades*, THE WASHINGTON POST (Aug. 29, 1997).

[73] *See* J. Nordstrom, *Eugenics in the Nordic Countries*, NORDICS INFO (Sept. 24, 2019), https://nordics.info/show/artikel/eugenics-in-the-nordic-countries; Laura Llach & Lucia Riera, *How Did Sweden Sterilize up to 30,000 People Against Their Will in the Cause of Eugenics?* EURONEWS (June 9, 2023); Stephen Bates, *Sweden Pays for Grim Past*, THE GUARDIAN (Mar. 6, 1999).

[74] Don Hill, *Sweden's Sterilization Program Has Plenty of* Company, RADIO FREE EUROPE/RADIO LIBERTY (Aug. 29, 1997).

[75] *Id.*

[76] *See* Stephanie Hyatt, *A Shared History of Shame: Sweden's Four-Decade Policy of Forced Sterilization and the Eugenics Movement in the United States*, 8 IND. INT'L & COMP. L. REV. 475 (1998).

[77] *See* William Branigin, *Va. Apologizes to the Victims of Sterilization*, THE WASHINGTON POST (May 3, 2002).

[78] *Id.*

[79] *Va. Gov. Apologises for Eugenics Law*, UNITED PRESS INTERNATIONAL (May 2, 2002).

[80] Riddick v. Craig, 469 U.S. 826 (1984). *See Attorney for a Woman Who Was Ordered Sterilized*, UNITED PRESS INTERNATIONAL (Oct. 2, 1984).

Winston-Salem Journal published a series entitled "Against Their Will," which exposed the state's history of eugenics.[81] In its wake, Governor Easley apologized and established a task force that considered individual compensation, the first American state to do so. The compensation efforts took a torturous fifteen years, but in 2018, approximately 220 living survivors of the 7,600 people sterilized received the final installment of their compensation, which totaled $45,500.[82] Though many details remain controversial, North Carolina was the first American state to have compensated victims of its eugenics program.[83]

Once again, this action prompted other movement. Other states also began to apologize, including Oregon in 2002 and California in 2003.[84] North Carolina's redress payments also began to have an effect. Although in 2002 Virginia's governor said he had been assured that the apology would not have any "legal repercussions," by 2015 Virginia changed course and gave $25,000 in compensation to those who had been wrongly sterilized.[85] California, with its notorious program of sterilization, came under increased pressure as others began to extend compensation to survivors. In July 2021, after years of consideration, California Governor Newsom finally signed the bill that explicitly acknowledged many of the wrongs that were done and extended compensation of approximately $35,000 each to the survivors of that state's eugenics program.[86]

Just as the eugenics practices were transnational, so too were the redress efforts. One result of this increasing global reach was that developments in Canada, Europe, and the United States had repercussions elsewhere. Japan had sterilized as many as 25,000 people under its *Eugenic Protection Law*, most of them women and in the absence of consent.[87] While challenges began in the

[81] Kevin Begos et al., Against Their Will: North Carolina's Sterilization Program and the Campaign for Reparations (2012).

[82] *See* Richard Craver, *Eugenics Victims Projected to Get Final State Compensation Payment Soon*, Winston-Salem Journal (Jan. 17, 2018); *Final Compensation Check Sent to NC Sterilization Victims*, Associated Press (Feb. 8, 2018). Survivors received two partial payments—$20,000 in October 2014 and $15,000 in November 2015. The third and final payment in 2018 was approximately $10,500.

[83] *See* Kim Severson, *Payment Set for Those Sterilized in Program*, The New York Times (Jan. 10, 2012); Eric Mennel, *Payments Start for N.C. Eugenics Victims, But Many Won't Qualify*, National Public Radio (Oct. 31, 2014).

[84] *See e.g. Joseph* Shapiro, *States Apologize for Forced Sterilizations*, National Public Radio (Dec. 2, 2002); Carl Ingram, *State Issues Apology for Policy of Sterilization*, Los Angeles Times (Mar. 12, 2003); Amanda Gokee, *90 Years After Vermont Eugenics Survey, Lawmakers Propose Apology to Those* Affected, VTDigger (Feb. 21, 2021); Joe Dougherty, *An Apology for the Wrongs of the Past: Eugenics in Utah*, Utah Department of Health & Human Services (Feb. 16, 2023), https://dhhs.utah.gov/featured-news/an-apology-for-the-wrongs-of-the-past-eugenics-in-utah/.

[85] Victims of Sterilization Fund Administration, 12 Va. Admin. Code § 35-240 (2015).

[86] *See* Cheri Mossburg, *California Will Compensate Survivors of Its Forced Sterilization Program*, CNN (Jul. 14, 2021). *See Recovery from Forced Sterilization*, California Victim Compensation Board, https://victims.ca.gov/for-victims/fiscp/#:~:text = How%20much%20money%20will%20survivors,income%20for%20state%20tax%20purposes (last visited Dec. 17, 2024).

[87] *See* Thisanka Siripala, *Japan's Forced Sterilization Victims Hit Back with a Wave of Lawsuits*, The Diplomat (May 25, 2018).

1970s, as with many other problems of historic injustice, real progress did not happen until decades later. In 1996, the *Eugenic Protection Law* was finally abolished. Then in 2004, under pressure from bar associations and courts, the legislature started to debate reparations. Compensation was initially rejected on the grounds that the sterilizations were legal at the time.[88] However, in 2016, the United Nations Committee on the Elimination of Discrimination Against Women recommended that Japan adopt measures to assist victims, including compensation and rehabilitation.

In 2018, survivors began to file civil lawsuits against the government seeking an apology and ¥11 million compensation.[89] In 2019, Prime Minister Shinzō Abe expressed "sincere regret" and "apologised wholeheartedly" on behalf of the government and offered the survivors each compensation of ¥3.2 million.[90] But this was viewed as insufficient by survivors, and a number of them sued for additional compensation. Then in February 2022, a Japanese court awarded damages to those who were forcibly sterilized under the eugenics law—the first court to do so since the decision in *Muir*. In a familiar pattern, the lower court had dismissed the claims for compensation on limitations grounds, but the Osaka High Court rejected the limitations defense. It found the eugenics law unconstitutional and ordered the government to pay a combined ¥27.5m to the three plaintiffs.[91] The government appealed, but the ruling was upheld by the Supreme Court, who criticized the ¥3.2 million as too little and ordered the state to compensate victims.[92] Parliament eventually passed a bill providing ¥15 million in compensation.[93]

This shifting approach to eugenics illustrates how much has changed for those seeking redress for old wrongs, even where the harmful acts were authorized by law. Early developments like the landmark decision in *Muir* and the Swedish reparations payments started to erode the idea that redress was out of the question because eugenics was done under the authority of law. Amplified by increasingly rapid communications, investigative journalism was also gaining greater transnational significance through outlets with global reach like *The Guardian*, *The New York Times*, and *Radio Free Europe*. This increased coverage of historic injustice meant that developments in one place resonated wherever that same

[88] *See* Justin McCurry, *Japan Apologises to Victims of Forced Sterilisation*, The Guardian (Apr. 24, 2019) [hereinafter McCurry, *Japan Apologises*].

[89] *See* Justin McCurry, *Japan Woman Sues Government over Forced Sterilisation*, The Guardian (Jan. 30, 2018).

[90] *See* McCurry, *Japan Apologises*, *supra* note 88.

[91] *See* Justin McCurry, *Japan Court Awards Damages to Victims of Forced Sterilisation for First Time*, The Guardian (Feb. 22, 2022).

[92] *See* Karin Kaneko, *Japan's Top Court Orders Compensation for Forced Sterilization Victims*, The Japan Times (July 3, 2024).

[93] *See* Karin Kaneko, *Parliament Clears Bill to Compensate All Victims of Forced Sterilization*, The Japan Times (Oct. 8, 2024) (Parliament also provided compensation for victims' spouses).

troubling history was shared. And so although it took many decades for survivors of eugenics to see any success, once that began to change, the domino effect was so powerful that even hold out jurisdictions like California and Japan undertook reparations. In the years since Leilani Muir won her surprising landmark victory, apologies, commemoration, and even individual reparations have finally been extended to many of the remaining survivors. And along the way, one of the key arguments that used to shield past acts from responsibility claims—"it was legal at the time"—was becoming a discredited defense that institutions invoked at their peril.

Redress for Wartime Atrocity: The 'Comfort Women'

This kind of complex interplay between investigative journalism, law, and politics was creating momentum on ever larger number of long-standing grievances. As some survivors of old injustices began to see progress, others renewed their own demands for redress. This resulted in some much-belated victories, even in the difficult case of state-sponsored injuries done under the color of law like eugenics. There were signs of progress on other challenging redress issues too. This included wrongs that arose in the complicated context of war. War has always been the site of horrific injuries. But since violence and harm are at the very heart of war, it is difficult terrain for reparative justice claims. Even where reparations have been extended, they have typically arisen out of state-to-state negotiations, with little heed to survivors' concerns with rectifying injustice.[94] But alongside other issues, even redress for some wartime wrongs was starting to look more plausible as long-suffering survivors found new hope in the resurgence of interest in historic injustice. There is no more powerful illustration of this than the much belated and complex activity surrounding the claims of the women forced by Japan into military sexual slavery during World War II, commonly referred to by the troubling term 'comfort women.'[95]

During World War II women—many of them Korean—were forcibly taken from Japanese occupied territory and incarcerated in 'comfort stations' used by the Japanese military. In these stations, hundreds of thousands of women were subjected to dozens of rapes a day as well as physical abuse. As the war neared its end, many were killed or forced to commit suicide—three quarters of them

[94] As noted earlier, this is true even in the landmark post–World War II German reparations program. *See generally* Colonomos & Armstrong, *supra* note 62.

[95] As noted earlier, while the term 'military sexual slaves' is more accurate and appropriate, the term 'comfort women' is the common description of the victims of the Japanese military's sexual slavery system during World War II. Where I use the conventional term, I mark my concern about it with scare quotes. *See also* Jimin Kim et al., *Teaching About the Comfort Women During World War II and the Use of Personal Stories of the Victims*, 24 ASIAN LIT. HUMAN. & SOC. SCI. 58 (2019).

were estimated to have died. There was no resolution of the issues at either the Tokyo Tribunal or the Military Trials of War Criminals in the Netherlands East Indies. While the San Francisco Peace Treaty referred to reparations, the postwar payments that Japan ultimately made to Korea were for industrial development, not individual compensation.

However, after decades of near silence and at the very time that other issues concerning the past were starting to surface, there was some movement. In 1991, three South Korean women sued the Japanese government. In a surprising 1998 ruling, a Yamaguchi District Court Judge "called the army's actions an example of sexual and ethnic discrimination and a 'fundamental violation of human rights'" and awarded each of the three survivors the equivalent of $2,300 USD.[96] Even before the verdict, however, it was becoming clear that the context was changing. Part of this was due to the controversial publication of *My Wartime Crime* by Seiji Yoshida, a Japanese novelist who had been stationed in Korea at the end of World War II.[97] Then, in 1993, shortly after the claim was filed and due in part to it, the International Commission of Jurists created a mission to study the issue.[98]

The pressure led to Japan's Chief Cabinet Secretary issuing the 1993 Kono Statement—the first official acknowledgment of the horrific treatment of the women and of government involvement. The Statement expressed the government's "sincere apologies and remorse" and called for further study and commemoration.[99] In 1995, Prime Minister Murayama expressed his "heart-felt apology" for Japan's wartime atrocities.[100] Also, in 1995, the Governments of Korea and Japan invited the United Nations Human Rights Commission's Special Rapporteur on violence against women and girls to "study in depth the issue of military sexual slavery in wartime."[101] That same year saw the creation of the Asian Women's Fund, which supported women forced into wartime prostitution. It eventually distributed approximately $42,000 USD, along with an apology, to each of sixty-one survivors. However, survivors pointed out that

[96] See *Japan Court Backs 3 Brothel Victims*, THE NEW YORK TIMES (Apr. 28, 1998). Though the decision was eventually overturned on appeal, the judge's framing of the issue as "illegal and unconstitutional" had significant impact. *See* Timothy Webster, *Japan's Transnational War Reparations Litigation: An Empirical Analysis*, 63 HARV. INT'L L.J. 181, 222 (2022) [hereinafter Webster, *Japan's Transnational War Reparations Litigation*].

[97] *See* David Sanger, *Japanese Veteran Presses Wartime-Brothel Issue*, THE NEW YORK TIMES (Aug. 8, 1992).

[98] *See* INTERNATIONAL COMMISSION OF JURISTS, COMFORT WOMEN: AN UNFINISHED ORDEAL (1994).

[99] *Statement by the Chief Cabinet Secretary*, MINISTRY OF FOREIGN AFFAIRS OF JAPAN (Aug. 4, 1993), https://www.mofa.go.jp/a_o/rp/page25e_000343.html.

[100] *See* Anna Fifield, *A (Very) Short History of Japan's War Apologies: Japanese Prime Minister Shinzo Abe Will Deliver a Statement on the 70th Anniversary of the End of World War II. But How Apologetic Will It Be?* THE WASHINGTON POST (Aug. 12, 2015).

[101] *See* Special Rapporteur on violence against women and girls, Radhika Coomaraswamy, *Report on the Mission to the Democratic People's Republic of Korea, the Republic of Korea and Japan on the Issue of Military Sexual Slavery in Wartime*, U.N. Doc. E/CN.4/1996/53/Add.1 (Jan. 4, 1996).

the money came from private donations and not the government, and therefore many refused to accept it, continuing instead to press for more meaningful redress.[102] Partly in response to this furor, in 2000, a people's tribunal called the Women's International War Crimes Tribunal sat in Tokyo to consider the criminal liability of high-ranking Japanese officials as well as state responsibility for rape and sexual slavery as crimes against humanity.[103] The tribunal broke new ground, gathering testimony from survivors as well as vast amounts of other evidence. Its novel work laid the foundation for the continued advocacy over the following decades.[104]

Controversy around the issue erupted again in 2007, when in response to a request from the surviving women for an official apology, Prime Minister Shinzo Abe denied any government role. The uproar that followed soon did lead to an official apology.[105] However, in 2014 another Japanese official expressed skepticism.[106] It was the ensuing furor around this that led to the important 2015 Agreement between Japan and South Korea, the first such post–World War II agreement in the region.[107] Under its terms, the Japanese government paid ¥1 billion (almost $9 million USD) to a South Korean foundation, which then compensated thirty-four of the forty-seven survivors.[108] A research institute was also created in South Korea.[109] But the 2015 Agreement sparked more controversy for lack of consultation, the nature of the apology, and the issue of the 'comfort women' statue. Twelve survivors sued the South Korean government for absence of consultation, and the issue helped lead to the downfall of President Park Geun-hye.[110] Korea's new president struck a task force to investigate the agreement and threatened to revoke it, but after consulting with survivors, "barely" affirmed it in 2018.[111] In June of that same year, a Korean

[102] *See* Brigit Katz, *Taiwan Unveils Its First Statue Honoring "Comfort Women,"* Smithsonian Magazine (Aug. 17, 2018). Other survivors received compensation from their home governments, including South Korea. *See* Chris Hogg, *Japan's Divisive "Comfort Women" Fund*, BBC News (Apr. 10, 2007).

[103] *See* Christine M. Chinkin, *Women's International Tribunal on Japanese Military Sexual Slavery*, 95 Am. J. Int'l L. 335 (2001).

[104] *See id.*

[105] *See* Justin McCurry, *Japan Rules Out New Apology to "Comfort Women,"* The Guardian (Mar. 5, 2007).

[106] Martin Fackler, *Japan Stands by Apology to Wartime Sex Slaves*, The New York Times (Mar. 14, 2014).

[107] *See Full Text: Japan-South Korea Statement on "Comfort Women,"* The Wall Street Journal (Dec. 28, 2015); Webster, *Japan's Transnational War Reparations Litigation*, *supra* note 96, at 183.

[108] *See* Celeste Arrington, *South Korea Ended Its Review of Its "Comfort Women" Deal with Japan. Here's What You Need to Know*, The Washington Post (Jan. 11, 2018).

[109] *See Korea to Form Institute to Commemorate "Comfort Women,"* The Korea Times (May 17, 2018). *See* KYEOL Research Institute on Japanese Military Sexual Slavery, https://kyeol.kr/en (last visited May 29, 2025).

[110] *See Court Dismisses Comfort Women's Suit Against Government for Signing 2015 Agreement with Japan*, Hankyoreh (Oct. 19, 2019).

[111] *See* Yuki Tatsumi, *The Japan-South Korea "Comfort Women" Agreement Survives (Barely)*, The Diplomat (Jan. 11, 2018).

court acknowledged flaws in the 2015 Agreement but dismissed the damages claims of the survivors.[112]

Later in 2018, and in the context of escalating tension with Japan on related World War II issues of slave labor, the South Korean government disbanded the fund set up by the 2015 Agreement, which it described as flawed.[113] It also created a day of commemoration, and on the first such day in 2018, more than 20,000 people protested outside the Japanese Embassy in Seoul, prompting Japan to issue a travel advisory for the region.[114] That same day, Taiwan also saw the unveiling of its first 'comfort woman' statue, designed to commemorate the Taiwanese women who suffered the same fate. Japan's efforts to get such statues removed have only had the paradoxical effect of inspiring a worldwide push to erect them, and there are now numerous such statues not only in Korea and Taiwan but all over the world.[115] In November 2018, a United Nations panel called on Japan to fully investigate issues including the actual number of victims and noted the lack of adequate reparations to survivors.[116] Ongoing litigation in Korea has continued to produce complicated rulings, with some courts rejecting immunity-based arguments and holding the Japanese government liable for the system because the cases involved such "serious breaches of human rights" that they nullified such immunity, while other courts accepted immunity-based arguments and rejected liability.[117] Then in 2023, the Seoul High Court overturned a lower court decision that had dismissed a claim brought by sixteen victims on the grounds of sovereign immunity. The High Court ordered Japan to pay compensation.[118]

In a familiar pattern with historic injustice claims, this belated activity on the sexual slavery issue has also influenced other long-standing World War II reparations claims against the Japanese government and corporations. Although these other slave labor and related cases have not received much attention, for

[112] *See Court Dismisses Comfort Women's Suit*, *supra* note 110.

[113] *See* Joyce Lee, *South Koreans Protest, Unveil Memorial in "Comfort Women" Row with Japan*, Reuters (Aug. 14, 2019).

[114] *Id.*

[115] *See "Comfort Women" Statue to Go up on Italian Shore, the 14th Outside of Korea*, Hankyoreh (June 24, 2024) ("[a]s of June 2024, there are around 30 memorials, commemorative plaques and Statues of Peace honoring the victims of Japan's 'comfort women' system around the world"); Julian Ryall, *"Comfort Woman" Statue in Berlin Angers Japan*, DW (Oct. 1, 2020); Seth Berkman, *The Fight over Berlin's Comfort Woman Statue*, The Nation (U.S., July, 18, 2022).

[116] *See* Wooyoung Lee, *U.N. Panel Recommends Japan to Compensate Comfort Women Victims*, United Press International (Nov. 19, 2018), https://www.upi.com/Top_News/World-News/2018/11/19/UN-panel-recommends-Japan-to-compensate-comfort-women-victims/5241542685715/.

[117] *See South Korean Court Dismisses Ex-Comfort Women's Suit Against Japan*, Kyodo News (Apr. 21, 2021); Takuya Suzuki, *Seoul Orders Tokyo to Reveal Assets in "Comfort Women" Decision*, The Asahi Shimbun (June 16, 2021).

[118] *See* Lou Newton, *Japan Ordered to Compensate Wartime "Comfort Women,"* BBC News (Nov. 23, 2023).

decades these survivors too have sought redress from Japan for World War II atrocities, highlighting the broader colonial reckoning at play. In the absence of the kinds of transnational agreements that have been employed to respond to World War II atrocities elsewhere, litigation also remains their dominant tool resulting in a massive volume of lawsuits across the region.[119] As the sexual slavery issue was receiving more attention, spillover effects started to appear in some of this other World War II litigation, particularly in Korean courts, which amplified the colonial resonance of these issues.

In one dramatic example, in 2018 (after a torturous twenty-years of litigation), the South Korean Supreme Court ruled that the Japanese corporation Nippon Steel & Sumitomo Metal Corp must pay four steel workers 100 million won (about $76,700 USD) each for their forced labor during the war. Echoing the reasoning in some of the sexual slavery cases and in the Holocaust reparations approach, it held that the postwar agreements that apparently precluded claims were not an impediment to suing private corporations.[120] A year later, the same court ordered Mitsubishi to pay between 80 and 150 million won ($68,000–$127,000 USD) to each of ten people who worked for the company during World War II.[121] It was in the context of this escalating dispute between the two countries, that the South Korean government took the step discussed above of formally dissolving the Reconciliation and Healing Foundation set up by the 2015 Agreement.[122] When the Japanese companies refused to compensate the victims, South Korea decided to compensate the victims instead, a move that has sparked outrage.[123] But this only amplified the conflict, with dozens of Japanese World War II cases before Korean courts.[124] A new milestone was reached early in 2024 when, after a positive ruling by the Supreme Court of South Korea, a Japanese company paid compensation for forced labor, the first such payment (although

[119] As of the time of writing, there were dozens of World War II reparations lawsuits against Japan in Korean courts. *See generally* Webster, *Japan's Transnational War Reparations Litigation*, *supra* note 96; Timothy Webster, *The Price of Settlement: World War II Reparations in China, Japan and Korea*, 51 N.Y.U. J. INT'L L. & POL. 301 (2019). Though the emphasis here is on the Japanese-Korean issues, there was also movement in China. In the wake of an adverse finding in a Chinese lawsuit, in 2016 Mitsubishi announced a multimillion-dollar settlement with hundreds of Chinese forced laborers. In addition to publicly apologizing, it also set up what Webster calls "Asia's most elaborate war reparations scheme." *See* Webster, *Japan's Transnational War Reparations Litigation*, *supra* note 96, at 184, citing Austin Ramzy, *Mitsubishi Apologizes to Chinese World War II Forced Laborers*, THE NEW YORK TIMES (June 1, 2016).

[120] *See* Choe Sang-Hun & Rick Gladstone, *How a World War II-Era Reparations Case Is Roiling Asia*, THE NEW YORK TIMES (Oct. 30, 2018).

[121] *See* Joyce Lee, *South Korean Forced Labor Victims to Seek Japan's Mitsubishi Asset Sale*, REUTERS (July 16, 2019).

[122] *See Japan-Funded "Comfort Women" Foundation in South Korea Formally Closed*, KYODO NEWS (July 5, 2019).

[123] *See* Jean Mackenzie & Nicholas Yong, *South Korea to Compensate Victims of Japan's Wartime Forced Labor*, BBC NEWS (Mar. 6, 2023).

[124] *See* Webster, *Japan's Transnational War Reparations Litigation*, *supra* note 96, at 184.

the details are controversial).[125] Given the volume and significance of all of this activity, it is not surprising that experts are urging a more comprehensive resolution that includes reparations programs, processes for acknowledgment and apology, as well as commemoration. Suggestions along these lines are very much inspired by the kind of transformative justice approach that we saw at work in the residential schools agreement, which not coincidentally is also a reparations issue bound up with a larger colonial legacy.[126]

The sexual slavery example serves to illuminate the complexity of remedial issues in cases like these, an issue that we will return to below. It is also another dramatic illustration of how the attitude toward past wrongs has shifted. Even apart from the complications arising from the passage of time, the fact that the injuries were inflicted in the context of war would until recently have made claims of responsibility very difficult. But increasingly, neither the passage of time nor the complicated context of war and international relations seem as certain to defeat redress demands as they once would have been.[127] This case also illustrates the impact when harrowing narratives like these grip the public imagination. Propelled by a complex combination of media coverage, litigation, and broader engagement, they often generate surprising momentum. Once this happens, such narratives can be very hard to control. Indeed, when Japan tried to prevent efforts to publicize the sexual slavery issue within the country, it only had the effect of bolstering the profile of the issue.[128] After Japanese authorities canceled an art display and a film focused on the 'comfort women,'[129] memorials and statues started popping up in very far-flung places. On the same week as cancellations in Japan, a 'comfort woman' statue was erected near Washington D.C., joining many other statues and memorials in the United States and elsewhere.[130] It is also noteworthy that the 'comfort women' play *The Apology* based on accounts of survivors, debuted in London in 2022, making clear that the issue still has considerable momentum more than eighty years after the events took place.[131]

[125] *See* Jack Kim, *South Korea Forced Labor Victim Gets "Compensation" from Japan Firm, Lawyer Says*, REUTERS (Feb. 21, 2024).

[126] *See e.g.* Timothy Webster, *A Formula to Resolve the South Korea-Japan Wartime Forced Labor Issue*, UNITED STATES INSTITUTE OF PEACE (Aug. 18, 2022), https://www.usip.org/publications/2022/08/formula-resolve-south-korea-japan-wartime-forced-labor-issue#:~:text = First%2C%20 the%20mechanism%20should%20pay,laborers%20and%20offer%20an%20apology.

[127] *See* Sang-Hun & Gladstone, *supra* note 120.

[128] *See Japan's Controversial Comfort Women Sculpture Is Going on View Again Despite Protests and Intimidation*, "COMFORT WOMEN" JUSTICE COALITION (July 25, 2022), https://remembercomfortwomen.org/japans-controversial-comfort-women-sculpture-is-going-on-view-again-despite-protests-and-intimidation/.

[129] *See Tokyo Art Exhibit Featuring "Comfort Women" Statue to Be Restaged After Right-Wing Obstruction*, HANKYOREH (Mar. 28, 2022); *Japanese Festival Shows "Comfort Women" Film After Controversy*, KYODO NEWS (Nov. 5, 2019).

[130] *Civic Groups Successfully Erect 5th Comfort Woman Statue in US*, HANKOYOREH (Oct. 29, 2019).

[131] *See* Arifa Akbar, *The Apology Review—Powerful Tale of Wartime "Comfort Women,"* THE GUARDIAN (Sept. 21, 2022).

Conclusion

As these examples illustrate, private law's insistence that wrongs must be righted—the old idea of reparative justice—was increasingly being liberated from the limits that had once confined its operation to discrete recent wrongs. One result was that the demand to make amends for old wrongs was felt with increasing force, not just in courts but also across many institutions forced to grapple with their complicated histories. Among the most ambitious realizations of this was Canada's residential schools settlement. Even beyond its vast scale, the settlement pioneered a model of transformative justice that started to make ideas like reparations, apologies, and truth commissions relevant to rectifying historic wrongs in stable regimes. Developments like these also began to implicate other historic wrongs, resulting in complex reckonings, even for harmful acts that were legal at the time, like eugenics, or done in the context of war, like sexual slavery and forced labor. The bright line between the transitional regimes with evil pasts and the rest of us was dissolving.

Before moving on to a closely related set of developments, let us summarize how these demands to rectify historic wrongs have garnered such contemporary currency. The development of reparations style private law claims was vitally important because of how it enabled survivors to press their cases before courts. With their harrowing accounts of wrongful injuries and harms that in many cases stretched over a lifetime, these claims often held surprising power. And as we saw, this power could even lead courts to set aside limiting doctrines and stretch to get to the substance of the claims.

The development of these reparations style private law claims has been important in part because of how it has empowered survivors. Unlike with criminal law, survivors can initiate these legal actions themselves and in so doing both make the account public and force an authoritative body to listen. But something deeper is at play as well—as survivors have been able to push past procedural obstacles to the substance of the claim, they have leveraged private law's unique ability to personalize injustices as vast and terrible as the taking of generations of children, forced sterilization, or sexual slavery. Criminal law focuses on the accused, constitutional law focuses on the state, but private law's focus on the plaintiff means that survivors of old wrongs finally have a voice—a voice that has turned out to be hard to ignore.

These cases also illustrate that while the passage of time often makes things harder for claimants, its effect is complex. Once survivors are finally able to air the substance of their claims, it underscores the seriousness of the wrongs. Moreover, the cruel impact of those wrongs is no longer speculative—the pain, the shame, and the effects are inscribed on the lives of those who survived, and on the absences of those who did not. In that sense, the survivors are an especially powerful kind of living proof of the life-altering nature of some wrongs and the most powerful counter to the old adage that time heals all wounds. Moreover, the fact that these wrongs were never righted until incredibly late means that the survivors are old—as they said in the sexual slavery cases, they are our grandmothers. Their vulnerability only adds to the tragic fact that even if there is some redress now, it will be too late to change the course of their lives. That is not to say that it does not matter—it is rather that it adds to both the urgency and the poignancy of redress that most cases of historic injustice are brought by elderly fragile survivors who serve as the few remaining voices for their many fellow sufferers.

The distinctive nature of these cases is also evident in their trajectories. While they often begin with a focus on the traditional private law elements that provide the legal structure for their claims, as they develop their reparations qualities come to the fore. They emphasize their seriousness by drawing in human rights, constitutional and international law norms, especially those that protect the integrity of the person and prohibit discrimination. The residential schools cases drew in the United Nations Declaration on the Rights of the Child and the Rights of Indigenous Peoples, the eugenics cases drew in the Convention on the Rights of People with Disabilities, and the 'comfort women' drew in the prohibition against slavery and the Convention on the Elimination of All Forms of Discrimination Against Women. In so doing, these claims call attention to their significance and their divergence from 'garden variety' private law. If the law's commitment to repair injustices means anything, they seem to say, it must encompass wrongs that are so egregious, so damaging, and so profoundly at odds with our most fundamental legal and moral norms. The lofty ambitions of the cases are also apparent in what they seek. Though monetary damages—private law's mechanism for vindicating violated rights—are indeed critically important, so too are more transformational elements like apology, commemoration, and truth-seeking processes that tilt toward transitional justice.

While the trajectory of redressing old wrongs owes a great deal to the rise of these novel and ambitious private law actions, law is by no means the only critical element in cases like these. Journalists are especially pivotal in raising awareness through investigative reporting. Without that reporting, it is unlikely that the developments surrounding Catholic Church sexual abuse or the history of eugenics, for instance, would have garnered the attention they did. The impact of such reporting was also amplified because of the rapid shifts in communication taking place at the same time that concern with historic wrongs was on the rise. The resulting conversation became increasingly transnational, bringing together media, advocates, academic, lawyers, and institutions, not only across jurisdictions but increasingly across a growing array of issues as well. Residential schools survivors and advocates were inspired by the South African Truth and

Reconciliation Commission, and the reparations processes in the Settlement Agreement were informed by redress efforts in Ireland and elsewhere. The eugenics movement was propelled by powerful investigative journalism across continents and led to sophisticated digital archives that continue to be used across the globe. The 'comfort women' spurred a transnational movement that deployed the arts and gave voice to issues of sexual violence, slavery, and colonialism, among other things. The conversation concerning redress for historic wrongs also ensured that local developments had a much broader impact. We noted how the success in *Muir* and Sweden's reparations program turned the spotlight on other jurisdictions that had remained silent on their history of eugenics, placing them under increasing pressure to respond. And in this changing environment, demands to make amends for old wrongs were also increasingly touching upon issues that had always been thought to be beyond the reach of responsibility such as those that arose from law or policy or even from the conduct of war.

Thus far we have focused on the branch of redress for old wrongs involving injuries to the person. However, examples like the Holocaust and colonialism remind us that the terrible harms inflicted on people were often accompanied by a massive theft of their belongings. And so, as the idea of reparations started to come to the fore to respond to injuries to the person, it should not be surprising that a related set of reparative justice demands focused on the violent takings that so often accompanied that violence. Those demands took up the old private law idea of restitution, and it is to them that we will now turn.

5

Lost and Found: The Restitution Revolution

Introduction

Recent decades have witnessed a surge of claims for historic wrongs and, as we have seen, demands for redress that would once have been considered far-fetched are increasingly plausible. So far, however, we have focused only on the issues of historic injustice that involve grievous personal injuries. But at the same time that these developments in reparations were unfolding, and often closely connected to them, the venerable doctrine of restitution was also experiencing dramatic new life.[1] The most powerful early application of this new kind of restitution claim was found in looted art cases, particularly in those that addressed the Nazi plunder that accompanied the Holocaust. These claims to restore wrongfully taken property began to breathe new life into the rather arcane principle of restitution, in the process reshaping it to make it more apt to address other old wrongs. The fact that reparative justice and restitution go hand in hand in the Holocaust example also showed something else—the willful destruction of people and communities was often accompanied by efforts to steal their property and obliterate their culture. The means of redress had to tackle both.

In the case of restitution, echoing what we noted with reparations claims, the thin edge of the wedge that opened the door to new responsibility for old wrongs was found in the cases that had most in common with ordinary private law. And though still far from easy, early looted art cases did share many of the features that characterized the traditional law of restitution. Then in the 1990s, the Holocaust litigation began to refashion private law to try to capture some of the systemic wrongfulness of that vast evil and the doctrine of restitution was at the heart of many of those claims. These cases, and their dramatic effects, helped to inspire what has been termed a 'restitution revolution'.[2] As the doctrine was gradually liberated from some of its traditional confines, its underlying principle—the

[1] As discussed in the previous chapter, reparative justice is the animating idea behind the redeployment of the old international law concept of reparations to ground claims for redress of grievous personal injuries. Restitution with its demand that wrongdoers repair or undo the consequences of their wrongs is also based on reparative justice. The division between the two kinds of reparative justice claims is not neat and, as discussed below, many of the most serious problems of the past, such as the Holocaust, colonialism, and slavery, often involve both. Similarly, claims such as slave labor are sometimes framed in terms of reparations, and sometimes in terms of restitution.

[2] Bénédicte Savoy, *The Restitution Revolution Begins*, The Art Newspaper (Feb. 16, 2018).

Making Amends for Historic Wrongs. Mayo Moran, Oxford University Press. © Mayo Moran 2025.
DOI: 10.1093/9780190927295.003.0005

owner's right of return of that which was wrongfully taken—received greater weight. In this way, the evolution that began with the Holocaust cases can be traced through to responses to settler societies and colonial-era takings. Old claims that had languished for decades or sometimes even centuries suddenly began to see movement. In the process, as we shall see, a conception of restitution more responsive to the vast scope of some especially serious historic wrongs began to take its place alongside its more conventional counterpart.

Holocaust Restitution

The idea that the wrongful taking of objects and other precious or meaningful property grounds a demand for return or restitution is a venerable one. In its simplest terms, if property is wrongfully taken, restitution demands that it be returned to the rightful owner. But as a private law cause of action linked to unjust enrichment, restitution traditionally had a closely confined sphere of operation. It was understood to apply primarily in civil relations and was certainly not viewed as having any purchase in the complicated context of war or colonialism. However, the underlying restitutionary impulse is by no means new, even in those contexts.

Famous examples of forceful takings and claims to 'give it back' abound. The fact that *Time Magazine* lists the "Top Ten Plundered Artifacts" attests to the power of the idea of restitution in cases as diverse as the Parthenon marbles, the skull of Geronimo, the Chinese Bronzes, and the Louvre's Egyptian Frescoes, among many others.[3] But in recent decades, the view that such issues might actually involve restitutionary *claims* has emerged, threatening major institutions and coming to the forefront of public debate. While the taking of property was once seen as a prerogative of war, many of those historic takings are now viewed as injustices and hence vulnerable to claims of restitution. Here too the shift began in earnest with the efforts to respond to the horrors of the Holocaust. Dramatic examples such as *Woman in Gold*, alongside other high-profile litigation such as that involving the work of Pissarro and Egon Schiele, began to raise awareness of Nazi theft and to test the power of restitution.

Holocaust Thefticide and Early Restitution Efforts

Among its other horrors, the Holocaust included the systematic and legislated Nazi plunder of Jewish art and property as part of a larger program of cultural

[3] *Top Ten Plundered Artifacts*, TIME MAGAZINE, https://content.time.com/time/specials/packages/article/0,28804,1883142_1883129_1929080,00.html (last visited Jan. 11, 2025).

destruction.[4] Both in method and in scale, the devastation of property and its accompanying way of life, sometimes termed "thefticide,"[5] became one of the distinguishing features of the Holocaust. As part of an explicit policy of "Ayranization," an array of legislation and decrees forced the closure of Jewish businesses, with the result that tens of thousands of them were transferred, and untold amounts of personal and other property were transferred or lost.[6] The nature of the human destruction and its impact means that it is difficult to estimate what was lost and destroyed, but commentators have suggested that it amounted to over $150 billion in tangible and intangible assets,[7] including over 600,000 works of art.[8]

The Nazi confiscations also stood out because of the efforts to cloak them with the appearance of legality. They created complex legislative schemes that involved assigning non-Jewish "trustees" to oversee the forced sale of Jewish property to non-Jews.[9] The acquisition of the property of desperate émigrés was also accomplished in part through an exorbitant exit tax—the "Reich flight tax."[10] Under these provisions, Nazi Germany collected hundreds of millions, their favored citizens were enriched, and Jewish émigrés lost virtually all their property.[11]

Given the scale of the devastation both in human and proprietary terms, and the fact that it was carried out so systematically using the apparatus of the law, it is not surprising that the idea of restitution surfaced quite quickly in this context. As the nature and scale of the looting and dispossession started to become apparent, efforts to respond began. As early as 1941, Britain took measures to prevent looted art seized in Belgium and Holland from being sold in the United States. In 1943, the Allies signed the Inter-Allied Declaration against Acts of Dispossession Committed in Territories under Enemy Occupation and

[4] *See* Leora Bilsky, *Transnational Holocaust Litigation*, 23 Euro. J. Int'l L. 349 (2012); Irwin Cotler, *The Holocaust, "Thefticide" and Restitution: A Legal Perspective*, *in* The Plunder of Jewish Property During the Holocaust 66 (Avi Beker ed., 2001).

[5] Cotler, *supra* note 4.

[6] *See "Aryanization,"* Holocaust Encyclopedia (Oct. 24, 2017), https://encyclopedia.ushmm.org/content/en/article/aryanization.

[7] Greg Bradsher, *Turning History into Justice: Holocaust-Era Assets Records, Research, and Restitution* (War and Civilization Lecture University of North Carolina—Wilmington, North Carolina, Apr. 19, 2001), National Archives, https://www.archives.gov/research/holocaust/articles-and-papers/turning-history-into-justice.html.

[8] *Id.*

[9] *See "Aryanization," supra* note 6.

[10] *Nazi Restrictions, Special Taxes Strip Jews of Wealth*, Jewish Telegraphic Agency (Dec. 25, 1938), https://www.jta.org/1938/12/25/archive/nazi-restrictions-special-taxes-strip-jews-of-wealth.

[11] For an overview of looting during World War II and efforts to preserve and restitute looted property, *see* Commission for Looted Art in Europe, Introduction to The National Archives' Records on Nazi-Era Looted Cultural Property, 1939–1961 (2011).

Control.[12] Among other things, that "London Declaration" reserved the right to declare transfers invalid, including those that were "apparently legal in form, even when they purport to be voluntarily effected."[13] This was natural terrain for restitution. Beginning in 1944, the Inter-Allied Commission for the Protection and Restitution of Cultural Material (the Vaucher Commission) gathered information on art that had been looted in each country and on the agents, dealers, and Nazi individuals and agencies involved in the looting and trading.[14] Then, in the aftermath of war, the Allies set up a complex legal system for the restitution of stolen property, marking the first such systematic post-war effort. Though those efforts are largely viewed as failures, they did begin a shift in the conversation about restitution, one that has continued to this day.[15]

To understand the nature of this shift, it is important to recall the way that restitution was commonly understood when these efforts began. The idea of restitution, or the imperative to return something wrongfully taken, can be traced back at least as far as the Roman law idea that no one should benefit at the expense of another.[16] This is expressed in common law systems through the use of restitution as a remedy for unjust enrichment.[17] Civil law systems also draw on the old Roman idea of "unjustified enrichment" as the grounding for claims of restitution.[18] But traditionally, the understanding of what made a transaction unjust, unjustified, or wrong was closely circumscribed and typically focused on whether there was a legal reason for the enrichment, such as a law, consent, or consideration.[19] What English law calls "the unjust factor" analysis, for example, was thus not generally viewed as drawing in a robust sense of wrong.[20] Moreover, claims for restitution were susceptible to being defeated by claims of third parties, particularly the bona fide purchaser for value without notice.

[12] *See* Nicholas M. O'Donnell, A Tragic Fate: Law and Ethics in the Battle over Nazi-Looted Art 7–8 (2017).

[13] *Id.* at 8.

[14] *See* Commission for Looted Art in Europe, *supra* note 11, at 5–7.

[15] *See Implementation of Restitution Policy in Europe*, *in* Presidential Advisory Commission on Holocaust Assets, Plunder and Restitution: Findings and Recommendations of the Presidential Advisory Commission on Holocaust Assets in the United States and Staff Report 8 (December 2000) [hereinafter Presidential Advisory Commission on Holocaust Assets].

[16] *See* Faizal Kurniawan et al., *Elaboration on Concepts of Restitution and Compensation as a Form of Liability in Private Law*, 131 Advances in Soc. Sci., Ed. & Hum. Research 85, 87 (2017).

[17] *See* American Law Institute, Restatement, Third, Restitution and Unjust Enrichment §1 (2011) ("[a] person who is unjustly enriched at the expense of another is subject to liability in restitution").

[18] *See e.g.* the comparative overview in Gerhard Dannemann, The German Law of Unjustified Enrichment and Restitution: A Comparative Introduction (2009).

[19] *See* Peter Birks, Unjust Enrichment (2d ed. 2005); Deutsche Morgan Grenfell Group plc v. IRC, [2006] UKHL 49.

[20] *See* Lutz-Christian Wolff, *Law of Unjust Enrichment or Law of Unjust De-Enrichment?*, *in* Rethinking Unjust Enrichment: History, Sociology, Doctrine, and Theory 201, 205–9 (Sagi Peari & Warren Swain eds., 2023).

The infamous case of *Bernstein v. Van Heyghen Freres Societe Anonyme* illustrates just how strictly the confines of restitution were drawn in the immediate aftermath of World War II and how difficult it was to use the legal doctrine of the day to rectify even egregious Holocaust takings. Arnold Bernstein owned a shipping line whose assets included a ship called the *Gandia*.[21] He was arrested by the Gestapo in Hamburg in 1937 and imprisoned for over two and a half years. While imprisoned, "Nazi officials" threatened him with "bodily harm, indefinite imprisonment and death," as well as business ruin, compelling him to transfer the shares of his shipping line to Marius Boeger—a "non-Jewish trustee." Boeger transferred the shares of Bernstein's shipping line to Van Heyghen for the equivalent of $90,000 USD and immediately thereafter the *Gandia* was insured for $350,000 USD.[22] In 1946, Bernstein sued Van Heyghen in New York for restitution of the insurance proceeds ($400,000 USD) that had been paid upon destruction of the ship.[23] Bernstein's claim was rejected by the trial court and that rejection was upheld by the Second Circuit Court of Appeals, in a decision authored by none other than Justice Learned Hand.

Under New York law, Bernstein's action was entitled to proceed to trial unless it was clear that he "must ultimately fail."[24] Despite this, Learned Hand J ruled to dismiss. He appeared protective of the defendant's rights as a third-party recipient, ignoring the evidence that the transfer was not made for fair market value. New York law, he said, would not countenance the argument that the defendant knew the transfer was discriminatory because it was "exceedingly fragile."[25] Then after noting the duress imposed by "Nazi officials," he held that even assuming a German court would have held the transfer unlawful, a US court "will not undertake to pass upon the validity under the municipal law of another state of the acts of officials of that state."[26] The result was that Nazi officials who used duress to force Jews to transfer property would be protected under the Act of State doctrine unless the Executive had indicated otherwise, something that Learned Hand J concluded had not been done.

Clark J dissented, troubled by the heavy burden that the majority held "must be overcome before acts of Nazi oppression can be questioned in our courts."[27] But his real quarrel with Learned Hand J focused on the idea that acts of Nazi officials were the kind of acts of a foreign sovereign that demanded respect.

[21] Bernstein v. Van Heyghen Freres Societe Anonyme, 163 F.2d 246 (2d Cir. 1947).

[22] Victor House, *The Law Gone Awry: Bernstein v. Van Heyghen Freres*, 37 CAL. L. REV. 38, 39 (1949). *See also* Michael Allen, *The Limits of Lex Americana: The Holocaust Restitution Litigation as a Cul-de-Sac of International Human-Rights Law*, YALE LAW SCHOOL STUDENT SCHOLARSHIP PAPERS (2009), http://digitalcommons.law.yale.edu/student_papers/93.

[23] House, *supra* note 22, at 39.

[24] Bernstein v. Van Heyghen Freres Societe Anonyme, 163 F.2d 246 (2d Cir. 1947).

[25] *Id.*

[26] *Id.* at 249.

[27] *Id.* at 253.

The Act of State precedents, he stressed, do not deal with the case where the Executive declares the acts of another nation "as wrongful and void, to be wiped out by a tremendous war effort and by acts of restitution and retribution at the war's end."[28] Clark J closed with the worry that the United States' allies may be "mystified by what must seem the vagaries of a policy looking to restitution to the Jews in Germany at the same time that it accepts the acts of Nazi oppression of the Jews as binding in American courts."[29] All the evidence suggested, in his view, that the Executive had clearly repudiated the acts of Nazi Germany, which were therefore no longer entitled to respect in the courts of the United States.

The decision in *Bernstein* was greeted by intense criticism from the legal community.[30] Commentators questioned Learned Hand J's discussion of notice and pointed to his failure to address the evidence that the defendant had not given fair value for the ship and hence was not a purchaser for fair value.[31] The conclusion that an American court owed respect to the Nazi officials who terrorized the Jewish population and stole their property was greeted with outrage.[32] The furor reached the State Department, which responded in 1949 with a letter from Acting Legal Advisor, Jack B. Tate. It stated that the government had "consistently opposed the forcible acts of dispossession of a discriminatory and confiscatory nature practised by the Germans."[33] It clarified that American courts were relieved of "any restraint upon the exercise of their jurisdiction to pass on the validity of the acts of Nazi officials" when claims were asserted in the United States for "restitution" of property lost through "forced, coercion, or duress as a result of Nazi persecution."[34] In 1954, the Second Circuit reversed its 1947 decision and finally allowed Bernstein's case to proceed.[35] In 1955, *The New York Times* reported "Bernstein Suit Settled at Last" for an undisclosed but "substantial" sum.[36]

[28] *Id.*

[29] *Id.* at 255.

[30] *See* House, *supra* note 22, at 38. House describes the criticism of the case as "spontaneous, widespread and continuous," citing *Should Judicial Respect Be Accorded to Nazi Acts of State?* 47 Col. L. Rev. 1061 (1947); *Judicial Recognition of Nazi Acts of State*, 15 U. CHI. L. Rev. 415 (1947); *"Act of State" Immunity*, 57 Yale L.J. 108 (1947); *Recent Cases*, 60 Harv. L. Rev. 1351, 1351 (1947); *Notes*, N. Y. U. L. Q. Rev. 298, 311 (1948). House also notes that "[l]etters from law teachers and leaders of the bar received by the writer, who was of counsel to the plaintiff in the litigation, are uniformly critical of the decision." House, *supra* note 22, at 38.

[31] *See supra* note 30 and sources cited therein.

[32] *See supra* note 30 and sources cited therein.

[33] Quoted in Bernstein v. V. Nederlandsche-Amerikaansche Stoomvaart-Maatschappij, 210 F.2d 375 (2d Cir. 1954).

[34] O'Donnell, *supra* note 12, at 15.

[35] Bernstein v. V. Nederlandsche-Amerikaansche Stoomvaart-Maatschappij, 210 F.2d 375 (2d Cir. 1954).

[36] *Bernstein's Suit Settled at Last: Fight over Nazi-Era Sale of Ship Properties Ends as Court Approves Terms*, The New York Times (Mar. 17, 1955). Background on Bernstein's remarkable life is found in *Arnold Bernstein*, Immigrant Entrepreneurship (Aug. 22, 2018), https://www.immigrantentrepreneurship.org/entries/arnold-bernstein/#_edn60.

The *Bernstein* decision was striking in part because of its tension with the restitution efforts of America and her Allies in the aftermath of Germany's defeat. Following the London Conference, the Allies promulgated a number of military laws to facilitate the restitution of Jewish property.[37] In 1947—the same year that *Bernstein* was decided—the US government enacted Military Government Law No. 59 Restitution of Identifiable Property (Military Law 59).[38] Applying to the United States' zones of occupation in Germany, it was designed to ensure the "speedy restitution of identifiable property" to persons who were wrongfully deprived of it during the Nazi era—the very issue the New York court addressed in *Bernstein*.[39]

Military Law 59 contrasts sharply with *Bernstein's* approach to restitution. It opens by stating that its purpose is to "effect to the largest extent possible the speedy restitution" of property to those who were "wrongly deprived" during the Nazi era including for reasons of race and religion.[40] It underscores this "basic principle" by making it clear that the law should be interpreted to achieve as much restitution as possible.[41] The opening section also rules out the common defences of absence of notice and good faith purchase, as well as explicitly rejecting technical definitions of matters such as confiscation and duress.[42] Importantly, it creates a presumption of confiscation where the individual "belonged to a class of persons which . . . was to be eliminated in its entirety from the cultural and economic life of Germany by measures taken by the State or the [Nazi Party]."[43] It also explicitly addresses the "cloak of legality' "commonly employed by the Nazis, rejecting reliance on legal orders or other acts that exploit the fact that the targeted classes of individuals were unable to protect their interests.

The terms of Military Law 59 do seem to go a considerable distance toward establishing a restitution model responsive to the oppressive context of the Nazi state. But its promise was never achieved, in part because even the Western Allies could not agree on a single approach. The result was at least four different regimes, which created great complexity as well as conflict of laws problems

37 *See* Stephen A. Denburg, *Reclaiming Their Past: A Survey of Jewish Efforts to Restitute European Property*, 18 B.C. Third World L.J. 233 (1998), discussing among other sources, Ronald W. Zweig, German Reparations and the Jewish World: A History of the Claims Conference 40–41 (1987).

38 Military Government, United States Area of Control, Germany, Law No. 59: Restitution of Identifiable Property (1947), https://www.dfs.ny.gov/system/files/documents/2019/02/us-military-law-59.pdf.

39 *Id.* § 1(1).

40 *Id. See also* Monroe Karasik, *Problems of Compensation and Restitution in Germany and Austria*, 16 L. & Contemp. Probs. 448, 452–57 (1951).

41 *See* Karasik, *supra* note 40, at 453.

42 Military Government, *supra* note 38, §§ 1(2), 2(1).

43 *Id.* § 3(1)(b).

between the various zones and authorities.[44] Moreover, and troublingly, restitution was not made to the individuals that lost the property but rather to organizations and to countries—ironically including Germany, the very state that had carried out the discriminatory confiscations in the first place. Then as alliances shifted, the will to pursue restitution quickly vanished in the face of emerging Cold War politics. So despite Military Law 59's promise and the restitution undertaken in the immediate post-war period, a vast amount remained to be done.[45] But for several decades, restitution took a back seat to other issues and almost disappeared from the legal and political agenda.

The Wall Falls and the Modern Era of Restitution Begins

When the Berlin Wall fell and Germany was reunited, global political dynamics changed and restitution started to resurface.[46] In the mid-1990s, a campaign by the World Jewish Congress led to US Senate hearings on the dormant accounts of Holocaust victims held in Swiss banks.[47] The Swiss banks claims, filed in the mid-1990s, picked up on this activity and were then joined by slave labor and other claims including looted art. As noted earlier, the claims were eventually consolidated into *In Re Holocaust Victims Asset Litigation* and were heard by Judge Korman of the Eastern District Court of New York.[48] Restitution was also at the forefront of two separate commissions which were created to study the role of Swiss banks in the persecution of victims of the Nazis. The Swiss Parliament appointed the Bergier Commission, and the Independent Committee of Eminent Persons (Volker Committee) was created by the Swiss Bankers Association, the World Jewish Restitution Organization, and the World Jewish Congress.[49]

All of this meant that the *Holocaust Victims Asset Litigation* proceeded against an extraordinary background of related activity. The litigation itself was spearheaded by Professor Bert Neuborne of New York University law school.[50]

[44] *See* Karasik, *supra* note 40; *Implementation of Restitution Policy in Europe, in* PRESIDENTIAL ADVISORY COMMISSION ON HOLOCAUST ASSETS, *supra* note 15; Wilhelm Wengler, *Conflicts of Laws Problems Relating to Restitution of Property in Germany*, 11 INT'L & COMP. L.Q. 1131 (1962).

[45] *See Implementation of Restitution Policy in Europe, in* PRESIDENTIAL ADVISORY COMMISSION ON HOLOCAUST ASSETS, *supra* note 15; Karasik, *supra* note 40, at 452–57.

[46] *See* O'DONNELL, *supra* note 12, especially chapter 1 discussing pre-Washington Conference claims involving stolen art such as Chagall's *Le Paysan a L'echelle* (Menzel v. List, 49 Misc. 2d 300 (N.Y. Sup. Ct. 1966).

[47] *See* LEORA BILSKY, THE HOLOCAUST, CORPORATIONS, AND THE LAW: UNFINISHED BUSINESS 36–39 (2017).

[48] *See Overview of Litigation and Settlement*, HOLOCAUST VICTIM ASSETS LITIGATION (SWISS BANKS) (Apr. 14, 2020), https://www.swissbankclaims.com/Overview.aspx.html.

[49] *Id.*

[50] Neuborne served "as both counsel to the entire plaintiff class and as Lead Settlement Counsel." In re Holocaust Victim Assets Litigation, CV 06-0983 (FB) (JO), CV 96-4849 (ERK) (JO), consolidated with CV 99-5161 and CV 97-0461, 7 (E.D.N.Y. Mar. 15, 2007).

In 1998, a $1.25 billion global settlement was reached involving the Swiss Banks, and the massive effort of implementing the plan began. The same group of lawyers also launched class actions against German corporations for forced and slave labor. These lawsuits were ultimately settled for approximately $5 billion USD.[51] Though both categories of claims involved some element of restitution, the slave labor cases are focused more on reparations for personal injuries where, as noted in the chapter above, they were instrumental in inspiring a new wave of activity seeking redress for grievous personal injury. The Swiss banks litigation by contrast focused more directly on the loss of property, and for that reason it was particularly influential in sparking a new wave of activity based on the old legal idea of restitution.

There were also related developments underway. Here too, the media played a critically important role. In 1992, Lynn Nicholas published *The Rape of Europa: The Fate of Europe's Treasures in the Third Reich and the Second World War.* This groundbreaking work received a great deal of attention, and it formed the basis of an award-winning documentary.[52] It was followed shortly thereafter by Hector Feliciano's *The Lost Museum*, which focused on Holocaust-looted art in France.[53] The publicity that these works received drew attention to how little Nazi-looted art had ever been returned to the rightful owners.

Then in the late 1990s, the drama around Schiele's *Portrait of Wally* put Holocaust restitution on the public radar in a new way. Before the Holocaust, the painting had been owned by Lea Bondi, a Jewish art dealer in Vienna. She had been forced to turn it over to the Nazis. After the war, she tried to get it back, including by enlisting the help of one of Austria's foremost collectors, Dr. Rudolph Leopold. But Leopold, himself a voracious collector of Schiele, managed to procure it for his own collection while ostensibly assisting with Bondi's restitution claim. The Austrian government eventually purchased his collection, including *Wally*, created the Leopold Museum, and named Leopold as director for life.

[51] *See* Bilsky, *supra* note 47, at 36–41.

[52] Lynn H. Nicholas, The Rape of Europa: The Fate of Europe's Treasurers in the Third Reich and the Second World War (1995). *See also* Donald Cameron Watt, *Hitler's Sticky Fingers*, The New York Times (Aug. 7, 1994); Michael Sheridan, *Cut Price Picassos and Cyanide Champagne: "The Rape of Europa"—Lynn H Nicholas: Macmillan, 20 pounds*, The Independent (Sept. 9, 1994). The documentary was nominated for and won various awards, see *The Rape of Europa Awards*, IMDB, https://www.imdb.com/title/tt0997088/awards/ (last visited Jan. 11, 2025).

[53] Hector Feliciano, The Lost Museum: The Nazi Conspiracy to Steal the World's Greatest Works of Art (1998). It was also widely reviewed. *See* Richard Bernstein, *Nazis and Their Allies in Art Theft*, The New York Times (June 18, 1997); Jonathan Petropoulos, *Petropoulos on Feliciano, "The Lost Museum: The Nazi Conspiracy to Steal the World's Greatest Works of Art,"* H-German (March 1998), https://networks.h-net.org/node/35008/reviews/43582/petropoulos-feliciano-lost-museum-nazi-conspiracy-steal-worlds-greatest.

In 1997, *Portrait of Wally* was among several paintings lent to New York's Museum of Modern Art (MOMA) for an exhibit entitled "Egon Schiele: The Leopold Collection." Shortly before the show was scheduled to close, *The New York Times* published a special report entitled "The Zealous Collector." Written by Judith Dobrzynski, it told the story of Leopold's obsession with Schiele and exposed the provenance of *Wally*.[54] The report created a furor. Early in 1998, just as the paintings were being prepared for return to Vienna, the Manhattan District Attorney subpoenaed *Wally* on the ground that it was Nazi-looted art.[55] The complicated legal proceedings dragged on for over a decade. Finally in 2009, a New York court rejected the claim that Leopold's acquisition was innocent and found that there was enough evidence for a trial to proceed.[56] The ruling precipitated a settlement, and in 2010, perhaps not coincidentally the year that Leopold died, the Bondi family accepted $19 million for the painting, which was then returned to the Leopold Museum.[57] The museum now has an extensive note on the *Wally* dispute on its website, but interestingly it makes no mention of Leopold's troubling role.[58] The *Wally* litigation also became the subject of a documentary, and the drama of the case, widely reported in the press, focused more attention on Holocaust restitution.[59]

The shock waves caused by the seizure of *Wally* also reverberated throughout the art world, prompting calls for alternatives to litigation for such disputes. Barely a month after the seizures, the Association of Museum Directors announced a Task Force that aimed to develop guidelines "to resolve individual ownership claims arising from the seizure of artworks before, during and immediately after World War II."[60] By mid-February, the House Banking Committee was holding hearings on looted art.[61] Throughout 1998, the fallout from *Wally* continued with developments in Austria, Germany, the Netherlands, and elsewhere.[62] Unsurprisingly, it was especially intense in Austria. In March,

[54] Judith H. Dobrzynski, *The Zealous Collector—A Special Report; A Singular Passion for Amassing Art, One Way or Another*, The New York Times (Dec. 24, 1997).

[55] *See Freezing the Schiele Paintings*, The New York Times (Jan. 9, 1998).

[56] United States v. Portrait of Wally, 663 F. Supp. 2d 232 (S.D.N.Y. 2009).

[57] *See* Press Release, United States Attorney for the Southern District of New York, *United States Announces $19 Million Settlement in Case of Painting Stolen by Nazi* (July 20, 2010), https://www.justice.gov/archive/usao/nys/pressreleases/July10/portraitofwallysettlementpr.pdf; O'Donnell, *supra* note 12, at 59–82.

[58] *Egon Schiele, Portrait of Wally Neuzil*, Leopold Museum, https://www.leopoldmuseum.org/en/collection/highlights/147 (last visited Jan. 11, 2025).

[59] *See The Multidimensional Fate of a 1912 Schiele Portrait*, The New York Times (May 10, 2012).

[60] Judith H. Dobrzynski, *Museums Call for System to Address Nazi Booty: Museums Address Ownership of Booty*, The New York Times (Feb. 5, 1998).

[61] *Id.*

[62] *See Art Advisory* Board, Bundesministerium Kunst, Kultur, öffentlicher Dienst und Sport, https://provenienzforschung.gv.at/en/ (last visited Jan. 12, 2025); Sarah MacDonald, *On Ethics and Effectiveness: German Museums, Nazi Art Confiscation, and International Restitution Efforts*, 3 The iJournal 1 (2017); *Art Restitution Cases*, Monument Men and Women,

Austria's culture minister announced the creation of a new approach to restitution. Austrian investigative journalists also began to highlight how Austria had capitalized on Nazi crimes.[63] The issue continued to gain momentum, creating pressure for a more comprehensive solution.

Then late in 1998, the United States State Department hosted the Washington Conference on Holocaust-Era Assets. Under the leadership of Stuart Eizenstat—at the time Under Secretary of State for Economic, Business, and Agricultural Affairs—the conference was attended by the representatives of over forty nations. Secretary of State Madeline Albright opened the proceedings, insisting that "our goal must be justice, even though justice in this searing context is a highly relative term."[64] Lynn Nicholas was among the historians who gave an overview of the scope and nature of Nazi looting. Ultimately, the conference adopted a set of guidelines that have become known as the Washington Principles.

The Washington Principles

Created over half a century after the end of the Holocaust, the Washington Principles were the first internationally agreed-upon framework focused on the return of Holocaust-looted art. Signed in December 1998 by forty-two countries and a number of interest groups, the eleven principles were intended to expedite the return of art looted by Nazis to the rightful owners—in their now famous wording, to find a "just and fair solution" to the problem of Holocaust-looted art. Given the backdrop of the *Wally* seizures and litigation, it is not surprising that much of the emphasis was on developing alternatives to litigation.

It is easy and even understandable now, many decades later, to be critical of several features of the Washington Principles. But whatever those weaknesses, the Principles remain the most important overarching policy innovation in Holocaust restitution. The conference and the principles put Holocaust restitution on the agenda in a new way, and their pragmatic emphasis on finding just and fair solutions helped to launch what has become known as the 'restitution revolution.' The most significant developments in the decades since can largely be traced back to those principles, which have served as the touchstone of restitution

https://www.monumentsmenandwomenfnd.org/resources/art-restitution-cases#:~:text = In%20 February%202006%2C%20after%20years,and%20during%20World%20War%20II (last visited Jan. 12, 2025).

[63] *See* Jane Perlez, *Austria Is Set to Return Artworks Confiscated from Jews by Nazism*, THE NEW YORK TIMES (Mar. 7, 1998) (in 2006, the Dutch government returned over 200 pieces).

[64] Secretary of State Madeline J. Albright, *Remarks at Opening of Washington Conference on Holocaust-Era Assets* (Dec. 1, 1998), https://www.lootedart.com/web_images/pdf2014/12-01-98%20Secretary%20Albright%20(Opening%20ceremony%20address).pdf, cited in O'DONNELL, *supra* note 12, at 30.

initiatives and advocacy. They resulted in a dramatic uptick in restitutions, and tens of thousands of works have been returned since they were adopted.[65] While a great deal remains to be done, this was a major accomplishment.

One key aim of the Washington Principles, particularly in light of the events surrounding *Wally*, was to prompt individual jurisdictions to adopt alternative processes to expedite the return of Holocaust-looted art. Some of the most affected jurisdictions in Europe did so, and unsurprisingly they have been responsible for most of the subsequent restitution activity. Unfortunately, as of the twentieth anniversary of the Washington Principles, only five of the forty-two signatories had set up such processes—the United Kingdom, France, Germany, Austria, and the Netherlands.[66] To the dismay of Stuart Eizenstat, even the United States, the 'home' of the Washington Principles, did not create an alternative to litigation. Although the national processes all had their flaws, they have been especially important in accelerating the pace of restitution, in part by avoiding the cost and delays associated with litigation. And as time has passed, those processes have also been the subject of revision in response to some of the challenges that have emerged.

The Washington Principles have also changed how museums, galleries, and cultural institutions operate. They stressed the importance of transparency, particularly in relation to studying and publicizing information about the provenance of objects that may have had ties to the Nazi period. In their wake, museums, galleries, and other institutions began, however slowly, to undertake provenance review and to be more transparent about their collections. Today major auction houses like Christie's and Sotheby's have restitution departments that explicitly support the Washington Principles and engage in extensive provenance research.[67] Stuart Eizenstat, in his role as Special Expert Advisor to the State Department on Holocaust Issues, observed that it is now standard practice to check the ownership history of new acquisitions or gifts, and that databases are being developed to assist claimants looking for looted art. Eizenstat also noted the large number of works that had been returned as of 2018, the twentieth anniversary of the Washington Principles: "Austria has restituted over 30,000 artworks [and other objects], Germany over 16,000."[68] However, he also

[65] *See Reclaiming Lost History: 25 Years of the Washington Principles on Nazi-Confiscated*, Christie's (Jan. 26, 2023), https://www.christies.com/en/stories/reclaiming-lost-history-anniversary-of-the-washington-principles-b3cde6088c1c4acd81b4c2e65262081b.

[66] Talya Zax, *The World Set Rules for Returning Nazi-Looted Art. Are They Working?* Forward (Dec. 3, 2018). As noted earlier, in the mid-2020s, Switzerland and Flanders both began to set up processes.

[67] *See Reclaiming Lost History*, *supra* note 65; Gareth Harris, *Reflect, Restore, Rebuild: Restitution at Sotheby's*, Sotheby's (Feb. 23, 2023), https://www.sothebys.com/en/articles/reflect-restore-rebuild-restitution-at-sothebys.

[68] Zax, *supra* note 66.

observed how much remained to be done—as he put it, "[w]e must candidly confront the unfulfilled promises we solemnly made."[69]

As this suggests, while their effect was certainly significant, the Washington Principles have in the estimation of most observers, including Eizenstat himself, not lived up to their promise. While the number of signatories is impressive, the text also reflects the compromises that were necessary to achieve that support. Most crucially perhaps, the Washington Principles are non-binding or "soft law." Moreover, while the ambitions are lofty, the actual wording is vague. Unlike Military Law 59, the Washington Principles do not expressly set out a right of restitution.[70] The term itself barely appears, referred to only in the negative ("not subsequently restituted"). In contrast with the forthright opening declarations of Military Law 59, the governing norms of the Washington Principles are stated more generally and are somewhat buried near the end. It is not until Principle 8 that we get the first expression of the governing and now famous language of "just and fair" solutions. The Principles also stress the great variety of legal systems—in fact, they begin with this recognition. The result was that most claimants had little choice but to pursue costly and time-consuming litigation—the very thing that the Washington Principles sought to avoid.[71]

Ironically, although the Washington Principles sought to avoid litigation, it could be argued that landmark cases on the issue—uneven though the results certainly have been—have played an equally important role in putting restitution on the radar. In part because of their powerful narratives, these compelling cases attracted a great deal of media interest.[72] But some of them did much more than that. As we have seen, the events and litigation surrounding *Wally* played a major role in sparking the conference that gave birth to the Washington Principles. Another landmark case in Holocaust restitution got underway when Maria Altmann began her struggle for the return of the Klimt portrait of her aunt, subsequently immortalized in the award-winning film *Woman in Gold.*

Woman in Gold was Klimt's portrait of Adele Bloch-Bauer, a member of Vienna's cultivated and affluent Jewish community. She died in 1925, and in her will, she asked her husband Ferdinand to leave the painting to the Belvedere Gallery in Vienna. In 1938, the Nazis invaded and Ferdinand fled to Switzerland:

[69] William D. Cohan, *Five Countries Slow to Address Nazi-Looted Art, U.S. Expert Says*, The New York Times (Nov. 26, 2018).

[70] Contrast Military Law 59, which begins with its purpose: "to effect to the largest extent possible a speedy restitution of identifiable property . . . to persons who were wrongly deprived . . . ." Military Government, *supra* note 38, § 1(1).

[71] *See* O'Donnell, *supra* note 12, at 58.

[72] *The New York Times* alone has hundreds of articles on the topic. *See Art Restitution*, The New York Times, https://www.nytimes.com/topic/subject/art-restitution (last visited Jan. 11, 2025).

> In his absence, according to the complaint, the Nazis "Aryanized" the sugar company he had directed, took over his Vienna home, and divided up his artworks, which included the Klimts at issue here, many other valuable paintings, and a 400-piece porcelain collection. A Nazi lawyer, Dr. Erich Führer, took possession of the six Klimts. He sold two to the Gallery in 1941 and a third in 1943, kept one for himself, and sold another to the Museum of the City of Vienna. The immediate fate of the sixth is not known.[73]

Ferdinand died in 1945, and many other members of the family perished in the Holocaust. Ferdinand's will made no mention of the painting, and he left his entire estate to his nephew and two nieces, one of whom was Maria Altmann. Altmann had managed to flee to the United States shortly after the Nazis took over. In the immediate aftermath of the war, her brother and fellow heir tried to get back the property stolen from their uncle, but he was thwarted by the unscrupulous Austrian lawyer he retained. The matter then went quiet for a very long time.

However, events in Austria decades later brought their restitution efforts back to life, and investigative journalism was again a pivotal factor. In 1998, journalist Hubertus Czernin discovered documents in the Belvedere Gallery's files that showed that they knew that neither Adele nor Ferdinand had donated the paintings. He noted that Klimt's portrait of Adele, "which all the [Gallery] publications represented as having been donated to the museum in 1936," was actually purchased in 1941, and it was accompanied by a letter from Führer signed "Heil Hitler."[74]

Upon discovery that the Gallery had in fact acquired the Adele painting from Führer, Maria Altmann sought its return under the new restitution law that Austria had enacted in the aftermath of Czernin's revelations. The Austrian Committee agreed to return some items, but not the Klimt paintings. Altmann wanted to challenge this in Austrian courts but could not afford their prohibitive costs, so she turned to the California courts. The Austrian government claimed sovereign immunity. The District Court rejected that claim, and so did the Court of Appeal, based in part on the Tate memorandum's clarification that American courts were not required to respect to the acts of Nazi officials.[75] In 2004, the Supreme Court agreed, ruling in Altmann's favor.[76] The parties then agreed to arbitration in Austria, and in 2006, Altmann was awarded five of the six paintings.[77] Because the Austrian government had rejected a term of the

[73] Republic of Austria v. Altmann, 541 U.S. 677, 682 (2004) (Stevens J.) [citations omitted].

[74] *Id.* at 684.

[75] *Id.* at 685–88.

[76] *Id.* at 688–700.

[77] *See* Patricia Cohen, *The Story Behind "Woman in Gold": Nazi Art Thieves and One Painting's Return*, The New York Times (Mar. 30, 2015).

arbitration that would have allowed it the first right of purchase at market price, Altmann consigned the painting to Christie's, which sold it to Ronald Lauder in a private sale, purportedly for $135 million. All of the Bloch-Bauer paintings set records, with the remaining four Klimts selling for $192.7 million.[78]

The dramatic story of *Woman in Gold* is often dominated by the litigation twists and turns and the price tag of what became the world's most expensive painting. But its meaning is deeper—*Woman in Gold* is in many ways an archetypal story of Holocaust restitution. It was considered an Austrian national treasure, one of the most important pieces in their national museum. But the nation that treasured the painting of Adele also destroyed her family, gaining the glorious portrait of her in the process. Moreover, the person demanding return was not some distant descendant—it was the niece who remembered the portrait hanging in the family home before it was brutally torn apart by the horrors of the Nazis era. *Woman in Gold* was in that sense much more than simply a beautiful and valuable piece of stolen art. Its journey from Klimt's studio to the Bloch-Bauer's gracious living rooms in cultured Vienna to the hands of the Nazi authorities who seized those quarters and terrorized the family to the Austrian national collection at the Belvedere was a personal history of the Holocaust. Austria's unwillingness to return the painting also epitomized something larger—its refusal to acknowledge its deeper responsibility. Maria Altmann's case captured public imagination, in part because it made the moral argument for return more forcefully than a legal argument ever could. It also showed why restitution was about so much more than an object. It was about a violently destroyed way of life, linked to a more grievous form of guilt. But that link also connected the question of return to the possibility of making amends, however belated and partial they might be. The result was that cases like these started to lend more resonance to the imperative of restitution, not only in the context of litigation but also in the realm of institutional practice, public policy, and, importantly, public opinion.

It is therefore unsurprising that litigation and other restitution-related activity saw a sharp uptick in the wake of events like the *Wally* case, the birth of the Washington Principles, and the *Woman in Gold* saga. While the activity is now so vast that it is difficult to track, a review of *The New York Times* coverage does provide a kind of timeline of how attention to the issue has accelerated over this period. The ten pages that list *The New York Times* articles on "Art Restitution" currently contain over 470 articles organized chronologically, beginning with a 1964 article about fraudulent restitution claims by an Austrian lawyer.[79] Between 1964 and 1990, there were very few articles on the topic at all, and only one

[78] *See* Christopher Michaud, *Christie's Stages Record Art Sale*, REUTERS (Aug. 9, 2007).
[79] *See Austrian Who Owns 2 U.S. Papers Seized in Bonn*, THE NEW YORK TIMES (Nov. 18, 1964).

focused on Holocaust restitution.[80] But here too things began to change with the fall of the Berlin Wall.

In the early 1990s, the coverage of Holocaust restitution increased slowly, much of it initially focusing on Russia. But beginning late in 1997, the pace of coverage picked up dramatically. That was the year, as *The New York Times* reported, that the World Jewish Congress created the Commission for Art Recovery with Ronald S. Lauder as Chairman.[81] And it was at the end of 1997 that Judith Dobrzynski published "The Zealous Collector" about Leopold and his obsession with Egon Schiele.[82] Partly triggered by the *Wally* case, in 1998 alone, *The New York Times* published at least seventeen articles focused on Holocaust restitution, including a December editorial that referred to the birth of the Washington Principles.[83] Over the years since, the pace of coverage has continued to grow, with signal events prompting increased discussion.

Despite the uncertainty that continues to characterize the outcome of individual restitution claims, the general level of restitution-related activity is vastly larger than it was before the fall of the Berlin Wall. The sense that restitution needs to be addressed has also undergone a significant transformation. The increased activity has been fueled by legislative interventions that tackled the challenges faced by plaintiffs seeking return, especially in the United States, which remains the forum of choice.[84] The Holocaust Expropriated Art Recovery Act of 2016, or HEAR Act, focused on issues—especially limitations—that the Nazi-looted art cases faced in US courts.[85] In 2018, the US Congress passed the Justice for Uncompensated Survivors Today Act (JUST Act) that mandates a comprehensive assessment of the compliance of signatories to the Terezin Declaration on Holocaust Era Assets and Related Issues.[86] The World Jewish Restitution Organization welcomed what it described as the first ever comprehensive review of this issue, while at the same time noting that the report shows that many European countries have not met their commitments to provide restitution or compensation for property that was wrongfully taken from them during World War II.[87]

[80] *See* Douglas C. McGill, *Treasurers Seized by Nazis Are Coming out of the Closet*, The New York Times (Dec. 9, 1984).

[81] *See* Judith H. Dobrzynski, *For What Nazis Stole, A Longtime Art Hound*, The New York Times (Nov. 29, 1997).

[82] *See* Dobrzynski, *The Zealous Collector*, *supra* note 54.

[83] *See Art Restitution*, *supra* note 72.

[84] Nicholas O'Donnell's *A Tragic Fate* devotes an entire section to limitations challenges in US courts—Part Three: Out of Time. *See* O'Donnell, *supra* note 12.

[85] Pub. L. No. 114–308, 130 Stat. 1524 (2016).

[86] Pub. L. No. 115–171, 132 Stat. 1288 (2018).

[87] *See The World Jewish Restitution Organization (WJRO) Welcomes Groundbreaking US Government Report on Property Restitution*, World Jewish Restitution Organization, https://wjro.org.il/the-world-jewish-restitution-organization-wjro-welcomes-groundbreaking-us-government-report-on-property-restitution/ (last visited Jan. 11, 2025).

Then in 2024, in recognition of the twenty-fifth anniversary of the Washington Principles, twenty-five countries endorsed the Best Practices for the Washington Conference Principles on Nazi-Confiscated Art.[88] First and importantly, they clarify that Nazi confiscated art includes "forced sales and sales under duress," in other words flight sales.[89] Second, they specify that a sale by a persecuted person is equivalent to an involuntary transfer of property, creating what looks like a presumption of confiscation for sales by Jews during the Nazi period.[90] Third, in contrast with the vague wording of the original Principles, the best practices are far more direct about what they aim at:

> "Just and fair solutions" means just and fair solutions first and foremost for the victims of the Holocaust (Shoah) and other victims of Nazi persecution and for their heirs. In principle, as set out in the Terezin Declaration, the primary just and fair solution is restitution, among other just and fair solutions.[91]

All of this activity on Holocaust restitution was also having a wider effect. As the twentieth anniversary of the Washington Principles approached, another important development was on the horizon.

Expanding the Reach of Restitution: The Sarr–Savoy Report and Colonial Legacies

During the decades following the creation of the Washington Principles, national Holocaust restitution processes generated return-related activity as well as considerable media coverage. The 2012 Gurlitt Trove discovery of over 1,200 artworks in Germany was one especially dramatic reminder of the scale of how much had been stolen and how little returned.[92] Policy changes and high-profile litigation also kept restitution in the spotlight and increased the pressure to be proactive. By 2018, a combination of these factors was leading to a "steady trickle of returns":

> In October, for instance, officials in New York organized the return of Renoir's "Deux Femmes Dans Un Jardin" to Sylvie Sulitzer, heir of the art collector Alfred

[88] *Best Practices for the Washington Conference Principles on Nazi-Confiscated Art*, U.S. Department of State (Mar. 5, 2024).
[89] *Id.* § B.
[90] *Id.* § C.
[91] *Id.* § D.
[92] *See generally Gurlitt Trove*, Claims Conference WJRO: Looted Art & Cultural Property Initiative, https://art.claimscon.org/work-provenance-research-archives/gurlitt-collection/ (last visited Jan. 11, 2025).

> Weinberger; that same month the Virginia Museum of Fine Arts returned the 16th-century painting "Madonna and Child Enthroned With Saints Nicholas of Tolentino and Sebastian" to Marei von Saher, heir of the Dutch Jewish art dealer Jacques Goudstikker.[93]

This increased attention also raised a challenging question—why only the Holocaust? Other historical takings also seemed ripe for restitution. As former colonial powers and settler societies were coming under pressure on this very issue, France's President Macron set off what has been described as a "tectonic shift."[94] He commissioned a report to examine France's colonial legacy in Africa, in the process giving rise to a new chapter in the restitution revolution.

The idea that Holocaust restitution might have broader implications was certainly not a new one. In 1994, when President Mitterand thanked Chancellor Helmut Kohl for Germany's restitution of twenty-seven French paintings stolen by the Nazis, he observed that museum curators must worry that it may not be possible to contain the example and that a "contagion" may result.[95] And indeed as Holocaust restitution activity and associated publicity ramped up, attention naturally also started to turn to colonial artefacts, especially the vast European collections that were the material legacy of colonialism in Africa.

This was already becoming a heated issue when newly elected French President Emmanuel Macron made his first visit to Africa. He began in Burkina Faso, where he gave a speech at the University of Ouagadougou. He described himself as a new generation who have never known a colonized Africa: "I am from a generation of French people for whom the crimes of European colonization cannot be disputed and are part of our history."[96] In the context of a long speech, he said the following:

> I cannot accept that a large share of several African countries' cultural heritage be kept in France. There are historical explanations for it, but there is no valid, lasting and unconditional justification. African heritage cannot solely exist in private collections and European museums. African heritage must be showcased in Paris but also in Dakar, Lagos and Cotonou; this will be one of my priorities. Within five years I want the conditions to exist for temporary or permanent returns of African heritage to Africa.[97]

[93] Zax, *supra* note 66.
[94] Savoy, *supra* note 2.
[95] *Id.*
[96] President Emmanuel Macron, *Emmanuel Macron's Speech at the University of Ouagadougou*, ÉLYSÉE (Nov. 28, 2017), https://www.elysee.fr/emmanuel-macron/2017/11/28/emmanuel-macrons-speech-at-the-university-of-ouagadougou.en.
[97] *Id.*

A few months later, he commissioned a report from Felwine Sarr and Bénédicte Savoy, and *The Restitution of African Cultural Heritage. Toward a New Relational Ethics* was published in November 2018.[98] Two days later, President Macron announced that he would be returning to Benin twenty-six artworks that France had had since the colonial period, a restitution request that had been rejected only a few years earlier.[99] He also pledged "a temporary or definitive restitution of African heritage to Africa" over the next five years, though as discussed below only halting progress has in fact been made on that promise.[100]

The Sarr–Savoy Report argues for a moral right of restitution of cultural heritage, observing that approximately 90% of all cultural heritage from Sub-Saharan Africa is in Western collections.[101] The report places restitution in the context of larger questions of memory and reparations, exploring in some detail the connection between French colonial administration and the acquisition of African cultural treasures by French institutions. It explicitly points to the deep connection between plunder of precious objects and projects of empire:

> Polybius describes the dual pain that the conqueror inflicts on the conquered by not only depriving him of his cultural heritage, but then inviting him to partake in the humiliating spectacle of passing through the various cities where his home country's objects have now become the mere spoils of plundering.[102]

It explores how "the return of African cultural heritage items can be effectuated," arguing that unless it could be proven that the objects were acquired legitimately, returns not loans are the appropriate response.[103] The argument is that in this colonial context at least, the default assumption should be that colonial takings were wrongful and the burden of persuading otherwise should be borne by the colonial institutions, not the countries of origin.

While on its surface the Sarr–Savoy Report only concerned France, its forceful articulation of the restitutionary imperative in the colonial context was greeted with concern, not only in France but also in other countries that had been colonial powers. Museum directors saw special reasons to worry about the implications for their collections. France's former culture minister Jean-Jacques

[98] Bénédicte Savoy and Felwine Sarr, The Restitution of African Cultural Heritage. Toward a New Relational Ethics (Drew S. Burk trans., 2018).

[99] *See* Clara Cassan, *The Sarr-Savoy Report & Restituting Colonial Artifacts*, Center for Art Law (Jan. 31, 2019), https://itsartlaw.org/2019/01/31/the-sarr-savoy-report-restituting-colonial-artifacts/#_edn2.

[100] *See* Vincent Noce, *France Retreats from Report Recommending Automatic Restitution of Looted African Artefacts*, The Art Newspaper (July 5, 2019).

[101] Savoy & Sarr, *supra* note 98, at 3.

[102] *Id.* at 7.

[103] *Id.* at 5.

Aillagon wrote a piece entitled "Museums have a vocation to keep their African collections." He feared the radical propositions of the report "would empty the museums, and especially the Musée du quai Branly-Jacques Chirac, where the works would be replaced by copies!"[104] A more measured response came from the Museums Association, which noted that the report would "add to growing pressure on museums across Europe to re-examine their approach to the repatriation or restitution of colonial-era objects."[105]

Amid this activity, the 2020 murder of George Floyd heightened the urgency of addressing historic wrongs involving racism. The fact that it followed on the heels of the Sarr–Savoy Report focused attention on colonialism and brought new demands that former powers reckon with their history. It was becoming increasingly untenable to argue that that colonial takings should be treated entirely differently than restitution claims for Nazi-looted art. Those formerly separate domains began to elide along with the acknowledgment that both were "periods of great historical injustice" and the return of colonial takings was also a "moral obligation."[106]

As a result, colonial-era restitution claims gained new levels of traction in the years following 2020. This was particularly true in those jurisdictions that were already grappling with a history of racism and injustice, like both the former European colonial powers and the settler societies that they had established in the 'new world.'[107] By 2024, ARTnews heralded the changing landscape with an editorial entitled "Welcome to the New Era of Restitution and Repatriation."[108] A December 2023 piece in *Town & Country Magazine* summarized the restitutions and repatriations in that year alone.[109] The timeline includes over 100 restitution events and illustrates the range of situations in which the imperative of return was being felt. The month of January, for example, includes returns to Egypt, the Palestinian Authority, Italy, Thailand, descendants of Holocaust victims, and Indigenous communities—a complex mix, with returns coming from museums, countries, and individuals. Among the many striking facts about

[104] *Restitution Report: Museum Directors Respond,* The Art Newspaper (Nov. 27, 2018).

[105] Geraldine Kendal Adams, *Macron Report Advocates Permanent Return of Colonial-Era African Objects,* Museums Association (Nov. 28, 2018), https://www.museumsassociation.org/museums-journal/news/2018/11/28112018-macron-report-repatriation/#.

[106] For an overview of the issue, *see* Amanda Buonaiuto, *From Stolen Heritage to Restitution: The Story Behind Looted Art,* Center for Art Law (May 6, 2024), https://itsartlaw.org/2024/05/06/from-stolen-heritage-to-restitution-the-story-behind-looted-art/.

[107] The British Museum has more than 200,000 African objects, the Weltmuseum in Vienna holds 37,000, the Royal Museum for Central Africa in Belgium has 180,000, the Humboldt Forum has 75,000, and France's leading ethnographic museum, the Quai Branly in Paris has 70,000. *See* Savoy, *supra* note 2.

[108] *Welcome to the New Era of Restitution and Repatriation,* ARTnews (Feb. 19, 2024).

[109] Emily Burack, *Was 2023 the Year Looted Art Returned Home? A Timeline of All the Artwork Repatriated This Year,* Town & Country Magazine (Dec. 15, 2023).

the timeline is the degree of involvement of New York District Attorney Alvin Bragg.[110]

While the level of restitutionary activity is too great to fully cover, highlighting two especially salient examples can illuminate the scope and significance of the changes that are afoot. We will begin with an issue that exemplifies the new era of pressure on European colonial powers and institutions—the Benin Bronzes. The changing view of colonial-era holdings from Africa reverberated throughout Europe, taking many by surprise. The fallout also had special implications for Indigenous belongings in settler societies like those in the United States, Canada, Australia, and New Zealand. Examining the impact of this new era of restitution in that context highlights another important aspect of the changing landscape. These two examples illustrate that the shift cannot be reduced to fact that there are more restitutions, though there certainly are. It is also that in the process of encounters with such profound historic wrongs, the doctrines of restitution themselves are also being reshaped. Just as the pressure from those who had suffered institutional abuse began to reshape private law responsibility, so too has the encounter with historic wrongs been transformative for restitution, giving rise to a new variant more apt to the difficult contexts in which it is increasingly invoked.

The Benin Bronzes

The nineteenth-century looting of the treasures of the Kingdom of Benin looms large in contemporary discussions of restitution. The "Benin Bronzes" are approximately 3,000 items (not all of which are bronzes) taken by the British from the Kingdom of Benin—now part of present-day Nigeria. In 1897, Benin City was sacked by British Forces as punishment for the killing of British citizens in a trade dispute. The city was burned to the ground, thousands were killed, and the Oba (king) was imprisoned. His palace was stripped of precious plaques and statues crafted out of brass, wood, and ivory. These "Bronzes" were sold to museums and private collectors in Britain, Europe, and America. They are considered outstanding works of art, and most of them now reside in important museums—the largest collection is in the British Museum, which holds over 900, and as many as 500 are in the Humboldt Forum in Berlin.[111] They also ended up

[110] For example, Bragg's office played a key role in the return of eleven Schiele artworks over a multiyear period. *See* Tom Masberg & Graham Bowley, *Schiele Artworks Returned to Heirs of Owner Killed by Nazis*, THE NEW YORK TIMES (Sept. 20, 2023); Eileen Kinsella, *Manhattan DA Returns 11th Nazi-Looted Egon Schiele Artwork to Grünbaum Heirs*, ARTNEWS (July 26, 2024).

[111] *See* Alex Greenberger, *The Benin Bronzes, Explained: Why a Group of Plundered Artworks Continues to Generate Controversy*, ARTNEWS (Apr. 2, 2021).

in the hands of private collectors, including the Rockefellers, Fords, Rothschilds, and even Picasso.[112]

The Bronzes are highly symbolic. As one commentator put it, few artefacts "embody this history of rapacious and extractive colonialism better than the Benin Bronzes."[113] For decades, Nigeria—where the historic Kingdom of Benin was located—has been pressing for return. In the 1970s, the Nigerian government asked the British to return the important Queen Idia mask for a cultural festival, but they refused.[114] The year 2010 saw the creation of the Benin Dialogue Group, which brought together Nigerian representatives and European museums, but it was focused on access and loans, not return.[115] And so despite increasing pressure on institutions like the British Museum and the Humboldt Forum, the status quo remained largely undisturbed. But this started to change following the Sarr–Savoy report and the Floyd murder.

Perhaps the most telling example is found in Germany where issues of historic wrongs have special salience. During its period of colonial rule in Namibia, Germany was responsible for what is now considered the first genocide of the twentieth century. Although obscured until recently by the focus on the Holocaust, the increased attention being paid to historic injustices and colonialism was starting to bring these terrible events out of the shadows. Then, the combination of Macron's speech, the Sarr–Savoy Report, and the Floyd murder put new pressure on Germany to respond to its colonial legacy. Even though Britain, not Germany, bore responsibility for the looting, the attention had significant implications for the large collection of Bronzes in Germany's Humboldt Forum and led to dramatic developments that helped to reshape the model for colonial restitution.

Although the ground was shifting even before 2020, the museum world seemed slow to respond. Hermann Parzinger, the president of the foundation that held most of Germany's Benin Bronzes, is a striking example. In 2018, Parzinger proclaimed, "[i]t is too simple to say that they were all stolen and to send them back."[116] But he would not maintain this stance for long. He oversaw the Humboldt Forum which was designed to bring together several collections in a reconstructed Baroque palace in the center of Berlin. The project initially sparked anger because it involved demolishing the former parliament of East

[112] *See* Alex Marshall, *This Art Was Looted 123 Years Ago. Will It Ever Be Returned?* The New York Times (Jan. 29, 2020).

[113] Chris Browne, *Radicals in Conversation*, Pluto Books (2020), https://www.plutobooks.com/blog/podcast-brutish-museums-benin-bronzes-decolonisation/ (last visited Jan. 12, 2025).

[114] *See* Victor Ehikhamenor, *Give Us Back What Our Ancestors Made*, The New York Times (Jan. 28, 2020).

[115] *See* Thomas Rogers et al., *How Germany Changed Its Mind, and Gave the Benin Bronzes Back*, The New York Times (Dec. 22, 2022).

[116] *Id.*

Germany. But the concerns soon also turned to what the new museum would hold, including about 500 Benin Bronzes. In 2017, Bénédicte Savoy, coauthor of what would become the Sarr–Savoy Report, resigned from the Humboldt Forum's advisory board over the approach to Germany's colonial legacy. University of Hamburg historian Jürgen Zimmerer accused the Forum's leaders, including Parzinger, of having "colonial amnesia."[117]

During 2018, Germany began to respond to some of these challenges, including by returning nineteen skulls, five full skeletons, as well as bone and skin fragments to Namibian descendants.[118] In that same year, it also expanded the mandate of the German Lost Art Foundation beyond issues of Nazi and Stasi-looted art to include provenance research into art looted from former colonies.[119] But concerns continued to grow and as the 2019 opening of the Forum approached, then German Chancellor Angela Merkel convened a group of historians and experts to discuss restitution. Their assessment was that Germany needed to reach an agreement with Nigeria about the Bronzes before the Forum's opening.[120] Germany's federal and state cultural ministers quickly approved guidelines for items from "colonial contexts." Those guidelines stipulated that all objects that had been obtained unethically would be liable for return and directed institutions to produce inventories and make them public.[121] Parzinger acknowledged his own changed views, noting that the Bronzes had become "symbolic for colonial-era cultural theft."[122] Zimmerer pointed out how the restitution of Holocaust-looted art had laid the foundation for Germany's groundbreaking change of approach—"[p]eople know that looted art is something you give back," he said.[123]

Pressure for return increased again in 2020 when the Nigerian government announced that it was constructing the Edo Museum of West African Art in Benin City. Germany signed a memorandum of understanding with Nigeria in 2021, and the agreement was finalized in July 2022, just weeks before the Humboldt

[117] *Id. See also* Philip Olterman, *"Inconvenient Truths": Berlin's Humboldt Forum Faces Up to Its Colonial Past*, The Guardian (Sept. 19, 2022).

[118] *See* Shola Lawal, *How to Pay for Genocide: Namibian Victims of German Colonialism Want a Say*, Al Jazeera (Dec. 23, 2023).

[119] *See* Franziska Boehm, *Normative Expectations and the Colonial Past: Apologies and Art Restitution to Former Colonies in France and Germany*, 2 Glob. Stud. Q. 1, 9 (2022).

[120] *See* Rogers et al., *supra* note 115.

[121] *See* Framework Principles for Dealing with Collections from Colonial Contexts Agreed by the Federal Government Commissioner for Culture and the Media, the Federal Foreign Office Minister of State for International Cultural Policy, the Cultural Affairs Ministers of the Länder and the Municipal Umbrella Organizations, Auswärtiges Amt (Eng. trans., Mar. 13, 2019), https://www.auswaertiges-amt.de/resource/blob/2210152/b2731f8b59210c77c68177cdcd3d03de/190412-stm-m-sammlungsgut-kolonial-kontext-en-data.pdf. *See also* Christopher F. Schuetze, *Germany Sets Guidelines for Repatriating Colonial-Era Artifacts*, The New York Times (Mar. 15, 2019).

[122] Rogers et al., *supra* note 115.

[123] *Id.*

Forum's ethnological exhibits opened.[124] As part of this initiative, Germany also pioneered a model for large-scale restitution that enabled the transfer of legal ownership in advance of any artefacts changing hands. Importantly, the transfer of ownership in advance of physical return enabled restitution to the community of origin even where it was not yet in a position to store and exhibit the items.[125] As a result, the Humboldt Forum still displays several dozen Benin Bronzes with signage clarifying that the objects belong to Nigeria. Late in 2022, Germany's foreign minister traveled to Nigeria with twenty of the Benin Bronzes. At the ceremony in Abuja, she handed them to Nigerian officials, saying "[i]t was wrong to take the bronzes, and it was wrong to keep them for 120 years."[126] Many other objects remain in Germany on long-term loan awaiting Nigeria's decisions about their fate.

The German announcement that it would be pursuing restitution both encouraged and pressured others. Just days afterward, Jesus College Cambridge and the University of Aberdeen became the first UK institutions to restitute Bronzes, doing so in consecutive handover ceremonies in October 2021.[127] The master of Jesus College said that the restitution was simply "the right thing to do."[128] Aberdeen University's principal and vice-chancellor echoed this saying that "[i]t would not have been right to have retained an item of such great cultural importance that was acquired in such reprehensible circumstances."[129] Later that year, France made its first real progress on President Macron's 2017 promise by returning twenty-six cultural treasures to Benin.[130] The Smithsonian followed suit in 2022, returning objects that "were stolen from Nigeria during the 1897 British raid on Benin City."[131] The Smithsonian agreement, following the German model, transferred ownership to representatives of Nigeria's National Commission for Museums and Monuments even before the physical transfer was accomplished.[132] A loan agreement allowed nine artworks from Benin

[124] *Id.*

[125] *Id.*

[126] Rogers et al, *supra* note 115.

[127] *See* Vivienne Chow, *After Years of Debate, Two Universities Have Become First U.K. Institutions to Restitute Benin Bronzes*, ARTNET NEWS (Oct. 29, 2021); Alex Greenberger, *Scottish University Becomes First to Repatriate Benin Bronze to Nigeria*, ARTNEWS (Mar. 25, 2021) [hereinafter, Greenberger, *Scottish University*].

[128] Chow, *supra* note 127.

[129] *Id.*

[130] *See France Returns 26 Treasures Looted from Benin*, AL JAZEERA (Nov. 9, 2021).

[131] *Smithsonian Returns 29 Benin Bronzes to the National Commission for Museums and Monuments in Nigeria*, SMITHSONIAN (Oct. 11, 2022), https://www.si.edu/newsdesk/releases/smithsonian-returns-29-benin-bronzes-national-commission-museums-and-monuments.

[132] According to the museum, "[t]he Smithsonian's Shared Stewardship and Ethical Returns Policy calls for the legal transfer of ownership of any artifacts that were acquired by stealing, looting or other questionable means. The transfer of ownership was formalized in a ceremony at the National Museum of African Art two years ago, and the artifacts were shipped to Nigeria a few months later." *See National Museum of African Art Displays Nine Benin Bronzes on Loan from the Government of*

City to remain at the Smithsonian.[133] In 2024, the Smithsonian hosted a special exhibition of those works.[134] The accompanying note refers to the items as originating from the "collection of the Oba of Benin, British raid of Benin 1897," acknowledging them as stolen.[135]

Amid this activity, eyes inevitably turn to the British Museum with the world's largest collection of Bronzes. While the Humboldt Forum and the Smithsonian were implicated because of holding the ill-gotten treasures, for Britain the issue is much more fundamental—their national museum has the Bronzes because their soldiers stole them during a violent raid. Yet despite Nigerian requests, the museum has still not made any significant movement toward return. It does, however, now have a lengthy entry on the Bronzes in a website section on "contested objects"—a section that also includes the Parthenon Marbles and other items.[136] The entry is frank, noting the "widespread destruction and pillage by British forces" as well as the "loot[ing]" by British forces of "thousands of objects of ceremonial and ritual value" taken to the UK as "spoils of war."[137] But it skirts the question of return by stressing the Benin Dialogue Group and its excellent partnerships with Nigerian institutions.[138] The institution's reluctance on this and other issues is one reason that the once-revered institution is now seen by many as an especially "brutish" museum.[139]

Other events have only made the issue more complex. First, came the revelation that a British Museum curator had stolen and sold thousands of items. This undercut the justification that the museum had always relied on—that they were best positioned to safeguard the world's treasures, reflected in the website language that says that the museum "cares for" the Bronzes.[140] When news of the thefts became public, the Government of Nigeria immediately renewed their request for return of the Bronzes.[141] Around the same time, more complexity was added to the mix when the outgoing Nigerian President announced that the returned Benin Bronzes had been given to Oba Ewuare II (enthroned in 2016),

Nigeria, SMITHSONIAN (May 23, 2024), https://www.si.edu/newsdesk/releases/national-museum-african-art-displays-nine-benin-bronzes-loan-government-nigeria.

[133] *Id.*

[134] *Id.*

[135] *Id.*

[136] *Contested Objects from the Collection*, THE BRITISH MUSEUM, https://www.britishmuseum.org/about-us/british-museum-story/contested-objects-collection (last visited Jan. 11, 2025).

[137] *Benin Bronzes*, THE BRITISH MUSEUM, https://www.britishmuseum.org/about-us/british-museum-story/contested-objects-collection/benin-bronzes (last visited Apr. 13, 2025).

[138] *Id.*

[139] DAN HICKS, THE BRUTISH MUSEUMS: THE BENIN BRONZES, COLONIAL VIOLENCE AND CULTURAL RESTITUTION (2020).

[140] *Benin Bronzes*, *supra* note 137.

[141] *See* Gareth Harris, *Nigeria Doubles Down on Restitution Demands Following British Museum Thefts*, THE ART NEWSPAPER (Aug. 25, 2023).

a direct descendant of the ruler that they had been stolen from, who would then determine what would happen to them.[142] While some institutions, such as Cambridge, saw this as a reason to hold off on further return, the Smithsonian took the position that the question of their fate in Nigeria was "none of the Smithsonian's business."[143]

While the fate of many of the Benin Bronzes remains uncertain, especially those in the British Museum, the dynamics have changed dramatically enough that a commentator said that "the move to send swathes of objects in British collections back to where they came from feels inexorable."[144] The long-awaited opening of the Museum of West African Art in Benin City late in 2024 has added to the existing pressure.[145] So too has the early 2025 announcement by the Netherlands that it is returning all of its Bronzes—the largest such return to date.[146] There are also indications that the current British Prime Minister, Keir Starmer, is generally more open to return than his predecessors have been. In the parallel case of the Parthenon Marbles, it has been reported that there is a more conciliatory approach from the newly appointed culture minister, who has indicated that decisions regarding the loan or return of the Parthenon Sculptures are now under review by the British Museum Trustees.[147] In late December 2024, it was reported that a deal that would see their return was "close."[148]

Settler Societies and Indigenous Belongings

As the case of the Benin Bronzes illustrates, connections were increasingly being drawn between Holocaust and colonial-era restitution. The idea that Holocaust restitution principles might apply to colonial contexts was also turning attention beyond Europe to settler societies where Indigenous peoples had been both displaced and dispossessed during the era of colonial expansion:

[142] *See* Alex Marshall, *Who Owns the Benin Bronzes? The Answer Just Got More Complicated*, The New York Times (June 8, 2023); Alicja Zelazko, *Benin Bronzes*, Encyclopedia Britannica (Nov. 23, 2024), https://www.britannica.com/art/Benin-Bronzes.

[143] Marshall, *supra* note 142.

[144] Zoe Strimpel, *Should We Really Send the Benin Bronzes Back to Slave Traders' Descendants?* The Telegraph (May 14, 2023).

[145] *See* Emily Allen, *Museum of West African Art Opens with a Bold Artistic Vision*, African Business (Nov. 22, 2024).

[146] Jonny Walfisz, *Netherlands to Return over 100 Benin Bronzes to Nigeria*, EuroNews (Feb. 20, 2025).

[147] *See Keir Starmer Moves to Return Sculptures to Greece in Bid to Strengthen EU Relations*, Greek City Times (July 30, 2024); Philip Chrysopoulos, *"Open to Return Parthenon Sculptures to Greece," UK Labour Leader Says*, Greek Reporter (July 4, 2024).

[148] *See* Sean Seddon & Kostas Koukoumakas, *Parthenon Sculptures Deal "Close", Ex-Greek Official Says*, BBC News (Dec. 3, 2024).

> The western world is under growing pressure to confront issues around the rightful ownership of art and artifacts as historians, Indigenous leaders and social justice advocates seek to address the historical wrongs that led to misappropriation—from the plundering of art by the Nazis to the systematic harvesting of Indigenous artifacts dating back to the earliest days of colonial exploration.[149]

The parallel between the Holocaust and colonial plunder seemed particularly apt in part because the effort to eradicate Indigenous peoples also involved large-scale confiscation of both human remains and other cultural belongings, often for display in far-flung places:

> [b]elieving the First Nations peoples were a disappearing race and that their sacred artifacts needed to be salvaged, the activities of anthropologists and ethnographers of the time led to the desecration of graves and the removal of totem poles and other traditional objects in order to study them and preserve them for future generations.[150]

A 2022 report by the Canadian Museums Association describes the "collecting frenzy" that accompanied the genocidal practices of colonial actors and observed how museums sought out and traded Indigenous artefacts.[151] This included the Vatican—in 1925, Pope Pius XI commissioned an exhibition of cultural belongings from Catholic missions all over the world, and over 40,000 of those objects became the permanent collection of the new Missionary Ethnological Museum.[152]

Indigenous peoples challenged many of these confiscations and had long advocated for return. But until recently, powerful institutions were reluctant to engage, and there was little progress. However, here too change was afoot, much of it coinciding with rise of activity in the burgeoning area of Holocaust restitution. Just after the fall of the Berlin Wall, the United States began its first serious engagement on Indigenous restitution with the 1990 passage of the *Native American Graves Protection and Repatriation Act* (NAGPRA). It created

[149] Jaela Bernstien, *Canada's Museums Are Slowly Starting to Return Indigenous Artifacts*, MacLean's (June 22, 2021).

[150] Jodi Simkin, United Nations Educational, Scientific and Cultural Organization & Canadian Commission for UNESCO, Creating a New Reality: Repatriation, Reconciliation and Moving Forward (2020), quoting Megan Gough, *The Changing Relationship Between First Nations Peoples and Museums. Our Legacy* (2008).

[151] Canadian Museum Association, Moved to Action: Activating UNDRIP in Canadian Museums 12 (2022).

[152] *Id. See also* the discussion of restitution and the Vatican archives in 39:2 Art Antiquity & L. (2024), including Mayo Moran, *Reparation and Return: Residential Schools, the Vatican Archives and Canada's Band Reparations Settlement*, 29 Art Antiquity & L. 115 (2024).

protocols for the return of human remains, funerary objects, and other holdings to tribes. Premised on the idea "that human remains must at all times be treated with dignity and respect," one of its aims was to "encourage a continuing dialogue between museums and Indian tribes and Native Hawaiian organizations" in order to "promote greater understanding."[153]

In 2007, the United Nations General Assembly adopted the United Nations Declaration on the Rights of Indigenous Peoples (UNDRIP).[154] Passed nearly a decade after the Washington Principles came into being, UNDRIP echoes some elements of those principles, particularly in the emphasis on mechanisms to facilitate return and redress. It affirms the cultural rights of Indigenous peoples and requires that "States shall provide redress through effective mechanisms, which may include restitution, developed in conjunction with indigenous peoples, with respect to their cultural, intellectual, religious and spiritual property taken without their free, prior and informed consent or in violation of their laws, traditions and customs."[155] It makes explicit that Indigenous peoples have "the right to the use and control of their ceremonial objects; and the right to the repatriation of their human remains."[156] It also places an obligation on states to "enable the access and/or repatriation of ceremonial objects and human remains in their possession through fair, transparent and effective mechanisms."[157]

While NAGPRA and UNDRIP were important innovations, progress remained slow for decades. Museums and other institutions were reluctant, and vast collections of Indigenous belongings as well as human remains stayed with those that had amassed them. In Canada, this was despite the fact that the 1996 Royal Commission on Aboriginal Peoples had called for repatriation measures and Indigenous control of interpretation and representation in museums.[158] In 2015, Canada's Truth and Reconciliation Commission underscored this, noting the importance of protecting Indigenous traditional knowledge and calling for a review.[159] In 2022, the Canadian Museums Association published *Moved to Action: Activating UNDRIP in Canadian Museums*. It estimated that 6.7 million Indigenous objects and human remains were held by Canadian institutions and made a range of recommendations.[160] Although there has been some progress, Canada is still without legislation on the issue, and (perhaps for that reason) return is happening more slowly than the Truth and Reconciliation Commission had hoped.

[153] S. Rep. No. 101-473 (1990) (submitted by Sen. Inouye, Select Committee on Indian Affairs).
[154] G.A. Res. 61/295, United Nations Declaration on the Rights of Indigenous Peoples (Oct. 2, 2007).
[155] *Id.* § 11(2).
[156] *Id.* § 12(1).
[157] *Id.* § 12(2).
[158] *See* Canadian Museum Association, *supra* note 151, at 19.
[159] See Truth and Reconciliation Commission of Canada, Calls to Action 8 (2015).
[160] *See* Canadian Museum Association, *supra* note 151, at 54.

A more encouraging approach to return of Indigenous materials is found in Australia. Many of the issues there involve Aboriginal and Torres Strait Islander ancestors and cultural heritage that was for centuries taken overseas and placed in museums, universities, and private collections. Repatriation and return had been on the agenda for some time when the federal government enacted the 2016 *Australian Government Policy on Indigenous Repatriation*. Explicitly referencing UNDRIP, it committed to "addressing the injustice of Australia's shared past as it relates to the removal of ancestral remains and secret sacred objects."[161] That policy charged the Australian Institute of Aboriginal and Torres Strait Islander Studies with responsibility for overseeing the implementation of the Return of Cultural Heritage policy.[162] Similarly, the repatriation process of the National Museum of Australia allows for "the unconditional return of remains and artefacts in line with the aspirations of traditional owners and custodians."[163] And paralleling what we noted with the Benin Bronzes in Germany and in the Smithsonian, the Australian National Museum also states that "[w]here custodians do not have the resources to take remains or secret and sacred objects, the Museum is able to hold them for safe-keeping on the community's behalf"—here too shifting legal title before physical transfer.[164] Individual states have also taken steps to effect return. In 2016, the State of Victoria passed legislative amendments to its Aboriginal Heritage Act 2006 that were described as a "seismic shift," requiring those who had "possession of Secret or Sacred Objects, to transfer the objects into the custody of Council."[165] The amendments also made it clear that "[l]egal ownership of Secret or Sacred Objects is held by the Traditional Owners."[166]

The issue of return of Indigenous material has also prompted some dramatic developments in the United States. Although NAGPRA had been in place since 1990, very little progress had been made. But new federal regulations, effective January 2024, gave institutions five years to prepare human remains and related funerary objects for repatriation. They also required consultation and incorporation of Native American traditional knowledge regarding treatment of human remains or cultural items.[167] But the most consequential of the new requirements

[161] Australian Government Department of Communications and the Arts, Australian Government Policy on Indigenous Repatriation 5 (2016).

[162] *Fact Sheet: International Repatriation of Aboriginal and Torres Strait Islander Ancestors*, Australian Government Department of Communications and the Arts (Nov. 20, 2024), https://www.arts.gov.au/publications/fact-sheet-international-repatriation/.

[163] *Repatriation*, National Museum Australia, https://www.nma.gov.au/about/repatriation (last visited Apr. 13, 2025).

[164] *Id.*

[165] *Secret or Sacred Objects*, Victorian Aboriginal Heritage Council (Feb. 13, 2023), https://www.aboriginalheritagecouncil.vic.gov.au/report-secret-or-sacred-objects.

[166] *Id.*

[167] 43 C.F.R. § 10 (2023).

was the need to "[o]btain free, prior, and informed consent" prior to "exhibition of, access to, or research on human remains or cultural items."[168]

When this new consent requirement came into effect, museums around the country scrambled to close or cover up displays of Native American materials. The American Museum of Natural History announced it would close two major halls that exhibited Native American objects. As the museum's president put it, "[t]he halls we are closing are artifacts of an era when museums such as ours did not respect the values, perspectives and indeed shared humanity of Indigenous peoples."[169] While that closure of nearly 10,000 square feet of exhibition space was the largest reaction, many others followed suit.[170] These dramatic responses reflect the unease of many contemporary institutions with the history behind their collections. *The New York Times* captured the magnitude of the changed understanding when it observed that collections were often amassed "through practices that are now considered antiquated and even odious, including through donations by grave robbers and archaeological digs that cleared out Indigenous burial grounds."[171] This recognition of the suspicious provenance of so much of these Indigenous collections and the fact that major institutions are acting on it tells us a great deal about how the issue has evolved. As we shall see, these changes also reflect larger shifts in the doctrines of restitution itself.

The Evolution of Restitution and the Emergence of the New Variant

The restitution-related activity we have explored is just the tip of the iceberg. But even this is enough to explain the references to the 'restitution revolution.' The term is apt, and not simply because of the dramatic increase in the number of restitutions. In the process of encounters with profound historic wrongs, the doctrine itself has begun to shift. Just as the pressure from those who had suffered institutional abuse started to reshape the core doctrines of private law responsibility, so too has the encounter with historic wrongs given rise to a new variant of the old doctrine of restitution—one more tailored to the difficult contexts in which the principle is increasingly invoked.

[168] *Id.* § 10.1(d)(3).

[169] Julia Jacobs & Zachary Small, *Leading Museums Remove Native Displays Amid New Federal Rules*, The New York Times (Jan. 27, 2024).

[170] *Id.* These include the Field Museum in Chicago, the Peabody Museum of Archaeology and Ethnology at Harvard University, the Cleveland Museum of Art, and the Metropolitan Museum of Art in New York.

[171] *Id.*

As a result, it is now possible to trace two quite different versions of restitution—the more traditional "transactional" version and the emerging "contextual" one.[172] While both are expressions of the underlying principle, there are important differences in how they operate and in what they demand by way of repair. Discussions of historic wrongs often employ both versions of restitution, but it is no accident that the contextual variant has emerged out of efforts to respond to wrongs such as the Holocaust and colonialism that are not only old but are also widespread and systemic in nature.

The transactional version of restitution most closely resembles its traditional legal operation. As the term transactional suggests, it focuses on whether there was a problem with free transfer in a particular transaction and relies on familiar legal concepts such as coercion, duress, and other failures of consent. Restitution claims such as these closely investigate the specific facts at the time of transfer to understand if there was evidence of a failure of consent such as coercion, duress, or fraud. Many modern art restitution cases, particularly those that involve high value works of art, rely on this narrower version of the legal principle. *Woman in Gold* is an example, as is much of the Parthenon Marbles debate, with its emphasis on the legality of Lord Elgin's removal of the Marbles and questions of consent.[173]

Arguments for the return of colonial and Indigenous materials often also invoke this transactional understanding of restitution. Speaking of Indigenous materials held in the Vatican Archives, the Inuit leader said he was not looking to repatriate items given freely but was focused instead on items of "murkier provenance," or those that were not freely given by Inuit to the Church.[174] Pope Francis also relied on the transactional variant when he spoke in favor of return to Indigenous peoples by invoking the Seventh Commandment—"[t]hou shalt not steal."[175]

But while this strand of restitution is undeniably powerful and while it does have an important role to play, it is also increasingly possible to see another variant of the doctrine at work in these cases. This is because the transactional version of restitution leaves in place the background presumption that the transfer was free unless proven otherwise. This means that the claimant seeking return typically has the burden of establishing the *absence* of consent by showing the

[172] I first set out this suggestion in Moran, *supra* note 152.

[173] *See generally* Alexander Herman, The Parthenon Marbles Dispute: Heritage, Law, Politics (2023).

[174] Tavia Grant, *The Pope Supports Restitution of Indigenous Items to Canada. So Why Haven't They Come Home?* The Globe and Mail (Mar. 30, 2024).

[175] *See* Nicole Winifield, *Pope Voices Willingness to Return Indigenous Loot, Artifacts*, Associated Press (Apr. 30, 2023); Grant, *supra* note 174; Elizabeth McSheffrey & Kylie Stanton, *"Overdue": B.C. First Nations Welcome Pope's Hint that Vatican Will Return Indigenous Artifacts*, Global News (May 3, 2023).

presence of force, fraud, duress, or coercion, for example. But while the transactional variant presumes that all transfers are free unless proven otherwise, some of the contemporary restitution developments seem to employ the opposite presumption. In those cases, the presumption instead seems to be that the larger context of a transfer may be so oppressive that it would be inappropriate to simply analyze individual transactions using otherwise ordinary legal ideas such as consent, free transfer, and gift. This 'contextual' approach to restitution instead shifts the default presumption and treats transfers as *not* free unless they are positively proven to be free. The result is that when the contextual approach applies, the holder of the good must affirmatively prove that they received it in a free transfer.

The contextual variant may sound novel but its lineage stretches back at least to Military Law 59's shift in the default presumption for transfers made by targets of Nazi oppression. However, it was not until decades later that this attentiveness to the context of the transfer would start to have broader significance, especially surrounding issues of colonial return. Under the traditional transactional variant, the burden of persuasion is upon the party seeking return to show that there was a flaw in the specific transaction at issue, as we saw in cases like *Woman in Gold* and *Portrait of Wally*. But as restitution was increasingly being asked to do a different kind of work, the assumptions of the traditional transactional approach started to be called into question.

Even before 2020, there were some indications of this shift. A relatively early example can be found in the Australian State of Victoria. Legislative amendments in 2016 made it clear that notwithstanding any purported transfer, legal title was held by the traditional holders of secret or sacred Indigenous materials. The amendments also imposed a blanket requirement that holders of those materials transfer them to the Victorian Aboriginal Heritage Council.[176] Far from the individualized analysis that characterizes the transactional variant, these provisions suggest that the default presumption against transfer of items like these is so strong that return is mandatory.

A similar approach to restitution is suggested in the Sarr–Savoy Report. Within the broader context of French colonialism in Africa, it identified situations in which it could be "presumed" that the objects had been "acquired through inequitable conditions," such as military aggression, from military personnel and through "scientific expeditions." For those kinds of acquisitions, the report recommended "[r]estitution in a swift and thorough manner without any supplementary research regarding their provenance or origins."[177] The shift in presumption, reflected in the almost automatic obligation of return in those

[176] *Secret or Sacred Objects*, *supra* note 165.
[177] SARR & SAVOY, *supra* note 98, at 61.

cases, suggests a move away from the traditional transactional approach in favor of a focus on the larger context of the transfer.

The shifting standards by which restitution would be judged, especially in the colonial setting, also goes some distance to explain why Herman Parzinger was caught off guard in the German discussion of the Benin Bronzes. When he argued that it couldn't be assumed that all of the Bronzes were wrongly acquired, he was relying on the traditional transactional understanding of restitution. While there was outrage at the idea that he was questioning whether the Bronzes had been looted, it seems more likely that he was suggesting that museums may have acquired some of the objects legitimately, presumably as gifts or purchases. But the approach to the Bronzes was being judged by a changing standard. And because the contextual variant is less sensitive to the holder's mode of acquisition, as we saw in the Australian model and as suggested in the Sarr–Savoy recommendation, the intricate analysis that traced exactly how the museums got the Bronzes turned out to be less relevant than the ethics of holding objects that still bore the stain of their original violent acquisition.

The German guidelines for items from colonial contexts also move toward a more contextual approach by casting the shadow of doubt far beyond illegal acquisition such as duress or coercion. Like the Sarr–Savoy recommendation, the guidelines modify the traditional transactional version, in its place creating an emphasis on return for all objects from colonial contexts that had been obtained unethically.[178] They explicitly acknowledge that the context involved "the violent appropriation of cultural objects in the wake of European colonialism" and respond to this oppressive context by adding an ethical standard to the ordinary legal one.[179] In so doing, they place a greater burden of persuasion on those seeking to retain colonial material. The resulting inquiry looks well beyond legal conceptions of consent and tracing of title, and focuses instead on the ethics of acquisition, especially the original acquisition. One of the lessons of the Holocaust, commentators noted, was that "looted art is something you give back."[180]

The case of the Benin Bronzes also points to another important contrast with the traditional approach. Under the transactional variant, as noted, a holder can defend against a claim by showing that they acquired it legitimately, by buying it at a fair price without notice, for example. But the developments with the Bronzes, like the State of Victoria's approach to sacred Indigenous belongings,

[178] Framework Principles for Dealing with Collections from Colonial Contexts, *supra* note 121, § 7 ("[i]dentifying cultural objects from colonial contexts which were appropriated in a way which is no longer legally and/or ethically justifiable and enabling their return is a moral and ethical obligation and an important political task for our age").

[179] *Id.* at 2.

[180] Rogers et al., *supra* note 115.

make it clear that such defences may not always be effective. As noted, Parzinger's efforts to defend retention of the Bronzes by invoking the museum's mode of acquisition missed the fact that this argument may not hold sway with such a violent original acquisition. Something similar was apparent when the University of Aberdeen returned its Bronze saying that it was not right for them to retain something "of such great cultural importance that was acquired in such reprehensible circumstances."[181] This was despite the fact that the item had been purchased at an auction. An approach along these lines suggests that sometimes the context of the original taking was so oppressive that its stain follows the object, and the only appropriate response is return.

The new NAGPRA regulations also underscore the force of the case for return when the context of the transfer was so oppressive that it generates a presumption against consent. The regulations are premised on the idea that the colonial setting in which Indigenous material was taken was such that it gave rise to a general presumption of Indigenous non-consent. This is what explains why the onus is placed on those who hold the material to affirmatively establish that they actually were given consent.[182] And as became clear, museums themselves seemed to lack confidence that they could comprehensively show they did have consent. Moreover, like the German guidelines and Victoria's legislation, the NAGPRA regulations are not concerned with the latest acquisition of the items but rather with the quality of the original transfer. The fact that some museums may well have purchased the items for fair value without notice or received them as gifts does not obviate the requirement for original consent. This makes it clear how much distance there can be between the traditional transactional approach to restitution and its contextual counterpart.

This emerging contextual approach to restitution has much in common with efforts to undo the massive theft from the Jewish population that accompanied the Holocaust. As noted above, American Military Law 59 was designed to ensure the speedy restitution of property from those who had been wrongly deprived of it during the Nazi era. Like some of the recent developments, especially in colonial contexts, it displaced the ordinary presumption, instead creating a presumption that some kinds of transfers were inherently suspect. By specifying that transfers between 1933 and 1945 from those who had been persecuted were prima facie "confiscations," it forced the party seeking to retain the property to show otherwise.[183] It also displaced other presumptions, including that of good faith purchase (other than where specifically provided for), and it rejected many purported transfers under power of law. Although Military Law 59 failed to

[181] Greenberger, *Scottish University*, *supra* note 127.
[182] 43 C.F.R. § 10.1(d)(3) (2023).
[183] Military Government, *supra* note 38, § 3(1).

achieve its objective for a range of reasons, it remains an important precedent and can be seen as a precursor to the adaptation of restitution that is now coming to the fore, particularly for takings from deeply oppressive contexts. It is testament to that approach that its spirit can now be felt at work in efforts such as those that aim to come to terms with colonial takings.

Conclusion

The restitution revolution has had a profound impact. Claims for return that had languished for decades or sometimes even centuries have started to gain traction, shaking institutions out of their complacency. From Holocaust cases involving stolen masterpieces to the Benin Bronzes scattered throughout the world's most important museums to Indigenous belongings held everywhere from the Vatican to the Museum of Natural History, the changed attitude to questions of retention and return is one very dramatic manifestation of how the wrongs of the past have come to be pressing contemporary problems of justice.

Institutions are coming under new and powerful pressure to understand the history of their holdings and that history is often unsettling. Issues of origin and provenance have gone from the margins of consideration to the very center. Museums, galleries, and auction houses are employing specialists in provenance, often with a special focus on Holocaust and colonial takings. Their websites are changing in important ways as well, and many of them now directly address concerns about the origins of what is in their collections. Those that were once reluctant such as the Humboldt Forum, the Rijksmuseum, and even the Vatican, are now engaging in return-related activities, sometimes at unprecedented levels. Even the British Museum—often now negatively viewed as an outlier on restitution—has a section on its website that has extensive discussions of the "contested objects" in its collection.

In this sense, the restitution revolution has rapidly become a very powerful and high-profile illustration of the imperative of making amends for historic injustice. And as issues such as the Holocaust and colonialism illustrate, it also has deep connections to the other reparations side of historic wrongs. These connections are dynamic, and developments on one issue often fuel demands on the other. This is particularly true for vast wrongs like colonialism and even slavery, and it is to that frontier of redressing old wrongs that we will now turn.

6
Reckoning with the Great Wrongs of History: Colonialism and Slavery

Introduction

Thus far we have traced the growing power of reparative justice and the increasingly wide array of historic wrongs it has engaged. And while the examples have been anchored in grievous wrongs to the person and to personal property, they often reach far beyond that. Cases such as those involving the Holocaust, institutional abuse, residential schools, eugenics, and the comfort women all recast those personal injury claims more forcefully in the language of injustice, as did the demands for the return of stolen belongings. But those claims, as we also noted, often connected particular wrongs to wider issues such as discrimination, dehumanization, genocide, and plunder. In this way, the reach into the past also began to force a reckoning with much vaster old wrongs like colonialism and slavery. And while the remedies for wrongs of this scale and antiquity inevitably differ in many ways from the response to those where the injuries are more particularized, even wrongs as vast as these are increasingly understood as injustices that demand some kind of repair.

Atoning for Colonialism

Until very recently the idea that there might be a duty to repair colonial abuses would have seemed very far-fetched. Like issues of war, colonial history was seen as well outside of the reach of reparative justice. The complications of time, distance, and scale, as well as the exploitation and violence at the very heart of the institution made it an unlikely context for arguments about redress. Here too however, things began to change and as in our other examples, the pace of that change picked up in the wake of 2020. Canada's residential schools settlement was an early harbinger of what was to come. It began to bring reparative justice demands to bear directly on colonial law and policy, in the process opening the door to the idea that colonialism itself could be the kind of wrong that demands repair. The years since that landmark settlement have seen the growth of other demands to atone both for colonial violence and for dispossession, matters that

Making Amends for Historic Wrongs. Mayo Moran, Oxford University Press. © Mayo Moran 2025.
DOI: 10.1093/9780190927295.003.0006

once seemed far outside of the duty to repair. Those demands have prompted some important efforts to make progress on redress and restitution although the magnitude of the issues and the complicated interactions between reparative justice and more distributive issues make remedy a very complex matter. Still the fact that reparative justice demands are being brought to bear, and with some success, on colonialism itself is testimony to the magnitude of the change in our understanding of the past.

Residential Schools and Colonial Reckonings

Canada's residential schools settlement, as we have noted, gave rise to the first truth commission in an established democracy as well as the first major reparations schemes for colonial abuse. In addition to this important role in shaping a new and transformative approach to historic institutional abuse, it also opened the door to a more direct reckoning with colonialism. The early residential schools claims focused on the grievous personal injuries suffered by Indigenous children. But by including claims based on acts that were legal at the time like the forced removal of children, they also reached beyond the grievous abuses of the system. The increasing emphasis on loss of language and culture began to implicate not just colonial law, but also the entire project with its avowed aim to "kill the Indian in the child."[1] Colonialism was a dominant theme in the *Final Report of the Truth and Reconciliation Commission*, the Common Experience Payment addressed colonial assimilation policy, and the prime minister's apology acknowledged that it was the whole system that was wrong. Other litigation also began to address the gaps in the original settlement and in 2023, the federal government signed an agreement with Indigenous bands that represented an entirely new phase in colonial reckoning.

The *Gottfriedson* class action was filed in 2012. The first part related to "day scholars" left out of the original agreement, and it settled in 2021.[2] The other branch—the "Band Reparations" claim—was a frontal assault on colonialism. It argued that the Government of Canada was responsible for damages caused by the Indian residential schools system, including "collective loss of language

[1] A commonly used phrase, it has been attributed to Duncan Campbell Scott, but Mark Abley attributes the phrase to an American military officer. *See* Andrew Stobo Sniderman, *The Man Wrongly Attributed with Uttering "Kill the Indian in the Child,"* MacLean's (Nov. 8, 2013). However, Campbell Scott, who served as the Deputy Superintendent of the Department of Indian Affairs, made similar comments and oversaw assimilationist policies toward Indigenous peoples. *See* Robert L. McDougall, *Duncan Campbell Scott*, The Canadian Encyclopedia (Jan. 18, 2008), https://www.thecanadianencyclopedia.ca/en/article/duncan-campbell-scott.

[2] *See* Residential School Day Scholars, https://www.justicefordayscholars.com/ (last visited Jan. 3, 2025); Settlement Agreement, McLean et al. v. Her Majesty the Queen in Right of Canada, No. T-2169-16 (Can. Fed. Ct., Mar. 12, 2019).

and culture and damage to the social fabric."[3] As the Federal Court of Appeal summarized it, "[t]he alleged fault is that the Crown conceived, implemented and administered a residential schools policy which was intended to and caused Indian day students to lose their identity."[4] The law and policy, the plaintiffs argued, were the legal wrongs.

This was a bold argument. Recall that early in the *Blackwater* litigation, the government *defended* itself by arguing that it was not the abuse but the system itself that caused most of the children's harm.[5] That "distasteful" argument reflected their confidence that the mere operation of the system could never give rise to damages because it was legal at the time. By the time of the Indian Residential Schools Settlement Agreement, the idea that the whole system was a wrong was gaining some traction. But the argument was not made head on until *Gottfriedson*. And even ten years into that litigation, the federal government was still arguing that while it "may have contributed" to the loss of language and culture, "such losses were not as a result of any unlawful acts or omissions of Canada or its employees or agents"—in other words, the same 'bad but legal system' argument that it had relied on for decades.[6]

But in 2021, hundreds of unmarked graves were discovered on the grounds of the former Catholic residential school that was in the traditional territory of lead plaintiff Shane Gottfriedson.[7] While this tragic discovery was not unexpected—and in fact many others followed—it created new momentum on many Indigenous issues. In January 2023, the parties announced the $2.8 billion dollar Band Reparations settlement.[8] That groundbreaking settlement directly compensated Indigenous communities for the first time for the loss of language and culture—the very results that were intended by the residential schools system. The Government of Canada said that it sought to "address the collective

[3] Waddell Phillips Professional Corporation, *Waddell Phillips Professional Corporation, Peter Grant Law, and Diane Soroka Advocate Inc.—First Nations Sign Historic Settlement Agreement with Canada to Address Collective Harms Caused by Indian Residential Schools*, Globe Newswire (Jan. 21, 2023).

[4] Gottfriedson v. Canada (Attorney General), 2014 FCA 55 (Can.), per Noel J.A., ¶ 1.

[5] As Brenner J. noted, "even the defendants concede" that the children were placed "in a severely compromised position by reason of their forced attendance" at Indian residential schools. Blackwater v. Plint, 2001 BCSC 997, ¶ 336 (Can.).

[6] Anna Bradley-Smith, *Canadian Federal Government Denies Reparations for Cultural Damage to Aboriginal People Caused by Residential Schools*, Top Class Actions (Feb. 16, 2022), https://ca.topclassactions.com/lawsuit-settlements/civil-rights/canadian-federal-government-denies-liability-reparations-for-cultural-damage-caused-by-residential-schools/.

[7] *See e.g. Calls to Find All Canada's Indigenous Unmarked Graves After School Discovery*, The Guardian (June 24, 2021); Ian Austen, *With Discovery of Unmarked Grades, Canada's Indigenous Seek Reckoning*, The New York Times (June 26, 2021).

[8] *See* Brett Forester, *Trial Put on Hold in Residential School Reparations Class Action After Parties Agree to Negotiate*, CBC News (Sept. 28, 2022); *Settlement Agreement Reached in Band Class Litigation*, Government of Canada (Jan. 23, 2023), https://www.canada.ca/en/crown-indigenous-relations-northern-affairs/news/2023/01/settlement-agreement-reached-in-gottfriedson-band-class-litigation.html.

harm" it had caused, particularly the loss of language, culture, and heritage.[9] The lead plaintiff said it was about "taking steps towards undoing the damage that was done to our Nations."[10] Marking the first such compensation for bands themselves, the settlement funds "the four pillars of revival, protection, promotion and wellness of Indigenous languages and cultures."[11] Until this settlement, most compensation was directed toward the abuses of the residential school system. The Band Reparations settlement targeted something very different—the ordinary and intended operation of the residential schools system, marking a new kind of reckoning with colonialism. Because of both this novelty and the broader implications for colonial reparations, the Band Reparations settlement was reported in news media all over the world.[12]

The Band Reparations settlement was certainly a striking development, but it took place in a context of wider efforts to press for a more direct reckoning with colonialism. Non-governmental organizations such as the International Center for Transitional Justice and the European Center for Constitutional and Human Rights had already expanded their mandates to include issues of historic injustice in non-transitional contexts. This was helping to connect the conversation about responsibility for historic wrongs with the legacies of colonialism.[13] At the same time, a different kind of "engaged history" had begun to turn a more critical lens on large scale historical events like colonialism and slavery.[14] And while this rankled some in the history establishment, it also resonated with advocates around the globe considering how to hold former colonial powers to account.[15] A striking early example and landmark development in the reckoning with

[9] *$2.8-Billion Settlement Reached in Class Action Lawsuit over Residential Schools*, CBC News (Jan. 21, 2023).

[10] Sabine Mannitz & Rita Theresa Kopp, *A Step Towards Justice: Canada Agrees to Compensate First Nations for Loss of Culture and Language*, PRIFF Blog (Jan. 31, 2023), https://blog.prif.org/2023/01/31/a-step-towards-justice-canada-agrees-to-compensate-first-nations-for-loss-of-culture-and-language/.

[11] *$2.8-Billion Settlement Reached*, *supra* note 9.

[12] *See e.g.* Ian Austen, *Canada Settles $2 Billion Suit over "Cultural Genocide" at Residential Schools*, The New York Times (Jan. 21, 2023); *Canada Settles Residential School Reparations Class-Action Lawsuit*, Reuters (Jan. 21, 2023); *Canada Settles Residential School Reparations Class-Action Lawsuit*, Reuters (Jan. 21, 2023); Mannitz & Kopp, *supra* note 10; *Canada Settles Residential School Reparations Lawsuit*, Al Jazeera (Jan. 22, 2023); Karen Graham, *$2.8-Billion Settlement Reached in Class-Action Lawsuit over Residential Schools*, Digital Journal (Jan. 22, 2023).

[13] The International Center for Transitional Justice was founded in 2001. While its early focus was understandably on regime change, as historic injustice issues outside of that context grew in significance, the Center broadened its work. *See Our Story*, International Center for Transitional Justice, https://www.ictj.org/our-story (last visited Jan. 3, 2025). *See also* European Center for Constitutional and Human Rights, Colonial Repercussions: Namibia—115 Years After the Genocide of the Ovaherero and Nama (2019).

[14] Adom Getachew, *Engaged History: An Introduction*, 127 Am. Hist. Rev. 793, 795 (2022). For the role of the engaged historian in the conflicts of the day, see The Engaged Historian: Perspectives on the Intersections of Politics, Activism and the Historical Profession (Stefan Berger ed., 2019).

[15] *See generally* David Frum, *The New History Wars: Inside the Strife Set Off by an Essay from the President of the American Historical Association*, The Atlantic (Oct. 30, 2022).

colonialism is found in the UK litigation against the British Government for the brutal suppression of the Mau Mau rebellion in Kenya that occurred over six decades before the case was finally brought to court.[16]

The United Kingdom and Kenya: *Mutua* and the Mau Mau Uprising

In 1952, years of growing discontent with British colonial rule in Kenya erupted into open rebellion in the "Mau Mau Uprising." The colonial administration brutally crushed the rebellion. Suspects were sent to concentration camps that employed abuse, torture, and summary execution. Even by the official count there was massive displacement, hundreds of thousands of arrests, 80,000 people detained, and nearly 12,000 rebels killed. But following independence in 1963, Kenya adopted a policy of "collective amnesia." Kenyans were told to "forgive and forget the past."[17] And for many decades, silence indeed did reign. But in 1998, a memoir describing brutal rapes by a British police officer in a detention camp shattered the silence.[18] In 2002, the Kenyan Human Rights Commission started cataloguing colonial-era violence, and when the ban on the Mau Mau was lifted in 2003, the Mau Mau War Veterans Association approached the Commission to help bring a lawsuit against the United Kingdom. In 2009, after many years of work, law firm Leigh Day brought a case in the United Kingdom on behalf of the veterans, demanding Britain compensate survivors for the torture they suffered.[19] As the case proceeded, the Kenyan Human Rights Commission and Leigh Day continued the investigations, eventually naming over 5,000 victims.[20]

Historians played a pivotal and controversial role in the case. In 2005, Harvard's Carolyn Elkins published her explosive first book, *Imperial Reckoning: The Untold Story of Britain's Gulag in Kenya*.[21] Based on oral testimony and the discovery of long hidden British archival material, it described "a murderous campaign to eliminate Kikuyu people, a campaign that left tens

[16] *See* Mutua v. Foreign & Commonwealth Office, [2011] EWHC (QB) 1913 (Eng.); Mutua v. Foreign & Commonwealth Office, [2012] EWHC (QB) 2678 (Eng.).

[17] Marc Perry, *Uncovering the Brutal Truth About the British Empire*, THE GUARDIAN (Aug. 18, 2016).

[18] WAMBUI OTIENO, MAU MAU'S DAUGHTER: A LIFE HISTORY (1998). *See also* Shola Adenekan, *Wambui Otieno Mbugua Obituary*, THE GUARDIAN (Oct. 18, 2011).

[19] *See The Mau Mau Claims*, LEIGH DAY, https://www.leighday.co.uk/International/Further-insights/Detailed-case-studies/The-Mau-Mau-claims/The-Mau-Mau-claimants (last visited Jan. 3, 2025); Jose Miguel Calatayud & Phil Moore, *"We are the Mau Mau": Kenyans Share Stories of Torture*, AL JAZEERA (May 5, 2016).

[20] *The Mau Mau Claims*, *supra* note 19.

[21] CAROLINE ELKINS, IMPERIAL RECKONING: THE UNTOLD STORY OF BRITAIN'S GULAG IN KENYA (2005).

of thousands, perhaps hundreds of thousands, dead."[22] When Elkins became an expert witness in the Mau Mau case, many in the history establishment were skeptical.[23] But on the eve of the trial, the government was forced to acknowledge that it did have thousands of secret colonial-era documents in a Hanslope Park repository.[24] Those documents validated Elkins's work, which was credited with laying "the ground for a legal case that has transformed our view of Britain's past."[25]

Early on, the government expressed confidence in their case based on "well-established aspects of constitutional and international law."[26] But that early confidence was misplaced. The judge said it was "dishonourable" when the government tried to distance itself from the massacre by pointing to the transfer of power to Kenyan authorities upon independence. The revelation about the secret Hanslope repository was another severe blow. Then, in July 2011, Justice McCombe said there was ample evidence of systematic torture and concluded "that the claimants have a properly arguable case that there was a duty of care owed by the UK Government."[27] The government then pivoted, arguing instead that the claimants had taken too long to bring their action.[28] But in a 2012 hearing, the judge disagreed and held that the claim could proceed to trial.[29] The government immediately moved to settle the case.

In that settlement, the United Kingdom agreed to pay £13.9 million, which amounted to £2,658 to each of the 5,228 victims.[30] It also paid £6 million to the Leigh Day law firm.[31] In Parliament, Foreign Secretary William Hague made British history when he stated as follows:

> ... I would like to make clear now and for the first time, on behalf of Her Majesty's Government, that we understand the pain and grievance felt by those who were involved in the events of the Emergency in Kenya. The British Government recognises that Kenyans were subject to torture and other forms of ill treatment at the hands of the colonial administration. The British Government sincerely regrets that these abuses took place, and that they marred Kenya's progress

[22] *Id.* at xv–xvi.

[23] *See* Perry, *supra* note 17; Tim Adams, Legacy of Violence: A History of the British Empire *by Caroline Elkins Review—The Brutal Truth About Britain's Past*, THE GUARDIAN (Mar. 13, 2022).

[24] *See* Perry, *supra* note 17.

[25] *Id.*

[26] Owen Bowcott, *Kenyans Sue UK for Alleged Colonial Human Rights Abuses*, THE GUARDIAN (Apr. 5, 2011).

[27] Mutua v. Foreign & Commonwealth Office, [2011] EWHC (QB) 1913 (Eng.), ¶ 138.

[28] *See* Daniel Leader, *The Mau Mau Litigation—Justice At Last*, OXFORD HUMAN RIGHTS HUB (Nov. 3, 2015), http://ohrh.law.ox.ac.uk/the-mau-mau-litigation-justice-at-last/.

[29] Mutua v. Foreign & Commonwealth Office, [2012] EWHC (QB) 2678 (Eng.).

[30] *See* Daniel Howden & Kim Sengupta, *59 Years Late—but Mau Mau Accept an Almost Apology*, THE INDEPENDENT (June 7, 2013).

[31] *Id.*

towards independence. Torture and ill treatment are abhorrent violations of human dignity which we unreservedly condemn.[32]

The government also supported the construction of a memorial to the victims. At the unveiling in Nairobi in 2015, the British High Commissioner made a public statement to members of the Mau Mau War Veterans' Association in Kenya, expressing Britain's "sincere regret for the abuses that took place."[33]

Mutua certainly broke new ground in the reckoning with colonialism, but it was not without serious difficulties. And while it raised the hopes of other survivors of colonial wrongs, it also highlighted concerns about litigating historic injustice.[34] The settlement itself was controversial because of the contrast between the very substantial legal fees and the very small awards to those who had suffered horrific injuries like castration, torture, and sexual abuse.[35] Worries about lawyer conduct were amplified in a second suit filed on behalf of as many as 40,000 claimants who said they had been left out of the first settlement.[36] The memorial erected in Nairobi was also controversial. The Mau Mau War Veterans Association objected to the lack of consultation and the portrayal of history, as well as to the presence of the United Kingdom High Commissioner at the unveiling.[37]

Despite these important concerns, *Mutua* was also seen as a critical milestone that held promise for moving forward the larger goals of redress for colonialism and slavery.[38] Shortly after the "stunning legal victory" in *Mutua,* Carolyn Elkins

[32] Foreign & Commonwealth Office, *Statement to Parliament on Settlement of Mau Mau Claims*, GOVERNMENT OF THE UNITED KINGDOM (June 6, 2013), https://www.gov.uk/government/news/statement-to-parliament-on-settlement-of-mau-mau-claims.

[33] Christian Turner, *Speech: UK-Kenya Shared History: Recognition and Reconciliation*, GOVERNMENT OF THE UNITED KINGDOM (Sept. 12, 2015), https://www.gov.uk/government/speeches/uk-kenya-shared-history-recognition-and-reconciliation.

[34] Owen Bowcott, *Claim that MP Lied About Kenya Massacre "May be in Contempt of Parliament,"* THE GUARDIAN (Mar. 21, 2017).

[35] The Law Society of Kenya challenged the fees on the ground that they were out of proportion with the compensation extended to survivors. *See* Patrick Sawer, *British Law Firm "Inflated" Mau Mau Compensation Costs to Taxpayer*, THE TELEGRAPH (Oct. 19, 2014).

[36] *See e.g.* Abiud Ochieng, *Mau Mau Case Hit by Row Among Lawyers*, DAILY NATION (Kenya, June 19, 2018). Kimathi & Ors. v. Foreign & Commonwealth Office, [2018] EWHC 2066 (QB), *aff'd* [2018] EWCA Civ 2213. *See* Chapter 7 on issues concerning lawyers.

[37] *See* Lydiah Nyawira, *Mau Mau Veterans Disown Freedom Monument*, THE SUNDAY STANDARD, https://www.standardmedia.co.ke/article/2000177509/mau-mau-veterans-disown-freedom-monument (last visited Jan. 4, 2025).

[38] *See* Jennifer Balint, *The "Mau Mau" Legal Hearings and Recognizing the Crimes of the British Colonial State: A Limited Constitutive Moment*, 3 CRIT. ANALYSIS L. 261 (2016); Juliana Appiah et al., *Architecture of Denial: Imperial Violence, the Construction of Law and Historical Knowledge During the Mau Mau Uprising, 1952–1960*, 14 AFR. J. LEG. STUD. 3 (2022); Regina Menachery Paulose & Ronald Gordon Rogo, *Addressing Colonial Crimes Through Reparations: The Mau Mau, Herero and Nama*, 7 STATE CRIME & COLONIALISM 369 (2018). The revelation about the Hanslope repository generated considerable interest. *See e.g.* John Darwin, *Last Days of Empire*, *in* THE ENDS OF EUROPEAN COLONIAL EMPIRES 268 (Miguel Bandeira Jerónimo & António Costa eds., 2015); Aoife Duffy, *Legacies of British Colonial Violence: Viewing Kenyan Detention Camps Through the Hanslope*

observed that it should be the first of many and that the "rest of the empire is still waiting."[39] Others considered Mau Mau-style actions for similar colonial brutality and for slavery.[40] As with residential schools, what started in the "particularist voice" of tort law marshaled that unique insistence to demand repair for the brutality of colonialism, in the process forcing "open the prism of the British colonial enterprise."[41] In this way, *Mutua* helped to make "reparative justice for colonial state crimes . . . a timely issue to discuss," one with vast implications.[42] And indeed issues of reckoning with colonialism have grown exponentially. Though the activity is now far too vast to explore in full, looking at some particularly important examples will serve to illuminate the larger dynamics. Let us begin with a prominent quest for colonial redress arising out of what is often considered to be the twentieth century's first genocide.

Germany and Namibia

In 1904 in what is now Namibia, the Herero and Nama peoples rose up against German settlers who were taking their land and cattle. They were met with a violent campaign of ethnic extermination in which tens of thousands of people were murdered, some in concentration camps. The quest for redress began immediately, and by the time of the Paris Peace Conference, the Herero and Nama peoples had already compiled the *Blue Book* report that helped convince delegates to deny Germany the return of its former colonies.[43] Sadly, the territory went instead to South Africa's white settler regime, which eventually introduced apartheid.[44] However, the Herero and Nama continued their quest, and in 1985, United Nations Special Rapporteur Benjamin Whitaker finally described the

Disclosure, 33 L. & HIST. REV. 489 (2015); Richard Drayton, *Britain's Secret Archive of Decolonisation*, HISTORY WORKSHOP (Apr. 19, 2012), http://www.historyworkshop.org.uk/britains-secret-archive-of-decolonisation/. One reporter allowed into the archive described "rows of historic documents on shelves with labels like 'Sierra Leone Arms Investigation,' 'Compensation of victims of Nazi persecution case files' . . . and 'Slave Trade Correspondence' from 1858–1859." Katie Engelhart, *The UK Government Has Opened Up Thousands of Secret Files to the Public*, VICE (May 14, 2014).

[39] Caroline Elkins, *Britain Has Said Sorry to the Mau Mau. The Rest of the Empire Is Still Waiting*, THE GUARDIAN (June 7, 2013).

[40] *See* Godfrey Mapondera, *Malawians Seek Compensation for Nyasaland Massacre During British Rule*, THE GUARDIAN (Apr. 20, 2015); Ben Fox, *Caribbean Nations Seeking Compensation for Slavery*, ASSOCIATED PRESS (Jul. 25, 2013).

[41] Balint, *supra* note 38, at 285.

[42] Paulose & Rogo, *supra* note 38, at 384.

[43] *See* Fabian Krautwald, *Namibia's Long History of Anti-Colonial Justice*, LONDON SCHOOL OF ECONOMICS (Feb. 9, 2023), https://blogs.lse.ac.uk/africaatlse/2023/02/09/namibias-long-history-of-anti-colonial-justice/.

[44] *Id.*

massacres as one of the twentieth century's first genocides.[45] However, Germany did not take the first step toward acknowledgment until 1998, and even then President Herzog did not apologize but only expressed regret. In 2004, on the 100th anniversary, the German development aid minister went further, officially accepting the state's "historic and moral responsibility" but avoiding the term genocide.[46] In 2007, the family of General von Trotha, who had ordered the killings of Herero people, came to Omaruru to publicly apologize, saying that the family was "deeply ashamed of the terrible events that took place 100 years ago."[47]

Although the Herero and Nama faced many obstacles, they were determined in their advocacy. This included launching two Alien Torts Statute claims in the United States against the Federal Republic of Germany and German companies, the first in 2001 and a second in 2017.[48] Although the actions did not succeed, the litigation helped to force the reluctant Namibian government into negotiations. In 2015, the German government and Namibia finally sat down to develop a more comprehensive response to the genocide. The 2021 "Reconciliation Agreement" included a detailed official apology for genocide as well as a €1.1 billion program for projects related to the "development of descendants of the particularly affected communities," as well as "projects on reconciliation, remembrance, research and education."[49] Germany, however, insisted that that "[r]eparations or individual compensations are not subject of the negotiations," noting that "[a]fter 100 years they would be unprecedented."[50]

Perhaps unsurprisingly, the Reconciliation Agreement was controversial. The question of who was at the table was especially fraught. The Herero and Nama were excluded from the negotiations, something they said was a violation of international law.[51] Descendants of survivors also argued they should have been

[45] U.N. Special Rapporteur of the Sub-Commission on Prevention of Discrimination and Protection of Minorities, Benjamin Whitaker, *Revised and Updated Report on the Question of the Prevention and Punishment of the Crime of Genocide*, U.N. Doc. E/CN.4/Sub.2/1985/6 (July 2, 1985).

[46] Andrew Meldrum, *German Minister Says Sorry for Genocide in Namibia*, THE GUARDIAN (Aug. 16, 2004).

[47] *German Family's Namibia Apology*, BBC NEWS (Oct. 7, 2007).

[48] Hereros ex rel. Riruako v. Deutsche Afrika-Linien Gmblt & Co., 232 Fed. Appx. 90 (3d Cir. 2007); Rukoro v. Federal Republic of Germany, 363 F. Supp. 3d 436 (S.D.N.Y. 2019), *aff'd* 976 F.3d 218 (2d Cir. 2020). *See Herero and Nama Groups Sue Germany over Namibia Genocide*, BBC NEWS (Jan. 6, 2017).

[49] Joint Declaration by the Federal Republic of Germany and the Republic of Namibia, United in Remembrance of Our Colonial Past, United in Our Will to Reconcile, United in Our Vision of the Future (Mar. 15, 2025); *Germany's Genocide in Namibia: Deal Between the Two Sides Falls Short of Delivering Justice*, THE CONVERSATION (Jan. 7, 2025), https://theconversation.com/germanys-genocide-in-namibia-deal-between-the-two-governments-falls-short-of-delivering-justice-246719.

[50] Philip Oltermann, *Germany Rules Out Financial Reparations for Namibia Genocide*, THE GUARDIAN (May 21, 2021).

[51] *See* Stefan Talmon, *Germany Not Answerable in U.S. Courts for Alleged Colonial Genocide*, GERMAN PRACTICE IN INTERNATIONAL LAW (Dec. 9, 2020), https://gpil.jura.uni-bonn.de/2020/

at the table and noted that, unlike in the Holocaust case, there was neither individual reparations nor land restitution.[52] In January 2023, after failed attempts to renegotiate elements of the agreement, the affected communities brought an action to nullify the agreement in the High Court of Namibia, stressing the absence of consultation and participation.[53] However, that action was postponed, and in December of 2024, Namibia announced that the two countries had reached a landmark decision "related to the signing of the Joint Declaration on the Genocide, Apology and Reparations between the Namibian and German governments."[54] While concerns remain and the fate of the amended agreement is uncertain, it has had an impact on the broader reckoning with colonialism. Among other things, the increased discussion of the genocide is leading institutions to begin to take steps to address their own legacies. The Berlin Ethnological Museum, for example, decided to return a collection of Namibian antiquities as "part of reparations for a period of colonial rule."[55]

Attention also began to turn to the larger issue of land restitution, and efforts appear to be underway to create the foundation for claims to redress those losses. The European Center for Constitutional and Human Rights in collaboration with the UK-based Forensic Architecture is using archival materials, photographs, and oral testimony to create "advanced 3D models of sites of atrocities" with the aim of generating "digital evidence that can be leveraged in support of demands for land restitution and reparations."[56] Groundbreaking coverage by *Der Spiegel*

12/germany-not-answerable-in-u-s-courts-for-alleged-colonial-genocide/; *Namibia Asks to Renegotiate Genocide Deal with Germany*, AfricaNews (Aug. 13, 2024).

[52] *See* Norimitsu Onishi & Melissa Eddy, *A Forgotten Genocide: What Germany Did in Namibia, and What It's Saying Now*, The New York Times (May 28, 2021); Nosmot Gbadamosi, *Namibia Calls for Reparations Talks with Germany*, Foreign Policy (Mar. 13, 2024), https://foreignpolicy.com/2024/03/13/namibia-calls-for-reparations-talks-with-germany/; *Viewpoint: Why German's Namibia Genocide Apology Is Not Enough*, BBC News (May 31, 2021). On the striking linkages between the Holocaust, eugenics, and colonialism, *see* Heike Becker, *Germany's Namibia Genocide Apology: The Limits of Decolonizing the Past*, Review of African Political Economy (June 22, 2021), https://roape.net/2021/06/22/germanys-namibia-genocide-apology-the-limits-of-decolonizing-the-past/.

[53] *See* Jemima Beukes, *Govt Sued over N$18BN Genocide Package*, Namibian Sun (Jan. 20, 2023); Kaamil Ahmed, *Descendants of Namibia's Genocide Victims Call on Germany to "Stop Hiding,"* The Guardian (Feb. 3, 2023).

[54] *Germany's Genocide in Namibia*, *supra* note 49; *High Court Postpones Genocide Agreement Challenge*, NBC (last visited Apr. 9, 2025); Natasha Booty, *Namibia Marks Colonial Genocide as Reparations Hang in the Balance*, BBC News (May 28, 2025).

[55] Jonny Walfisz, *Germany Returns Stolen Colonial Treasures to Namibia as Reparations Continue*, EuroNews (May 25, 2022).

[56] *Restitution Evidence: Genocide and Reparations in German Colonial Namibia*, Forensic Architecture, https://forensic-architecture.org/investigation/restituting-evidence-genocide-and-reparations-in-german-colonial-namibia-phase- (last visited Jan. 3, 2025). *See also From Museum to Courtroom: Investigative Commons Reinvents Legal Investigations*, European Center for Constitutional and Human Rights, https://www.ecchr.eu/en/case/investigative-commons/ (last visited Jan. 3, 2025).

also explored the issues left out of the 2021 Reconciliation Agreement, noting that it was not only a genocide but also a massive theft of land, the vast majority of which remains in the hands of the tiny minority of the population of European and German origin.[57] The case is being closely followed by other former colonial powers like France, Belgium, and Portugal—all of whom see uneasy parallels to their own legacies in the case of Germany and Namibia.[58]

The Broader Reckoning with Colonialism

Alongside developments in cases like *Mutua* and Namibia, larger events also started to bring more urgency to issues concerning the legacy of colonialism. Just as the Canadian discovery of hundreds of unmarked graves prompted renewed activity on Indigenous issues and residential schools, the tragic public murder of George Floyd in 2020 directed a new level of attention to racial violence, including the legacies of colonialism and slavery. Former colonial powers came under increased pressure to respond to their troubling histories. And as some of them started to take action, the pressure on others increased.

Belgium is an example. In 2020, Belgium's King Philippe expressed his "deepest regrets" for colonial abuses in the Democratic Republic of Congo, though he stopped short of a full-blown apology.[59] That same year, the Belgian government made history when it set up the Special Commission on the Colonial Past. In 2021, after hearing from hundreds of witnesses, the Commission published its nearly 700-page report, which detailed the history and spoke to the importance of apology, restitution of cultural property, and payment of the "colonial debt."[60] However, as it was wrapping up its work in December 2022, the Commission splintered and failed to pass its recommendations, which included an official apology, commemoration, declassification of archives, and an anti-racism action plan.[61]

[57] *See* Maximilian Popp & Bernhard Riedmann, *"It's As If We Never Existed": Namibia Continues Seeking Justice for Germany's Colonial-Era Genocide*, Spiegel International (Nov. 10, 2022).

[58] *See id.*

[59] *Viewpoint: Why German's Namibia Genocide Apology Is Not Enough*, *supra* note 52; *Belgian King Expresses "Deepest Regrets" for DR Congo Colonial Abuses*, BBC News (June 30, 2020).

[60] Gaëlle Ponselet, *Colonial Crimes: Experts Recommend that Belgium Compensate*, Justice Info (Nov. 2, 2021), https://www.justiceinfo.net/en/83944-colonial-crimes-experts-recommend-that-belgium-compensate.html. *See* Chambre des représentants de Belgique, Commission Spéciale Chargée D'examiner L'état Indépendant Du Congo Et Le Passé Colonial De La Belgique Au Congo, Au Rwanda Et Au Burundi, Ses Conséquences Et Les Suites Qu'il Convient D'y Réserver (2021).

[61] *See* Gaëlle Ponselet, *Belgian Colonial Past: Commission Fails on Apology to Victims*, Justice Info (Jan. 19, 2023), https://www.justiceinfo.net/en/111372-belgian-colonial-past-commission-fails-apology-to-victims.html. *See also* Mustafah Dhada, *Historical Scholarship and the Public Square: The Belgian Commission on Colonialism Through the Lens of Wiriyamu*, J. Afr. Hist. (2025).

This occurred on the same day that the Government of the Netherlands recognized its responsibility for its slavery past, asked for an apology and set up a reparations fund, increasing the pressure on Belgium.[62] Some advocates also turned to the courts. In a landmark January 2025 ruling, Belgium's highest court found that the "systematic kidnapping" of mixed-race children from their African mothers in Belgian-ruled territories was a crime against humanity. While the prime minister had apologized for this in 2019, the government had rejected claims for compensation.[63] But the Court of Appeal sided with the survivors, awarding each of the five plaintiffs €50,000. With tens of thousands more in a similar position, the ruling could lay the groundwork for a larger reparations initiative, and the comparison with Canada is being noted.[64] Amid uncertainty about how the government will respond, the country continues to struggle with "its colonial ghosts."[65]

The same could be said of its fellow former colonial powers. Just before Germany's most recent apology to Namibia, French President Emmanuel Macron asked for forgiveness for France's role in the 1994 Rwandan genocide, in which about 800,000 ethnic Tutsis and moderate Hutus died.[66] Responding to the French legacy in Algeria, however, has proven more complicated. President Macron described the events as a crime against humanity, but he refused to apologize. Then in 2022, under increasing pressure, Macron announced the creation of a "joint commission of historians, opening our archives and allowing us to look at the whole of this historical period."[67] Like the Belgian commission, this is another truth-style commission, a notable development in a continent that has until recently avoided any serious reckoning with the legacy of colonialism. President Macron also expressly referred to opening of the archives which, as *Mutua* showed, has been a contentious matter in colonial history. In 2024, an agreement was signed to "retrieve the Algerian archives from the colonial era and possessions of immeasurable historical value to the hearts of the Algerian people."[68] Since then, however, the relationship has

[62] Ponselet, *Belgian Colonial Past, supra* note 61; Jon Henley, *Dutch PM Apologizes for Netherlands' Role in Slave Trade*, THE GUARDIAN (Dec. 19, 2023).

[63] *See* Milan Schreuer, *Belgium Apologizes for Kidnapping Children from African Colonies*, THE NEW YORK TIMES (Apr. 4, 2019); Jennifer Rankin, *Court Ruling on Belgium's Conduct in Africa Hailed as Turning Point*, THE GUARDIAN (Jan. 12, 2025).

[64] Rankin, *supra* note 63.

[65] Ketrin Jochecová, *Belgium Still Struggling with Its Colonial Ghosts*, POLITICO (Mar. 30, 2024). *See also* Ciara Carolan, *People Are "Not Ready": Investigation into Belgium's Colonial Past at a Standstill*, THE BRUSSELS TIMES (Jan. 25, 2024).

[66] *Macron Asks Rwanda to Forgive France over 1994 Genocide Role*, BBC NEWS (May 27, 2021).

[67] *Macron Announces France-Algeria Historians Commission to Study "Painful" Colonial Past*, EURONEWS (Aug. 26, 2022).

[68] Abbas Maymouni, *Algeria, France Sign Agreement on Memory, Retrieval of Colonial Archives*, ANADOLU AJANSI (May 25, 2024).

come under unprecedented diplomatic strain, leaving the fate of the agreement uncertain.[69]

Steps like those taken by Germany, Belgium, Holland, and France have also increased the scrutiny, as well as the moral and political pressure, on other former colonial powers who may be reluctant to address the past. In Britain, in the years since *Mutua*, the intertwined histories of colonialism and slavery have prompted intense debate. There is, for example, a new Museum of British Colonialism and an increasing and very public discussion about the legacy of empire.[70] When Queen Elizabeth died in 2022, the colonial legacy was a prominent feature of coverage of her reign.[71] In his first state visit speech, King Charles acknowledged "the wrongs which have shaped our past" and expressed "profound sorrow" at elements of his country's history, though he stopped short of an apology for slavery and colonialism.[72] Still, a line can be traced from the British statement of regret in *Mutua*, through to the formal apology of Germany for the Namibian genocide in 2021 after decades of prevarication, to the increasing pressure on newly-crowned King Charles to apologize for Britain's colonial legacy.[73] Each development, however partial, turns the focus on other former colonial powers and brings with it demands for some kind of reckoning.

This increased pressure to make amends for the legacy of colonialism is due in part to the growth of a well-organized transnational advocacy movement.[74] Cities and institutions have begun to issue their own apologies and are taking steps to respond to their intertwined legacies of colonialism and slavery. This includes Amsterdam, Rotterdam, The Hague, Utrecht, Edinburgh, and the Bank

[69] *See Why Are Diplomatic Relations Between Algeria and France so Bad?* Al Jazeera (May 1, 2025).

[70] *See* The Museum of British Colonialism, https://www.museumofbritishcolonialism.org/ (last visited Jan. 3, 2025); Sunil Khilnani, *The British Empire Was Much Worse than You Realize*, The New Yorker (Mar. 28, 2022); Dylan Sullivan & Jason Hickel, *How British Colonialism Killed 100 Million Indians in 40 Years*, Al Jazeera (Dec. 2, 2022).

[71] *See* Jason Burke, *Personal Ties, Diplomacy and Charm: King Charles Will Need Them All to Win over Africa*, The Guardian (Sept. 10, 2022); *Pritika Chowdhry, King Charles III Must Do Better Than His Mother on Colonialism and Reparations. Will He?*, USA Today (Sept. 16, 2022); Alexander Tripp & Caitlin Mittrick, *Before Moving Forward, King Charles III Must Address the Commonwealth's Past with Africa*, Atlantic Council (Oct. 12, 2022), https://www.atlanticcouncil.org/blogs/africasource/before-moving-forward-king-charles-iii-must-address-the-commonwealths-past-with-africa/; *King Charles Condemns British Colonialism in First Major Speech as Monarch*, The News (Pakistan, Nov. 23, 2022).

[72] Jack Royston, *King Charles' Colonialism "Sorrow" Is "Empty" Without Apology, Reparations*, Newsweek (Nov. 23, 2022).

[73] *See* Nosmot Gbadamosi, *King Charles III Faces a Reckoning on Empire in Africa*, Foreign Policy (Sept. 14, 2022), https://foreignpolicy.com/2022/09/14/elizabeth-charles-britain-colonialism-empire-africa/.

[74] *See* Max Fisher, *The Interpreter: The Long Road Ahead for Colonial Reparations*, The New York Times (Aug. 27, 2022). There is even an Oxford handbook on the topic. *See especially* Robert Aldrich, *Apologies, Restitutions, and Compensation: Making Reparations for Colonialism*, *in* The Oxford Handbook of the Ends of Empire 714 (Martin Thomas & Andrew S. Thompson eds., 2017).

of the Netherlands.[75] The movement is also finding institutional expression, including through organizations like Colonialism Reparation, which aims to have former colonial powers "condemn colonialism acknowledging their behaviour as a crime, reconcile with their past, apologize, and compensate the colonized nations."[76]

Prominent among these institutional voices is the CARICOM Reparations Commission, developed over a decade ago by Caribbean nations. Its Ten-Point Plan for Reparatory Justice, which addresses the interconnected legacies of colonialism and slavery, is a touchstone on the issue of remedying the most egregious effects of these linked legacies.[77] In addition to familiar elements like an apology, rehabilitation (healing), and repatriation of cultural belongings, the Ten-Point Plan also encompasses larger structural remedies such as education, health, and economic support, including debt cancellation.[78] And unlike our earlier examples where the wrongs were particularized, individual compensation is not the focus. Though the language of reparations is often used because of the primacy it places on repairing a wrong, this is a more structural approach to remedying the past that employs many of the tools of distributive justice. In that sense it is closer to transitional justice than to the issues of redress for particular—even though often massive—historic wrongs we have been examining so far. An approach along these lines is underscored in the Report of the United Nations Special Rapporteur entitled *Transitional justice measures and addressing the legacy of gross violations of human rights and international humanitarian law committed in colonial contexts*.[79] It notes the difficulties of applying traditional notions of reparation to wrongs that have the scale and the age and the devastating impacts of colonialism.[80] It echoes the spirit of the Ten-Point Plan, stressing among other things the importance of addressing the deeper causes of colonial violence, including through "reparation programmes that remedy the structural inequalities suffered in particular by the victims."[81]

[75] *See e.g. Edinburgh Says Sorry for City's Role in Slavery and Colonialism*, BBC News (Oct. 27, 2022); *Newsletter 11/24—The Commonwealth Opens to Reparations*, Colonial Reparation, https://www.colonialismreparation.org/en/ (last visited Jan. 3, 2025).

[76] *Newsletter 11/24—The Commonwealth Opens to Reparations*, *supra* note 75.

[77] *See Historic Reparative Apology Guided by the UWI and CARICOM Reparations Commission*, CARICOM (Mar. 9, 2023), https://caricomreparations.org/historic-reparative-apology-guided-by-the-uwi-and-caricom-reparations-commission/.

[78] *CARICOM Ten-Point Plan for Reparatory Justice*, CARICOM, https://caricom.org/caricom-ten-point-plan-for-reparatory-justice/ (last visited Apr. 9, 2025).

[79] Special Rapporteur on the promotion of truth, justice, reparations, and guarantees of non-recurrence, Fabián Salvioli, *Transitional justice measures and addressing the legacy of gross violations of human rights and international humanitarian law committed in colonial contexts*, U.N. Doc A/76/180 (July 19, 2021).

[80] *Id.* ¶ 57.

[81] *Id.* ¶ 6.

Alongside the growing conversation about making amends for colonialism, important partnerships have also sprung up, including between CARICOM and the African Union. The African Union has also long worked on issues of reparations and plans to play a key role in developing a continental approach to "reparatory justice for historical injustices."[82] The 2023 Accra Conference on Reparations, which brought together heads of states from Africa and the Caribbean, the United Nations, NGOs such as CARICOM, and others, was part of the African Union's "renewed effort to advance the cause of reparations."[83] The proclamation that emerged affirmed that "reparations to Africans is a moral and legal imperative rooted in the principles of justice, human rights and human dignity," and that reparations would be a "concrete step towards remedying historical wrongs and fostering healing among the people of Africa and people of African descent."[84] Designed to build upon the larger momentum around issues of reparatory justice, the African Union's 2025 theme is "Justice for Africans and People of African Descent Through Reparations," and it has an ambitious schedule planned around it.[85]

This more concerted advocacy on redressing colonialism has led to some other notable milestones. In 2019, the European Parliament overwhelmingly passed a resolution addressed to making amends for colonialism. It called for "some form of reparations such as offering public apologies and the restitution of stolen artefacts to their countries of origin," declassification of colonial archives, and education about the history of colonialism and slavery and their legacy.[86] In that same year, a United Nations working group asked Belgium to apologize for its actions in the Congo.[87] In 2021, the United Nations Office of the High Commissioner for Human Rights called on states to confront their legacies, "including through accountability and redress."[88] In 2023, the United Nations Special Rapporteur on the promotion of truth, justice, reparation, and guarantees of non-recurrence, Fabián Salvioli, presented the important report that, as noted above, explored how transitional justice measures could be

[82] Isaac Kaledzi, *Africa Revives Push for Colonial-Era Reparations*, DW NEWS (Aug. 4, 2022).

[83] African Union, Executive Council, *Concept Note on the African Union Theme of the Year for 2025*, EX.CL/1528(XLV) Rev. 1, 5 (2024).

[84] *Id.* at 2, 5.

[85] *See AU Theme of the Year 2025*, AFRICAN UNION, https://au.int/en/theme/2025 (last visited Apr. 9, 2025).

[86] Resolution on Fundamental Rights of People of African Descent in Europe, EUR. PARL. DOC. 2018/2899(RSP) (Mar. 26, 2019).

[87] *See* James Crisp, *UN Tells Belgium to Apologise for Its Colonial Past in Congo*, THE TELEGRAPH (Feb. 19, 2019). It also criticized the newly renovated Musee D'Afrique for failing to address the legacy of Leopold and its colonial past even after a massive renovation focused on "decolonialisation."

[88] U.N. High Commissioner for Human Rights, *Promotion and Protection of the Human Rights and Fundamental Freedoms of Africans and of People of African Descent Against Excessive Use of Force and Other Human Rights Violations by Law Enforcement Officers*, U.N. Doc. A/HRC/47/CRP.1, at 78 (June 28, 2021).

adapted to help to respond to the legacies of colonialism. The report describes the need to address "truth, justice and reparation relating to colonial injustices" as "an ineluctable duty," but one that poses inherent challenges.[89] As noted, it suggests that reckoning with the legacies of colonialism requires a broader understanding of reparations, one that draws more heavily on transitional justice principles with their greater focus on structural remedies.

Some Concluding Thoughts on Redress for Colonialism

Until recently, colonialism was largely seen as an historic issue. But it is now viewed as an issue of injustice that poses daunting present day challenges. Those challenges were sharply put by *The New York Times* in 2022:

> What do former colonial powers owe the descendants of those they colonized?
> Is it enough to apologize and return cultural objects? If restitution is to be financial, how does one tabulate the debt for generations of exploitation, plunder and enslavement?[90]

In one sense this shift has been quite dramatic. While not too long ago it would have been unthinkable for heads of state to apologize for the colonial ambitions of their predecessors and to contemplate how to make amends for some of the most devastating consequences, it has now become increasingly common. Former colonial powers are also beginning to employ truth commission-style bodies and to return stolen belongings. At the same time, former colonies are working together to develop a more robust sense of what might count as reparatory justice with wrongs of this scale, duration, and consequences.

But while some previously unthinkable steps have been taken, the aims of former colonies, as we have noted, stretch well beyond apologies and go to the heart of the enterprise—they seek "repayment for the stolen labor and resources that drove Europe's rise at the colonized world's expense."[91] In this sense, colonial redress implicates issues far beyond transactional wrongs like assault or mass violence. As the Namibian example makes clear, it also engages deeper structural issues of distributive justice such as the unequal distribution of land.[92]

[89] Special Rapporteur on the promotion of truth, justice, reparations, and guarantees of non-recurrence, *supra* note 79, ¶ 2.

[90] Fisher, *supra* note 74.

[91] *Id. See also* Jason Hickel, *Enough of Aid—Let's Talk Reparations*, THE GUARDIAN (Nov. 27, 2015); Jason Hickel, *The Case for Reparations*, JASON HICKEL (Oct. 13, 2018), https://www.jasonhickel.org/blog/2018/10/13/the-case-for-reparations; Priya Sippy, *Is the Tide Turning on Reparations to Africa*, QUARTZ (June 8, 2021).

[92] *See* e.g. Special Rapporteur on contemporary forms of racism, racial discrimination, xenophobia, and related intolerance, E. Tendayi Achiume, *Ecological Crisis, Climate Justice and Racial*

It is certainly possible to identify demands in common across the entire spectrum of reparations for historic wrongs, including apology, acknowledgement, commemoration, and restitution of cultural belongings. But as the CARICOM reparations plan illustrates, vast wrongs with such a strong distributive element also demand different kinds of remedies, including forward-looking "constructive reparations."[93] And it is especially on these large-scale responses that, as Sir Hilary Beckles pointed out, movement has been very minimal.

Still the question of how to repair some of the large-scale injustices of colonialism is now a live one that both former powers and former colonies are grappling with. The same could be said of the closely connected issue of slavery. Like colonialism, not too long ago, most would have seen the terrible injustices of slavery as simply "too big to remedy." But this issue too is shifting. Let us now see what lessons that example might hold.

Reparations for Slavery

Colonialism had a terrible twin—slavery. The legacy of colonialism in Africa has deep connections to the struggle for redress for what is perhaps the most horrific of history's wrongs. The push for reparations for slavery is centuries old, but until recently there had not been many gains. However, over the past decade and especially since the murder of George Floyd, the ground has dramatically shifted, leading to what has been referred to as a new era in reparations for slavery.[94] In July 2023, *Time Magazine*'s cover announced "Slavery Reparations Are Coming," crediting Barbados with leadership on the global issue.[95]

The long-standing redress for slavery movement experienced the same modern upsurge as other reparative justice efforts during the late 1980s and

Justice, U.N. Doc A/77/549 (Oct. 25, 2022); Special Rapporteur on the promotion of truth, justice, reparation, and guarantees of non-recurrence, Fabián Salvioli, *International Legal Standards Underpinning the Pillars of Transitional Justice*, U.N. Doc A/HRC/54/24 (July 10, 2023).

[93] *See* Olúfẹ́mi Táíwò, Reconsidering Reparations (2022). He notes that while concepts like fault and cause are useful, they "aren't built to respond to things on the scale of global racial empire. While we can sometimes identify individual culpable parties for individual events or even eras of domination, we are often tracking the impacts of their actions across multiple generations in which complicated legacies often intersect." *Id.* at 122. This has consequences for appropriates remedies. *See* Olúfẹ́mi Táíwò & Michael Franczak, *Here's How to Repay Developing Nations for Colonialism—and Fight the Climate Crisis*, The Guardian (Jan. 14, 2022).

[94] Jaclyn Diaz, *How Reparation Efforts in Barbados Found an International Spotlight*, National Public Radio (Jan. 7, 2023). *See also* Nick Logan, *Will King Charles's Reign Open the Door for Slavery Reparations in the Caribbean?* CBC News (Sept. 15, 2022); Janell Ross, *Inside Barbados' Historic Push for Slavery Reparations*, Time (July 6, 2023).

[95] *Slavery Reparations Are Coming—A Historic Global Movement Gains Power in Barbados*, Time (July 24, 2023).

early 1990s. The 1993 Abuja Declaration was part of a larger movement that included many of the reparative justice issues we touched on earlier. It focused on reparations for African enslavement and colonization and emphasized "compensation for injustice"—in other words reparative or reparatory justice.[96] The modern international movement has grown exponentially since then, with the Caribbean emerging here too as a leading voice.

An estimated five million slaves were brought to the Caribbean to toil in brutal conditions on sugar plantations owned by colonial powers, especially Britain and France. The region was "at the core of the crime against humanity induced by the transatlantic slave trade and slavery."[97] This terrible legacy was the major impetus behind CARICOM's 2013 launch of its important Reparations Commission.[98] As noted, its 10-Point Reparation Plan for European governments included a full apology, health care and literacy programs, and debt cancellation, among other things.[99] In 2015, connections between the various reparations movements deepened when the National African American Reparations Commission brought together delegates from across the United States with twenty-two countries in the Caribbean, Europe, Africa, and Latin America, as well as CARICOM.[100] To support this work, a Centre for Reparations Research at the University of the West Indies began its work in 2017.[101]

In 2019, the American Society of International Law (ASIL) got involved, partnering with the University of the West Indies to commission an economic analysis of slavery by the Brattle Group. It was presented at a 2023 Reparations Symposium with an introduction by ASIL Honorary President Patrick Robinson. He argued that the illegality of slavery under international law gave rise to an obligation on those who benefited to make reparations to the descendants of those they enslaved.[102] The *Report on Reparations for Transatlantic Chattel Slavery in the Americas and the Caribbean* brought a new level of empirical and legal sophistication to the issue.[103] It quantified the harms legally cognizable under

[96] *See* Aldrich, *supra* note 74, at 715.

[97] A. Missouri Sherman-Peter, *The Legacy of Slavery in the Caribbean and the Journey Towards Justice*, UN Chronicle (Mar. 25, 2022).

[98] *The Global Reparations Movement*, CARICOM Reparations Commission, https://caricomreparations.org/the-global-reparations-movement/ (last visited Jan. 4, 2025).

[99] *10-Point Reparation Plan*, CARICOM Reparations Commission, https://caricomreparations.org/caricom/caricoms-10-point-reparation-plan/ (last visited Jan. 4, 2025).

[100] *See About NAARC*, National African-American Reparations Commission, https://reparationscomm.org/about-naarc/ (last visited Jan. 4, 2025).

[101] *See Centre for Reparation Research Furthers the Cause of Justice*, The University of the West Indies, https://www.uwi.edu/vcreport/2017-2018/st-reparation.php (last visited Jan. 4, 2025).

[102] Patrick Robinson, *Introduction*, *in* Report on Reparations for Transatlantic Chattel Slavery in the Americas and the Caribbean 1, 2–4 (2023).

[103] Coleman Bazelon et al., *Quantification of Reparations for Transatlantic Chattel Slavery*, *in* Report on Reparations for Transatlantic Chattel Slavery in the Americas and the Caribbean, *supra* note 102, at 21.

international law as amounting to $100–$131 trillion.[104] Also in 2023, as noted, the African Union and Caribbean countries joined forces to press European nations to pay for their "historical mass crimes," which included the intertwined issues of colonialism and slavery.[105] On the International Day of Remembrance of the Victims of Slavery and the Transatlantic Slave Trade in 2024, Sir Hilary Beckles' article on global reparations movement was featured in the *UN Chronicle*.[106]

In the backdrop was a growing interest in deploying law and especially international law. Leigh Day, the firm that represented the Mau Mau in *Mutua*, was initially retained to advise CARICOM on a potential action against the UK government.[107] Though that case was never brought, Leigh Day's work has continued, including convening a 2024 House of Commons reparations event with academics, advocates, lawyers, and journalists.[108] So far however Caribbean efforts to use the courts have been met with defeat. In July 2023, following two lower court defeats, France's highest court rejected a claim by descendants, mainly from Martinique, who sought reparations for the "transgenerational harm" of slavery.[109] The court pointed to limitations issues and said that there was no evidence of individual damage from the crimes that their ancestors had been subjected to.[110] The claimants plan to return to the European Court of Human Rights, which ruled their claims admissible in 2020.[111] Despite judicial obstacles, Caribbean nations are focusing on the European powers that dominated the slave trade—Britain, France, Holland, Spain, and Portugal. This pressure dramatically increased in 2020, bringing European nations under

[104] The estimate included harm during the period of chattel slavery ($77–$108 trillion) and continuing harm post-enslavement ($22.9 trillion). Bazelon et al., *supra* note 103, at 1–4, 35; Kenneth Mohammed, *Don't Listen to the Critics: Reparations for Slavery Will Right Historical Wrongs*, The Guardian (Aug 21, 2023).

[105] Amelia Gentleman, *African and Caribbean Nations Agree to Seek Reparations for Slavery*, The Guardian (Nov. 17, 2023).

[106] *See* Hilary McDonald Beckles, *From Local Movements to Global Movement: Reparations Mechanisms and a Development Framework*, UN Chronicle (Mar. 25, 2024).

[107] *See Reparations*, Leigh Day, https://www.leighday.co.uk/our-services/human-rights/reparations/ (last visited Jan. 4, 2025). Ironically, it appears that the current UK Attorney General worked on the potential reparations claim against the UK government. *See* Oliver Trapnell, *Starmer's Attorney General "Advised Caribbean Nations" on Slavery Reparations as Ex-Colonies Demand* £18tn Pay-Out, GB News.

[108] *See Time Has Come for Reparations Discussions, Say Lawyers Investigating Potential for Claims*, Leigh Day (Oct. 24, 2024), https://www.leighday.co.uk/news/news/2024-news/time-has-come-for-reparations-discussions-say-lawyers-investigating-potential-for-claims/.

[109] *France's Top Court Denies Appeal for Reparations by Descendants of Slaves*, Radio France Internationale (July 5, 2023).

[110] *See* Cara Anna, *France's Supreme Court Rejects Groups' Request for Slavery Reparations in Case from Martinique*, Associated Press (July 5, 2023).

[111] *See France's Top Court Denies Appeal for Reparations*, *supra* note 109; Magali Bessone, *Reparations Claims for Slavery in France: The Need for a Paradigm Shift*, African Futures Lab (Dec. 22, 2021), https://www.afalab.org/news/2021-12-22-reparations-claims-for-slavery-in-france-the-need-for-a-paradigm-shift/.

renewed scrutiny and giving rise to more intense demands to reckon with the legacy of slavery.[112] Although there is too much activity to cover in full, let us look at some especially salient examples, beginning with the United Kingdom.

The United Kingdom

The United Kingdom played a major role in the slave trade until it finally passed a law to abolish slavery in 1807.[113] However, slavery continued throughout British colonies in the Caribbean, and Britain continued to profit from it. Because it was such an important player in slavery, efforts to press the country to come to terms with that legacy are longstanding. As early as 2006, then-Prime Minister Tony Blair expressed his "deep sorrow" for slavery.[114] In 2023, under growing pressure to apologize, then-Prime Minister Rishi Sunak refused to formally apologize for slavery, saying that "trying to unpick our history" was not the way forward.[115] The new Labour government took a similar approach, and Prime Minister Kier Starmer garnered significant criticism for refusing to put the issue on the table at the 2024 meeting of the Commonwealth.[116] However, the United Kingdom did not prevail with Commonwealth leaders, who instead resolved "that 'the time has come' for a conversation on reparatory justice."[117] There are also indications that while the government continues to reject an apology or paying reparations, they may be more open to other types of "reparatory justice, such as restructuring financial institutions and providing debt relief."[118] Early in 2025, there were also rumors that the Foreign Office was planning to open talks on reparations with Caribbean delegations, but that was later denied.[119]

Despite the official government position, there have been a number of grassroots initiatives in the United Kingdom. An especially striking one is from

[112] *See* David Thomas, *Europe Must Pay Africa Reparations for Slave Trade, Says Akufo-Addo*, National African-American Reparations Commission (Aug. 5, 2022), https://reparationscomm.org/reparations-news/europe-must-pay-africa-reparations-for-slave-trade-says-akufo-addo/ ; Debora Guidetti & Clara Grosset, *Slavery and Reparation in France*, Open Society Foundations (May 9, 2013), https://www.opensocietyfoundations.org/VOICES/SLAVERY-AND-REPARATION-FRANCE.

[113] An Act for the Abolition of the Slave Trade 1807, 47 Geo. III Sess. 1, c. 36 (Eng.).

[114] Joshua Nevett, *Slavery: Rishi Sunak Rejects Call to Apologise and Pay Reparations*, BBC News (Apr. 26, 2023).

[115] *Id.*

[116] *See* Eleni Courea & Aamna Mohdin, *Starmer Says He Wants to "Look Forward" and Not Talk About Slavery Reparations*, The Guardian (Oct. 23, 2024).

[117] *See* Eleni Courea & Geneva Abdul, *"Time Has Come": Commonwealth Heads Agree to Reparatory Justice Dialogue Despite Reluctant UK*, The Guardian (Oct. 26, 2024).

[118] *See* Eleni Courea et al., *UK "Open to Discussing Non-Cash Form of Reparatory Justice" for Former Colonies*, The Guardian (Oct. 24, 2024).

[119] *See* David Maddox, *Government Denies Talks with Caribbean Nations Over Slave Trade Reparations*, The Independent (Feb. 8, 2025).

families with a legacy of slave-holding. In 2021, UK philanthropist, Bridget Freeman announced that she would be contributing $500,000 USD to the University of the West Indies' development fund as reparations for her family's involvement in slavery. Vice-Chancellor Sir Hilary Beckles quoted Freeman as saying that reparations should be paid by those who benefitted from the crime against humanity: "[w]e owe it . . . the giving back just seems so obvious."[120] Other individuals and families with connections to slavery have also come together to make amends and support the reparations movement. Alex Renton's book *Blood Legacy: Reckoning with a Family's Story of Slavery*, which investigated his family's slave-owning past, prompted other descendants of some of the United Kingdom's wealthiest slave owners to connect with him.[121] That resulted in the 2023 formation of the group Heirs of Slavery, which has urged the government to apologize for slavery and "begin a programme of reparative justice."[122] One of the founders, former BBC journalist Laura Trevelyan, has apologized for her ancestors' slave owning past in Grenada and that family has donated £100,000 for education projects in Grenada, where her family once owned slaves.[123]

Other public and private initiatives are also underway. In an historic move, in 2019 the University of Glasgow agreed to pay £20 million for "reparative justice," specifically to study slavery and its global impacts, following research that uncovered their links to the slave trade.[124] The program will fund a joint center for development research at the University of the West Indies.[125] Actions like this have pushed many other institutions to take their own steps. Cambridge University's Legacies of Enslavement project is part of a wide range of universities and other public institutions beginning to address the legacy of slavery.[126] University College London created The Centre for the Study of the Legacies of British Slavery,[127] and many UK institutions are now members of

[120] *UWI Receives US$500,000 Reparation Payment*, The University of the West Indies St. Augustine (Aug. 25, 2021), https://sta.uwi.edu/news/releases/release.asp?id = 22311.

[121] Alex Renton, Blood Legacy: Reckoning with a Family's Story of Slavery (2021).

[122] Amelia Gentleman, *Descendants of UK Slave Owners Call on Government to Apologise*, The Guardian (Apr. 24, 2023).

[123] *See* Aamna Mohdin, *Laura Trevelyan Quits BBC to Campaign for Reparative Justice for Caribbean*, The Guardian (Mar. 16, 2023).

[124] Palko Karasz, *Glasgow University Millions for "Reparative Justice" for Slavery Ties*, The New York Times (Aug. 24, 2019).

[125] *See* Severin Carrell, *Glasgow University to Pay £20m in Slave Trade Reparations*, The Guardian (Aug. 23, 2019).

[126] *See Cambridge Responds to Legacies of Enslavement Inquiry*, Cambridge University (Sept. 22, 2022), https://www.cam.ac.uk/stories/legacies-of-enslavement-inquiry. Trinity College, Cambridge has also announced its own research initiative and a £1m scholarship fund to support students from the Caribbean. *See* Tobi Thomas, *Cambridge College to Create Fellowship to Examine Slavery Links*, The Guardian (Mar. 18, 2023). Like others, this research and the initiatives have sparked controversy. *See* Samira Shackle, *The Backlash: How Slavery Research Came Under Fire*, The Guardian (June 1, 2023).

[127] *Centre for the Study of the Legacies of British Slavery*, University College London, https://www.ucl.ac.uk/lbs/ (last visited Jan. 4, 2025).

the global group Universities Studying Slavery.[128] The Church of England has also identified how one of its arms profited from slavery and agreed to set aside £100 million ($127.63 million USD) for a fund to address racial inequality.[129]

Some businesses also have begun to engage in their own forms of redress. Only a month after the murder of George Floyd, the owners of British pub chain Greene King publicly acknowledged that their founder was a vocal supporter of slavery and owners of a plantation and slaves.[130] They also announced a partnership with the International Slavery Museum in Liverpool and committed to funding other initiatives and to developing a diversity strategy.[131] Financial institutions have also begun to address their role in funding slavery. For example, in 2004 Lloyds of London successfully defeated a claim by descendants of enslaved people who were transported to North America on ships financed by Lloyds.[132] However, on the same day in 2020 that Greene King apologized, Lloyd's followed suit, committing to increase diversity and engage in research on its involvement in slavery.[133] Other financial institutions like the Royal Bank of Scotland and Barclays have also begun to take steps toward acknowledgment. The Bank of England mounted an exhibition entitled "Slavery and the Bank," which details its slave-owning past.[134] A domino effect has followed and a growing number of public and private institutions are also studying their involvement in slavery and beginning to explore ways to make amends.[135]

This increasing scrutiny has also turned attention to other links to the slave trade.[136] Shortly after the Floyd murder, the statue of Bristol slave trader Edward Colston was toppled into the Bristol Harbour. Among other consequences, this prompted the Scott Trust, which owns *The Guardian*, to investigate and publish their own involvement. After research uncovered extensive links to the slave trade, they apologized and announced a more than £10 million redress program.[137] Their research was shared in a special series called "Cotton Capital."[138] Then in 2023, one of the Cotton Capital researchers discovered a 1689 document

[128] *Universities Studying Slavery*, UNIVERSITY OF VIRGINIA, https://slavery.virginia.edu/universities-studying-slavery/ (last visited Jan. 4, 2025).

[129] *See* Ross, *supra* note 94.

[130] Olivette Otele & Mawuena Kattah, *More than Money: The Logic of Slavery Reparations*, THE GUARDIAN (Mar. 31, 2023).

[131] *Id.*

[132] *See* In re African American Slave Descendants Litigation, 471 F.3d 754 (7th Cir. 2006).

[133] Otele & Kattah, *supra* note 130.

[134] *See Slavery & the Bank*, BANK OF ENGLAND MUSEUM (Feb. 27, 2024), https://www.bankofengland.co.uk/museum/whats-on/slavery-and-the-bank.

[135] Otele & Kattah, *supra* note 130.

[136] *See e.g.* David Conn, *The British Kings and Queens Who Supported and Profited from Slavery*, THE GUARDIAN (Apr. 6, 2023).

[137] *See* Aamna Mohdin, *The Guardian and Slavery: What Did the Research Find and What Happens Next?* THE GUARDIAN (Mar. 28, 2023).

[138] *Cotton Capital: How Slavery Changed The Guardian, Britain and the World*, THE GUARDIAN, https://www.theguardian.com/news/series/cotton-capital (last visited Jan. 3, 2025).

that showed that Colston had transferred shares in the slave-trading Royal African Company to King William III.

The revelation prompted Buckingham Palace to go on the record as supporting research into the monarchy's involvement in the slave trade.[139] In 2021, before he ascended the throne, then Prince Charles had already denounced the "atrocity of slavery" and Britain's legacy of the slave trade.[140] But Prince William's controversial 2022 trip to the Caribbean prompted an open letter that called for an apology for slavery and colonialism and urged "recognition of the need for atonement and reparations."[141] As noted, it was a sign of the times that the role of the monarchy in slavery and colonialism was also one of the major themes in the coverage of the death of Queen Elizabeth II.[142] At the difficult 2024 Commonwealth meeting in Samoa, King Charles touched on the issue carefully, noting that "[n]one of us can change the past. But we can commit, with all our hearts, to learning its lessons and to finding creative ways to right inequalities that endure."[143] Although the word slavery was not mentioned, the King's comments were widely seen as speaking to the issue which was such a live one at the meeting.

Other Colonial Powers

The United Kingdom is not alone—other former colonial powers in Europe are also reckoning with their own legacies of slavery. In 2018, Denmark apologized to Ghana for its role in the transatlantic slave trade. During a visit to the Democratic Republic of Congo in 2022, the King of Belgium did not quite apologize, but did express his "deepest regrets for these wounds of the past."[144] The legacy of slavery has also become a subject of increasing national attention in Holland. In the context of the larger global conversion about slavery and

[139] *See* David Conn, *The Colston Connection: How Prince William's Kensington Palace Home Is Linked to Slavery*, The Guardian (Apr. 6, 2023); David Conn, Aamna Mohdin & Maya Wolfe-Robinson, *King Charles Signals First Explicit Support for Research into Monarchy's Slavery Ties*, The Guardian (Apr. 6, 2023).

[140] *See* Simon Perry, *Prince Charles Denounces "Appalling Atrocity" of Slavery as Barbados Becomes a Republic*, People (Nov. 30, 2021).

[141] *Open Letter from Jamaican Advocacy Group Requesting Prince William & the Duchess of Cambridge Kate Apologizes for UK Colonial Past*, Jamaicans, https://jamaicans.com/open-letter-from-jamaican-advocacy-group-requesting-prince-william-the-duchess-of-cambridge-kate-apologizes-for-uk-colonial-past/ (last visited Jan. 4, 2025). *See also* Jennifer Hassan, *Jamaica Set to Seek Compensation from Britain over Slave Trade*, The Washington Post (July 13, 2021).

[142] *Supra* note 71 and sources cited therein.

[143] Sean Coughlan, *Why the King Can't Say "Sorry" for Slavery*, BBC News (Oct. 25, 2024). *See also* Kate Lyons & Natricia Duncan, *Prince Charles Acknowledges "Painful" Past as Calls for Slavery Reparations Grow at Commonwealth*, The Guardian (Oct. 25, 2024).

[144] Ruth MacLean & Elian Peltier, *Belgian King Returns Mask to Congo in Landmark Visit*, The New York Times (June 8, 2022).

colonialism, in 2021, the Rijksmuseum in Amsterdam mounted an ambitious exhibition entitled "Slavery" that explored more than two centuries of Dutch participation in slavery. Designed to "right a historic wrong" and call attention to the Dutch role, the museum's ambitious effort shifted focus from the United States back to Holland's own role.[145] Following the Floyd murder, the Dutch government also set up an independent advisory panel that urged the government to apologize and pay reparations, noting that while it was not possible to turn history back, their aim was to correct the "historical injustice" as far as possible.[146] Then in December 2022, the Dutch prime minister made history by formally apologizing for his country's extensive involvement in the slave trade, the first European country to do so.[147] The government also announced the creation of a €200 million fund to increase "awareness and involvement and follow-up" regarding the country's role in slavery, although the prime minister stressed that the fund was not for reparations.[148] However, the apology was met with skepticism, in part because the descendants were not included, and demands for a more fulsome response including reparations have continued.[149]

Despite criticisms of the Dutch approach, many advocates see it as evidence of a turning point. Sir Hilary Beckles observed that "[t]he reparatory justice movement has moved in to a new phase" while also noting that the Netherlands "continues to be an imperial nation."[150] Six months after the Dutch apology in June of 2023, a new study revealed that Dutch rulers received the equivalent of €545 million from the practice.[151] Shortly afterwards, the Dutch King also personally apologized, calling the practice a "horror" and noting that the monarchy did nothing to stop it.[152] He pledged that "[a]fter acknowledgment and apology, we can work together on healing, reconciliation and restoration."[153] The King has also commissioned his own study, due in 2025, into the role of the Dutch royal family in slavery.[154] Such actions increase the pressure on others, which is

[145] Nina Siegal, *Telling Stories of Slavery, One Person at a Time*, The New York Times (June 4, 2021).

[146] *Panel Advises Dutch Government to Apologise for Slavery*, Reuters (July 1, 2021).

[147] *See* Claire Moses, *Dutch Prime Minister Apologizes for His Country's Role in the Slave Trade*, The New York Times (Dec. 19, 2022); *Dutch Formally Apologize for Slave Trade But Struggle to Battle Racism at Home*, Bloomberg (Dec. 9, 2022).

[148] Moses, *supra* note 147; Toby Sterling & Ank Kuipers, *Netherlands PM Rutte Apologises for Role of Dutch State in Slavery*, Reuters (Nov. 19, 2022).

[149] Moses, *supra* note 147; Sterling & Kuipers, *supra* note 148.

[150] Lyndon Mukasa, *Dutch Slavery Apology Shut Down*, The Voice (Mar. 10, 2023).

[151] *See* Matt Murphy, *Dutch King Willem-Alexander Apologises for Country's Role in Slavery*, BBC News (July 1, 2023).

[152] *Id. See also* Claire Moses, *Dutch King Apologizes for His Country's Role in the Slave Trade*, The New York Times (Jul. 1, 2023).

[153] Murphy, *supra* note 151.

[154] *See* Donna Ferguson, *Dutch King Apologises for Country's Historical Involvement in Slavery*, The Guardian (July 1, 2023).

the reason why many believe that reparations for transatlantic slavery is an issue that is "gaining momentum."[155]

American Chattel Slavery

The demand to reckon with the history of slavery, as we have seen, is global. But because of its scale, duration and after-effects, the American institution of chattel slavery has long been the site of especially intense activity.[156] And although it may be seen as newly topical, the quest for redress has been a live issue at least since Emancipation.[157] During the brief period of Reconstruction following the Civil War, the famous but short-lived "forty acres and a mule"[158] initiative was the first of many redress efforts. But those plans halted when Reconstruction came to an end.[159] Redress advocates turned to Congress, but when that failed, they launched the first slavery reparations lawsuit. The 1916 class action claimed the taxes collected on the cotton produced as a result of the "involuntary servitude" of former slaves. The Court of Appeals denied their claim based on governmental immunity, and the Supreme Court of the United States agreed.[160]

The movement to respond to the legacy of slavery continued however, and the 1980s also brought new momentum on this issue. Inspired by the Holocaust restitution cases, the South African Truth and Reconciliation Commission, and redress for Japanese-American internment, advocates reignited the struggle.[161] They pressed for a commission to examine slavery: Bill H.R. 40 was first

[155] Catarina Demony, *Slavery Reparations: Where do Europe and the Rest of the World Stand?* REUTERS (Oct. 25, 2024).

[156] There is a vast literature surrounding reparations for slavery in the United States, and I can only touch on the small part of it that has special relevance for my argument. The modern era of discussion began with BORIS BITTKER, THE CASE FOR BLACK REPARATIONS (1973). *See also* Keith N. Hylton, *Slavery and Tort Law*, 84 B.U. L. REV. (2004); REDRESS FOR HISTORICAL INJUSTICES IN THE UNITED STATES: ON REPARATIONS FOR SLAVERY, JIM CROW, AND THEIR LEGACIES (Michael T. Martin & Marilyn Yaquinto eds., 2007); OLÚFẸ́MI TÁÍWÒ, RECONSIDERING REPARATIONS (2022). I also discuss some of these issues along with relevant literature in Mayo Moran, *The Problem of the Past: How Historic Wrongs Became Legal Problems*, 69 U. TORONTO L. J. 421, 425–26 (2019).

[157] Ta-Nehisi Coates's important article, *The Case for Reparations*, THE ATLANTIC (June 2014), prompted a renewed and larger debate. *See e.g.* Ishaan Tharoor, *U.S. Owes Black People Reparations for a History of "Racial Terrorism," says U.N. Panel*, THE WASHINGTON POST (Sept. 27, 2016).

[158] Freedmen's Bureau Act of 1865, ch. 90, 13 Stat. 507 (1865).

[159] *See* Dinah Shelton, *The World of Atonement: Reparations for Historical Injustices*, 50:3 NETHERLANDS INT'L L. REV. L. 289, 319–23 (2003); Joe R. Feagin, *Documenting the Costs of Slavery, Segregation, and Contemporary Racism: Why Reparations Are in Order for African Americans*, 20 HARV. BLACKLETTER L.J. 49, 55 (2004); Miranda Booker Perry, *No Pensions for Ex-Slaves: How Federal Agencies Suppressed Movement to Aid Freedpeople*, 42:2 PROLOGUE MAGAZINE (Summer 2010).

[160] Johnson v. McAdoo, 45 App. D.C. 440, 441 (1916), *aff'd* 244 U.S. 643 (1917). *See also* Perry, *supra* note 159.

[161] *See* Alfred L. Brophy, *Some Conceptual and Legal Problems in Reparations for Slavery*, 58 N.Y.U. ANN. SURV. AM. L. 497, 499–501 (2002). *See also* ALFRED L. BROPHY, REPARATIONS PRO AND CON 19–40 (2006).

introduced in 1989, but despite some movement over the decades, that commission has not yet been struck.[162] And most other political efforts also faltered, particularly when it came to individual redress.[163] In part for that reason, attention began to shift to litigation.

United States Slavery Reparations Litigation

The era of modern judgments began in the 1990s with *Cato v. United States.* It was a claim against the federal government for $100,000,000 "for damages due to the enslavement of African Americans and subsequent discrimination against them, for an acknowledgement of discrimination, and for an apology."[164] The District Court dismissed it, and the Court of Appeals upheld the decision. The courts acknowledged the gravity of the wrongs but held that government was protected by sovereign immunity. They also noted difficulties posed by the passage of time and by the lack of a personal link between the plaintiffs and the wrong.[165] The question of redress, they said, was more appropriately addressed to the legislature.[166]

Despite this rather definitive loss, the litigation had some important effects, including helping to spur the slavery disclosure movement.[167] And since *Cato* only claimed against the government, beginning in 2002, a series of tort and unjust enrichment claims were filed against private insurance, railway, tobacco, and other companies that had been involved in slavery. Eventually consolidated into *In re African American Slave Descendants Litigation*, the claims were once again dismissed.[168] The District Court focused on problems with standing, holding that the plaintiffs could not show the requisite link between the defendants' wrongs and their harms. They also noted the passage of time. The Seventh

[162] Senator Booker reintroduced the legislation in January 2025. *See* H.R. 40, 119th Cong. (2025–2026); *Booker Reintroduces Legislation to Form Commission for Study of Reparation Proposals for African Americans*, Cory Booker (Jan. 9, 2025), https://www.booker.senate.gov/news/press/01/09/2025/booker-reintroduces-legislation-to-form-commission-for-study-of-reparation-proposals-for-african-americans.

[163] See *supra* note 156.

[164] Cato v. United States, 70 F.3d 1103, 1105 (9th Cir. 1995).

[165] *Id.* at 1107–10.

[166] *Id.* at 1111.

[167] *See* Jason Levy, *Slavery Disclosure Laws: For Financial Reparations or for Telling the Truth?*, 2009 Colum. Bus. L. Rev. 468 (2009). By 2009, eight major American cities (Berkeley, Chicago, Detroit, Los Angeles, Milwaukee, Oakland, Philadelphia, and San Francisco) as well as three states (Iowa, Illinois, and California) had similar legislation. Others have also followed suit, including Richmond, California; Maryland; Wayne, Michigan; Cleveland, Ohio; and Milwaukee, Wisconsin. *See Slavery Era Disclosure Laws*, Restitution Study Group, https://rsgincorp.org/legislation/ (last visited Jan. 5, 2025).

[168] In re African American Slave Descendants Litigation, 375 F. Supp. 2d 721 (N.D. Ill. 2005).

Circuit Court of Appeals upheld the dismissal, primarily because of problems with standing.[169]

Around the same time, *Alexander v. Oklahoma* was also making its way through the courts. It arose out of one of the United States' worst episodes of racial violence—the 1921 Tulsa massacre that destroyed the Black business district in Greenwood and left at least 10,000 Black people homeless and 300 dead. More than seventy-five years later, the Tulsa Race Riot Commission was created. Its 2001 report documented government involvement in the massacre and made recommendations. Their first recommendation was reparations to the survivors and descendants, which they said "would be good public policy and do much to repair the emotional and physical scars of this terrible incident in our shared past."[170] The Legislature adopted some recommendations but rejected reparations, leading advocates to turn to the courts.[171] The courts did acknowledge that the events were tragic, but held that the plaintiffs had brought their claims too late.[172]

As these cases illustrate, the slavery claims face distinctive hurdles. We have noted elsewhere that judges have sometimes found ways around procedural barriers like limitations and immunities. But not in the slavery cases. Some of the reasons echo the challenges that the Salvioli Report noted in the closely related issue of colonial reparations—the scale, age, and transformative impact of the injustice pose challenges for the kinds of remedies normally ordered by courts.[173] Chattel slavery lasted for nearly 250 years, enslaved millions, and formally ended over 150 years ago.[174] It implicated most major public and private institutions, was extensively regulated by law, enforced through the legal system, and accommodated by the Constitution.[175] As with colonial redress, many of the remedial ambitions reflect the fundamental nature of the wrongs inflicted by slavery and their structural impact.[176] We earlier saw how courts in the

[169] In re African American Slave Descendants Litigation, 471 F.3d 754 (7th Cir. 2006).

[170] Currie Ballard et al., Tulsa Race Riot: A Report by the Oklahoma Commission to Study the Tulsa Race Riot of 1921 ii (2001).

[171] Alexander v. Oklahoma, 382 F.3d 1206 (10th Cir. 2004).

[172] *Id.* at 1218.

[173] Special Rapporteur on the promotion of truth, justice, reparations, and guarantees of non-recurrence, *supra* note 79, ¶ 57.

[174] *See* Allan D. Cooper, *From Slavery to Genocide: The Fallacy of Debt in Reparations Discourse*, 43 J. Black Stud. 107, 108–109 (2012).

[175] *See* Phillip W. Magness, *The American System and the Political Economy of Black Colonization*, 37 J. Hist. Econ. Thought 187 (2015); Carlton Waterhouse, *Total Recall: Restoring the Public Memory of Enslaved African-Americans and the American System of Slavery Through Rectificatory Justice and Reparations*, 14 J. Gender Race & Just. 703, 713–14 (2011). U.S. Const. art. I, § 9, cl. 1. *See generally*, Kenneth Morgan, *Slavery and the Debate over Ratification of the United States Constitution*, 22 Slavery & Abolition 40 (2001); Helen J. Knowles, *The Constitution and Slavery: A Special Relationship*, 28 Slavery & Abolition 309 (2007).

[176] Notice of Filing, In Re African-American Slave Descendants' Litigation, No. 1:02-cv-00764, ¶ 3(c) (N.D. Ill. June 17, 2003).

residential schools context had difficulty grappling with the idea that the legal and political systems themselves were a central part of what was now understood as an historic wrong. Similar but greatly amplified challenges have led even some supporters to wonder if slavery is simply "too big to remedy."[177] But despite these complications and the losses in court, slavery redress efforts have accelerated.

Alexander illustrates some of these dynamics. With its more particularized claims, it drew on traditional causes of action and its powerful reparative justice underpinnings made it look more like some of the successful historic redress issues we examined earlier. So unlike the other large scale slavery claims, *Alexander* seemed tailor-made for getting beyond the limitations issue. Crucially, standing was not an issue—it was clear that the plaintiffs had suffered catastrophic damage that was intentionally inflicted. The Race Riot Commission report established the defendant's responsibility, noting that they "arrested based on race, not on danger to the Greenwood residents themselves."[178] In addition to the clear link between the defendant's wrong and the plaintiffs' injuries, there was even a helpful precedent. Only a few years earlier, a New York court had found a "continuing violation" exception to the limitations issue in a claim against French banks for expropriating Holocaust victims' funds. That court observed that the "plaintiffs could hardly have been expected to bring these claims at the end of World War II," and noted that they had been consistently thwarted since then.[179] The *Alexander* court also acknowledged that for decades the plaintiffs had no meaningful access to the courts.[180] But they found that those denials ended with the passage of the *Civil Rights Acts* in the 1960s, even though this entailed rejecting the Commission report that documented the ongoing racism and violence faced by the community.

Despite these judicial rejections, the way that *Alexander* marshaled the evidence and sharpened the reparative justice arguments had a powerful effect, highlighting slavery and its racist aftermath and putting the Tulsa massacre on the radar.[181] Then, as we shall see , the combination of the approaching

[177] *See* Kaimipono David Wenger, *Too Big to Remedy—Rethinking Mass Restitution for Slavery and Jim Crow*, 44 Loy. L.A. L. Rev. 177 (2010). Relevant background includes Eric A. Posner & Adrian Vermeule, *Reparations for Slavery and Other Historic Injustices*, 103 Columbia L. Rev. 689 (2003); Roy L. Brooks, *Getting Reparations for Slavery Right—Response to Posner and Vermeule*, 80 Notre Dame L. Rev. 251 (2004).

[178] Ballard et al., *supra* note 170, at 164.

[179] Bodner v. Banque Paribas, 114 F. Supp. 2d 117, 135 (E.D.N.Y. 2000).

[180] Alexander v. Oklahoma, 382 F.3d 1206, 1219 (10th Cir. 2004). *See* Kaimipono David Wenger, *From Radical to Practical (and Back Again?): Reparations, Rhetoric, and Revolution*, 25 J. Civ. Rts. & Econ. Dev. 697, 725 (2011); Elijah Schimelpfenig, *The Tulsa Race Massacre and the Substance of Law: Reconsidering Equitable Tolling/Estoppel in Cases of State Sponsored Civil Violence*, Harv Undergrad. L. Rev (2021).

[181] *See Statement to the Media by the United Nations' Working Group of Experts on People of African Descent, on the Conclusion of Its Official Visit to USA, 19–29 January 2016*, Office of the High Commissioner for Human Rights (Jan. 29, 2016), https://www.ohchr.org/en/statements/2016/01/statement-media-united-nations-working-group-experts-people-african-descent; Bayeté Ross

centennial of the massacre and the Floyd murder catapulted the issue back to the public attention and some very belated success.[182]

Slavery Redress Enters a New Era

Although the slavery litigation failed in court, the legacy of *Alexander* shows how important it was. It helped to develop both more sophisticated redress arguments and more fulsome evidence. It also fueled public discussion and debate. Advocates also began pressing their claims with institutions directly, and the information that emerged made the redress question increasingly hard to avoid. So even more than a decade before the murder of George Floyd, there was a new level of attention to redress for slavery. In 2008, Congress made history when it apologized for slavery and for the legacy of Jim Crow.[183] Many of the states that had slavery at the start of the Civil War also began to apologize.[184] A growing number of cities and other institutions also began to apologize, often in conjunction with other redress-oriented activity.[185]

In the years leading up to 2020, monuments and namings with a connection to slavery were also increasingly attracting critical scrutiny.[186] By 2017, there was already a growing list of Confederate monuments that were coming down, and the focus began to shift to how many remained.[187] Alongside this, public and

Smith & Jimmie Briggs, *Tulsa Race Massacre at 100: An Act of Terrorism America Tried to Forget*, THE GUARDIAN (May 31, 2021).

[182] *See* Brentin Mock, *Survivors of Black Wall Street Massacre Challenge Tulsa's Atonement Strategy*, BLOOMBERG (Nov. 17, 2022).

[183] *Congress Apologizes for Slavery, Jim Crow*, NATIONAL PUBLIC RADIO (July 30, 2008); Darryl Fears, *House Issues an Apology for Slavery*, THE WASHINGTON POST (July 30, 2008).

[184] *See e.g. Virginia Lawmakers Apologize for Slavery*, NBC NEWS (Feb. 24, 2007); *Maryland Issues Apology for its Role in Slavery*, NBC NEWS (Mar. 27, 2007); *North Carolina Senate Apologizes for Slavery*, NBC NEWS (Apr. 5, 2007); *Resolutions on Alabama's Role in Slavery*, AL.COM (Apr. 11, 2007), https://www.al.com/bn/2007/04/sjr54_expressing_profound_regr.html; Damien Cave & Christine Jordan Sexton, *Florida Legislature Apologizes for State's History of Slavery*, THE NEW YORK TIMES (Mar. 27, 2008); *New Jersey Apologizes for Slavery*, NATIONAL PUBLIC RADIO (Jan. 8, 2009); Matt Bittle, *Slavery Apology OKd by Delaware Legislative Panel*, BAY TO BAY NEWS (Jan. 13, 2016); Lindsey Holden, *State of Gavin Newsom Signs California Apology for Slavery and Discrimination*, POLITICO (Sept. 26, 2024).

[185] *See* Daniel Burke, *In Emotional Service, Jesuits and Georgetown Repent for Slave Trading*, CNN (Apr. 20, 2017); Melissa Gomez, *Charleston Apologizes for City's Role in Slave Trade*, THE NEW YORK TIMES (June 20, 2018).

[186] *See* Yoni Appelbaum, *Take the Statues Down*, THE ATLANTIC (Aug 13, 2017); Eliott C. McLaughlin, *Honoring the Unforgivable*, CNN (June 17, 2020).

[187] *From 2017: Confederate Monuments Are Coming Down Across the United States. Here's a List*, THE NEW YORK TIMES (Aug. 28, 2017); Giselle Rhoden, *73 Confederate Monuments Were Removed or Renamed Last Year, Report Finds*, CNN (Feb. 3, 2022). More than 200 Confederate memorials were taken down since George Floyd's murder and that 2,089 Confederate memorials remain. SOUTHERN POVERTY LAW CENTER, WHOSE HERITAGE? PUBLIC SYMBOLS OF THE CONFEDERACY 6 (3d ed. 2022).

private institutions had begun difficult processes of rethinking monuments and namings.[188] Efforts to commemorate and acknowledge the history of slavery and the contributions of the enslaved were also on the increase. The Slave Memorial at Mount Washington, created in 1983 by the students of Howard University, was an important early initiative.[189] National cultural institutions started to engage with the history of slavery, as exemplified in the Smithsonian's National Museum of African American History and Culture's 2016 exhibition, "Slavery and Freedom."[190] "Contemporary Monuments to the Slave Past" was one of several efforts to help "memorialize the slave past."[191] Alongside it and also opened in 2018, the National Memorial for Peace and Justice in Montgomery, Alabama is a comprehensive memorial described as demanding "a reckoning with one of the nation's least recognized atrocities"—the lynching of thousands of Black people.[192] The transitional justice resonance of such projects was becoming more audible in their aim to confront "the truth about our history" as "the first step towards truth and reconciliation."[193]

This increased focus on the legacy of slavery also began to prompt a rethinking of national history, paralleling what we noted in the issues involving residential schools and other colonial examples. *The New York Times'* important "The 1619 Project" told "a new origin story" centered on the role of slavery in the history of the country.[194] The impact of the series was profound, ranging from winning a Pulitzer prize to being banned from use in schools and generating one of newly re-elected President Trump's first executive orders.[195] One of the effects of this

[188] *See* Kaitlin M. Murphy, *Fear and Loathing in Monuments: Rethinking the Politics and Practices of Monumentality and Monumentalization*, 14 MEMORY STUDIES 1143 (2021).

[189] *The Slave Memorial*, GEORGE WASHINGTON'S MOUNT VERNON, https://www.mountvernon.org/george-washington/slavery/the-slave-memorial-at-mount-vernon (last visited Apr. 12, 2025).

[190] *Slavery and Freedom*, THE SMITHSONIAN, https://www.si.edu/exhibitions/slavery-and-freedom-event-event-exhib-4840 (last visited Apr. 12, 2025).

[191] CONTEMPORARY MONUMENTS TO THE SLAVE PAST, https://www.slaverymonuments.org/collections/show/12 (last visited Jan. 4, 2025). *See also* Petula Dvorak, *America's Missing Slave Memorials: It's Time to Truly Acknowledge Our Bloody Past*, THE WASHINGTON POST (Aug. 28, 2017).

[192] *The National Memorial for Peace and Justice*, THE LEGACY SITES, https://legacysites.eji.org/about/memorial/ (last visited Jan. 4, 2025). *See also* Kyle Gassiott, *Freedom Monument Park Tells Honest Story of Enslaved People*, NATIONAL PUBLIC RADIO (Apr. 22, 2024); Campbell Robertson, *A Lynching Memorial Is Opening. The Country Has Never Seen Anything Like It*, THE NEW YORK TIMES (Apr. 26, 2018).

[193] *National Memorial for Peace and Justice*, *supra* note 192.

[194] *The 1619 Project*, THE NEW YORK TIMES MAGAZINE, https://www.nytimes.com/interactive/2019/08/14/magazine/1619-america-slavery.html (last visited Jan. 2, 2025).

[195] *See* Adam Serwer, *The Fight over the 1619 Project Is Not About the Facts*, THE ATLANTIC (Dec. 23, 2019); Lauren Michele Jackson, *The 1619 Project and the Demands of Public History*, THE NEW YORKER (Dec. 8, 2021); Jake Silverstein, Letter to the Editor, *We Respond to the Historians Who Critiqued the 1619 Project*, THE NEW YORK TIMES (Jan. 19, 2021); Sarah Schwartz, *Lawmakers Push to Ban "1619 Project" From Schools*, EDUCATION WEEK (Feb. 3, 2021). Many US states have banned "critical race theory." *See Critical Race Theory Ban States 2025*, WORLD POPULATION REVIEW, https://worldpopulationreview.com/state-rankings/critical-race-theory-ban-states (last visited Apr. 12, 2025). President Trump appointed the 1776 Commission to counter *The 1619 Project* with a "patriotic" history and at the beginning of his second term, he reinstated the Commission. *See* Collin

reevaluation of national history was found in the fact that, after many years of focusing outside of their home jurisdiction, the US-based International Center for Transitional Justice began to turn attention to the domestic legacy of chattel slavery, noting that its mandate was not confined to government upheaval, but also encompassed "a long history of human rights violations and deeply-rooted injustice."[196]

This increased focus on the legacy of slavery led *The Washington Post*, even before the 2020 murder of George Floyd, to observe that reparations were already underway at the local level.[197] Georgetown University's ground-breaking reckoning with its infamous 1838 slave sale was a case in point. Following a 2016 student newspaper exposé, Georgetown's president commissioned a Working Group on Slavery, Memory, and Reconciliation.[198] In a move that changed the conversation, it recommended preferential admissions to the descendants of those it sold as slaves a century and a half earlier.[199] The university agreed, though few expected many living descendants. But the Georgetown Memory Project identified over 12,000 descendants—an illustration that it just might be much easier than expected to trace both the benefits and the burdens of slavery down through generations.[200] Reparative justice, this example made clear, could sometimes encompass cases with no living survivor.[201] Inspired by student

Binkley & Zeke Miller, *Trump's Orders Take Aim at Critical Race Theory and Antisemitism on College Campuses*, Associated Press (Jan. 30, 2025); President Donald J. Trump, Executive Order, *Ending Radical Indoctrination in K-12 Schooling*, White House (Jan. 29, 2025), https://www.whitehouse.gov/presidential-actions/2025/01/ending-radical-indoctrination-in-k-12-schooling/.

[196] International Center for Truth and Justice, Truth, Reconciliation, and Redress for Racial Injustice in the United States: Insights from Experiences of Commissions Around the World 5 (Dec. 2022).

[197] *See* Thai Jones, *Slavery Reparations Seem Impossible. In Many Places, They're Already Happening*, The Washington Post (Jan. 31, 2020).

[198] *See* Jesús A. Rodríguez, *This Could Be the First Slavery Reparations Policy in America*, Politico (Apr. 9, 2019); Nick Anderson, *Georgetown Plans to Apologize for its Role in Slavery*, The Washington Post (Sept. 1, 2016). *See also Georgetown University Tries to Make Amends for Profiting from Slavery*, PBS (Sept. 1, 2016).

[199] *See* Rachel L. Swarns, *Georgetown University Plans Steps to Atone for Slave Past*, The New York Times (Sept. 1, 2016).

[200] *See* John Murawski, *Georgetown University's Road to Slavery Reparations Was Paved with Good Intentions, Leading to a Can of Works*, National African-American Reparations Commission (July 13, 2022), https://reparationscomm.org/reparations-news/georgetown-universitys-road-to-slavery-reparations-was-paved-with-good-intentions/#:~:text = The%20university%20now%20offers%20preferred,rendering%20their%20descendants%20non%2Dpersons.

[201] *See* John J. DeGioia, *Racial Justice: A Georgetown Response, Continuing the Conversation*, Georgetown University Office of the President (Sept. 1, 2016), https://president.georgetown.edu/slavery-memory-reconciliation-report-remarks; *Georgetown Shares Slavery, Memory, and Reconciliation Report, Racial Justice Steps*, Georgetown University (Sept. 1, 2016), https://www.georgetown.edu/slavery-memory-reconciliation-working-group-sept-2016. Georgetown also formally apologized for its role in slavery and has renamed buildings to acknowledge slaves. *See* Adeel Hassan, *Georgetown Students Agree to Create Reparations Fund*, The New York Times (Apr. 12, 2019).

efforts, the university also created a fund to support descendants. All of this was part of what the university described as an ongoing and long-term process to more deeply understand and respond to their "role in the injustice of slavery."[202]

Georgetown's unprecedented effort to achieve some measure of reparative justice inevitably also increased the pressure on others. Universities like Brown, Harvard, Princeton, and Yale began to examine their own histories, many as part of the global consortium Universities Studying Slavery.[203] In 2019, the Princeton Theological Seminary broke new ground when it created a slavery reparations fund, followed by others such as the Virginia Theological Seminary.[204] On this front too, the Floyd murder created new pressure to extend meaningful redress. In 2021, undergraduate students at Brown University voted in favor of reparations to descendants of slaves who were affiliated with the school.[205] That same year, the Jesuits announced that they would create a $100 million fund to address their legacy of slavery and benefit descendants of enslaved people at Georgetown University.[206] Shortly thereafter in April 2022, Harvard University announced the creation of a $100 million Legacy of Slavery Fund, alongside other measures designed to respond to the legacy of slavery.[207] In 2024, Yale University also apologized for its ties to slavery and announced it would be taking a range of actions that focus "on systemic issues that echo in our nation's legacy of slavery."[208]

In other sectors too, there was an acceleration of slavery-related activity, especially after 2020. Evanston City Council made history when it developed a reparations program in the wake of a report that traced the city's history of discrimination.[209] In 2021, in a "likely first," Evanston created individual grants to

[202] *Georgetown Reflects on Slavery, Memory, and Reconciliation*, GEORGETOWN UNIVERSITY, https://www.georgetown.edu/slavery/ (last visited Jan. 4, 2025). *See also* Murawski, *supra* note 200; Hassan, *Georgetown Students Agree*, *supra* note 201.

[203] *Georgetown Reflects on Slavery*, *supra* note 202. *See also Universities Studying Slavery*, *supra* note 128. *See also* CRAIG STEVEN WILDER, EBONY AND IVY: RACE, SLAVERY, AND THE TROUBLED HISTORY OF AMERICA'S UNIVERSITIES (2013).

[204] *See* Ed Shanahan, *$27 Million Reparations over Slave Ties Pledged by Seminary*, THE NEW YORK TIMES (Oct. 21, 2019); Rachel L. Swarns, *The Seminary Flourished on Slave Labor. Now It's Planning to Pay Reparations*, THE NEW YORK TIMES (Sept. 12, 2019).

[205] *See* Randi Richardson, *Undergraduates at Brown Vote for University to Offer Reparations*, NBC NEWS (Mar. 29, 2021).

[206] *See* Rachel L. Swarns, *Jesuits Vow to Raise $100 million to Atone for Role in Slavery*, THE NEW YORK TIMES (Mar. 16, 2021).

[207] *See* Michela Moscufo, *Harvard Sets up $100 Million Endowment Fund for Slavery Reparations*, REUTERS (Apr. 26, 2022); Anemona Hartocollis, *Harvard Details Its Ties to Slavery and Its Plans for Redress*, THE NEW YORK TIMES (Apr. 26, 2022). The Harvard plan is vague however on the question of individual redress.

[208] *Yale Vows New Actions to Address Past Ties to Slavery, Issues Apology, Book*, YALE NEWS (Feb. 16, 2024), https://news.yale.edu/2024/02/16/yale-vows-new-actions-address-past-ties-slavery-issues-apology-book.

[209] Memorandum from City Clerk Devon Reid to Alderwoman Robin Rue Simmons re The Case for Reparations (Apr. 18, 2019), https://www.cityofevanston.org/home/showpublisheddocument/71150/637854525387270000; *Reparations Committee*, CITY OF EVANSTON, https://cityofevanston.civicweb.net/portal/members.aspx?id = 85 (last visited Jan. 5, 2025).

help redress discriminatory housing practices.[210] Other local governments also started reparations initiatives including Los Angeles, California; Providence, Rhode Island; Asheville, North Carolina; Burlington, Vermont; and Boston and Amherst, Massachusetts.[211] Many have apologized and are working on "a reparatory approach to confronting and dismantling structural and institutional racism."[212]

The force of these reparative justice demands also began to show up in the commercial sphere, in part as a result of the slavery disclosure requirements that came into force in the aftermath of the reparations litigation. As early as 2005, JP Morgan Chase, the largest bank in the United States, admitted that its predecessors accepted enslaved people as collateral on loans and established a $5 million scholarship program for Louisiana students that it described as reparations.[213] Wachovia followed suit shortly thereafter.[214] But in the wake of 2020, the pressure once again increased, particularly as central banks in the United Kingdom and Europe began to take action.[215] In 2021, Amalgamated Bank announced that it backed reparations and supported bill H.R. 40, becoming the first major American bank to do so.[216] In 2022, there was a congressional

[210] *See* Rachel Treisman, *In Likely First, Chicago Suburb of Evanston Approves Reparations for Black Residents*, NATIONAL PUBLIC RADIO (Mar. 23, 2021). A conservative group has sued the city, arguing discrimination. *See* Isabel Yip, *Evanston Faces Lawsuit over Reparations Payments to Black Residents*, NBC NEWS (June 4, 2024).

[211] *See* Madeleine List, *Providence Mayor Signs Order to Pursue Truth, Reparations for Black, Indigenous People*, THE PROVIDENCE JOURNAL (July 16, 2020); Zuri Hoffman, *The City of Burlington Establishes Reparations Task* Force, NBC 5 (Nov. 17, 2020); Neil Vigdor, *North Carolina City Approves Reparations for Black Residents*, THE NEW YORK TIMES (Jul. 16, 2020); Philip Marcelo, *A Price Tag on Trauma? College Town Weighs Black Reparations*, ASSOCIATED PRESS (Mar. 10, 2021); Michael Casey, *Council Votes to Study Reparations for Black Bostonians*, ASSOCIATED PRESS (Dec. 14, 2022).

[212] *Steinberg, 10 Other U.S. Mayors Commit to Develop Reparations Pilot Projects*, CBS NEWS (June 18, 2021). *See also 11 U.S. Mayors Commit to Developing Pilot Projects for Reparations*, NATIONAL PUBLIC RADIO (June 18, 2021); Kyle K. Moore & Stevie Marvin, *Why We Have to Keep Talking About Reparations in 2025*, ECONOMIC POLICY INSTITUTE (Feb. 19, 2025), https://www.epi.org/blog/reparations-in-2025/; Philip M. Albieri et al., *Racial Justice and Health Equity: Public Perspectives on Reparations in America*, AAMC CENTER FOR HEALTH JUSTICE (Apr. 16, 2024), https://www.aamchealthjustice.org/resources/policy/reparations.

[213] *See* Joshua Levs, *Bank Chain Apologizes for Involvement in Slavery*, NATIONAL PUBLIC RADIO (June 3, 2005); Ken Magill, *From J.P. Morgan Chase, an Apology and $5 Million in Slavery Reparations*, THE NEW YORK SUN (Feb., 1, 2005).

[214] *See* Joshua Levs, *Bank Chain Apologizes for Involvement in Slavery*, NATIONAL PUBLIC RADIO (June 3, 2005).

[215] *See Dutch Central Bank Apologises for Historic Links to Slave Trade*, AL JAZEERA (July 1, 2022); Jasper Jolly, *Barclays, HSBC and Lloyds Among UK Banks that Had Links to Slavery*, THE GUARDIAN (June 18, 2020); Kevin Rawlinson, *Lloyd's of London and Greene King to Make Slave Trade Reparations*, THE GUARDIAN (June 18, 2020); Jasper Jolly, *Bank of England Owned 599 Slaves in 1770s, New Exhibition Reveals*, NATIONAL AFRICAN-AMERICAN REPARATIONS COMMISSION (Apr. 18, 2022), https://reparationscomm.org/reparations-news/bank-of-england-owned-599-slaves-in-1770s-new-exhibition-reveals/; Otele & Kattah, *supra* note 130.

[216] *See* Justine Coleman, *Union-Owned Bank Backs Reparations for Black Americans*, THE HILL (Mar. 17, 2021). *See also* Zoe Thomas, *The Hidden Links Between Slavery and Wall Street*, BBC NEWS (Aug, 28, 2019).

hearing entitled "An Enduring Legacy: The Role of Financial Institutions in the Horrors of Slavery and the Need for Atonement."[217] Then, in 2023, Citigroup, the third largest bank in the United States, publicly acknowledged that its predecessors likely benefited from slavery and slave labor.[218] And although the political climate has certainly changed since the 2024 election, research on the deep connections between the financial industry and slavery continues to generate scrutiny on this issue.[219]

Another indication of the evolution of the debate about reparations for slavery has been the increased use of the kind of truth-seeking bodies that used to be more typical of the transitional justice context. We have already noted how former colonial powers, governments and other institutions were turning to bodies along these lines. But perhaps the most ambitious such initiative to date is the California Task Force to Study and Develop Reparation Proposals for African Americans—the first-ever in the nation and certainly the most important of the many recent developments on reparations for slavery.[220] Like the South African and Canadian Truth and Reconciliation Commissions, it prioritized hearing directly from those affected, held public meetings and gathered a vast amount of relevant material.[221] In mid-2023, it released its ambitious final report. At nearly 1,100 pages, it "surveys the ongoing and compounding harms experienced by African Americans as a result of slavery and its lingering effects."[222] After outlining the complicity of California, it sets out the general outlines of a reparations program including a formal public apology alongside over one hundred recommendations that span the reparations spectrum from direct payments to the descendants to the kinds of distributive justice based structural remedies found in the CARICOM plan that focus on fairer distribution of public goods like education and housing, as well as legal and other policy changes.[223]

In the fall of 2024, Governor Newsom signed into law a number of related measures, including an official apology, described as an "important step" toward

[217] An Enduring Legacy: The Role of Financial Institutions in the Horrors of Slavery and the Need for Atonement, Hearing Before the Subcommittee on Oversight and Investigations, 117th Cong. (2022).

[218] *See* Emily Flitter, *Citigroup Says Its Predecessors Likely Benefited From Slavery*, THE NEW YORK TIMES (July 27, 2023).

[219] *See* SHARON ANN MURPHY, BANKING ON SLAVERY: FINANCING SOUTHERN EXPANSION IN THE ANTEBELLUM UNITED STATES (2023).

[220] *See California Unveils the US's First Slave Reparations Report*, AL JAZEERA (June 1, 2022).

[221] *See* CALIFORNIA TASK FORCE TO STUDY AND DEVELOP REPARATION PROPOSALS FOR AFRICAN AMERICANS, INTERIM REPORT 37 (2022).

[222] *The California Reparations Report*, CALIFORNIA OFFICE OF THE ATTORNEY GENERAL, https://oag.ca.gov/ab3121/report (last visited Jan. 5, 2025). *See also* CALIFORNIA TASK FORCE TO STUDY AND DEVELOP REPARATION PROPOSALS FOR AFRICAN AMERICANS, FINAL REPORT (2023) [hereinafter CALIFORNIA TASK FORCE FINAL REPORT].

[223] CALIFORNIA TASK FORCE FINAL REPORT, *supra* note 222.

making amends for "the grave injustices of the past."[224] However, there has also been considerable controversy about the scope of reparations especially on the thorny question of individual compensation, and as of the end of 2024, there was no movement on this issue.[225] But whatever comes next, the California Task Force has undoubtedly changed the conversation about both the legacy of slavery and the need to make amends, as well as about what form those amends might take. It marks an historic moment in the evolution of the problem of historic wrongs—one that seemed almost unimaginable only a decade ago.

California's ambitious undertaking has also prompted others along similar lines. The San Francisco Reparations Committee made news in mid-2023 when it released its own report with over one hundred recommendations, including an official apology and $5 million lump-sum payments to eligible individuals. The City apologized early in 2024, but the mayor also made it clear that cash reparations were off the table at least for the time being, although other recommendations could be considered.[226] After Boston became the first major American city to apologize for slavery,[227] it established a Reparations Task Force that it charged with holding community hearings and studying racial disparities and "historic harms" to Black Bostonians. The Commission was asked to make recommendations for reparations and changes to laws and policies.[228] In 2024, New York became the second state to establish a truth seeking process focused on slavery. The New York State Community Commission on Reparations Remedies will explore the legacy of slavery and make recommendations to address longstanding inequities.[229]

Let us close this discussion about making amends for slavery and its aftermath by returning to the post-2020 developments concerning the Tulsa Massacre and the redress issues raised in *Alexander*. Despite the judicial rejections discussed above, the issue of redress for the massacre rose to prominence again in the wake of the Floyd murder. As the centennial massacre approached, there were several

[224] Shawn Hubler & Audra D.S. Burch, *California Will Formally Apologize for Being Complicit in Slavery*, The New York Times (Sept. 26, 2024). *See also* AB 3089: Chattel Slavery: Formal Apology, State Assembly, 2023–2024 Leg., Reg. Sess. (Cal. 2024) (enacted Sept. 26, 2024).

[225] *See* Hubler & Burch, *supra* note 224.

[226] *See* Joe Rivano Barros, *Mayor Nixes SF Reparations, but Black College Hub Still Possible*, Mission Local (Jan. 9, 2024), https://missionlocal.org/2024/01/there-will-be-no-reparations-in-san-francisco-will-there-be-an-hbcu/; Tim Arango, *Can Reparations Bring Black Residents Back to San Francisco?*, The New York Times (May 17, 2023).

[227] *See* Tovia Smith, *Boston Takes Rare Step of Apologizing for Its Role in Slavery and Its Lasting Harm*, National Public Radio (June 17, 2022).

[228] Boston, Mass., An Ordinance Creating a Commission to Study and Develop Reparation Proposals for African Americans (Feb. 2, 2022). *See also* Casey, *supra* note 211; *Task Force on Reparations*, City of Boston, https://www.boston.gov/departments/equity-and-inclusion-cabinet/task-force-reparations (last visited Apr. 12, 2025).

[229] James Sanders Jr., *New York Takes Historic Step: Reparations Commission Announced*, New York State Senate (Feb. 29, 2024), https://www.nysenate.gov/newsroom/press-releases/2024/james-sanders-jr/new-york-takes-historic-step-reparations-commission.

documentaries about it[230] as well as in-depth media coverage.[231] Human Rights Watch issued a major report on the massacre.[232] The House Subcommittee on the Constitution, Civil Rights, and Civil Liberties held a hearing commemorating the massacre and highlighting how "the injuries inflicted on the Greenwood community have continued to compound through the succeeding decades."[233] President Biden proclaimed May 31, 2021 a Day of Remembrance of the Tulsa Race Massacre.[234] A century after the massacre, survivors and descendants were finally gaining some traction.

Inspired by this activity, in 2020, the three remaining survivors and their descendants brought another lawsuit, this one modeled on Oklahoma's successful public nuisance claims against opioid manufacturers.[235] The court ruled that the three survivors—then aged 108, 107, and 101—were entitled to have their claims heard, though they dismissed the claims of descendants.[236] However, in June 2024, the Oklahoma Supreme Court dismissed the claims of the two remaining survivors, noting that the "continuing blight alleged within the Greenwood community born out of the Massacre implicates generational-societal inequities that can only be resolved by policymakers—not the courts."[237]

[230] Tulsa Burning: The 1921 Race Massacre (The History Channel 2021); Dreamland: The Burning of Black Wall Street (CNN 2021); and Tulsa: The Fire and the Forgotten (PBS 2021). *See 3 Documentaries You Should Watch About the Tulsa Race Massacre*, National Public Radio (May 30, 2021).

[231] *See e.g. What the 1921 Tulsa Race Massacre Destroyed*, The New York Times (May 28, 2021); *Tulsa Race Massacre Centennial: Greenwood's Destruction*, The Washington Post (May 28, 2021); Richard Luscombe, *Tulsa Massacre: Centennial of White Mob Rampage to be Commemorated in Oklahoma*, The Guardian (May 30, 2021).

[232] Human Rights Watch, The Case for Reparations in Tulsa, Oklahoma: A Human Rights Argument (2020); *US: Failed Justice 100 Years After Tulsa Race Massacre*, Human Rights Watch (May 21, 2021), https://www.hrw.org/news/2021/05/21/us-failed-justice-100-years-after-tulsa-race-massacre.

[233] Continuing Injustice: The Centennial of the Tulsa-Greenwood Race Massacre: Hearing Before the Subcommittee on the Constitution, Civil Rights, and Civil Liberties, 117th Cong. 1 (May 19, 2021).

[234] President Joseph R. Biden Jr., *Proclamation on Day of Remembrance: 100 Years After the 1921 Tulsa Race Massacre*, White House (May 31, 2021), https://bidenwhitehouse.archives.gov/briefing-room/presidential-actions/2021/05/31/a-proclamation-on-day-of-remembrance-100-years-after-the-1921-tulsa-race-massacre/ (last visited Oct. 18, 2025).

[235] *See* Maria Cramer, *Tulsa Massacre Survivors Sue City Nearly 100 Years After Attack*, The New York Times (Sept. 1, 2020).

[236] Press Release, *Historic Court Ruling—Last Living Survivors of 1921 Tulsa Race Massacre Entitled to Prove the Massacre Was a "Public Nuisance,"* Justice for Greenwood (Aug. 4, 2022), https://www.justiceforgreenwood.org/press-release-historic-court-ruling-last-living-survivors-of-1921-tulsa-race-massacre-entitled-to-prove-the-massacre-was-a-public-nuisance/; Daniela Ibarra, *Tulsa Race Massacre Lawsuit Moves Forward to Discovery Phase*, KTUL ABC 8 (Oct. 18, 2022). The claims of the descendants, however, were not allowed to proceed. *See* Ken Miller, *Judge: Tulsa Race Massacre Victims' Descendants Can't Sue*, Associated Press (Aug. 4, 2022).

[237] *See* Audra D.S. Burch, *Oklahoma Supreme Court Dismisses Tulsa Race Massacre Lawsuit*, The New York Times (June 12, 2024); Sean Murphy, *Oklahoma's Supreme Court Dismisses Lawsuit from Last 2 Survivors of Tulsa Race Massacre Seeking Reparations*, PBS News (June 12, 2024). The Court

But the case continued to reverberate, prompting ground-up redress initiatives by private individuals and foundations, who offered assistance to survivors and their families.[238] Ghana extended the remaining survivors royal names and citizenship.[239] In January 2025, the US Department of Justice issued a report on the Tulsa Massacre, saying that it "stands out as a civil rights crime unique in its magnitude, barbarity, racist hostility and its utter annihilation of a thriving Black community."[240] The report observes that even though "[l]egal limitations may have stymied the pursuit of justice," the "historical reckoning continues."[241] Then in June 2025, Tulsa's mayor announced a $105 million dollar reparations package designed to address the impact of the massacre. Although the plan did not specify direct cash payments to the remaining survivors (who were by then 110 and 111), the city confirmed that the Board of Trustees in charge of the trust could consider such payments.[242] Over one hundred years after those events, the reckoning is certainly underway.

Alexander illustrates just how persistent profound reparative justice claims can be. In part, this is because of how some injuries tend to compound, not diminish, over time.[243] But it also shows the strength of the commitment to achieve some measure of justice even a century after the atrocity and notwithstanding legal defeats. Like *Mutua*, the residential schools cases, and others, *Alexander* leveraged the power of private law in the aid of a much larger confrontation. Along the way, it created a compelling record and generated more research, features it shared with *Cato* and *Slave Descendants*.[244] Beyond this, however, the strength of

rejected a request by the plaintiffs to reconsider the dismissal. *See The Oklahoma Supreme Court Denies a Request to Reconsider Tulsa Race Massacre Dismissal*, Associated Press (Sept. 11, 2024). Commentators have suggested that the defendants have been dragging out the lawsuit in the hope that the survivors would die. *See* Deon Osborne, *OK Supreme Court Closes on Survivors. Will Biden Reopen It?* The Black Wall Street Times (Sept. 18, 2024).

[238] Tyler Butler, *Nonprofit Donates $1 Million to 1921 Tulsa Race Massacre Survivors*, KTUL ABC 8 (May 17, 2022).

[239] DeDeen L. Brown, *Tulsa Race Massacre Survivors, 108 and 102, Given Ghana Citizenship*, The Washington Post (Mar. 1, 2023); Oliver Slow, *Tulsa Race Massacre Survivors Granted Ghanaian Citizenship*, BBC News (March 2, 2023).

[240] Press Release, *Justice Department Announces Results of Review and Evaluation of the Tulsa Race Massacre*, U.S. Department of Justice (Jan. 10, 2025), https://www.justice.gov/archives/opa/pr/justice-department-announces-results-review-and-evaluation-tulsa-race-massacre.

[241] *Id.*

[242] *See* Audra D.S. Burch & Breena Kerr, *$105 Million Reparations Package for Tulsa Race Massacre Unveiled by Mayor*, The New York Times (June 1, 2025).

[243] Continuing Injustice: The Centennial of the Tulsa-Greenwood Race Massacre, *supra* note 233.

[244] *See e.g.* Alex Albright et al., *After the Burning: The Economic Effects of the 1921 Tulsa Race Massacre*, National Bureau of Economic Research (July, 2021), https://www.nber.org/system/files/working_papers/w28985/w28985.pdf; Andre M. Perry et al., *The True Costs of the Tulsa Race Massacre, 100 Years Later*, Brookings Institution (May 28, 2021), https://www.brookings.edu/research/the-true-costs-of-the-tulsa-race-massacre-100-years-later/. On the larger issues of the economic impact of slavery, *see e.g.* Mark Stelzner & Sven Beckert, The Contribution of Enslaved Workers to Output and Growth in the Antebellum United States, 77 Econ. Hist. Rev. 137 (2024); Slavery's Capitalism: A New History of American Economic

the link it drew between the defendant's wrong and the plaintiff's harms helped to force an ongoing reckoning with the massacre and its legacy. *Alexander* in that sense shows the capacity of especially powerful reparative justice claims to press open even those doors of history that seem most firmly closed.

While the issue of atoning for slavery is in considerable flux, it is clear that the conversation has evolved very rapidly over the past decade or two. Until recently the idea of reparations for something as vast, old, and central to American history as slavery seemed like a "pipe dream" even to advocates.[245] But despite predictions to the contrary, a national reckoning with the legacy of slavery—something which had seemed almost impossible a few short years ago—is underway. And while it is controversial and very much in its infancy, the change is a fundamental one. In much public debate, slavery has gone from being a horrific historical event to an injustice that demands some kind of present-day effort at repair. The question of just how to repair wrongs that are so vast, so old, and so deeply intertwined with centuries of law, politics, and the economy is inevitably a very difficult one that eludes easy responses. But the question has now been sharply posed and despite the political turmoil it has generated, it is unlikely to go away.

Conclusion

When Ta-Nehisi Coates was interviewed by *The New Yorker* in 2019 about his important 2014 article, "The Case for Reparations," he said "my notion wasn't

Development (Sven Beckert & Seth Rockman eds., 2016); Greg Timmon, *How Slavery Became the Economic Engine of the South*, History Channel (Apr. 2, 2024), https://www.history.com/news/slavery-profitable-southern-economy; Joseph E. Inikori, *The Slave Trade, Imperialism, Colonialism and Neocolonialism: The Rise of the Western World Economy, and Unjust Enrichment*, *in* Accounting for Colonialism: Measuring Unjust Enrichment and Damages in Africa 9 (Richard F. America ed., 2024); Daniel Tetteh Osabu-Kle, *A Rough Ball Park Estimate—Damages and Unjust Enrichment from Abuses of Dominance*, *in* Accounting for Colonialism, *supra* note 244, at 195; William A. Darity Jr. & A. Kirsten Mullen, From Here to Equality: Reparations for Black Americans in the Twenty-First Century (2d ed. 2022). This work spurred a great deal of discussion. *See e.g.* V.P. Franklin, *William A. Darity Jr., and A. Kirsten Mullen,* From Here to Equality: Reparations for Black Americans in the Twenty-First Century, *Chapel Hill: University of North Carolina Press, 2020,* 106 J. Afr. Am. Hist. 766 (2021). On tracing the effects of slavery forward to the present, see e.g. Juliana Menasce Horowitz, *Most Americans Say the Legacy of Slavery Still Affects Black People in the U.S. Today*, Pew Research Center (June 17, 2019), https://www.pewresearch.org/fact-tank/2019/06/17/most-americans-say-the-legacy-of-slavery-still-affects-black-people-in-the-u-s-today/; Ronald W. Walters, *The Impact of Slavery on 20th- and 21st-Century Black Progress*, 97 J. Afr. Am. Hist. 110–30 (2012); Gwendolyn Scott-Jones & Mozella Richardson Kamara, *The Traumatic Impact of Structural Racism on African Americans*, 6 Dela. J. Public Health 80 (2020); William Darity Jr. et al., *The Cumulative Costs of Racism and the Bill for Black Reparations*, 36 J. Econ. Perspectives 99, 116–17 (2022).

245 Moore & Marvin, *supra* note 212.

that you could actually get reparations passed, even in my lifetime. My notion was that you could get people to stop laughing."[246] Perhaps more than any other example, the ongoing reckoning with slavery illustrates the dramatic change in our attitude to past wrongs, even when they are the most challenging of our shared history. Like colonialism, the scale of slavery is vast, it stretched across centuries, and in many respects it made us what we are today. That is why, not too long ago, critics dismissed the idea of reparations for slavery or colonialism as far-fetched and implausible. But as we have seen, this began to be replaced by a growing sense that such grievous injustices do not disappear just because they are old. Time does not heal them and, as we are learning, nor does trying to ignore them make them go away. They demand to be reckoned with, in whatever form that might take.

Litigation proved a useful tool with wrongs that could be wedged—even if somewhat awkwardly—into a tort-like framework. The same could not be said, however, of wrongs like colonialism and slavery whose scale and significance placed even more strain on the tort analogy. Yet as we have seen, the failure to attract judicial support does not necessarily diminish the force of reparative justice. Instead, it often proves powerful when brought to bear on institutions directly without the intersession of law. From governments to businesses to churches and universities, the moral force of well-developed reparative justice arguments about colonialism and about slavery have proven surprisingly hard to resist. People certainly disagree about questions concerning both if and how to repair as wrongs as vast as colonialism or slavery, but to put it in Coates' terms, no one is laughing any more.

[246] *Ta-Nehisi Coates Revisits the Case for Reparations*, The New Yorker (June 10, 2019).

7
Heroes or Villains? Lawyers and Historic Wrongs

Introduction

We have traced how the wrongs of the past have gone from being a source of sorrow or shame to something very different—an injustice. Recent decades have witnessed a growing awareness that time does not heal all wounds and that many wrongs do not simply fade away over time. Some old injuries actually fester and grow. Along with this insight, as we have seen, have come new and pressing demands to make amends. No longer convinced that we should just "let sleeping dogs lie," there is a growing sense that wrongdoers must try to repair harm they did, even if it was a long time ago.

This changed approach to old wrongs has had a profound impact on a wide range of institutions from governments, churches, and corporations, to universities and museums, among many others. They find themselves in unfamiliar territory—struggling to understand their pasts and to respond. They face serious consequences, and not only because of the financial cost of making amends. Grappling with a problematic past consumes significant time and energy and often creates difficult internal and external dynamics. It may also profoundly affect the way an institution is viewed, sometimes even calling its very existence into question. In light of these high stakes, let us now ask what lessons we can learn to help us better respond to demands to redress historic injustices.

We will begin by focusing on an issue that has been especially significant across many cases of historic wrongs—the role of lawyers. We have observed the critical role that law plays in putting these issues on the radar. For this reason, lawyers occupy central roles both for survivors and for defending institutions. Many of the historic wrongs that are widely acknowledged today would never have come to light had it not been for lawyers who stepped up to represent survivors in the face of terrible odds. Lawyers play another central role too—inside institutions that are challenged, they typically have the most influential voices and end up being critical not only in litigation but also in broader strategy and decision-making.

But there is also another less salutary reason that issues with lawyers warrant serious attention. Some of the biggest challenges in historic injustice cases

Making Amends for Historic Wrongs. Mayo Moran, Oxford University Press. © Mayo Moran 2025.
DOI: 10.1093/9780190927295.003.0007

revolve around them. All too often, lawyers acting for justice-seekers, particularly those as vulnerable as survivors of old wrongs, enrich themselves at the expense of survivors. Across a wide range of cases from residential schools to colonial redress, lawyer misconduct takes a devastating toll, undermining the integrity of reparative measures and damaging broader goals like reconciliation. There is also a second more subtle problem with lawyers, one that arises on the side of defendant institutions. When faced with historic wrongs, legal counsel often automatically defaults to an extreme protective stance that they think will benefit the institution. But they frequently do so without grasping either important ethical considerations or the larger context. As a result, they often press 'attack doglitigation strategies that end up undermining the very institution they are so keen to defend.

While these challenges are extremely important, most lawyers do an admirable job for their clients. As a result, before turning to the challenges, it is useful to remind ourselves that without them many of the most significant cases of historic wrongs would never have moved forward at all. In that sense, the lawyer is a complex figure—sometimes hero, sometimes villain. So let us begin by looking at why lawyers matter so much in cases like these before turning to some of the challenges that come along with that centrality.

Unlikely Heroes

Lawyers are often critical players in cases of historic injustice. The transformative cases of righting historic wrongs almost always depend on lawyers taking on "lost causes" for little or no pay. Leilani Muir's ground-breaking eugenics case against the Alberta government is a telling example. When she discovered that she had been the victim of eugenic sterilization, she decided to sue the government. It was a bold and probably rash decision. She was barely getting by as a part-time cashier and had none of the critical evidence. And because the prospects for success were incredibly low, she was repeatedly turned down, not only by law firms but even by the feminist advocacy group, the Women's Legal Education and Action Fund (LEAF). But nearly a decade into Ms. Muir's search for representation, LEAF asked lawyer Myra Bielby to meet with her, which she did in 1989:

> As Bielby recalls Muir arrived at Field's downtown Edmonton office "with shopping bags full of materials" along with a complicated and startling story. After talking to her, Bielby decided while "it didn't look too promising, there was something here." Before taking the case Bielby had to get clearance from her Firm's senior management because some disbursements would be charged to the Firm's accounts. When she approached the managing partner Bob Teskey

> she recalls him saying rather enigmatically "Well Myra, God is with you". Bielby "took that as a yes" and proceeded with the case.[1]

During the years it took to prepare for trial, Bielby became a judge and other lawyers from the firm stepped in. In 1996, more than seven years after that original meeting, the stunning verdict in Muir's favor changed the landscape for her and for thousands of other survivors, something that never would have happened without the years of support from the lawyers and the firm. When Leilani Muir died in 2016, the litigator who had presented her case to the court said that that it was "a chance to represent a hero."[2]

A committed lawyer working against all odds was also critical to the restitution of *Woman in Gold.* When Maria Altmann decided to sue for return of the painting under a new Austrian law, her choice was unexpected—rather than a high-flying firm, she chose a young attorney who was the grandson of composer Arnold Schoenberg. He did work at a law firm, but he agreed to the contingency arrangement Altmann proposed. He would receive nothing if he lost—which "everyone predicted he would"—but he would be entitled to 40% of the value of the Klimts if he won.[3] Schoenberg worked for almost nothing for years in the face of extremely poor odds and eventually had to leave his law firm.[4] Yet, after eight years of torturous transnational litigation, Schoenberg secured the return of the Klimts to Altmann.[5] As in the case of Leilani Muir, without his commitment the paintings would certainly have remained in the hands of the Austrians who stole them in the first place.

At the same time, this case also highlights another complicated dimension of the role lawyers play in cases like these. Schoenberg's commitment to the return of *Woman in Gold* was probably an objectively unreasonable decision. It took over his professional and personal life and financial ruin looked far more likely than financial gain. Yet, as things turned out, when the paintings sold for a record $326 million, Schoenberg reportedly ended up with $139 million.[6] Even for

[1] Geoff Ellwand, *Forced Sterilization—How the Law Righted an Ugly Wrong in Alberta History*, The Canadian Bar Association Alberta Branch, https://lawmatters.cba-alberta.org/MediaGallery/NM/Law-Matters-Archived-Issues/law-matters_summer-2017_web.pdf at 14 (last visited Oct. 18, 2025).

[2] *Id.*

[3] Tom Tugend, *Real-Life Lawyer Behind "Woman in Gold,"* Forward (Apr. 3, 2015), https://forward.com/schmooze/218047/real-life-lawyer-behind-woman-in-gold/.

[4] *See* Mike Boehm, *Lawyer E. Randol Schoenberg Likes Being Film Fodder for Ryan Reynolds*, Los Angeles Times (Jan. 30, 2015), https://www.latimes.com/entertainment/arts/culture/la-et-cm-ryan-reynolds-helen-mirren-woman-gold-klimt-randol-schoenberg-20150128-story.html; Kevin Lang, *Woman in Gold: History vs. Hollywood*, History vs. Hollywood (May 7, 2015), https://www.historyvshollywood.com/reelfaces/woman-in-gold/.

[5] *See* Tugend, *supra* note 3.

[6] *Id.*

eight years of unpaid labor, this is a very large—perhaps outsize—reward. And in retrospect, it might be tempting to view Schoenberg as a profiteer. However, evaluating whether lawyer conduct amounts to undue self-interest is a complex matter in cases like these.

As *Altmann* and *Muir* illustrate, landmark historic wrongs cases are usually viewed at the outset as far-fetched "losers." Individuals who sue powerful institutions for old wrongs typically face almost insuperable obstacles. They have problems with proof because the critical evidence is almost always in the hands of the defendant institutions. As we have seen, they typically have to break new legal ground on multiple difficult issues. These include the all-important limitations periods, questions about where the legal action should be brought and who should be sued, as well as more conceptual matters of institutional responsibility. All of this gives defendants many plausible preliminary challenges, which forces plaintiffs to expend considerable time and money before they ever get to the substantive issues at the heart of the case. This is why these cases are unusually prone to delay and cost escalation. So survivors need lawyers who are prepared to take a risk on their cases, and like Leilani Muir, most of them struggle to get someone willing to do so.

Challenges with delay and expense are of course not unique to cases involving historic wrongs—they arise in all litigation. However, there are at least two reasons why they loom even larger in these cases. First, the longer it takes to get to the substantive issues, the greater the risk that direct survivors will die before they see resolution. The *Alexander* litigation involving the Greenwood massacre survivors is an especially poignant example—at age 109 and 110, the two survivors that were still alive continued to fight for "their day in court," a reminder of the profound importance of being able to tell your story.[7] The ramifications of disappearing survivors, however, go beyond the significant individual loss. Direct survivors always have the strongest redress claims, and recovery is often limited to them.[8] Direct survivors are also the most powerful way of making courts and others understand the gravity of the wrong, as cases like *Muir*, *Altmann*, and *Alexander* remind us. This especially matters in these challenging cases because courts need to be sufficiently motivated to set aside procedural and other obstacles. So in this context, the

[7] As noted in the chapter above, their tenacity was not enough, however. The Oklahoma Supreme Court dismissed their claims and rejected a request by the plaintiffs to reconsider the dismissal. *See The Oklahoma Supreme Court Denies a Request to Reconsider Tulsa Race Massacre Dismissal*, Associated Press (Sept. 11, 2024). However, at the beginning of June 2025, the mayor of Tulsa announced the reparations package discussed in the chapter above. *See* Audra D.S. Burch & Breena Kerr, $105 Million Reparations Package for Tulsa Race Massacre Unveiled by Mayor, The New York Times (June 1, 2025).

[8] See also for example *Mutua*, *Alexander*, and the residential schools cases discussed in Chapter 6, where compensation went mainly to direct survivors only.

fact that defendants can bring multiple early challenges creates a serious risk that survivors may not live long enough to be able to speak to the substance or benefit from any resolution.

A sad example is found in the thirty-five-year saga involving the Catholic Church's Mount Cashel orphanage sexual abuse scandal.[9] Reports of abuse emerged in 1989, and the legal action was launched in 1999. The diocese brought motion after motion. After the Supreme Court dismissed their final appeal, the diocese declared bankruptcy.[10] By that time, the lawyer for the survivors had already spent two decades on the case and would spend several more years to get compensation in the context of the bankruptcy proceedings.[11] It took from 1999 until 2016 for the trial to commence, and only late in 2024 did a court finally rule that survivors should at least receive a portion of their awards. By that time, 15% of the claimants had died.[12] As this extreme example shows, defendants in historic injustice claims have many opportunities to delay, and it is not hard to imagine that the disappearance of direct survivors may be viewed as one very significant advantage of stretching out the litigation timeline. It also makes these extremely challenging cases for lawyers to assume.

The complex nature of litigation like this also results in very high costs. Virtually all historic wrongs claims are brought against institutions. Governments are common defendants, as are religious, educational, and cultural institutions. And because defendants are institutions, often with insurers behind them, they can vastly outspend the impoverished survivors that are typically on the other side of the litigation. This in turn creates another serious risk for lawyers considering taking on claims for historic wrongs.

The fact that cases like these are so challenging for legal counsel is one reason why contingency fee arrangements are important in this context. Indeed, high-risk and potentially high-reward claims are one important reason why contingency arrangements are thought to further access to justice.[13] As the Honorable

[9] *See* Kevin Clarke, *After 35 Years, a Final Settlement Reached in the Mount Cashel Orphanage Sex Abuse Cases*, AMERICA MAGAZINE (July 11, 2024).

[10] Roman Catholic Episcopal Corporation of St. John's v. John Doe (G.E.B. #25), et al., 2021 CanLII 1097 (Can. S.C.C.) (dismissing leave to appeal). *See also* Terry Roberts, *N.L. Court Approves 1st Payment of $22M for Abuse Survivors*, CBC NEWS (Oct. 9, 2024); Clarke, *supra* note 9.

[11] *See* Roberts, *supra* note 10; Barb Sweet, *Supreme Court of Canada Decision in Favour of Mount Cashel Victims Will Have Sweeping Implications: Lawyers*, THE CHRONICLE HERALD (Can., Jan. 15, 2021).

[12] *See* Roberts, *supra* note 10.

[13] See for example the detailed American Bar Association formal opinion regarding contingency fees. American Bar Association Standing Committee on Ethics and Professional Responsibility, *Formal Opinion 94-389: Contingent Fees*, AMERICAN BAR ASSOCIATION (Dec. 5, 1994), https://www.americanbar.org/content/dam/aba/publications/YourABA/201203_94-389.authcheckdam.pdf. *See also Fee Arrangements*, CANADIAN BAR ASSOCIATION, https://www.cba.org/Publications-Resources/Practice-Tools/Retainers-and-Fees-Toolkit/Fee-Arrangements (last visited Jan. 26, 2025). *See also* David Luban, *Speculating on Justice: The Ethics and Jurisprudence of Contingency Fees*, *in* LEGAL

Frank Iacobucci, who played a key role in Canada's residential schools agreement, observed, "class actions can facilitate the substantive element of access to justice because the class as a whole is stronger than individual claimants when facing a defendant with considerable resources to defend itself."[14] Indeed, in the absence of contingency arrangements, most historic injustice claims would never have been raised. At the same time, these arrangements do pose risks and for that reason often require judicial approval.[15] As discussed in the section below, such vigilance is essential if survivors are to get the benefits that contingency arrangements promise. Still, it is important to bear in mind that lawyers taking on claims like the ones we have discussed have very poor prospects of winning. Survivors need to find lawyers who are willing to take a leap of faith for them—a leap that entails many years of work with no pay and low chances of success.

That is why the lawyers who are willing to take on claims in the face of so many of these challenging factors do have a heroic quality, as we see in cases like *Muir*, *Altmann*, and the Mount Cashel litigation, among many others. Without lawyers like these and their years of difficult work, we would not have had the efforts to undo some of the horrors of the Holocaust, we would not have museums around the world reflecting on their colonial pasts, we would not have had truth and reconciliation processes in places like Canada, the United States, Finland, and elsewhere. We would not have education for children about these issues, and we would not have commemorations that warn us not to forget. We would understand less of our pasts.

So as these and many other examples show, lawyers are often critical advocates for claimants in cases of historic wrongs, taking on cases that seem like lost causes and devoting many years to pursuing justice for survivors. And as we shall see, even when reparative processes do get underway, lawyers frequently end up having to go to court for survivors who would often otherwise never see the benefits that should be coming their way. But there is also another side to the lawyer equation. Cases of historic wrongs lawyers are also replete with lawyers who, far from being heroes, too often appear as villains who prey on vulnerable survivors for their own benefit. In order to draw some lessons about how to preserve the benefits of lawyer involvement while limiting the risks, we need to better understand the nature of this kind of lawyer misconduct as well. Let us now turn to some of these troubling examples.

Ethics and Legal Practice: Contemporary Issues 88 (Stephen Parker & Charles Sampford eds., 1996).

[14] The Hon. Frank Iacobucci, *What Is Access to Justice in the Context of Class Actions?* 53 Sup. Ct. L. Rev. (2d) 17, 21 (2011).

[15] *See generally* Luban, *supra* note 13.

The Self-Serving Villain

Our earlier discussion explored a number of cases that broke new ground for survivors of historic wrongs, including Canada's residential schools settlement and the United Kingdom action by survivors of colonial violence in Kenya. Both of those cases resulted in individual compensation alongside more comprehensive responses, including apologies, commemoration, and even a truth and reconciliation commission in Canada's case. They were important victories that opened the door for other efforts to rectify historic wrongs. Yet, both examples also illustrate the threat that lawyer misconduct poses in situations like these where there are vulnerable old survivors, well-resourced institutional defendants, and money to be made by lawyers. Examining what went so wrong in these two important cases helps to illuminate how we can do a better job of responding to historic injustice.

The "Biggest Winners": Lawyer Problems in Canada's Residential Schools Settlement

Canada's historic residential schools agreement was notable for its pioneering Truth and Reconciliation Commission and two ambitious compensation processes. Unfortunately, it also stands out for less positive reasons—the scale of lawyer misconduct and exploitation of claimants, and the repeated failures of the mechanisms that should have protected them. A fitting place to begin understanding the dynamics at play in cases like these is with Tony Merchant, the lawyer who became known as the residential schools agreement's "biggest winner."[16]

As residential schools issues were starting to surface, Merchant began aggressively recruiting survivors, many of whom had never even spoken about their experiences.[17] Indigenous leaders complained, and he was sanctioned as a result.[18] He was undeterred, however, and was suspended twice for this behavior.[19] But his aggressive recruitment paid off—by most counts Merchant ended up with more claimants than any other lawyer.[20] As the Settlement Agreement

[16] Jonathan Gatehouse, *The Residential Schools Settlement's Biggest Winner: A Profile of Tony Merchant*, MACLEAN'S MAGAZINE (April 4, 2013).

[17] *See Lawyer Says Native Leaders Have Failed Abused Students*, TEKAWENNAKE NEWS (July 21, 1999).

[18] *See* Gatehouse, *supra* note 16; Merchant v. Law Society of Saskatchewan, 2002 SKCA 60, ¶ 119 (Can.).

[19] *See* Arthur White-Crummey, *Law Society Suspends Tony Merchant for 8 Months*, REGINA LEADER POST (Oct. 1, 2020); Alec Salloum, *Tony Merchant Wins Appeal Against Law Society of Saskatchewan*, REGINA LEADER POST (Jan. 11, 2022).

[20] Reliable numbers are hard to find but at various times, Merchant has claimed to have represented over 10,000 survivors. *See* Gatehouse, *supra* note 16. The firm's website also claimed at

was being negotiated in 2006, Merchant seemed confident that he would profit handsomely:

> Merchant is sure what his take should be: $40 million upfront, and tens of millions more once special tribunals start handing out additional compensation to former students who were physically or sexually abused. In the past, he has publicly mused about hitting the $100-million mark.[21]

And even though there were serious concerns about Merchant from the very outset, he remained one of the most prominent players.[22] As he predicted, alongside the upfront fee of $40 million, the individual compensation process did prove extremely lucrative for Merchant. The huge caseload that resulted from his early troubling recruitment practices ensured that Merchant had a dominant voice in the negotiations. One of the key items in those negotiations was the design of the "special tribunal process." And as it turned out, the process that Merchant had a strong say in negotiating did end up conferring huge benefits on lawyers, Merchant himself prominent among them.[23]

That process—the Independent Assessment Process (IAP) discussed earlier—was a unique and ambitious one that generated important benefits for claimants. But its complexity also meant that claimants needed legal counsel.[24] To address this, the Canadian government agreed to pay both for the award itself as well as for a further 15% of the award amount for legal fees.[25] But the Settlement Agreement did not explicitly limit the fees lawyers could charge to Canada's 15% Though many did not charge more than 15%, others saw opportunity. Some lawyers sought to maximize revenue by minimizing service, and courts had to clarify that the 15% fee award assumed acceptable service and that

one point to represent half of the claimants, though that claim has now disappeared from the website. *See Merchant Law Firm to Get $40M in Residential School Fees*, CBC NEWS (May 8, 2006). It is an irony that without Merchant's troubling recruitment tactics driving up claimant numbers, there might never have been the political will to forge an agreement.

[21] Gatehouse, *supra* note 16.

[22] For this reason, Merchant's fees were subject to a special verification requirement. *See* Indian Residential Schools Settlement Agreement, Schedule V (May 8, 2006) [hereinafter *IRSSA*]. After MLG was paid $25 million of the upfront fee, Canada sought return of some of the monies on the basis of fraudulent billing practices, which resulted in protraccted litigation. *See* Canada (Attorney General) v. Merchant Law Group, 2017 SKCA 62 (Can.), leave to appeal denied, 2018 CanLII 12948 (Can. S.C.C.). *See also* Baxter v. Canada (Attorney General), 83 O.R. (3d) 481, 2006 CanLII 41673, ¶¶ 66–78 (Can. Ont. S.C.).

[23] For example, Merchant was the only firm with guaranteed membership on the important National Certification Committee and National Administrative Committee. *See IRSSA*, *supra* note 22, §§ 4.09, 4.11.

[24] Schedule D itself states that one of the "Core Assumptions" of the process is that "parties have legal representation." *IRSSA*, *supra* note 22, Schedule D at 7.

[25] *Id.*

lower fees could be awarded. Some lawyers also argued that 30% fees (15% from Canada and 15% from the claimant) had to be rubber stamped by adjudicators.[26] The Chief Adjudicator was forced to clarify that 30% was reserved "for the most difficult or time-consuming cases."[27] One result of all of this was lawyers' fees consumed far too much time and energy in the early years of the process.[28]

Many of these problems resulted from gaps in the Settlement Agreement. Besides not limiting fees, the Settlement Agreement lacked a mechanism for reviewing legal fees. This allowed high-volume practices with large numbers of claimants to extract excessive fees for minimal service in the expectation that vulnerable claimants would have difficulty objecting. The Settlement Agreement was also silent on another serious issue—lawyer misconduct, especially fraud. Without a complaint mechanism, claimants were left to go to law societies or launch court actions against their lawyers on their own. And even when they did manage to complain, sluggish responses too often left them at the mercy of self-serving lawyers, some of whom walked away with tens of millions of dollars. David Blott, who at one point had thousands of claimants in the IAP, serves as a dramatic illustration.

Blott and his "business associate" were on the lookout for a lucrative opportunity when they heard about the possibility of the IAP. They exploited their connection with an Indigenous tribe, paying community members to sign up claimants. They gave a bonus for sexual abuse claims and charged a hefty fee if claimants decided to change lawyers.[29] The plan paid off—Blott amassed over 5,600 IAP claimants, even though he only had one associate.[30] Unsurprisingly this did not serve claimants well. They went into hearings unprepared, often meeting their lawyer for the first time that day.[31] Blott also extended claimants high interest loans—some in excess of the 60% "criminal" rate.[32] Some claimants

[26] Winnipeg lawyer Howard Tennenhouse, for instance, retained 30% of any award obtained. On forty-seven occasions, he appropriated more than the Government of Canada's 15%, acquiring for himself nearly $1 million. The Law Society of Manitoba disbarred him in 2012. *See* The Law Society of Manitoba v. Tennenhouse, 2012 MBLS 14 (Can.).

[27] Chief Adjudicator, *GP1R3: Factors to Consider in the Exercise of Adjudicators' Responsibilities to Review Legal Fees Under IAP*, Indian Residential Schools Adjudication Secretariat (2013), http://www.iap-pei.ca/guidance-eng.php?act = gp-1r3-lf-gp-b-eng.php.

[28] *See* Independent Assessment Process Oversight Committee, Final Report 34, 52–54 (2021).

[29] The courts reacted slowly. It was not until 2014—two years after the IAP application deadline had passed—that the Manitoba Court of Queen's Bench confirmed that those "form filler" contracts were null and void, as were contracts requiring claimants to pay non-lawyers for legal services. Not including Blott, seven law firms with roughly 2,250 cases were affected by this decision. *See* Fontaine et al. v. Canada, 2014 MBQB 113 (Can.).

[30] *See* Fontaine v. Canada (Attorney General), 2012 BCSC 839, ¶¶ 33–35 (Can.).

[31] *Id.* ¶¶ 62, 76.

[32] When the Law Society of Alberta finally investigated in 2014, it concluded that there were grounds to believe that the Blott's interest rates may have been criminal. *See* Law Society of Alberta v. Blott, 2014 ABLS 7, ¶ 27, Exhibit 5(D), ¶ 67 (Can.). *See also Lawyer David Blott Disbarred*

reported that by the time the settlement arrived there was almost nothing left.[33]

David Blott was eventually removed from the IAP and later disbarred. But his case is a cautionary tale. He operated from 2006 until 2012, even though the Law Society of Alberta received a complaint about him as early as 2007 and had received ten complaints by the time he was removed.[34] Yet, it was the Chief Adjudicator of the IAP—not the Law Society of Alberta—that began the process that led Blott's removal. And not until two years after that did a Law Society of Alberta panel finally accept his resignation and disbar him, noting that the "victims of the residential school system were effectively revictimized and treated less like human beings and more like cattle" and describing his practice as a "factory of gross self-interest."[35] Still Blott walked away a rich man. His company that hired community members to fill out forms took away $6 million, and Blott himself reportedly made $21 million from Canada's contribution to legal fees alone, not including what he extracted from claimants.[36]

In response, the Chief Adjudicator published a set of practice expectations, which targeted issues like those in the cases of Merchant, Blott, and others.[37] But both the lawyer misconduct and the regulatory failure persisted, as the troubling case of lawyer Stephen Bronstein illustrates. By 2009, complaints were coming in about Bronstein. Community members said that he was using a convicted murderer to pressure people to sign up with him.[38] Again, despite the complaints, it was not the courts nor the law society, but the Chief Adjudicator that initiated the investigation. The investigation revealed that Bronstein's whole enterprise was set up to maximize clients and minimize service. Yet, the judge allowed him to remain in the process under supervision, even though she described his conduct as "improper and blameworthy."[39] Bronstein eventually admitted to

Following Law Society's Acceptance of Resignation, LAW SOCIETY OF ALBERTA (June 13, 2014), https://www.lawsociety.ab.ca/wp-content/uploads/2017/01/blott-media-statement-june-13-2014.pdf.

[33] Fontaine v. Canada (Attorney General), 2012 BCSC 839, ¶¶ 59, 78 (Can.). *See also* Meghan Grant, *"Revictimized" Residential School Survivors Can Sue Disgraced Lawyer in Class-Action*, CBC NEWS (Oct. 3, 2019); Law Society of Alberta Resignation Committee, *Resignation Committee Report in the Matter of the Legal Professions Act re David J. Blott* 3 (June 30, 2014), https://documents.lawsociety.ab.ca/wp-content/uploads/2017/02/22165850/Blott-Resignation-Report.pdf.

[34] Law Society of Alberta Resignation Committee, *supra* note 33, at 10–11.

[35] *Id.* at 3. *See also* Grant, *supra* note 33.

[36] *See* Amy German, *Class Action Suit to Go Ahead for Thousands of Swindled Residential School Victims*, NATION (Can., Oct. 25, 2019).

[37] *Expectations of Legal Practice in the IAP*, INDIAN RESIDENTIAL SCHOOLS ADJUDICATION SECRETARIAT (October 3, 2013), http://www.iap-pei.ca/expectations-eng.php.

[38] In the matter of the Legal Profession Act SBC 1998 c. 9 and a hearing concerning Stephen John Bronstein, 2021 LSBC 19, ¶¶ 33–53 (Can.) [hereinafter Bronstein].

[39] As the court put it, "[s]everal subsequent [Requests for Direction] were brought in regard to Bronstein's adherence to the terms of the 2013 Order." *See* Fontaine v. Canada (Attorney General), 2015 BCSC 717, ¶ 3 (Can.). The court held that "Bronstein has demonstrated a capability to reform

pressuring claimants, providing inadequate representation, and to illegal financial transactions. The response of the Law Society of British Columbia—twelve years after the original concerns were raised—was a one-month suspension and a $4,000 costs award, something described by the dissenting Indigenous member of the hearing panel as "grossly inadequate."[40] The chief of the nation targeted by Bronstein said that the "outcome makes a mockery of justice" and that the system had once failed Indigenous peoples.[41] Stephen Bronstein made as much as $40 million from the process.[42]

Chief Alfonse's emphasis on the system was well-placed. In the Merchant, Blott, and Bronstein cases, as in many others, both the courts and the regulators failed to protect survivors from unscrupulous lawyers. And while most lawyers did a good job for claimants, the few lawyers who engaged in this kind of misconduct intentionally amassed very large caseloads and ended up representing a large percentage of the survivors. The sad result was that for many survivors the healing that the process aimed at was profoundly undermined both by self-interested lawyers and by the failure of those who were supposed to regulate them.

Colonial Violence and Lawyer Misconduct—The Case of the Mau Mau

The troubling behavior of lawyers in the residential schools processes is not an isolated example. We have noted how the fact that these cases involve vulnerable old survivors and well-resourced institutional defendants also means that they often attract self-serving lawyers. The second Mau Mau case provides another illustration. In the litigation that followed *Mutua's* ground-breaking settlement, the lawyer misconduct was so grave that it brought an end to the claims of tens of thousands of other Mau Mau survivors, some of whom may well have fared better had they had diligent representation.

its practice" and that "with continual supervision, it can provide service to its clients that is consistent with IAP best practices." *Id.* ¶ 116.

[40] Bronstein, *supra* note 38, ¶ 304.

[41] Jason Proctor, *Tŝilhqot'in Nation Slams "Failure" to Condemn Lawyer for Misconduct on Residential School File*, CBC News (June 11, 2021).

[42] Canada's 15% amounted to $10,541,898.95 in legal fees, which it paid Bronstein for the 624 IAP claims at issue between 2009 and 2015. Bronstein, *supra* note 38, ¶ 90. Since Bronstein also charged an additional 10 to 15% from the claimants, he would have made something close to double this figure on those 624 cases alone. But Bronstein had more than 1,400 IAP claims in total. *See* Fontaine v. Canada (Attorney General), 2015 BCSC 717, ¶ 1 (Can.). If he made the same amount on those claims as on the 624 addressed in the Law Society decision, Canada would have paid him over $23.6 million. Including the contingency he charged claimants, his take from the IAP could easily have exceeded $40 million.

Mutua was a striking victory for survivors of colonial-era violence in Kenya and was seen as a moment of reckoning.[43] As discussed earlier, after two unexpected judicial wins for claimants, the United Kingdom settled with a statement of regret, a memorial, and compensation for over 5,000 survivors. Of the nearly £20 million settlement total, the law firm received £6.6 million, while survivors each received £2,600. Criticisms soon surfaced. The Law Society of Kenya sued the firm, saying that its fees were inflated and "out of proportion."[44] The law firm, which had partnered with the Kenyan Human Rights Commission, pointed out that they had had 20 Kenyan lawyers analyze 15,000 claims and that the United Kingdom legal proceedings took 4 years.[45] The Kenyan courts sided with the law firm, but there was a lingering sense of grievance, fueled in part by the many potential claimants left out of that first case.[46] The lawyers were again described as the "biggest beneficiaries."[47] And although the 30% fees were at the lower end of standard contingency fee spectrum,[48] the amount that went to the firm contrasted uncomfortably with the low individual compensation for castration, torture, and sexual assault. *Mutua* in this way suggests that without attentiveness to individual compensation, it may be difficult to defend law firm fees, even with such an historic win.[49]

Lawyer issues in *Mutua* may have been in a grey area, but there was no such uncertainty in the case that followed. Known as the Mau Mau Group Litigation,[50] from the beginning that second case was marred by lawyer misconduct, fighting over claimants, and infighting among counsel. But there was even more to it. Behind the amassing of nearly 40,000 claimants lurked a complex legal fraud scheme that eventually resulted in bankruptcies, disbarments, and even prison sentences. Mau Mau survivors in Kenya were caught in the crosshairs, and many ended up being revictimized.

[43] *See* Jennifer Balint, *The "Mau Mau" Legal Hearings and Recognizing the Crimes of the British Colonial State: A Limited Constitutive Moment*, 3 Crit. Analysis L. 261 (2016).

[44] *See Law Society of Kenya Sues Top UK Human Rights Firm*, Global Legal Post (Oct. 20, 2014); Patrick Sawer, *British Law Firm "Inflated" Mau Mau Compensation Costs to Taxpayers*, The Telegraph (Oct. 19, 2014).

[45] *See* Martin Plaut, *Who Represented the Mau Mau? Another Side to the Story*, Martin Plaut (Oct. 20, 2014), https://martinplaut.com/2014/10/20/who-represented-the-mau-mau-another-side-to-the-story/.

[46] *See High Court Dismisses Mau Mau Governing Council over Sh2 Billion Settlement*, The Sunday Standard, https://www.standardmedia.co.ke/article/2000135470/court-dismisses-mau-mau-council-over-sh2b-payment (last visited Jan. 26, 2025).

[47] *Mau Mau UK Lawyers to be Paid Sh780 Million*, Business Daily Africa (Dec. 24, 2020); *UK Agrees to Pay Kenya Freedom Fighters $31m*, The East African (Aug. 5, 2020). *See also Mau Mau Legal Fees Uprising*, LawFuel (Oct. 20, 2014).

[48] At the same time, apparently the local lawyers charged nothing and were not paid. *See Mau Mau UK Lawyers to be Paid Sh780 Million*, *supra* note 47.

[49] *Id.*

[50] This is the usual description for the second Mau Mau cases. There are many judgements, but see for example Kimathi & Ors v. The Foreign and Commonwealth Office, [2018] EWHC 2066 (QB) (Eng.).

In 2011, the year of the first promising *Mutua* judgment, law firms Ashton Fox and the brand new and closely allied firm of Tandem Law began paying "introducers" in Kenya, such as Griffin, to register new Mau Mau claimants.[51] As word of an expected *Mutua* settlement surfaced, recruitment efforts for a second case reached a fever pitch, with multiple firms vying for survivors and issuing threats.[52] The contending firms eventually sued each other over tactics, fees, and client transfers.[53] In Kenya, communities expressed concern about "the sudden influx of lawyers competing to sign up clients."[54] The Law Society of Kenya said elderly people had been targeted by imposter lawyers and defrauded of savings. The Kenya Human Rights Commission set up an emergency hotline for the survivors who were targeted: "[w]e said to the old men and women, 'If you are threatened, call us.' Some did and we intervened."[55]

In this second case characterized by a competitive numbers game, there was no *Mutua*-like selection process. Instead, firms were paying for claimants. And in contrast with *Mutua's* limitation to serious physical injuries, the claims they framed were so broad that they extended to arguing that fear itself was a personal injury (which the court rejected).[56] With over 40,000 claimants in the second case, the tactics used to push up numbers in one sense achieved their goal. But the way that these numbers were generated also turned out to be fatal. As the case that became known as the Mau Mau Group Litigation proceeded, the presiding judge noted that, unlike in *Mutua*, the evidence was not carefully vetted and was instead often gathered using questionnaires with leading questions.[57] The result was that, in 2018, after a trial spanning 232 hearing days, oral evidence from more than sixty witnesses, and sixteen reserved judgments, Justice Stewart dismissed the Mau Mau Group Litigation on limitations grounds.[58]

This is not surprising. Our earlier examples—including *Mutua* itself—showed the critical role of credibility in moving judges to set aside obstacles like limitations periods and immunities. And although his dismissal focused on unfairness to the defendant, Justice Stewart repeatedly pointed to the profound evidentiary challenges posed by the huge class. Unlike the narrower classes in ordinary

[51] *See* Abiud Ochieng, *How Court Wars for Mau Mau Billions Have Delayed Payouts*, DAILY NATION (Kenya, July 2, 2020).

[52] *See Lawyers Locked in Epic Battle over Mau Mau Billions as Old Age Claims More Survivors*, DAILY NATION (Kenya, July 2, 2020); Ochieng, *supra* note 51.

[53] *See Lawyers Locked in Epic Battle over Mau Mau Billions*, *supra* note 52; AVH Legal LLP v. Raballa & 8 others (Civil Appeal (Application) 117 of 2018), [2023] KECA 232 (K.L.R.) (Kenya).

[54] Katie Engelhart, *40,000 Kenyans Accuse UK of Abuse in Second Mau Mau Case*, THE GUARDIAN (Oct. 29, 2014).

[55] *Id.*

[56] Kimathi & Ors v. The Foreign and Commonwealth Office, [2018] EWHC 2066 (QB), ¶ 16 (Eng.); Kimathi & Ors v. The Foreign and Commonwealth Office, [2018] EWHC 1305 (QB) (Eng.).

[57] Kimathi & Ors v. Foreign and Commonwealth Office, [2018] EWHC 2066 (QB), ¶¶ 69–76 (Eng.).

[58] *Id.*

group litigation, he noted, here the evidence involved over 40,000 claims, many detention camps, a huge geographical area, and an eleven-year period.[59] And this was not just unwieldy—Justice Stewart pointedly observed that with such a large class "unreliable allegations" were unavoidable.[60] This was unlike *Mutua* where it "was accepted" that the claimants "had suffered torture and other mistreatment at the hands of the colonial administration."[61]

The claimants appealed their loss but that too failed and the appeal court's reasons echoed Justice Stewart's skepticism. They pointed out the contrast between the Group Litigation and *Mutua* where, as they noted, the claimants gave reasons "for showing that their allegations were true (perpetrators, named camps and times of detention were precisely identified)."[62] The Group Litigation law firms were subsequently sued by claimants who argued that there may have been a different conclusion on limitations had the judge had "proper evidence" and a properly vetted test claim before him.[63] And while the court dismissed the claim against the law firms, it did allow that there was an "arguable case that the Defendants did not adduce any, or any adequate, evidence."[64]

These problems with the Mau Mau Group Litigation were not, however, simply the result of bad lawyering, though that was certainly on ample display. As it turned out, there was a complex legal financing fraud behind the push for claims. Shortly before law firm Ashton Fox began amassing Mau Mau claims, it had started to receive money from Cayman-based Axiom, a group litigation investment fund. Within two years, Axiom had funneled over £40 million to Ashton Fox and two other law firms. To keep up with the Axiom loans, Ashton Fox had to continually find new cases, which helps to explain why it was scrambling so hard for the Mau Mau claimants.[65]

But Axiom was later found to be a fraud scheme masterminded by "utterly dishonest" former British policeman and solicitor Timothy Schools.[66] Schools was the principal of Axiom, a director of Ashton Fox and he had an undisclosed interest in all three of the firms that received Axiom funding.[67]

[59] *Id.* ¶¶ 426–28.
[60] *Id.* ¶ 426.
[61] *Id.* ¶ 174.
[62] Kimathi & Ors v. Foreign and Commonwealth Office, [2018] EWCA Civ 2213, ¶ 8 (Eng.).
[63] Murithi & Ors v. AVH Legal LLP (t/a Tandem Law) & Ors, [2023] EWHC 1245 (KB), ¶¶ 104–105 (Eng.).
[64] *Id.* ¶ 29.
[65] *See* Solicitors Regulatory Authority v. Richard Emmett et al., Solicitors Disciplinary Tribunal Case No. 11659-2017 (Eng. Oct. 29, 2018).
[66] *Solicitor Jailed for Fraud Was "Utterly Dishonest,"* Jonathan Goodwin Solicitor Advocate, https://jglaw.co.uk/solicitor-jailed-for-fraud-was-utterly-dishonest/ (last visited May 28, 2025); Sam Tobin, *"Get-Rich-Quick" Scheme: "Egregious" Axiom Fraud Left Investors with Nothing*, Law Society Gazette (U.K., Aug. 11, 2022).
[67] *See Solicitor Jailed for Fraud Was "Utterly Dishonest," supra* note 66.

He used this law firm influence to divert the Axiom loans for personal use, leaving the investors with nothing.[68] Ashton Fox went into receivership in 2013. But just before it did so, it transferred 4,000 Mau Mau claims to Tandem Law. Tandem continued the same approach to acquiring Mau Mau claimants. In quick succession, Tandem and Axiom both also ended up in receivership. The receiver described many of the cases as of "poor quality," but they were more optimistic about the millions that might be realized from the Mau Mau claims.[69] After the law firm failures, Antony Hodari Solicitors acquired all of the Mau Mau claims, which were viewed as promising assets of the failed firms.[70] The amassing continued, and Antony Hodari Solicitors ended up with over 20,000 of the Mau Mau Group Litigation claims, which proceeded under the name Tandem Law in the case that was eventually dismissed by Justice Stewart.[71]

This sorry backdrop, though not mentioned in the decision, helps to explain the apparently careless approach to gathering claims for the Mau Mau Group Litigation. The case was not driven by the interests of the claimants nor the reliability of the evidence but was instead designed to generate as many claimants as possible in a scramble for maximum profit. The Solicitor's Disciplinary Tribunal that disbarred Timothy Schools said that the "whole funding setup was designed to produce the maximum profit for those involved heedless of the interests of the clients."[72] In 2022, Schools was convicted of a number of fraud-related offenses and sentenced to fourteen years in prison.[73] Axiom's investment manager was also convicted of fraud,[74] and at least six solicitors were struck off as a result.[75] Viewed against this backdrop of malfeasance, self-interest and fraud, the skepticism of the court about the nature of the class, and the related reliability of the evidence goes a good way to explaining why the case fared so poorly, despite the fact that there may well have been viable claims among the tens of thousands that came before the court.

[68] *Id.*

[69] GRANT THORNTON, AXIOM LEGAL FINANCING FUND—A SEGREGATED PORTFOLIO OF JP SPC 1; AXIOM LEGAL FINANCING FUND MASTER, SP—A SEGREGATED PORTFOLIO OF JP SPC 4 (BOTH IN RECEIVERSHIP) 6 (Apr. 17, 2015).

[70] *PI Diversification Continues as Anthony Hodari Snaps Up Tandem Law*, LEGAL FUTURES (U.K., May 9, 2013).

[71] *See* Neil Rose, *High Court Dismisses Negligence Claim over Failed Group Action*, LEGALFUTURES (May 30, 2023).

[72] *Lawyer Struck Off for Naming His Firm After a Cash Machine*, ROLLONFRIDAY (Sept. 9, 2014).

[73] Tobin, *supra* note 66.

[74] *Axiom Legal Financing Fund: "David Kennedy Fraud Conviction" (U.K. SFO News Release)*, OFFSHORE ALERT (May 3, 2024), https://www.offshorealert.com/axiom-legal-financing-fund-david-kennedy-fraud-conviction-u-k-sfo-news-release/.

[75] *See* Neil Rose, *Axiom Fund Claims Victim Number Six as Solicitors Who "Misused" £3mis Struck Off*, LEGALFUTURES (Dec. 6, 2016).

A Fine Balance—Maximizing the Good of Lawyers and Minimizing the Bad

We have noted the critical role of law in forcing the uncomfortable confrontation with historic wrongs. Without the lawyers who risked bringing 'far-fetched' claims for survivors of old injustices, it is unlikely that we would be witnessing the current surge of efforts to redress historic wrongs. That is why so many of these lawyers are rightly viewed as heroic figures. But as we have also seen, a closer look reveals the troubling role that lawyers too often play. This raises the question of whether there is some way to maximize the good that lawyers can do in this context while minimizing the risk they also pose.

It seems clear that a significant subset of lawyers *will* behave very badly, which in turn means that it is critical to be on alert for this in cases of historic wrongs. While most lawyers do an admirable job for their clients, it is also clear that cases like these do attract those who will do anything to enrich themselves. And although they may be small in number, their impact is very significant because amassing many claimants is typically at the heart of their profit-making strategy. Moreover, success compounds this risk. The aftermath of the early victories in *Mutua* shows both how serious this 'ambulance chaser' risk is and the damage it can do. This is especially worrisome because survivors of historic wrongs are especially poorly positioned to protect themselves from bad lawyers. The risk of bad lawyer behavior is especially serious where there are redress schemes for survivors like those we saw in the residential schools process, the Australian and Irish redress schemes, and many others. In cases like these, it is critical for both the systems and the individuals to anticipate that some lawyers will try to exploit survivors and to minimize that risk. One way to accomplish this would be to try to keep lawyers away from redress processes like those that we have examined. But while this would eliminate the risk of lawyer exploitation, looking more closely at some purely claimant-driven processes suggests that this solution is not as straightforward as it may seem.

Claimant-Driven Processes

Most redress processes do not make an allowance for private counsel fees, and many explicitly steer claimants away from legal support. Given what we observed in the residential schools process, this is hardly surprising. But while this may seem like an easy solution, the evidence suggests otherwise. In fact, processes that rely on the claimants themselves to complete applications and to navigate processes typically do a poor job of getting the intended benefits to survivors. Because of the challenges in getting information out to possible claimants, the rates of participation tend to be far below the estimates of the class size. Moreover, even the best attempts at plain language application processes are daunting for most survivors. Left to their own devices, claimants struggle to complete the documentation and marshal the necessary documentation. This is compounded by the fact that the processes often end up relying on overly bureaucratic reasoning. The result is that survivors typically fare poorly in claimant-driven processes and failure rates tend to be very high. Ironically, many claimants only secure their promised benefits when they retain lawyers to challenge some of the difficult elements of these processes.

An example is found in California's ground-breaking eugenics compensation program discussed earlier. In 2021, the California State Legislature approved a reparations scheme to "acknowledge the wrongful sterilization of thousands of vulnerable people."[76] The process relied on claimants themselves to fill out the forms and provide the necessary documentation. Despite the fact that advocacy groups helped in drafting the application and assisted with outreach, the failure rate was extremely high. As the program neared its end in 2023, only around 500 of the approximately 800 eligible individuals had applied, and only 108 were approved.[77] This extremely high failure rate prompted public concern, negative media, and eventually lawsuits.[78] Community legal clinics stepped up, observing that the Victim Compensation Board was "acting like insurance adjusters" and finding excuses to deny claims.[79] A woman who had her application rejected four times sued the Compensation Board, and the judge ruled that the board had wrongfully denied her reparations.[80] Shortly thereafter and with more lawsuits pending, the governor extended the appeal window for survivors denied reparations.[81] Ironically, only by turning to lawyers and filing lawsuits were many claimants able to secure benefits under what was supposed to be a claimant-driven process.

These are unfortunately common challenges in such systems. After decades of advocacy, Ireland finally apologized and agreed to compensate women detained in the "Magdalene Laundries"—coercive institutions that imprisoned 'fallen'

[76] Cayla Mihalovich, *"I Would Have Been a Great Mom": California Finally Pays Reparations to Woman It Sterilized*, CALMATTERS (Oct. 7, 2024), https://calmatters.org/justice/2024/10/reparations-forced-sterilization/; *California Launches Program to Compensate Survivors of State-Sponsored Sterilization*, STATE OF CALIFORNIA, https://www.gov.ca.gov/2021/12/31/california-launches-program-to-compensate-survivors-of-state-sponsored-sterilization/ (last visited Jan. 29, 2025).

[77] *See* Cayla Mihalovich, *Survivors of California's Period of Forced Sterilizations Denied Compensation*, KQED (Nov. 1, 2023), https://www.kqed.org/news/11965926/survivors-of-californias-forced-sterilization-denied-reparations.

[78] *See* Mihalovich, *"I Would Have Been a Great Mom," supra* note 76.

[79] Mihalovich, *Survivors of California's Period of Forced Sterilizations Denied Compensation*, *supra* note 77.

[80] *See* Mihalovich, *"I Would Have Been a Great Mom," supra* note 76.

[81] *Id.*

women and used them for forced labor.[82] However, the reparations scheme suffered from many of the same weaknesses as California's forced sterilization process. Survivor advocates pointed to narrow technical exclusions, the absence of support in the application process, and the failure of outreach.[83] The issue was finally referred to the Ombudsman. His report, *Opportunity Lost*, described a "flawed administrative process" where women applied without being told the criteria, where the eligibility criteria were narrowly interpreted, and "where great reliance was placed on the congregations' records" over other evidence.[84] While the scheme was "intended to bring healing and reconciliation," he observed that for some it has "served instead to cause further distress."[85] His report made a number of recommendations, including extending the scheme. Eventually some survivors took the state to court, arguing they were wrongly denied benefits under the scheme. After a decision in their favor, the government relented and extended the scheme.[86] So as in the California process, survivors fared very poorly in the supposedly claimant-centered system. Once again, it was only outside advocacy in the form of an ombudsman's report and litigation that enabled them to secure more of the promised benefits.

Examples like these are very common, which suggests that processes that rely on claimants alone to navigate the system will do poorly in meeting their reparative objectives. Most claimants need some professional support to successfully navigate application processes and marshal the evidence. And as we have seen, they also often need outside advocates including lawyers to ensure that the processes are consistent with reparative aims, rather than the kind of bureaucratic reasoning and technical exclusions that seem to creep into such processes. This suggests that the best approach is likely found neither in the complete absence of advocates nor in a generously funded system for private counsel like the residential schools example. It is probably in recognition of this that there have been some interesting efforts between these two extremes. Though this is an area

[82] However, while the pope apologized in 2018, the religious congregations that run the laundries have all refused to participate in the scheme. *See* Sarah MacDonald, *Extension of Compensation to Women of Ireland's "Magdalene Laundries" Adds to Healing*, Global Sisters Report (Dec. 13, 2018), https://www.globalsistersreport.org/news/trends/extension-compensation-women-irelands-magdalene-laundries-adds-healing-55700.

[83] *See Magdalene Restorative Justice Scheme: Resources for Survivors*, Justice for Magdalenes Research, https://jfmresearch.com/wp-content/uploads/2017/03/Survivor-Guide-to-Magdalene-Restorative-Justice-Scheme.pdf (last visited Oct. 18, 2025).

[84] Office of the Ombudsman, Opportunity Lost: An Investigation by the Ombudsman into the Administration of the Magdalen Restorative Justice Scheme 4 (2017).

[85] *Id.* at 5.

[86] *See* Seosamh Gráinséir, *High Court: Minister's Decision to Exclude Women from Magdalen Compensation Scheme Violated Right to Justice*, Irish Legal News (July 4, 2017); MacDonald, *supra* note 82.

that requires more study, let us look briefly at two other models that may hold some promise.

The Class Counsel Model

Perhaps the most obvious alternative to the extremes outlined above is found in processes that use class counsel to assist claimants. Such counsel are typically private firms specializing in class actions, or group litigation as it is called in places like the United Kingdom. Since class counsel will already be familiar with the claim and the class, there is logic in having them support claimants in any follow-up process. However, there also appear to be serious risks in this model. A prominent illustration is found in the early reparations efforts in what are sometimes called the "Black Farmers" cases.

These decades-long efforts to secure redress for the United States Department of Agriculture's (USDA) historic discrimination against Black farmers in the provision of loans began in the late 1990s with *Pigford v. Glickman (Pigford I)*.[87] The settlement of the first cases resulted in a two-track process with some similarities to the residential schools IAP. However, while residential schools claimants chose their own private counsel and the defendant helped support the cost, in the *Pigford* settlement class counsel was appointed. But the process was nonetheless plagued with similar challenges, including a rush to sign up claimants, very high fees, and egregious failures of representation. The presiding judge described class counsel's performance as "dismal" and bordering on "legal malpractice."[88] He suggested that perhaps they had been too busy filing "three new sister class actions" against the Department.[89] After a series of escalating fines failed to alter their behavior, the court made an emergency request to the American Bar Association Committee on Pro Bono and Public Services to "assemble a team of *pro bono* lawyers to assist class counsel on an emergency basis."[90] Class counsel who made nearly $15 million USD eventually acknowledged that they never intended to meet the deadlines.[91] The Court of Appeal observed that the intended beneficiaries suffered a "double betrayal: first by the [USDA] . . ., and then by their own lawyers."[92] The lead lawyer was described by

87 Pigford v. Glickman, 185 F.R.D. 82 (D.D.C. 1999).

88 Pigford v. Veneman, 144 F. Supp. 2d 16, 17, 19 (D.D.C. 2001).

89 *Id.* at n. 3. *See also* Neely Tucker, *A Long Road of Broken Promises for Black Farmers: USDA Fights Claims After Landmark Deal*, The Washington Post (Aug. 13, 2002).

90 *Pigford*, 144 F. Supp. 2d at 20.

91 Tucker, *supra* note 89.

92 Pigford v. Veneman, 292 F.3d 918, 927 (D.C. Cir. 2002).

claimants as a "snake in the reparations grass," and the major farmers organization brought an action to have the court fire him for incompetence.[93]

Problems with the program have continued as have subsequent attempts to set things right.[94] The most recent such attempt involved a move away from the private counsel model and toward a more public interest delivery model. In 2022, another program was set up to try to address USDA discrimination. The danger of more lawyer fraud loomed large. The USDA website explicitly warned about lawyers and contingency arrangements. It also stressed that there was no filing fee and that lawyers were not needed.[95] It directed claimants instead to organizations that would assist them for free. The process also forced lawyer disclosure. For example, the application form required lawyers to fill out a page stating their fee and certifying that they had informed the claimant that filing is free. Having learned from what went wrong in the past, there are now elements built into the system that help to protect claimants and deter lawyer misbehavior.[96] Attentiveness to the risk of lawyer misconduct can, as this illustrates, help to shape the process in ways that will help to minimize and deter such behavior.

Another more recent example involving the use of class counsel reveals some similar challenges. Canada's $1.47 billion CAD Indian Day Schools Settlement was a follow-up process for those left out of the residential school's compensation processes. No doubt in response to some of the IAP difficulties and for cost reasons discussed earlier, the Day Schools process was based on a written application, awarding from $10,000 for attendance at day schools and up to $200,000 for the most extreme abuse. The Gowling law firm was appointed class counsel, receiving $55 million for its work on the settlement and $7 million for claimant support over four years.[97] However, mirroring the issues in the Black Farmers' process, serious concerns were raised about their service. Many survivors pointed to trouble getting through to class counsel. As a result, they said they just applied for the lowest level of compensation. Some went to court to get the

[93] Tucker, *supra* note 89.

[94] *See* Kali Holloway, *How Thousands of Black Farmers Were Forced Off Their Land*, The Nation (U.S., Nov. 1, 2021).

[95] *See Avoid Scams Related to USDC Financial Assistance for Farmers Facing Discrimination*, U.S. Department of Agriculture (Sept. 2023), https://www.farmers.gov/sites/default/files/documents/farmersgov-factsheet-ira-avoid-scams.pdf. This is only one of many warnings about scams and fraud which indicates how pervasive the concern is. For more on the application process, *see Financial Assistance Application Opens for USDA Farm Owners Who Have Faced Discrimination*, U.S. Department of Agriculture (July 7 2023), https://www.usda.gov/about-usda/news/press-releases/2023/07/07/financial-assistance-application-process-opens-usda-farm-loan-borrowers-who-have-faced.

[96] The IAP did not have fee disclosure or review built into the process. Some lawyers objected to any review of fees and other arrangements as a violation of the lawyer–client relationship, wasting great deal of time, and leaving claimants without protection.

[97] *See* Olivia Stefanovich, *Day School Settlement Has Paid Out $5.7B in Claims. Supreme Court Petition Says Survivors Were Shortchanged*, CBC News (Mar. 5, 2024).

right to be represented by independent counsel rather than class counsel, citing poor service and the "heartless" call center approach.[98] Survivors also asked the courts to reopen the process on the basis that the law firm did not represent their interests, but they were refused.[99] In 2024, Gowling threatened to end its free legal services for claimants unless it received an additional $6 million, and after litigation the parties settled on an additional $3 million.[100] Survivors also raised familiar concerns about the administrator, Deloitte, who they said was acting like these were "insurance claims."[101] As in California's eugenics reparations scheme, here too the concerns resulted in an extension.[102] A lead plaintiff has requested a review, and the former Minister of Justice who signed the deal acknowledged the seriousness of the concerns that survivors had raised.[103]

As these cases suggest, although the class counsel model provides support to plaintiffs while perhaps avoiding the worst elements of the IAP's private lawyer approach, serious problems remain. Even apart from the high cost, the temptation to maximize profit by scrimping on service is an unavoidable risk associated with relying on a for-profit entity to provide support. Moreover, when common problems arise like unduly technical interpretations of the program, the close relationship between the defendant and class counsel makes it unlikely that class counsel will advocate for the claimants' interests. Indeed, it is telling that in these and other examples claimants had to privately pay outside lawyers in order to secure their promised benefits. As a result, while the class counsel model could be improved, it appears to have unavoidable elements that risk jeopardizing survivor support. Let us look finally at an alternative that may hold greater promise in balancing the good of legal counsel while minimizing some of its pathologies.

The Community Legal Center Model

The community legal center model may offer a helpful alternative to paying private counsel or relying on claimants themselves. An experiment with this approach is found in Australia's National Redress Scheme for survivors of institutional abuse. That scheme, which was a key recommendation of the Royal Commission into Child Sexual Abuse, began its ten-year period of operation in 2018. An alternative to civil litigation, it offers survivors compensation,

[98] *See* Patrick Quinn, *Day School Survivors Now Able to Have Individual Legal Representation in Class Action Settlement*, NATION (Can., July 31, 2020).

[99] *See* Stefanovich, *supra* note 97.

[100] *Id.*

[101] *Id.*

[102] *See* Ka'nhehsí:io Deer, *As Extension Period for Indian Day Schools Settlement Comes to an End, Concerns Remain*, CBC NEWS (Jan. 11, 2023).

[103] *See* Stefanovich, *supra* note 97.

counselling support, and the option of "direct personal responses" from the responsible institution. Compensation is capped at $150,000 AUD, which although significant is below the level of at least some court awards. Responsible institutions are required to join the scheme, and those who fail to do so risk losing their charitable status and government grants.[104] Although many institutions have joined the scheme, not all have done so and the government remains a "funder of last resort."[105] As of September 2024, the scheme had received 48,953 applications of the more than 60,000 anticipated.[106] Of these, nearly 20,000 applications had been resolved with 16,665 payments totaling approximately $1.49 billion AUD. More than 27,000 applications are yet to be determined.[107] Concerns about the looming 2028 deadline have prompted extensive media attention.[108] And in a 2024 parliamentary report titled *Redress: Journey to Justice* made a number of recommendations, including extending the timeline for the scheme.[109]

The key elements of the redress scheme are set out in the Royal Commission's 2015 Report on Redress and Civil Litigation. It specified that the scheme should provide funding for "support services and community legal centres to assist applicants to apply for redress."[110] As a result, "Knowmore" became the primary source of information and support for those pursuing redress. Originally established in 2013 to provide free legal advice and assistance for those engaging with the Royal Commission, Knowmore is now an independent charity funded by the Australian government. It provides free advice and support to survivors of sexual abuse, including through the redress scheme.[111] Knowmore also advocates on behalf of survivors in various fora on issues such as civil litigation and criminal justice reform, sexual violence, and human rights.[112] The parliamentary inquiry found that Knowmore was "highly regarded for the

[104] *See National Redress Scheme*, Australia Government Department of Social Services (Nov. 28, 2024), https://www.dss.gov.au/national-redress-scheme. A good overview of the scheme is found in Chapter 2 of Joint Standing Committee on the Implementation of the National Redress Scheme, Redress: Journey to Justice (2024).

[105] *Id.* at 15, 36–37.

[106] Royal Commission into Institutional Responses to Child Sexual Abuse, Redress and Civil Litigation Report 22 (2015); *November/December Update 2024*, National Redress Scheme, https://www.nationalredress.gov.au/node (last visited Jan. 26, 2025).

[107] *November/December Update 2024*, *supra* note 106.

[108] *See e.g.* Christopher Knaus, *"Dangerous Crunch Point": Risk Abuse Survivors Will be Denied Justice Due to Delays in Australia's Redress Scheme*, The Guardian (Nov. 26, 2024).

[109] Joint Standing Committee on the Implementation of the National Redress Scheme, *supra* note 104, at 1–9.

[110] Royal Commission into Institutional Responses to Child Sexual Abuse, *supra* note 106, at 40.

[111] *See Legal Advice & Assistance*, Knowmore, https://knowmore.org.au/services/legal-advice/ (last visited Jan. 26, 2025).

[112] *See Submissions*, Knowmore, https://knowmore.org.au/leading-change/submissions/ (last visited Jan. 26, 2025).

quality of their work." However, they also noted that Knowmore was having difficulty keeping up with the demand associated with the growing number of applicants.[113] Among its many other recommendations, the Joint Standing Committee on Implementation of the National Redress Scheme recommended additional funding to support claimants.[114]

While this approach seems promising, it is not without challenges. Even though there is free legal support, unscrupulous lawyers continue to target survivors. The Joint Standing Committee report devoted significant attention to unethical behavior by private law firms looking to exploit survivors. As in the residential schools and the Mau Mau cases (among others), this included lawyers paying "claim farmers" who badgered survivors with unrealistic promises, pressuring them into signing complex contracts with hidden costs.[115] The Joint Standing Committee saw this issue as so egregious that it asked that governments "*urgently* change laws to address claim farming and exploitative practice."[116] To add another layer of complexity, one of those private firms launched a suit against Knowmore, saying that it "encouraged" claimants to accept lower redress payments rather than going to court.[117] That firm is advertising for clients and is taking the case on a contingency basis. They acknowledge it will take years.

Despite these complexities, the community legal center model that is used in Australia redress scheme does appear promising. The model seems to balance free support for claimants while remaining at arm's length from the process and the funder. There is no doubt that the model is expensive, although it is likely considerably less so than private firm alternatives. And although there are many concerns about the Redress Scheme, the quality of Knowmore's services and supports seems clear. As a result, this appears to be a model that warrants closer study, particularly as it is still in progress. The issues that continue to arise even in this model, especially the continued risk of lawyer misconduct, also help to point toward those areas where there is a special need for attentiveness on the part of the regulators—that is typically courts and law societies or bar associations.

The Need for Vigilance

While most lawyers are professional and serve their clients admirably, our cases make it unfortunately apparent that there is also a subset of self-serving lawyers

[113] Joint Standing Committee on the Implementation of the National Redress Scheme, *supra* note 104, at 21.
[114] *Id.* at 25.
[115] *Id.* at 157–63.
[116] *Id.* at 23 [emphasis added].
[117] Kristian Silva, *Knowmore Legal Taken to Court, Amid Claims Sex Abuse Survivors Were Short-Changed by Compensation Scheme*, ABC News (Austl., Jul. 17, 2024).

who will do almost anything to make money. And though their number may be small, the damage they can do is significant. As we have seen, process design can do a great deal to address this risk, particularly in any compensation processes. At the same time, even the best model will not eliminate all of the risks of lawyer misconduct, which is why it is so important that all parties, but especially courts and regulators, are alive to this danger. While we cannot fully explore the large topic of regulation of lawyer conduct, let us look at some of the issues most relevant to historic injustice cases in order to see what lessons they might yield.

Unethical Recruitment and the Role of Regulators

Aggressive recruitment of survivors, typically through paid third parties, is one of the most vexed issues in historic injustice cases. We saw this at work in a range of cases from residential schools, to the Mau Mau survivors, to institutional abuse cases. Because this kind of misconduct is so pervasive and so egregious, there have been several efforts to address it, most of them aimed at regulatory solutions. As such, it serves as a helpful example to explore the efficacy of regulatory systems in addressing some of the most troublesome issues in historic injustice cases.

Australia's Final Report of the Joint Standing Committee on Implementation of the National Redress Scheme is among the most ambitious efforts to respond to this kind of lawyer misconduct. It devoted an entire chapter to "claim farming," addressing unethical approaches, pressure tactics and misrepresentations, hidden fees, inadequate representation, and other common forms of unethical behavior. As noted, they were so concerned that they asked governments for urgent law reform.[118] They recommended precluding contingency fees and limiting other fees, requiring lawyers to attest that they had informed claimants about the free legal advice, making solicitation an offence, and establishing a set of national standards for lawyers in the redress scheme.[119] Their recommendations echo some of the common elements of other efforts to address unethical recruiting and related issues. The 2022 changes to the Black Farmers compensation process described above, added several similar elements including lawyer attestations to enable better policing of the process. And one of the responses to unethical recruitment and other abuses in Canada's residential schools context was a set of guidelines for recruiting and representing survivors

[118] Joint Standing Committee on the Implementation of the National Redress Scheme, *supra* note 104, at 23 [emphasis added].

[119] *Id.* at 23–24.

that was passed by the Canadian Bar Association and subsequently adopted by a number of provincial law societies.[120]

While recommendations along these lines are certainly helpful, they require the active engagement of regulators, courts, and others if they are to make a meaningful difference. But regulators have often shown themselves to be both slow and weak in this context. The responses to the Australian Joint Standing Committee's urgent recommendations are a sobering example. The Australian federal government said that it supported the recommendations in principle but had "limited levers . . . to regulate private law firms."[121] States and territories did have the regulatory responsibility but indicated they had "limited visibility over the conduct of private law firms."[122] There was a similarly weak response in Canada when the Indigenous Bar Association (IBA) warned about lawyer exploitation of Indigenous peoples and recommended capping fees, revising the code of conduct, and developing mandatory training. They asked for regulation of the high fees some firms were charging Indigenous clients, but the federal government said that might be a conflict of interest. Unreasonable fees, they suggested, would be "best raised with the appropriate provinces and professional associations who regulate firms."[123] But, as noted, the provincial law societies have done a poor job of responding to complaints about even the most egregious lawyer misconduct. As an example, when Indigenous advocates sought to protect future claimants by asking which lawyers had been disciplined in the residential schools process, law societies refused, citing confidentiality. They recommended checking all of the websites of all of the law societies in the country.[124]

Responses like these, particularly with claimants who are so obviously vulnerable, underscore the worry that the approach to regulation does a better job of protecting lawyers than the public. Commentators have long pointed out that self-regulation gives rise to an inherent conflict of interest that results in a "very strong temptation and even likelihood that the lawyers' interests will come before the public interest."[125] This is underscored by the fact that lawyers tend to

[120] *Guidance for Lawyers Acting for Survivors of Indian Residential Schools* (Resolution 07-09-M), Canadian Bar Association (Feb. 17, 2007), https://cba.org/getmedia/1416bc56-0943-49ad-a7f6-0102fee6c677/07-09-MC.pdf (last visited Oct. 18, 2025). *See also* Trevor. C. W. Farrow, *Residential Schools Litigation and the Legal Profession*, 64 U. Toronto L. J. 596 (2014).

[121] Joint Standing Committee on the Implementation of the National Redress Scheme, *supra* note 104, at 162.

[122] *Id.*

[123] Patrick White, *Ottawa Won't Regulate How Lawyers Bill First Nations Clients After Concerns Raised over "Unfair" Fees*, The Globe and Mail (Aug. 17, 2023).

[124] *See* Kathleen Martens, *B.C. Lawyer Facing Residential School Discipline Now Signing Up '60s Scoop Survivors*, APTN News (Dec. 27, 2017).

[125] Anita Balakrishnan, *Self-Regulation: The End of an Era? Lawyer Discipline and the Role of Law Societies*, Canadian Lawyer Magazine (Nov. 14, 2019). *See also* William McDonald, *The Case for*

aggressively protect their own interests when regulators do act. Recall for example, that Knowmore was being sued by a private law firm who said that the free community legal clinic wasn't giving potential claimants an accurate picture of how much they could receive from civil litigation. Similarly, after fifty-seven of Doug Keshen's residential schools clients filed formal complaints against him, the Law Society of Ontario finally ordered him "to receive corrective advice and guidance" and dismissed the case against him.[126] But Keshen struck back against even this weak sanction, suing the Law Society of Ontario and saying it destroyed him. The case was eventually settled.[127] The Law Society of Ontario admitted that the case revealed systemic issues and commissioned yet another report by an Indigenous leader.[128] An advocate for survivors also tried to get the federal Department of Justice to investigate the Law Society of Ontario process, but to no avail.[129] All of this serves as a reminder of how difficult it is to get serious action from regulators even in the face of helpful recommendations that would reduce exploitation of survivors. Instead, governments and regulators often seem to point to each other leaving survivors at the mercy of unscrupulous lawyers.

In this, survivors of historic wrongs are not alone. A study of forty years of American Bar Association recommendations aimed at protecting clients victimized by their lawyers found that many states had declined to adopt the recommendations. And because courts also tended to defer to the state bar associations, clients were left with little protection from lawyer malfeasance. If courts were not going to protect ordinary clients, the author concluded, legislatures should do so.[130] Other work also supports the thesis that the conflicts inherent in self-regulation leave clients with little protection from lawyer misconduct.[131] Legislative interventions therefore are one important route to improving the situation for all "ordinary clients" of legal services, especially those as vulnerable as survivors of historic injustice. Legislative options to protect

Stronger Self-Regulation by Lawyers, THE REGULATORY REVIEW (Apr. 4, 2024), https://www.theregreview.org/2024/04/04/mcdonald-the-case-for-stronger-self-regulation-by-lawyers/.

[126] Elizabeth Raymer, *LSUC Reaches Agreement with Lawyer over Residential School Settlement*, CANADIAN LAWYER MAGAZINE (Apr. 28, 2017).

[127] *Id.*

[128] *See* Jon Thompson, *How the Legal System Failed Residential School Survivors, According to a Major New Report*, TVO (July 3, 2018), https://www.tvo.org/article/how-the-legal-system-failed-residential-school-survivors-according-to-a-major-new-report; REVIEW PANEL ON REGULATORY AND HEARING PROCESSES AFFECTING INDIGENOUS PEOPLES, REPORT OF THE REVIEW PANEL ON REGULATORY AND HEARING PROCESSES AFFECTING INDIGENOUS PEOPLES (2018).

[129] *See* Matt Prokopchuk, *Residential School Survivor Wants Probe of How Ontario Law Society Handled Lawyer's Conduct Review*, CBC NEWS (Jan. 17, 2019).

[130] *See* Leslie C. Levin, *Ordinary Clients, Overreaching Lawyers, and the Failure to Implement Adequate Client Protection Measures*, 71 AM. U. L. REV. 447 (2021).

[131] *See* Anita Anand, *Governance Gone Wrong: Examining Self-Regulation of the Legal Profession*, 21 LEG. ETHICS 99 (2019).

clients and the public interest also quite naturally bring scrutiny to the issue of self-regulation. In an increasing number of jurisdictions, including California, England and Wales, and Australia, legislators have introduced moves away from it.[132] Monitoring the impact of some of those relatively recent changes will be important for determining whether they do a better job of protecting the public interest, especially for vulnerable clients. However, the Australian responses to the Joint Standing Committee's recommendation about the redress process suggest that more may well be needed.

While the topic of lawyer regulation is a large one that cannot be resolved here, lawyer misconduct with extremely vulnerable populations like survivors of historic wrongs underscores hard questions about the best model for the regulation of the legal profession. But since our examples make it obvious that without considerable reform, the regulators of lawyers are unlikely to provide a solution to the exploitation of vulnerable survivors, let us also examine some other avenues to address the issue.

Contingency Fees—The Role of Courts and Others

We have seen that lawyers' own regulatory systems have typically done a poor job of responding to lawyer misconduct. And while legislative interventions are often advocated, to date they have been relatively modest and their impact uncertain. This makes courts especially important in protecting survivors of historic wrongs from lawyer misconduct. In order to examine this role, let us explore an issue that often raises worries about lawyer misconduct in historic injustice cases—contingency fee agreements. We have already noted that while such arrangements can increase access to justice for the disadvantaged, they are also especially likely to be manipulated by lawyers who have expertise and resources on their side. This is why increased regulation is often viewed as important if the benefits are to be realized while avoiding the pathologies.[133] But in the absence of meaningful action from regulators, courts often play an especially critical role for survivors.

In Canada, as we have noted, the issue of how lawyers engage with Indigenous people in historic wrongs cases has been a focus of particular concern. The

[132] *See* Andrew Boon & Avis Whyte, *"Trusted to the ends of the earth?": An Analysis of Solicitors' Disciplinary Processes in England and Wales from 1994 to 2015*, 28 Int'l J. Leg. Prof. 129 (2021); Noel Semple et al., *A Taxonomy of Lawyer Regulation: How Contrasting Theories of Regulation Explain the Divergent Regulatory Regimes in Australia, England and Wales, and North America*, 16 Leg. Ethics 258 (2014).

[133] *See* Noel Semple, *Regulating Contingency Fees: A Consumer Welfare Perspective*, *in* The Justice Crisis: The Cost and Value of Accessing Law 304 (Trevor C.W. Farrow & Lesley A. Jacobs eds., 2019).

Indigenous Bar Association has noted that on multiple occasions courts have found that "unscrupulous lawyers have engaged in exorbitant contingency fee agreements with Indigenous clients."[134] These were not isolated incidents, and as noted, the IBA advocated reforms to existing rules and codes of conduct as well as greater judicial scrutiny.[135] And some courts do seem to be paying attention to the argument that these cases warrant heightened vigilance. This makes them more willing to reject settlements or substitute their own judgment regarding reasonable fees. In a treaty dispute, the Tallcree First Nation agreed to pay a law firm at least 20% of any resolution amount. Just over two years later, a $57.6-million settlement was finalized, and the law firm claimed a fee of $11.5 million. Tallcree contested and the initial reviewing officer found that the fee, though very high for the work done, was "not 'unexpectedly unfair.'"[136] But the chambers judge who reviewed that decision noted that contingency arrangements are often relied on by vulnerable people who would otherwise have no access to justice. The question, he said, was not whether the fee was unexpectedly unfair or clearly unreasonable, but rather whether it was "reasonable."[137] Had the hours been billed, the client would have paid just under $400,000. Since the $11.5 million fee was unreasonable, he revised the fee to $3 million, or roughly 5%. The appeal court agreed that the fee in the contingency agreement was unreasonable and upheld the $3 million fee.

As this suggests, increased vigilance focused on the nature of the class could serve as one important element in limiting the ability of self-seeking lawyers to exploit survivors of historic wrongs. Supervising judges in particular occupy an especially critical role, as we saw in the Black Farmer's settlement. Recall that in the face of egregious failures of representation by class counsel, the exasperated supervising judge tried escalating fines and other measures before finally issuing an emergency call for other legal assistance. Then the courts stepped in again when claimants asked for an extension to the filing deadline because so many were prejudiced by class counsel's negligence. The defendant US Department of Agriculture lawyers conceded that class counsel committed what "appeared to be malpractice," but they argued against an extension, saying that "[c]lients must be held accountable for the acts and omissions of their attorneys."[138] The correct remedy, they insisted, was for the farmers to sue their lawyers. The Court of Appeals disagreed, noting the distinctive nature of this case and refusing to

[134] Indigenous Bar Association, Indigenous Bar Association in Canada 2021–2021 Annual Report 21 (2021).

[135] *Id.*

[136] Tallcree First Nation v. Rath & Company, 2022 ABCA 174, ¶ 34 (Can.), quoting Reviewing Officer.

[137] *Id.* ¶ 39.

[138] Pigford v. Veneman, 292 F.3d 918, 925 (D.C. Cir. 2002).

sanction what it said would be a "double betrayal."[139] It is worth noting that the courts in this case had to be very vigilant not only about class counsel but also about the USDA's own attorneys, an issue we will turn to below. It also illustrates how judges who are attentive to the vulnerability of survivors and willing to keep lawyers in line can play a critical role in ensuring that the benefits of settlements do reach those they were intended for.

Alongside judges, there are often influential others who play a lead role in the implementation of ongoing and complex settlements of the kind often found in historic injustice cases. Such individuals may therefore also be in a position to help to minimize lawyer self-dealing. An example is found in Stuart Eizenstat's role in the Holocaust reparations processes discussed earlier. Among these processes was the settlement of the Nazi-era slave labor lawsuit, which was estimated to include more than a million victims who were forced into labor.[140] The lawyers were paid from a separate fund, but there was consternation about the amount of money that they received, especially in comparison to the victims. A *New York Times* article that covered the issue opened by drawing attention to the discrepancy between the payments to the victims and what the lawyers received:

> Lawyers who represent Nazi-era slave laborers split more than $52 million in legal fees for work on a case that will bring Holocaust victims $5,000 to $7,500 each.[141]

As discussed in the Mau Mau case and other examples, while this metric may not be in the foreground of standard contingency fee analysis, in human rights cases with large numbers of victims the comparison is an important one that must be attended to. But in the slave labor case, Eizenstat defended the fees by pointing out that they were far below the standard 33% contingency fees. The lawyers acknowledged, he said, that such fees would be "unseemly" and so they agreed to take only 1 to 1.5% of the total, although because of the large global amount and number of beneficiaries, the lawyers still received millions. And while criticism remained about the discrepancy between the awards to survivors and the lawyer fees, compared to the vast majority of arrangements, the fee that Eizenstat helped to broker does seem defensible as "both modest and fair."[142] It also seems plausible that in the absence of Eizenstat's guiding hand, there would very likely have been very different fee arrangements.

[139] *Id.* at 927.
[140] *Slave Labour Class I*, Holocaust Victim Asset Litigation (Swiss Banks), https://www.swissbankclaims.com/SlaveLaborI.aspx.html (last visited Jan. 26, 2025); *Slave Labour Class II*, Holocaust Victim Asset Litigation (Swiss Banks), https://www.swissbankclaims.com/SlaveLaborII.aspx.html (last visited Jan. 26, 2025).
[141] Jane Fritsch, *$52 Million for Lawyers' Fees in Nazi-Era Slave Labor Suits*, The New York Times (June 15, 2001).
[142] *Id.*

The fact that Eizenstat was so important in restraining the self-interest of the lawyers illustrates what a crucial role those in such positions can play in protecting survivors. Another example can be found in the residential schools example where lead negotiator and former Supreme Court of Canada judge Frank Iacobucci played an important role in trying to restrain Tony Merchant's fees. He insisted that the settlement agreement require proof that Merchant's firm had indeed done at least $25 million worth of work.[143] Yet, despite Iacobucci's efforts, in an echo of what we have repeatedly seen, law societies sided with the lawyer, not the survivors. Despite the explicit clause in the agreement, it was a struggle to get Merchant to provide the proof required under the settlement agreement's special verification process. Merchant managed to get several provincial law societies to agree with him that the audits were a violation of solicitor–client privilege.[144] On the basis of what records were obtained, the government sued to recover some of the funds, citing "fraud, fraudulent misrepresentation and deceit." A Saskatchewan Court struck out the claim, observing that Canada should not have entered into the agreement if it was so concerned about the legitimacy of Merchant's billings.[145] However, that holding was overturned by the Court of Appeal, and Merchant's appeal was dismissed by the Supreme Court.[146]

While this difficult saga serves as yet another illustration of how aggressive lawyers can be when facing consequences, it also shows the important role that parties like negotiators and others in protecting survivors (and defendants) from lawyer misconduct. Without Iacobucci, it would have been impossible to challenge Merchant's legal fees—indeed, even with him it continued to be an uphill battle across many issues and jurisdictions. And perhaps more than anything else, this example is also a sobering reminder of just why so much vigilance is required on the part of courts, regulators, and those involved in compensation processes. In its absence, as we have seen, unscrupulous lawyers too often end up walking away with the benefits intended for survivors.

The Other Lawyer Problem—'Attack Dog' Institutional Lawyers

The lawyer problems we have discussed so far have focused on private lawyers exploiting survivors for their own benefit. This is a very serious issue and one

[143] *See* Paul Barnsley & Kathleen Martens, *Residential Schools Settlement Agreement Under Fire*, APTN NEWS (May 19, 2016).

[144] *See* Jonathon Gatehouse, *Residential Schools Settlement Enriches Lawyer*, THE CANADIAN ENCYCLOPEDIA (Dec. 16, 2013), https://www.thecanadianencyclopedia.ca/en/article/residential-schools-settlement-enriches-lawyer.

[145] Attorney General of Canada v. Merchant Law Group, 2016 SKQB 25 (Can.).

[146] *Canada (Attorney General) v. Merchant Law Group LLP*, 2017 SKCA 62, leave to appeal to SCC dismissed, No. 37794 (March 15, 2018) (Can.).

that casts a long shadow over many of the landmark cases of historic wrongs. And while the solution to these issues is not simple, there are lessons to be learned. But not all of the problems with lawyers concern their self-interested exploitation of survivors. In many historic injustice cases, the behavior of lawyers on the defendant side is equally problematic. Too often characterized by an excess of zeal and a deficit of ethics, defendant lawyers frequently end up undermining the very institutions they seek to preserve.

When faced with demands to make amends for historic wrongs, most institutions turn reflexively to their lawyers. And whether those lawyers are inside the institution or on retainer, they often end up with the loudest voices not only on legal issues but also on strategy. Looking at the nature of their advice and tactics across many cases suggests another pattern of troubling lawyer behavior that is a mirror image of excessive self-interest discussed above. They too often suffer from excessive institutional protectiveness, focusing on legal tactics and seemingly missing both the ethical issues and the larger context. From the Catholic Church litigation to residential schools issues to the Black Farmers settlements to the Austrian government in *Altmann* among many other examples, myopic institutional lawyers often press legalistic, questionable, and morally tone-deaf arguments that end up working against the larger objectives of the very institutions they are striving to protect. An example is found in how Canadian government lawyers in residential schools cases kept raising the 'bad but legal system' defense, in spite of how it undermined the larger reconciliation efforts of the government they served. In order to explore some of the challenges with institutional lawyering in more depth, let us look more closely at Australia's *Ellis* case, which offers insight into how far lawyers will go to defend their clients and serves as a cautionary tale.

The earlier discussion of how the Catholic Church handled the sexual abuse crisis made it apparent that it had a playbook to avoid liability. As set out in the report of the Pennsylvania Grand Jury, that playbook relied on a series of strategies to keep victims silent, avoid liability, and keep disputes in-house.[147] And when that failed to prevent victims from filing legal actions, there was another kind of playbook that seemed to govern the Church's litigation strategy. It involved a troubling willingness to aggressively exploit every possible defense no matter how far-fetched or morally troubling. An infamous example of this behavior was made the subject of a case study by the Australian Royal Commission into Institutional Child Abuse. Because the Commission examined the Church's legal

[147] *See Pennsylvania Diocese Victims Report*, Office of the Attorney General for the Commonwealth of Pennsylvania (Aug. 14, 2018), https://www.attorneygeneral.gov/report/. *See also Scott Dodd, Pennsylvania Grand Jury Says Church Had a "Playbook for Concealing the Truth,"* The New York Times (Aug. 14, 2018).

behavior in depth and held hearings in which key parties were cross-examined, it provides unique insight into institutional lawyering gone radically wrong.

John Ellis had been sexually abused as a teenage altar boy by Father Duggan. Ellis later became a lawyer and, after a series of struggles associated with his abuse, at the age of forty-one he brought a complaint forward in the "Towards Healing" process of the Sydney Archdiocese. After two and a half frustrating years in what the Royal Commission later found to be a flawed process with an "absence of justice," Ellis turned to litigation. He launched tort and fiduciary duty claims against Cardinal Pell, the Diocese, and the perpetrator.

The law firm Corrs, which had been the Church's lawyers for decades, advised the Church to "vigorously defend" the case, in part to deter others.[148] Cardinal Pell accepted this advice.[149] In the earlier healing process the Church had accepted that Ellis had been abused by Father Duggan, but the lawyers advised challenging that. Before the Royal Commission, the Church lawyer explained as follows:

> . . . the decision to dispute the fact of Mr Ellis's abuse was taken because it put the Trustees and the Archbishop in a tactically advantageous position with regard to the question of prejudice in the limitation hearing. That is, by disputing that Mr Ellis had been abused, the Trustees and the Archbishop could argue that they would suffer severe prejudice if the limitation period was extended because the crucial witness in this case—namely, Father Duggan—was dead.[150]

The Royal Commission was scathing about this tactic—it said the Archdiocese had "contrived an outcome" that would be strategically beneficial in litigation even though they knew and had earlier accepted that he had been abused.[151] The Church maintained this argument throughout the litigation, even though they had become aware of witnesses and other complaints. The decision to dispute the abuse had another effect—the Church's lawyers cross-examined Ellis for two full days, including asking him whether he had previously had "homosexual conduct," to which he replied that he was only fourteen.[152] At the Royal Commission hearing, the Church accepted, "with regret and apology" that the refusal to admit the abuse "resulted in Mr Ellis being cross-examined for longer than was necessary, in circumstances which were hurtful and painful to him."[153]

148 ROYAL COMMISSION INTO INSTITUTIONAL RESPONSES TO CHILD SEXUAL ABUSE, REPORT OF CASE STUDY NO. 8: MR JOHN ELLIS'S EXPERIENCE OF THE TOWARDS HEALING PROCESS AND CIVIL LITIGATION 11 (2015).

149 *Id.*

150 *Id.* at 78.

151 *Id.* at 12.

152 *Id.* at 85.

153 *Id.* at 13.

There was another element to the "vigorous defense" that the Church lawyers advised—they said the Church "should not help" Ellis identify a suitable defendant, and again the Church agreed. Ultimately, it was the failure to identify a proper defendant that defeated Ellis's claim.[154]

The Royal Commission's criticism of how the Church conducted its litigation was devastating. The case study report detailed how the "Archdiocese failed to conduct the litigation with Mr. Ellis in a manner that adequately took account of his pastoral and other needs as a victim of sexual abuse."[155] At the hearing, the Cardinal was forced to concede that they "did not act fairly from a Christian point of view in the conduct of the litigation against Mr Ellis."[156] The *Ellis* litigation strategy also attracted exactly the kind of negative publicity that Cardinal Pell had sought to avoid. A *Sydney Morning Herald* headline reads "Questionable ethics of Cardinal Pell's lawyers go under microscope."[157] The Ellis hearings, it said, were a "spellbinding display of the moral vacuum at the heart of two mighty institutions—the Roman Catholic Church and the law."[158] It recounted how Cardinal Pell pointed to his lawyers, saying they told him it was "a legally appropriate tactic, strategy," while the lawyers said they were acting on instructions from the Cardinal.

The reporting on the case referred to the approach to Mr. Ellis as a "morally bankrupt legal strategy."[159] Commissioners demanded that the lawyers explain how they could countenance these tactics, with the lawyers recognizing that "[t]rying to tear Ellis' legs off in court, when his attackers knew the truth of his claim, should never have happened."[160] It was all part of the "attack dog strategy" that the lawyers advised and the Cardinal accepted, and then the law firm "prosecuted it with gusto."[161] While the firm may have won the case, reporters pointed out how it had failed its duty to the client by not making it clear that the strategy would damage the Church's moral standing and violate its duty to the court.[162] The commentary stressed that lawyers needed to ensure that they didn't let their duty to a client lead them "to lose sight of other important and

[154] Trustees of the Roman Catholic Church v. Ellis, Court of Appeal of the Supreme Court of New South Wales, [2007] NSWA 117 (Austl.), leave to appeal refused [2007] HCA 697.

[155] Royal Commission into Institutional Responses to Child Sexual Abuse, Report of Case Study No. 8, *supra* note 148, at 17.

[156] *Id.*

[157] Richard Ackland, *Questionable Ethics of Cardinal Pell's Lawyers Under Microscope*, The Sydney Morning Herald (Austl., March 27, 2014).

[158] *Id.*

[159] *Pell Was Wrong to Blame the Lawyers, But They Aren't Blameless*, The Conversation (Apr. 2, 2014), https://theconversation.com/pell-was-wrong-to-blame-the-lawyers-but-they-arent-blameless-25016.

[160] Ackland, *supra* note 157.

[161] *Pell Was Wrong to Blame the Lawyers*, *supra* note 159. *See also* Helen Davidson, *Pell: Vigorous Defence Against Ellis Was to Deter Other Claimants*, The Guardian (Mar. 26, 2014).

[162] *Pell Was Wrong to Blame the Lawyers*, *supra* note 159.

overarching duties. Lawyers need to question their judgements, to step back and consider things from different points of view."[163] As the Sydney Morning Herald observed, the moral stature of both the Church and the law suffered from the approach that was taken in the *Ellis* saga.

The Church sustained serious damage from this exposure of its over-zealous pursuit of success by any means. Even beyond the damage to its moral standing, the legal strategy also backfired. As noted earlier, the Royal Commission recommended significant reforms to the law in response to the Church tactics exposed in the *Ellis* case study, including abolishing not only the limitations defense but also the "*Ellis* defence."[164] The Commission also recommended the "Model Litigant" approach in child abuse cases, something designed to preclude exactly the kind of legal tactics used in *Ellis*. This approach employs institutional guidelines "designed to minimise potential re-traumatisation of claimants and to avoid unnecessarily adversarial responses to claims."[165] It also stresses the "obligation on the institution to provide assistance to claimants and their legal representatives in identifying the proper defendant."[166]

As a result of the *Ellis* saga, Cardinal Pell's name became inextricably linked with the Church's unfair tactics in child sexual abuses. A separate Royal Commission report documented how he repeatedly failed to act on other complaints about dangerous priests. Then, in the same year that the Royal Commission released its landmark report, Pell himself was also charged and convicted of child abuse and spent thirteen months in prison, becoming the highest-ranking Catholic official to serve prison time. In 2020, the High Court of Australia overturned the jury verdict, saying there was reasonable doubt, and Pell was set free.[167]

The law firm did not emerge unscathed either. Corrs had had a sixty year relationship with the Catholic Church, and the child abuse work was described as "lucrative" for the firm and the lead church lawyer.[168] But the firm severed the relationship in 2022 amid rumors that its reputation had suffered from its work for the Church, particularly with a generation of lawyers who placed more value on corporate responsibility.[169] Reporting on this issue referred to the firm's role

[163] *Id.*

[164] *See* ROYAL COMMISSION INTO INSTITUTIONAL RESPONSES TO CHILD SEXUAL ABUSE, FINAL REPORT RECOMMENDATIONS 88, 90 (2015).

[165] *Id.* at 90.

[166] *Id.*

[167] *See* Melissa Davey, *George Pell: Australian Cardinal Released from Bail After High Court Quashes Child Sexual Abuse Convictions*, THE GUARDIAN (Apr. 7, 2020).

[168] Hannah Wootton, *Catholic Church's Go-To Lawyer Joins Rival Firm After Corrs Saga*, FINANCIAL REVIEW (Jan. 18, 2023).

[169] *See* Cameron Houston, *Law Firm Dumps Catholic Church After 60 Years, But Won't Say Why*, THE AGE (July 31, 2022), https://www.theage.com.au/national/victoria/law-firm-dumps-catholic-church-after-60-years-but-won-t-say-why-20220729-p5b5ot.html.

in establishing the "*Ellis* defence" and noted that some lawyers were uneasy with the nature of the work the firm did for the Church in child sex abuse cases.[170]

The work of the Royal Commission also generated follow-up in Australia on these issues. In 2016, the Catholic Church's Truth, Justice and Healing Council, which coordinated its response to the Royal Commission "with a commitment to justice and compassion for survivors," released *Guidelines for Church Authorities in Responding to Civil Claims for Child Sexual Abuse*.[171] These guidelines speak directly to many of the issues at play in the *Ellis* saga, including the obligation to assist with identifying a defendant, not contesting a matter that the Church knows to be true, confining the scope of legal proceedings, and limiting both reliance on the limitations defenses and appeals, among other elements.[172] The Guidelines came into effect in Australia in 2016 and are described by the Truth, Justice and Healing Council as designed "to promote justice and consistency in the way Church authorities conduct litigation in relation to child sexual abuse."[173] It is worth noting that the United Kingdom's Independent Inquiry into Child Sexual Abuse came to similar conclusions, among other things recommending that governments and insurers "produce codes of practice for responding to civil claims of child sexual abuse."[174] Adoption of such guidelines, which has been done by some governments in Australia could make a significant positive difference in many cases of historic injustice and not only those involving the Catholic Church.

Despite the pressure to adopt a model litigant approach, the'attack dog' legal tactics appear to remain in use by the Catholic Church at least. An example is found in the use of "stay applications" to circumvent limitations period reforms. This was part of the Church's *Ellis* strategy to circumvent limitations reform. And it appears that across multiple jurisdictions, and despite the censure of the Royal Commission and conflict with its own guidelines, the Church has continued to argue that the death of a perpetrator brings all actions including civil ones to an immediate end, even if the limitations period has not expired. In 2019, the Supreme Court of Canada unanimously rejected that argument. It observed that it would frustrate the objective of limitations reforms that were designed to avoid

[170] *See* Houston, *supra* note 169. *See also* Christopher Niesche, *Partners Defect from Australia's Corrs After Firm Drops Catholic Church*, LAW.COM INTERNATIONAL (Jan. 19, 2023), https://www.law.com/international-edition/2023/01/19/partners-defect-from-australias-corrs-after-firm-drops-catholic-church/?slreturn = 20241226192604.

[171] *Guidelines for Church Authorities in Responding to Civil Claims for Child Sexual Abuse*, THE CATHOLIC ARCHDIOCESE OF CANBERRA AND GOULBURN, https://cgcatholic.org.au/services-directory/professional-standards/guidelines-church-authorities-responding-civil-claims-child-sexual-abuse/ (last visited Jan. 29, 2022).

[172] *Id.*

[173] *Id.*

[174] INDEPENDENT INQUIRY INTO CHILD SEXUAL ABUSE, ACCOUNTABILITY AND REPARATIONS INVESTIGATION REPORT 105 (2019).

the injustice of "allowing sexual abusers to go on with their lives without liability and granting them repose while the victims continue to suffer the consequences of the abusers' actions and remain psychologically unable to act."[175] However, this censure did not stop efforts to use the same tactics in other jurisdictions. A headline in *The Guardian* on the topic sounded eerily familiar—"Strategy used to deny compensation is a 'stark example' of Catholic clergy prioritising the advice of lawyers over moral leadership."[176] The former chief executive of the Australian Church's Truth, Justice and Healing Council described this as an example of the Church again failing to exercise moral leadership, and instead taking "the advice of lawyers and insurance companies, whose job is to tell them what the law states, not what the moral law says."[177] Not long after this reporting, the High Court of New South Wales issued a "damning judgment" on what the press described as the "Catholic Church's tactics in abuse cases."[178] Again the troubling role of lawyers and legal advice attracted concern, with one headline stating "NSW to consider action over Catholic church abuse legal tactics."[179] And the Church's no holds barred approach to litigation seems to have backfired once more as jurisdictions like New South Wales consider enacting legislation to "further restrict churches and other institutions from using stay applications to prevent abuse survivors having their cases heard."[180]

The work of the Australian Royal Commission gave unprecedented insight into the complex dynamics that can develop between defending institutions and their lawyers, particularly with large-scale issues that are very likely to repeat themselves and hence to have broader effects. But while, as we have noted before, the Catholic Church may well be a particularly egregious example of these dynamics, they are by no means alone. Government lawyers too often adopt an excessively defensive stance that can end up undermining not only their own credibility but also the very healing processes set up and funded by the governments they represent. We saw this all too clearly in the residential schools cases and in the Black Farmers processes, and these are but two examples of a much larger phenomenon. They also serve as a reminder for lawyers and institutions that checking one's moral impulses is a critically important element of providing good legal representation.

[175] L'Oratoire Saint-Joseph du Mont-Royal v. J.J., 2019 SCC 35, ¶ 133 (Can.), citing M. (K.) v. M. (H.), [1992] 3 S.C.R. 6 (Can.).

[176] Christopher Knaus, *'It Crucifies You Every Time': The 'Crushing' New Tactic the Church Uses to Block Claims by Abuse Survivor*, The Guardian (Mar. 21, 2023).

[177] *Id.*

[178] Christopher Knaus, *NSW to Consider Action over Catholic Church Abuse Legal Tactics*, The Guardian (Nov. 2, 2023), discussing GLJ v. The Trustees of the Roman Catholic Church for the Diocese of Lismore, [2023] HCA 32 (Austl.).

[179] Knaus, *supra* note 178.

[180] Christopher Knaus, *High Court Decision to Limit Catholic Church Abuse Legal Tactics to Become Law Under NSW Proposal*, The Guardian (May. 8, 2024).

Conclusion

This reminds us that the behavior of lawyers working for institutional defendants can be just as problematic as that of self-interested claimant counsel. In both cases, as we have seen, systems must be devised with the challenges that they pose in mind. In both cases as well, there seems to be a consensus that guidelines to address the unique nature of litigation concerning historic wrongs cases can serve as one important tool to address the issues. At the same time, it is obvious that such measures alone will not be enough. Vigilance and enforcement of more appropriate norms of behavior will clearly continue to be of paramount importance in restraining the excesses that the legal profession seems overly prone to. Courts and regulators need to play a much more active role in cases like these. The absence of an understanding of the appropriate guardrails for mounting a defense also suggests that more proactive measures are also needed, in legal education in particular. The duty to the client, as commentators noted in the *Ellis* case, is not a simple one, and nor is the duty to the court. Lawyers therefore are likely to continue to figure as both heroes and villains in these cases. Continued vigilance will therefore certainly remain essential.

8
How to Make Amends

Introduction

We have traced a radical shift in how we understand the terrible events of our pasts. Violence, abuse, assault, rape, torture, and looting have of course historically been seen as sources of shame and regret. However, despite long-standing efforts of survivors and descendants, they were not generally viewed as injustices. But that has changed. Many of the most grievous problems of our collective pasts are now treated not as simply bad but as injustices. That means that they cannot just be ignored—they demand some effort at repair. This raises the difficult question of how to right wrongs and repair injuries that are so enduring and life-altering.

A decade or two ago, it would have seemed strange to even pose this question, let alone to try to answer it. But while it is certainly daunting to answer, there is nothing unfamiliar about the question itself anymore. New lawsuits are regularly launched for injustices that occurred decades ago. Media ask what we owe for the sins of the past and how we can repair enduring harms, even for wrongs as vast as colonialism and slavery. Museums, galleries, and auction houses review their holdings amid anxiety about how their collections were amassed. Governments around the world ask for forgiveness for the harms they inflicted and strike truth-seeking bodies tasked with understanding long past injustices. Terms like "reparations" and "restitution" are now common in mainstream media and public debate, testifying to the new importance of reparative or reparatory justice. This quest to right old wrongs is making itself felt in institutions large and small, from churches to museums and galleries to auction houses, universities, cities, and states. These difficult issues, as we have seen, elude easy answers and often prompt controversy. But even the strength of the backlash prompted by this focus on righting old wrongs, particularly with the re-election of President Trump in the United States, is itself a kind of testimony to just how central the problems of the past have become.

Alongside the emergence of this new kind of problem, we have also witnessed a wide range of efforts to set things right, to make amends, and to achieve a sense of justice. As these efforts proliferate, there are positive lessons to be learned. To begin with, it is helpful to recall how redress for historic wrongs became a contemporary problem, particularly for the complex category of reparations style

Making Amends for Historic Wrongs. Mayo Moran, Oxford University Press. © Mayo Moran 2025.
DOI: 10.1093/9780190927295.003.0008

claims that will be the focus here. We saw how such claims borrow their legal structure from private law's duty of repair and then amplify that duty with loftier norms drawn from human rights, constitutional and international law, as well as the transformational ambitions of transitional justice. Understanding this background helps to clarify survivors' remedial ambitions and assists in fashioning better responses to these complex claims, which are neither private law, nor ordinary human rights claims, nor transitional justice, but a complex mix of all three.

Some of the remedial elements that we have seen at work in these cases, particularly those drawn from transitional justice, are well explored in other literature. An important example is found in the increasing use of truth-seeking bodies to grapple with a problematic past beyond the context of regime change. We noted this novel use of such bodies beginning in earnest with Canada's Truth and Reconciliation Commission, but now extending to many other such processes, including California's Task Force on Reparations for Slavery, Norway's Truth and Reconciliation Commission on the Sami People, Belgium's investigation of its colonial past, France's recent announcement of a Franco-Haitian body, and many others. While such processes play an important and complex role in cases of historic wrongs, they will not be the focus here, since they are well explored in other literature.[1]

In order to draw out the lessons that are most germane to these cases of redress for historic wrongs, the emphasis here will instead be on those remedial elements that not only pose the greatest challenges but also hold the most opportunities to learn. From both the survivor and the institutional perspective, some of the greatest remedial complexity is found in the reparations-style claims that demand individual compensation—typically interchangeably referred to as reparation or redress. As the most controversial element of repair, money—particularly when it takes the form of individual compensation—looms large in these cases, but its significance is not well understood.[2] Our examples can help to cast some light on this critical aspect of making amends for grievous old wrongs. Alongside money, apology and commemoration are two symbolic elements of repair that are typically also identified as critical. These non-material elements are vitally important to survivors and can either enhance or diminish the value

[1] *See e.g. Truth and Memory*, THE INTERNATIONAL CENTER FOR TRANSITIONAL JUSTICE, https://www.ictj.org/truth-and-memory (last visited May 17, 2025); *The Truth and Reconciliation Commission*, STORTINGET (June 1, 2023), https://www.stortinget.no/en/In-English/About-the-Storting/News-archive/Front-page-news/2022-2023/the-truth-and-reconciliation-commission/.

[2] *See* the discussion in Leora Bilsky, *Transnational Holocaust Litigation*, 23:2 EURO. J. INT'L L. 349 (2012). In the transitional justice context as well, commentators have noted that reparations or individual redress has also been the most neglected element, both in the literature and in practice. *See generally* Pablo de Greiff, *Justice and Reparations*, in THE HANDBOOK ON REPARATIONS (Pablo de Greiff ed., 2006); Special Rapporteur, Pablo de Greiff, *Report of the Special Rapporteur on the Promotion of Truth, Justice, Reparation and Guarantees of Non-Recurrence*, U.N. Doc. A/69/518 (Oct. 14, 2014) [hereinafter de Greiff, *Report of the Special Rapporteur*].

of compensation. Accordingly, we will also explore what our examples can tell us about how to do a better job of this important dimension of redress.

These core elements of repair remind us that, even when they involve many people, at the heart of most cases of redress of historic injustice is the survivor who suffered abuse, assault, torture, rape, or dispossession. These claims focus in the first instance on the individual past and by insisting the wrongdoer make amends to someone for some particular injustice, they bring the survivor, and sometimes their descendants, into sharper focus. And so while the last chapter warned of the dangers of listening too much to lawyers, the overarching theme of this chapter can be seen as the counterpart to that injunction. While there is no simple solution to how to make amends, listening closely to survivors in shaping the core reparative efforts turns out to be critically important to doing a better of redressing historic wrongs.

Listening to Survivors

The importance of listening to survivors should be obvious given that it is their determined pursuit of justice that drives these cases forward, but it is often overlooked. Special Rapporteur Pablo de Greiff's important report on reparations emphasized that, as distinct from broader reparations programs, the right to reparation itself focuses on "measures that may be employed to redress the various types of harms that victims may have suffered."[3] Because as a mechanism of justice, reparation is so sharply focused on survivors, their input is critical to its success. Without it, as we shall see, efforts to make amends tend to founder.

To begin with, it is worth noting that for survivors who have been dehumanized and excluded, having a voice is itself a form of repair because of how it underscores that survivors have rights that matter. When survivors have a sense of agency in the process that furthers reparative justice because of how it conveys the message of respect for their rights of personhood. This is why survivor involvement must be handled with care and why respect for survivors is of the utmost importance. Unfortunately, the value of engagement as a good in itself is often most evident in its absence—particularly when survivors feel that redress processes fail to respect their experiences, perspectives, and needs.

While survivors' voices are important across both material and non-material elements of redress, they loom especially large in the symbolic or non-material

[3] de Greiff, *Report of the Special Rapporteur*, *supra* note 2, ¶ 19. For simplicity, I generally use the term survivor here, although on occasion (such as with many claims related to slavery or colonialism), the claimants may well be the direct survivors and/or descendants.

elements, particularly issues of commemoration and apology. We have already noted how often survivors and descendants raise concerns about not being consulted. In the Mau Mau case, for example, the veterans complained about the memorial planned and designed by the British government, in consultation with the Kenya Human Rights Commission, arguing it did not accurately portray history and the sacrifices of the freedom fighters.[4] Similarly, the Dutch government's apology for its involvement in the slave trade was criticized because the descendants were not consulted.[5] Because survivor and descendant voices matter so much in cases like these, the media often cover their expressions of concern, and the results can undermine the other reparative efforts. Looking more closely at their engagement in these symbolic elements helps to illustrate the critical difference it can make and shows how the results can either support or undermine other redress efforts. We will begin with the important role of survivors in apologies before touching on commemoration.

Apology

Survivors want the wrongdoer to acknowledge the wrong they did and the harm it caused them and to take responsibility for it. This typically takes the form of an apology, ideally as a complement to the critical element of monetary redress that will be discussed below. There is now a very extensive literature on the question of what makes a public apology meaningful as a broader matter, but it is useful to look briefly at some of the key elements that are especially significant in cases of historic wrongs. The de Greiff report emphasizes the justice function that apology can serve by strengthening the status of survivors "not just as victims but as rights holders."[6] The International Center for Transitional Justice similarly notes that apology can be a form of reparation that addresses "moral damages" when it acknowledges the wrongs that were perpetrated and addresses their consequences.[7] The van Boven principles, which address reparation for victims of gross violations of international human rights law, stress the significance of similar elements, noting the importance of "acknowledgement of the facts and acceptance of responsibility."[8] Australia's Report on Redress and Civil Litigation echoes this,

[4] *See* Lydiah Nyawira, *Mau Mau Veterans Disown Freedom Monument*, THE SUNDAY STANDARD (Kenya, Sept. 25, 2015).

[5] *See* Jon Henley, *Dutch PM Apologises for Netherlands' Role in Slave Trade*, THE GUARDIAN (Dec. 19, 2022).

[6] de Greiff, *Report of the Special Rapporteur*, *supra* note 2, ¶ 39.

[7] INTERNATIONAL CENTER FOR TRANSITIONAL JUSTICE, MORE THAN WORDS: APOLOGIES AS A FORM OF REPARATION 8 (2015).

[8] G.A. Res. 60/147, *Basic Principles and Guidelines on the Right to a Remedy and Reparation for Victims of Gross Violations of International Human Rights Law and Serious Violations of International Humanitarian Law*, U.N. Doc. A/RES/60/147 (Dec. 16, 2005).

noting that for survivors to have a "sense of achieving justice," the institution has to make a "genuine apology," which must include a description of the wrong, a clear recognition that it was wrong, and an acknowledgment of the harm it caused.[9]

As this suggests, if apologies are to provide the validation and accountability that are so critical to the survivor's sense of justice, the wrongdoer must clearly acknowledge the wrong that was done, the harm it caused, and take responsibility for it. And in relation to each of these elements, the engagement of survivors is critical to ensuring a positive outcome. In order to draw out some of the lessons surrounding this complex element of redress in the context of historic wrongs, it is helpful to look at how apologies played out in two of the examples discussed earlier, one that has had a more positive outcome and one that has not.

Canada's residential schools context provides a relatively positive example of an official apology for a grievous historic wrong. The example is not all positive however—the well-received 2008 apology was not the first attempt at an official government apology. In 1998, as part of the response to the Report of the Royal Commission on Aboriginal Peoples, the minister of justice delivered a "Statement of Reconciliation" alongside a $350 million healing fund. However, it was not well received, in part because, far from engaging positively with survivors, at the time the government was aggressively litigating their claims in court. Moreover, the reparation component was viewed as inadequate and the apology itself as "a kind of watered-down apology that came from a cabinet minister and not the prime minister."[10]

The 2008 apology was very different. It followed the multibillion-dollar residential schools agreement that, as discussed earlier, created the Truth and Reconciliation Commission as well as two individual compensation systems, among other things. The apology was delivered by the prime minister. It described the wrongs of residential schools and the lasting impact on survivors. It unequivocally acknowledged that it was not only the abuse that was wrong—it was also the whole system itself. The apology was a ceremonial event in the House of Commons that fully incorporated survivors. Phil Fontaine, a survivor and former Grand Chief of the Assembly of First Nations who was the key Indigenous negotiator, was seated at the head of a circle of Indigenous leaders and survivors at the front of the House of Commons. He delivered an official response in full Indigenous regalia, saying "[f]inally we heard Canada say it is sorry."[11] He recounted the

[9] Royal Commission into Institutional Responses to Child Sexual Abuse, Redress and Civil Litigation Report 136 (2015) [hereinafter Redress and Civil Litigation Report].

[10] Katherine Walker, *An Apology: Finally, I Thought, They Understand*, CBC News (June 12, 2008).

[11] *Indian Residential Schools Statement of Apology—Phil Fontaine, National Chief, Assembly of First Nations*, Government of Canada (Sept. 15, 2010), https://www.rcaanc-cirnac.gc.ca/eng/1100100015697/1571589725919.

suffering his people endured in residential schools and said "[t]his day will help us to put that pain behind us" and that it signified a "respectful" relationship going forward.[12] While an apology that addresses such grievous wrongs will understandably be impossible for some survivors to accept, the general response was positive.

A contrasting example involves the 2015 apology to the 'comfort women' As in the residential schools case, the 2015 apology followed earlier efforts. The first effort was the 1993 Kono Statement of the Chief Cabinet Secretary. It acknowledged both Japanese military involvement and that the practice was conducted "generally against" the will of the women.[13] Prime Minister Murayama echoed this statement in 1995:

> The problem of the so-called wartime comfort women is one such scar, which, with the involvement of the Japanese military forces of the time, seriously stained the honor and dignity of many women. This is entirely inexcusable. I offer my profound apology to all those who, as wartime comfort women, suffered emotional and physical wounds that can never be closed.[14]

The vague wording of these 1990s apologies prompted concern. The Asian Women's Fund that accompanied the apologies was also criticized by survivors because the money came from private donations, not from government. Only seven survivors accepted it. The issue continued to foment until 2015, when there was an effort to solve it "finally and irreversibly" with a comprehensive agreement that included $8.3 million for survivor support from the Japanese government and another apology. Delivered by the foreign minister on behalf of the prime minister at a press conference held jointly with the Korean foreign minister, the apology read, in part:

> The issue of comfort women, with an involvement of the Japanese military authorities at that time, was a grave affront to the honor and dignity of large numbers of women, and the Government of Japan is painfully aware of responsibilities from this perspective. As Prime Minister of Japan, Prime Minister Abe expresses anew his most sincere apologies and remorse to all the

[12] *Id.*

[13] *Statement by Chief Cabinet Secretary Yohei Kono on the Result of the Study on the Issue of "Comfort Women,"* DIGITAL MUSEUM: COMFORT WOMEN ISSUE AND THE ASIAN WOMEN'S FUND (Aug. 4, 1993), https://www.awf.or.jp/e6/statement-02.html.

[14] *Statement by Prime Minister Tomiichi Murayama on the Occasion of the Establishment of the "Asian Women's Fund,"* DIGITAL MUSEUM: COMFORT WOMEN ISSUE AND THE ASIAN WOMEN'S FUND (July 18, 1995), https://www.awf.or.jp/e6/statement-08-2.html.

women who underwent immeasurable and painful experiences and suffered incurable physical and psychological wounds as comfort women.[15]

The photos of the press conference show a formal room with government parties on both sides of the table and no obvious involvement of survivors.[16] Shortly after the press conference, Prime Minister Abe restated his oft-repeated remarks that there was no evidence that the women were coerced and that all legal issues had been settled in the 1965 treaty.[17]

The 2015 agreement and the apology immediately ignited controversy. The survivors protested, stressing that it was concluded without input from them. Only thirty-six of the forty-seven women alive at the time accepted funds.[18] Korean Prime Minister Park Geun-hye was called "traitorous" for her role in the agreement and was impeached on corruption charges less than a year later.[19] All of the Korean political parties, which rarely agreed on anything, supported a task force to review the agreement.[20] The task force adopted "a victim-centered approach," and its 2017 report concluded that the agreement mainly reflected the government's position, "without sufficiently listening to, and incorporating, the victims' opinions."[21] United Nations bodies concurred, noting that the agreement lacked the essential "victim-centered approach."[22] Ten years later, the 'comfort women' issue remains unresolved, and the 2015 agreement and apology are prominent among the reasons why.

The contrast between these two apologies makes it abundantly clear how critical it is, both symbolically and substantively, to have meaningful engagement with survivors. Let us begin with the symbolism that is so central in the case of

[15] *Announcement by Foreign Ministers of Japan and the Republic of Korea at the Joint Press Occasion*, Ministry of Foreign Affairs of Japan (Dec. 28, 2015), https://www.mofa.go.jp/a_o/na/kr/page4e_000364.html.

[16] *See* Hyun-Soo Lim, *Not "Final and irreversible": Explaining South Korea's January 2018 Reversal on the "Comfort Women" Agreement*, Yale J Int'l L (Feb. 1, 2018), https://yjil.yale.edu/posts/2018-02-01-not-final-and-irreversible-explaining-south-koreas-january-2018-reversal-on-the.

[17] *See* Sarah Kim, *Abe Denies Forcing of Sex Slaves Again*, Korea JoongAng Daily (Jan. 19, 2016).

[18] *See* Choe Sang-Hun, *South Korean Court Orders Japan to Pay Compensation for Wartime Sexual Slavery*, The New York Times (Jan. 7, 2021); Task Force on the Review of the Korea-Japan Agreement on the Issue of "Comfort Women" Victims, Report on the Review of the Korea-Japan Agreement of December 28, 2015 on the Issue of "Comfort Women" Victims 12–13 (2017).

[19] *See* Jonathan Soble & Choe Sang-Hun, *South Korean and Japanese Leaders Feel Backlash from "Comfort Women" Deal*, The New York Times (Dec. 29, 2015); Celeste Arrington, *South Korea's President Was Just Impeached. This Is What It Means and What Comes Next*, The Washington Post (Dec. 12, 2016).

[20] *See* Arrington, *supra* note 19.

[21] Task Force on the Review of the Korea-Japan Agreement on the Issue of "Comfort Women" Victims, *supra* note 18, at 21, 24.

[22] *Id.* at 22, citing Committee on the Elimination of Discrimination Against Women, *Concluding Observations on the Combined Seventh and Eighth Periodic Reports of Japan*, U.N. Doc. CEDAW/C/JPN/CO/7-8 (Mar. 7, 2016).

non-material elements of redress like apologies. Since it was the Canadian government that had devalued the rights of Indigenous people, it was deeply significant that during the ceremony, Indigenous survivors and their leadership sat at the very center of Parliament. Given that residential schools were an effort to eradicate their culture, it was similarly meaningful that they sat in a circle and wore traditional regalia and brought their own ceremonies into the House of Commons. Indigenous leaders played an active role in responding to the apology, something that symbolically brought them into the circle of power and, as Phil Fontaine noted, established the relationship of respect and equality that was so lacking.

There was a sharp contrast with the 'comfort women' apology. For such an important official act, it was marked by the absence of ceremony and of survivor involvement. The setting was not official but rather a fifteen-minute press conference. The apology was not delivered directly by the prime minister, but by a minister on his behalf. Similarly, it was not delivered directly to the survivors, who waited elsewhere to hear what the televised press conference would say. Media coverage of survivors' responses drew attention to their exclusion. One survivor said, "I want to hear the apology directly," and another questioned "Why don't they ask us? It's about us."[23] Survivors said they felt "left behind."[24] When government officials visited a survivors' organization the next day, they were attacked and asked, "[s]houldn't you meet with the victims before (the agreement)?"[25] The exclusion of the survivors was one central focus of the uproar—an exclusion that was evident in the format of the event itself.

The contrasting approach to survivor involvement was also evident in the substance of the apologies. When survivors are engaged, it helps to ensure that the wording of the apology addresses the core issues. The involvement of Phil Fontaine on behalf of the most important Indigenous organization in Canada was part of the reason that the wording of the apology was responsive to the survivors' desire for justice. It detailed the operation of residential schools, their harms, and the lasting effects for survivors. It clearly stated that it was not simply the abuse that was wrong but rather the colonial mentality that underlay the whole system—"[t]oday, we recognize that this policy of assimilation was wrong, has caused great harm, and has no place in our country."[26] Though this point was extremely important to survivors and Indigenous communities, it was not understood more generally, and its inclusion shows how survivor involvement

[23] *Critical Reflections on "Comfort Women" 75 Years On*, POSITIONS POLITICS, https://positionspolitics.org/nothing-about-us-without-us/ (last visited May 17, 2025).
[24] *Id.*
[25] *Id.*
[26] *Indian Residential Schools Statement of Apology—Prime Minister Stephen Harper*, GOVERNMENT OF CANADA (Sept. 15, 2010), https://www.rcaanc-cirnac.gc.ca/eng/1100100015677/1571589339246.

can help to ensure that the language correctly names the wrongs. Survivor input is similarly crucial to ensuring that appropriate language is used to take responsibility. The language used in the residential schools apology was direct and unequivocal—"[t]he Government of Canada sincerely apologizes and asks the forgiveness of the aboriginal peoples of this country for failing them so profoundly. We are sorry."[27]

Just as the active engagement of survivors positively impacted the residential schools apology, so too did the absence of survivor input make itself felt in the substance of the 2015 Japanese apology. The survivors had long been clear about what mattered to them. They reiterated it after the apology, saying that they wanted the Japanese government to "expressly acknowledge its legal and state responsibility for the war crime of the 'comfort women' of the Japanese military."[28] But the 2015 apology was terse and vague, echoing the 1993 apology's description as "the issue of comfort women, with an involvement of the Japanese military authorities."[29] The 2015 apology also avoided the central issue of coercion, something that was especially concerning given Prime Minister Abe's public expressions of doubt. All of this meant that the acknowledgment of wrong was sorely lacking. On the question of expressly taking responsibility, the apology said only that the state was "painfully aware of responsibilities."[30] The failure to acknowledge legal responsibility was immediately identified by the survivors and the public, who said it was flawed on that score and hence the money was not official reparations.[31] At the news conference, one survivor said, "[t]he agreement does not reflect the views of former comfort women . . . I will ignore it completely."[32] As noted, many of them did not accept the money, and the issue has continued to foment.

Commemoration

As these contrasting examples indicate, the engagement of survivors is one important way to ensure that an apology—something that is critically important to all survivors—goes some distance to fulfilling its role as a symbolic element of reparation. The centrality of engaging survivors can also be seen in another element of symbolic redress—commemoration (also called memorialization).

[27] *Id.*
[28] Task Force on the Review of the Korea-Japan Agreement on the Issue of "Comfort Women" Victims, *supra* note 18, at 22.
[29] *Id.* at 10.
[30] *Id.*
[31] *Id.* at 13.
[32] Choe Sang-Hun, *Japan and South Korea Settle Dispute over Wartime "Comfort Women,"* The New York Times (Dec. 28, 2015).

Commemoration is another feature that is of great significance to survivors, in part as a tribute, especially to those who are lost. But for many survivors, commemoration also especially matters because it responds to their determination to avoid recurrence through a public statement of "never again." This can take many different forms and commonly includes everything from physical memorials to days of commemoration to educational initiatives. Physical memorials can include not only memorials and museums but also preserved sites of atrocity like residential schools and death camps, as well as archives and art installations such as the "comfort woman" statues.[33] Days of commemoration, often part of larger educational initiatives, are also another significant way to memorialize historic wrongs, and there are many such examples, including Australia's "Sorry Day" commemorating the "Stolen Generations," and the two-day gathering "Dublin Honours Magdalenes."[34] Particularly because memorials depict their life-altering experiences, listening to the voices of survivors is essential. In the absence of this, efforts at commemoration easily backfire.

California's redress program for wrongful sterilization discussed earlier provides both negative and positive lessons about the role of survivor engagement in commemoration. The landmark 2021 reparations law provided for individual redress of $35,000 USD, as well as $1 million USD for memorialization.[35] Survivors envisaged a "collaborative and reparative process with the state" where they could meaningfully contribute.[36] The justice significance of this was noted by an advocate who said that "[i]t could have been a historic moment where people who were greatly harmed could have gained a form of reparation through the process and that was lost."[37] Although the memorialization funding was premised on consultation, after being pressed for a more survivor-centered process, the consultation requirements and the budget were both reduced.[38] Survivors who said they felt silenced undertook their own memorialization

[33] *See e.g.* Ed O'Loughlin, *Ireland's Last "Magdalene Laundry" Will Become a Memorial*, The New York Times (Mar. 31, 2022); Genocide Archive of Rwanda, https://genocidearchiverwanda.org.rw/ (last visited May 17, 2025); *Indian Residential Schools National Monument*, Government of Canada, https://www.canada.ca/en/canadian-heritage/services/art-monuments/upcoming-projects/residential-school.html (last visited May 17, 2025); Auschwitz-Birkenau Memorial and Museum, https://www.auschwitz.org/en/ (last visited May 17, 2025); *Statute of Peace*, Project Sonyeo, https://www.projectsonyeo.com/statueofpeace (last visited May 17, 2025).

[34] *See Dublin Honours Magdalenes*, Justice for Magdalenes Research, http://jfmresearch.com/home/restorative-justice/dublin-honours-magdalenes/ (last visited May 17, 2025); *National Sorry Day*, Reconciliation Australia (May 25, 2020), https://www.reconciliation.org.au/national-sorry-day-2020/.

[35] *California Launches Program to Compensate Survivors of State-Sponsored Sterilization*, Governor Gavin Newsom (Dec. 31, 2021), https://www.gov.ca.gov/2021/12/31/california-launches-program-to-compensate-survivors-of-state-sponsored-sterilization/.

[36] Cayla Mihalovich, *Forced Sterilization Survivors Undertake Own Healing After Feeling "Silenced Again" by State*, KQED (Oct. 11, 2024).

[37] *Id.*

[38] *Id.*

projects, but they also did something else—they created a document of examples outlining where survivors were "active partners."[39] One example they pointed to was Los Angeles General Medical Center's "Sobrevivir."[40] The large scale memorial, which incorporates survivor quotes, is described as an "ode to survivors" and part of the state's apology to them.[41] The artist said that the "biggest part for me was to listen and hear from the survivors."[42] These contrasting examples illustrate how survivor involvement creates justice in the process and helps to ensure that the efforts are positively received.

"Dublin Honours Magdalenes" is another example that illustrates the power of survivor engagement in both apology and commemoration. The two-day event was held in Dublin in 2018 in fulfillment of two recommendations of the Quirke Report. First, it provided an opportunity for survivors to meet other survivors, and second, it created a "listening exercise" to gather survivors' views about how the Magdalene Laundries should be remembered. The survivor advocacy group, Justice for Magdalenes, was centrally involved in the planning of the event. People lined the streets of Dublin to welcome survivors, holding up signs that said, "We honour you" and "Welcome home."[43] The impact was profound. One survivor said, "[i]t was like we were being welcomed back into society, or whatever. It's like we were being forgiven. Accepted again, that we're humans."[44]

The president of Ireland hosted survivors at his residence, and although there had already been an official apology, he personally delivered a fulsome apology to them:

> Ireland failed you . . . . I want to acknowledge again the wrong that has been done to you, the pain that has been caused in your lives and the opportunities that have been lost to you as a result of your mistreatment . . . . as President of Ireland, mar Uachtarán na hÉireann, I apologise to you—survivors of the Magdalene regime.[45]

The minister of justice also apologized. The listening exercise was held at the official residence of the Lord Mayor of Dublin, and the results were published.

[39] *Id.*

[40] *Id.*

[41] Gitanjali Mahapatra & Nate Perez, *LA County-USC Medical Center Unveils Artwork Apologizing to Women Forcibly Sterilized There*, LAIST (July 12, 2022).

[42] Yazmin Cruz, *"Art is Healing": LA County General Hospital Monument Tells "Dark Past" of Sterilizations*, SPECTRUM NEWS 1 (Aug 21, 2022).

[43] KATHERINE O'DONNELL & CLAIRE MCGETTRICK, DUBLIN HONOURS MAGDALENES LISTENING EXERCISE REPORT, VOL 1: REPORT ON KEY FINDINGS 11–13 (2020).

[44] *Id.* at 11.

[45] Michael D. Higgins, President of Ireland, *Speech to Women Who Worked at the Magdalene Laundries*, Áras an Uachtaráin (June 5, 2018), https://president.ie/en/media-library/speeches/speech-to-women-who-worked-at-the-magdalene-laundries.

Survivors stressed the critical importance of education and commemoration of what happened as a way of ensuring that it did not happen again.[46] They also spoke in detail about ways to commemorate the laundries, a number of which have been taken up since.[47] Though the event certainly did not resolve all of the outstanding issues, survivors described it as deeply meaningful, not only for them but also for the people of Ireland who rallied behind them. Dublin Honours Magdalenes stands out as an especially ambitious process for engaging survivors in commemoration and apology. It also shows that when done well, such engagement can be deeply meaningful in bringing a measure of justice both to the survivors and to the broader community.

Doing Redress Better

So far, we have focused on the important role of survivor engagement in the more symbolic aspects of making amends. However, individual material redress is also central to the survivors' quest for justice, and their input on this dimension of repair is equally critical to ensuring that redress achieves its aims. As Special Rapporteur de Greiff noted, "[v]ictim participation can help increase the 'fit' between the benefits on offer and the expectations of victims."[48] He goes on to point out that if reparations benefits "fail to speak to their intended targets," they risk "floundering completely," something that holds true for both material and symbolic reparations.[49] The many examples we reviewed earlier underscore this, including the central role of survivors in the multi-decades Holocaust reparations efforts, the role of prominent survivors in negotiating Canada's residential schools agreement, and the deep involvement of the survivor group Justice for Magdalenes in the development of the redress scheme and commemoration efforts.

An example of how meaningful engagement with survivors can help to shape a more effective approach to compensation can be found by looking at another dimension of the redress scheme that came out of the Australia Royal Commission on Institutional Child Sexual Abuse. We have already noted several of the strengths of that scheme which came out of the Commission's *2015 Redress and Civil Litigation Report.* That report was based on a very robust consultation process which, at the time of its publication, included twenty-eight public hearings on case studies, consultation on a wide array of issues through written

46 *See* O'Donnell & McGettrick, *supra* note 43, at 33–40.
47 *Id.* at 41–47.
48 *See* de Greiff, *Report of the Special Rapporteur*, *supra* note 2, ¶ 77.
49 *Id.*

submission, private roundtables, and many other options.[50] The Commission also published a consultation paper and conducted additional hearings before finalizing the report.[51] It also made special arrangements for survivors who might wish to tell their stories. By mid-2015, nearly 10,000 survivors had already chosen to do so, either by participating in private sessions or by providing a written account.[52] While a process like this involves substantial resources, it also helps to avoid the kind of missteps that, as we have seen, so often plague responses that do not sufficiently engage with survivors. In this case, the effort paid off with a positive reception both for the report itself and for the redress scheme that came out of it. Moreover, as with the Dublin Honours Magdalenes event, this illustrates how the consultation process itself can do more than simply enhance the chance of a positive result–the opportunity to share their experiences can also itself serve an important reparative function for survivors.

As these examples illustrate, working closely with survivors and listening to their voices is the most important way to ensure that redress matters and achieves its aims. It is equally true that the failure to do so can undermine redress efforts, even when other aspects of the approach seem significant. With this understanding in hand, let us now look more closely at the question of individual material redress. Though often—and incorrectly—reduced to the issue of money, individual redress is simultaneously of primary importance to most survivors as well as the most controversial and least understood element of making amends for old wrongs.

The Quest for Individual Redress

The sheer determination of survivors to achieve what can realistically be, at best, a modicum of justice is perhaps the most striking aspect of cases of old wrongs. We have repeatedly seen how survivors persist, despite terrible odds and in the face of high costs, both personally and financially. After decades of failed efforts to reclaim property wrongfully held in Swiss banks, Holocaust survivors and their descendants finally brought legal actions in the mid-1990s, half a century after the end of World War II.[53] Similarly undaunted by repeated failures to get redress, in 2020 nearly a century after the events, the last three remaining survivors of the Tulsa massacre launched a new case in public nuisance, even

[50] Redress and Civil Litigation Report, *supra* note 9, at 83–90.

[51] *See* Royal Commission into Institutional Responses to Child Sexual Abuse, Consultation paper: Redress and Civil Litigation Report (2015).

[52] Redress and Civil Litigation Report, *supra* note 9, at 83–84.

[53] *See Overview of the Litigation and Settlement*, Holocaust Victim Assets Litigation (Swiss Banks) (Apr. 14, 2020), https://www.swissbankclaims.com/Overview.aspx.html.

though they were all over one hundred years old.[54] The remaining survivors of the infamous Mount Cashel orphanage continued to pursue their cases against the Catholic Church during the more than three-decade-long court case, despite the loss of many of their members along the way.[55] In 2023, when the Seoul High Court ordered Japan to compensate women held as sexual slaves, a ninety-five-year-old survivor and activist who had endured repeated defeats said that she "wished she could tell all the victims who passed away about the verdict."[56] These survivors refuse to accept defeat, persisting for decades in their quests for justice, carrying on as their compatriots die. The quests shape their lives, and the price they pay is terrifyingly high. What is it that they seek?

Examining the survivors' claims more closely and listening to what they say reveals a strong pattern that can help to fashion better responses to historic wrongs. It is useful to begin by reminding ourselves of the complex genealogy of these claims. Beginning with the Holocaust reparations litigation of the late 1980s, we noted how these novel cases leveraged private law's commitment to repair of wrongs by fashioning claims in tort and unjust enrichment to redress the horrific harms involving mass wrongdoing. They then fortified these demands for repair by drawing in public law norms from human rights and constitutional and international law. In the complex cases of personal injury in particular, the kind of amplified private law claim that resulted often used the language of reparations and reparative or reparatory justice to express their serious nature and complex ambitions.

This complex mix of private law duties of repair and lofty public law norms is reflected in the range of remedies survivors seek. In keeping with the reparative justice underpinnings of these claims, material compensation in the form of either damages to repair harm or return of that which was wrongly taken is a core remedial ambition. We saw this across virtually all of the cases that we examined, from the Holocaust to the Mau Mau veterans to the comfort women. But while reminding ourselves of how these historic injustice cases are founded on private law duties of repair explains some of the significance of material redress, it only takes us part way to understanding what survivors seek. As one commentator put it, "[g]roups that advocate for reparations almost never seek only money."[57] Some of the reasons are obvious. Survivors of historic wrongs wait decades for redress. Their injuries are such that money was never going to do a good job of

[54] *See The Historic Lawsuit*, JUSTICE FOR GREENWOOD, https://www.justiceforgreenwood.org/legal/ (last visited May 17, 2025).

[55] *See* Kevin Clarke, *After 35 Years, a Final Settlement Reached in the Mount Cashel Orphanage Sex Abuse Cases*, AMERICA MAGAZINE (July 11, 2024).

[56] Lou Newton, *Japan Ordered to Compensate Wartime "Comfort Women,"* BBC NEWS (Nov. 23, 2023).

[57] For an excellent article on repair, *see* Olivette Otele & Mawuena Kattah, *The Logic of Slavery Reparations*, THE GUARDIAN (Mar. 31, 2023).

putting them back in the position they were in before their injuries, and with the passage of time even that low possibility of repair diminishes. Think for example of the surviving ninety-five-year-old comfort woman activist, the aged Holocaust survivors, the centenarian survivors of racial violence in Tulsa, the eighty-seven-year old recipient of eugenics compensation from Virginia, and the Mau Mau veterans.[58]

This calls our attention to two distinct features of these claims. First, while money does matter, it matters very differently. Its justice significance comes to the fore, especially in the face of material value that is less able to effect repair. This fact makes the symbolic aspects even of material redress itself matter much more than usual. And second, reflecting how these cases draw in broader norms, as we have seen, the claimants' ambitions stretch beyond ordinary private law damages to the important symbolic elements of redress, especially the issues of apology and commemoration that we have already discussed.

So while survivors care deeply that a serious effort be made to repair their injuries, what counts as repair is complicated in cases such as these. Alongside the growth of issues of historic wrongs, has come an increasing interest in broader conceptions of repair. But it is noteworthy that compensation itself receives so little serious attention, particularly given its importance to survivors and the fact that it is so often subject to critical commentary. However, listening to what survivors say about the form of reparation they seek suggests how we can also do better on this element of making amends. So let us turn to the thorny question of how money matters in cases like these.

Why Money Matters

Money does matter to survivors of the kinds of grievous harms that are at the heart of historic injustice cases. Our examples illustrate the importance survivors place on individual compensation, something that is also reflected in the commentary. As the International Center for Transitional Justice notes, most "victims see reparations as the most direct and meaningful way to obtain justice."[59] Special Rapporteur de Greiff also stresses the importance of the individual "right to reparation" as a key justice measure for victims of gross violations of human rights.[60] Australia's Report on Redress and Civil Litigation similarly identifies "monetary payments as a tangible means of recognising the wrong survivors have suffered"

[58] *See e.g. Virginia Eugenics Victims Compensated for Sterilisation*, BBC NEWS (Feb. 27, 2015).

[59] *Reparations*, INTERNATIONAL CENTER FOR TRANSITIONAL JUSTICE, https://www.ictj.org/reparations (last visited May 17, 2025).

[60] *See* de Greiff, *Report of the Special Rapporteur*, *supra* note 2, ¶¶ 17–18.

as one of the three key elements of effective redress.[61] Despite this, observers and survivors frequently note that reparations to victims are "rarely prioritized" and poorly funded. The de Greiff Report describes the implementation of the right to reparation as "scandalous" and the record dismal.[62] The Salvioli Report points out how survivors that seek reparations "are stigmatized and are perceived as 'taking advantage' of the situation."[63] While these concerns focus on the transitional justice context, there are many echoes of such sentiments in historic injustice cases.

As we have seen, claimants seeking reparations for historic wrongs are often criticized, and individual reparations are typically the most strongly resisted element of efforts at repair.[64] Recall that the first recommendation of the Tulsa Massacre Task Force Report was to extend individual reparations. Although the state accepted many other recommendations, it rejected reparations payments, a decision that led to decades of litigation that lasted until all but two of the survivors were dead. Similar hostility is also apparent in many of the eugenics cases where the apologies often came long before the individual compensation. When Virginia became the first US state to apologize, the governor stressed that it would not lead to reparations payments, although this approach was later revisited.[65] Similarly, Germany stressed that its multibillion dollar settlement with Namibia was not reparations. The Japanese government made the same point in the context of the 2015 agreement with Korea, provoking ire among the survivors and their advocates. In President Macron's 2025 announcement of a truth commission to study the French-Haitian relationship, including the impact of the devastating debt France imposed on the colony to buy its way out of slavery, the topic of reparations was carefully avoided.[66] This fear of making reparations payments certainly springs in part from concern about setting a precedent and the financial implications that could have. However, as cases like Germany and Japan illustrate, even when payments are extended, there is often reluctance to accompany those payments with anything that appears to be an acknowledgment of responsibility. Sometimes this aversion to anything that looks like reparations payments is so strong that institutions continue to fight even when, as in the Tulsa case and many others, the cost of the fight far outweighs the payments themselves.

[61] REDRESS AND CIVIL LITIGATION REPORT, *supra* note 9, at 8.

[62] *See* de Greiff, *Report of the Special Rapporteur*, *supra* note 2, ¶ 6.

[63] Special Rapporteur, Fabián Salvioli, *Report of the Special Rapporteur on the Promotion of Truth, Justice, Reparation and Guarantees of Non-Recurrence*, U.N. Doc. A/HRC/42/45 (July 11, 2019), ¶ 27 [hereinafter Salvioli, *Report of the Special Rapporteur*].

[64] The de Greiff report explores some of the reasons for this. *See* de Greiff, *Report of the Special Rapporteur*, *supra* note 2, ¶¶ 48–63.

[65] See the discussion above in Chapter 6. *See also* Matthew Engel, *State Says Sorry for Forced Sterilisations*, THE GUARDIAN (May 4, 2002).

[66] *See* Roger Cohen & Ségolène Le Stradic, *France Acknowledges Devastating Effect of Debt Imposed on Haiti for Freedom*, THE NEW YORK TIMES (Apr. 19, 2025).

If defendants resist individual reparation payments because of how they link money and responsibility, those very reasons are exactly what make such payments so significant for survivors. While survivors do value the practical benefits of such payments, the much more important reason they matter to survivors springs from how they function as a mechanism of justice. Compensation paid by the wrongdoer to the person they injured helps to fulfill the legal obligation to take the violation of rights seriously.[67] Though such compensation can never actually repair the wrongful harm (something that is also true in many ordinary tort cases), that does not diminish its importance to survivors. The way they speak about it is telling. While insisting on the importance of individual redress and often fighting quite literally to their deaths to secure it, they also say that it is not about the money.[68] They stress that money can never undo the harm they suffered and insist that "no amount of money could ever compensate them for what they had been through."[69] Indeed, this is pointed to by skeptics who sometimes suggest that survivors seeking damages are opportunistic and that accepting damages debases the gravity of the harm in cases like the Holocaust.[70] However, in focusing on the practical effect of money, such comments miss how it serves as the law's mechanism for enacting reparative justice.

When survivors insist that compensation is important and yet that the money itself is not what matters, this apparent ambivalence is better understood as a reflection of the complex relation between money and reparative justice. Reparative justice expressed through mechanisms like private law damages protects the core rights of physical integrity and autonomy—two of the central interests of persons—from wrongful injury. By requiring that those who violate these rights make a serious effort at repair, it affirms the value of personhood.[71] When the Belgian Court ordered that the state pay compensation to the Congolese women forcibly taken from their parents as children, one of the survivors described its significance as follows: "[t]his decision says that we have a certain value in the

[67] *See* de Greiff, *Report of the Special Rapporteur, supra* note 2, ¶¶ 10–11.

[68] *See* LAW COMMISSION OF CANADA, RESTORING DIGNITY: RESPONDING TO CHILD ABUSE IN CANADIAN INSTITUTIONS 92 (2000). *See also* Kathleen Daly, *Money for Justice? Money's Meaning and Purpose as Redress for Historical Institutional Abuse*, in THE SEXUAL ABUSE OF CHILDREN: RECOGNITION AND REDRESS 160 (Yorick Smaal et al. eds., 2016); Katheleen Daly, *Redress for Historical Institutional Abuse of Children*, in THE PALGRAVE HANDBOOK OF AUSTRALIAN AND NEW ZEALAND CRIMINOLOGY, CRIME AND JUSTICE 449 (Antje Deckert & Rick Sarre eds., 2017).

[69] INDEPENDENT INQUIRY INTO CHILD SEXUAL ABUSE, ACCOUNTABILITY AND REPARATIONS: INVESTIGATION REPORT 14 (2019).

[70] *See* the discussion of such arguments in Bilsky, *supra* note 2.

[71] For an account of how private law protects the key incidents of personhood, *see* Mayo Moran, *The Mutually Constitutive Nature of Public and Private Law*, in THE GOALS OF PRIVATE LAW 17 (Andrew Robertson & Tang Hang Wu eds., 2009); HANOCH DAGAN, PROPERTY: VALUES AND INSTITUTIONS (2011); Mayo Moran, *The Problem of the Past: How Historic Wrongs Became Legal Problems*, 69 U. TORONTO L.J. 433 (2019).

world. We are recognised."[72] Like these and so many other survivors of historic wrongs who have suffered injury precisely because their personhood was not valued, individual compensation affirms their status as rights-holders, and, in so doing, vindicates that personhood.

There is also another related reason that individual compensation especially matters in cases like these. Reparative justice is founded on the unique and critical link between what private law theorists sometimes refer to as the "doer" and the "sufferer."[73] The payment of damages to the sufferer is important not only because it is an effort to undo the wrongful harm, but also because by requiring the doer of that harm to pay those damages, it holds him accountable as a matter of justice. So it matters not just that the sufferer receives money, but critically also that the doer of the harm pays it. This correlativity feature and its resulting accountability function is the other deeply connected reason why money matters to survivors as the "most direct and meaningful way" to achieve justice.

The importance of the accountability function of damages is underscored by another feature of cases of historic injustice. While accountability is a primary goal of survivors and a key demand of justice, it is often thought of as criminal responsibility, in other words retributive justice. However, this ignores the fact that its private law counterpart, reparative justice, imposes its own powerful form of accountability for wrongdoing. This especially matters in historic injustice cases because it is often also the only form of accountability available. There are two reasons for this. The first is the obvious point we noted earlier in cases like sexual abuse—because it takes so long for survivors to come forward and longer still to see any success, individual perpetrators are almost always dead. That means that criminal law accountability will rarely be available in cases of historic wrongs.

However, the deeper and more important reason that reparative justice accountability assumes such prominence in these cases turns on the nature of the wrongs. Most of the terrible wrongs involved in cases of historic injustice from the Holocaust to residential schools, eugenics, institutional and colonial violence, and slavery cannot be reduced to the individualist model of accountability found in criminal law. We noted earlier how the wrongs in such cases typically involve many individuals and collectivities acting together, but often in different and overlapping ways. The deeply institutional character of these injustices means that they are not apt to be captured by criminal law responsibility.[74] One survivor who testified before the United Kingdom Independent Inquiry into Child Sexual Abuse spoke of the "need to hold to account the systems" noting

[72] Jennifer Rankin, *Belgium Found Guilty of Crimes Against Humanity in Colonial Congo*, The Guardian (Dec. 2, 2024).

[73] *See* Ernest Weinrib, The Idea of Private Law (2012); Ernest Weinrib, *Causation and Wrongdoing* 63 Chi.-Kent L. Rev. 407 (1987).

[74] *See also* Bilsky, *supra* note 2 for a related argument focused on the use of the class action in transnational Holocaust litigation.

that "the systems failed us."[75] It was this institutional character of such wrongdoing, manifested for example in the Catholic Church sexual abuse crisis, that drove courts to begin to reshape private law responsibility. And as the Canadian Prime Minister acknowledged in his apology for residential schools, it was the system itself that was wrong, not just the abuses within it.

The deeply institutional character of the wrongdoing in historic injustice cases is also the most important reason why reparative justice and its concomitant insistence on the payment of damages matters so much in these cases. It offers both the only and a uniquely meaningful form of legal accountability to survivors of old injustices. This in turn helps to explain what we noted earlier—the apparent ambivalence of survivors who persist for decades in their reparations quests but who also insist that it is "not about the money." The payment of money by the wrongdoer affirms respect for the violated rights of those survivors and hence is the best means by which to meet the demands of justice in these difficult cases.

Improving the Practical Significance of Redress

Recognizing this significance of compensation can help to improve how redress is accomplished. While the elements of redress are deeply interconnected, let us first focus on how to do a better job with individual compensation and complementary services designed for survivors. Attending to how such material forms of redress can best improve the lives of survivors and restore some of the life chances they lost due to wrongdoing is one important element of doing redress well. And when damages are in this way responsive or proportional to the severity of injury, they also play a critical role in the justice function.

The stories of survivors of eugenics, childhood abuse, violence, and wartime sexual abuse, among others, remind us of the terrible lifelong impact of the harm caused in most historic injustice cases. Practically, damages may assist a person prevented from flourishing because of a life-altering wrong to pursue some of what they lost and to find some peace and security, even if very late in life. Survivors of childhood abuse who spoke to the UK Inquiry said that while true repair was not possible, they hoped "that the money might go some way towards helping them to achieve the things that they had been unable to because of the effects of the abuse."[76] Many of them "spoke of a lost education and the inability to live fulfilled lives."[77] The victims of historic wrongs very often count among those who are vulnerable and dehumanized, whether because of race, religion, ethnicity, gender, ability, or myriad other reasons. The wrongs, which

[75] Independent Inquiry into Child Sexual Abuse, *supra* note 69, at vii.

[76] *Id.* at 3.

[77] *Id.*

often targeted the young, were life-altering. Such serious lifelong injuries make it difficult to flourish, and survivors often struggle with physical and mental health issues, addiction, and poverty. The dire quality of life that therefore characterizes many survivors reminds us of the practical value of compensation, even if survivors insist that it is not about the money.

Survivors often use the term "meaningful" to describe compensation that is significant enough to have practical value and hence to achieve some of the justice functions we noted earlier. While this will vary greatly given the context, background entitlements, and the like, and while the views of survivors themselves are especially important here, it is worth noting some important elements that are repeatedly referred to in considering how to ensure meaningful material redress. Survivors who speak about redress often emphasize the importance of elements such as basic necessities, care, and healing, as well as providing access to lost opportunities.[78] For this reason, finding ways to respond to the needs of survivors beyond the rather blunt mechanism of money is an important way to bolster the effectiveness of compensation itself. One way that redress schemes sometimes recognize lifelong impact is through the use of pensions. Pensions were provided to some survivors in a number of Holocaust redress programs, and the survivors of the Magdalene Laundries received weekly pensions from the state in addition to the lump sum that attempted to compensate them to some degree for their forced labor.[79] Recall also that pensions were the form of redress sought by former slaves in the early reparations case of *Johnson v. McAdoo.*

The provision of healthcare and similar supports is another element that is often identified by both experts and survivors as among the most significant non-monetary element of any reparative efforts because it can have such a positive impact on survivors.[80] As Special Rapporteur Salvioli observed, "if there are transformative opportunities for victims in the right to reparation" then this is "one of the measures most likely to deliver on them."[81] Special arrangements to extend health and other therapeutic supports to survivors can therefore improve both the efficacy of the material redress program and enhance the meaning of those elements, in part because of how they serve as an acknowledgment that needs of survivors matter. This is why redress schemes for historic wrongs often make separate provision for extending enhanced supports for healthcare, counseling, and other therapeutic services to survivors.[82]

[78] *See e.g.* REDRESS AND CIVIL LITIGATION REPORT, *supra* note 9, at 13–19.

[79] *See Survivor Guide to the Magdalene Restorative Justice Scheme*, JFM RESEARCH, http://jfmresearch.com/wp-content/uploads/2017/03/Survivor-Guide-to-Magdalene-Restorative-Justice-Scheme.pdf (last visited May 17, 2025).

[80] *See* Salvioli, *Report of the Special Rapporteur*, *supra* note 63, ¶¶ 98–107.

[81] *Id.* ¶ 98.

[82] For instance, as part of the New South Wales reparations scheme for Stolen Generation survivors, the government created a special health card for victims and committed to providing better access to medical services and reducing the cost of medication and gap fees payable under

Thus, in the residential schools example, the Settlement Agreement included arrangements for healthcare and related healing supports, both as independent measures as well as in the compensation process.[83] Australia's Royal Commission also stressed the importance of providing counseling and psychological care as a central element of redress.[84] The provision of increased homecare for Holocaust survivors was also a successful funding priority in the 2023 Claims Conference negotiations with the German government.[85] Similarly, survivors of the Magdalene Laundries pressed for "enhanced health care" as an important element of the redress package. This is a reminder that arrangements aimed at specific practical or therapeutic needs arising from the wrong may be especially meaningful for survivors, as they combine a response to an immediate need with symbolic recognition of the priority the redress program places on survivors' health and well-being.

Precisely because the provision of therapeutic supports for survivors can be very powerful, where material redress fails to accomplish even this, it also threatens to fail not only in its pragmatic purposes but also in its symbolic ones. In this context, it is worth noting the grounds on which commentators on the settlement in *Mutua* criticized the very low set payment the claimants received for extremely egregious violations, including castration and torture. In pointing to the inadequacy of the redress (particularly in contrast with the lawyer's fees, as discussed earlier), commentators emphasized that the payment was not sufficient to cover even minimal needs for the claimants in Kenya, describing it as a "small settlement" that had done "little to alleviate the poverty endured by most Mau Mau veterans."[86] It is also important to note that supports cannot be considered reparation for a wrong if they are nothing more than the ordinary background entitlements.[87] This was evident in the case of the survivors of the Magdalene Laundries who worked hard to secure a special healthcare package

the state's subsidized medical plan. *See* New South Wales Government, Unfinished Business—NSW Government Response to the General Purpose Standing Committee 3 Report into Reparations for the Stolen Generations 12 (2016).

[83] *Indian Residential Schools Resolution Health Support Program*, Government of Canada (July 15, 2022), https://www.canada.ca/en/health-canada/services/first-nations-inuit-health/health-care-services/indian-residential-schools-health-supports/indian-residential-schools-resolution-health-support-program.html. The example of the Magdalene Laundries discussed below provides another illustration.

[84] *See* Redress and Civil Litigation Report, *supra* note 9, at 13–19.

[85] *See Holocaust Survivors Will Continue to Receive Additional One-Time Payments from the German Government Until 2027 as a Result of Claims Conference Negotiations*, Claims Conference (June 15, 2023), https://www.claimscon.org/2023/06/holocaust-survivors-will-continue-to-receive-additional-one-time-payments-from-the-german-government-until-2027-as-a-result-of-claims-conference-negotiations/.

[86] *Kenya's Mau Mau Veterans Seek Royal Redress from Charles III*, Africanews (Aug. 13, 2024).

[87] *See* de Greiff, *Report of the Special Rapporteur*, *supra* note 2, ¶ 36.

only to discover to their deep disappointment that it was "essentially nothing more than" the routine service provided to everyone.[88] This underscores both the practical and symbolic importance of such services and the role they can play in either enhancing compensation payments or detracting from the effectiveness of the entire redress scheme.

Improving the Symbolic Significance of Redress

The practical value of material redress matters to ensuring that it is "meaningful" but, as we have noted, in cases such as these it is the symbolic value of compensation that looms especially large. When reparative justice demands that the wrongdoer make a serious effort at repair by paying the claimant damages, it simultaneously reasserts respect for the plaintiff's violated personhood and demands accountability for that violation from the defendant. In this important sense, "reparations provide recognition to victims not only as victims but, importantly, also as rights holders."[89] The importance of this validation was apparent when one of the few remaining survivors of Virginia's eugenics program received his $25,000 USD reparations payment. The eighty-seven-year old said he "welcomed" it, observing that he couldn't have a family like others and commenting that "they took my rights away."[90] Since damages cannot actually restore many of the plaintiff's lost life chances in historic redress cases, this validation of personhood looms especially large. This is why survivors so often stress the symbolic element of monetary redress and, in particular, its justice significance. Paying close attention to this justice significance can help to increase the symbolic significance of monetary payments.

The justice significance of compensation largely derives from how damages simultaneously strive to repair the survivor's wrongful injury and hold the wrongdoer accountable. To accomplish this, compensation must go at least some distance toward expressing both the severity of the injury and the gravity of the wrong. The Australian Royal Commission drew attention to the survivor side of this proportionality requirement when it noted that one purpose of monetary payments was to provide "tangible recognition of the seriousness of the hurt and injury that a survivor has suffered."[91] And as discussed compensation will only be responsive to the gravity of the survivor's injury if it is "meaningful" such as, for example, when it makes "a tangible difference in survivors' lives."[92] Where it

[88] Patsy McGarry, *Magdalene Survivors Insist State Not Fulfilling Terms of Compensation Scheme*, The Irish Times (June 25, 2020).
[89] de Greiff, *Report of the Special Rapporteur*, *supra* note 2, ¶ 9.
[90] *Virginia Eugenics Victims Compensated for Sterilisation*, *supra* note 58.
[91] Redress and Civil Litigation Report, *supra* note 9, at 225.
[92] *Id.* at 223.

meets this threshold, redress may well be considered to go some distance toward expressing the seriousness of the harm suffered by the claimant.

The other proportionality demand focuses on the relationship between the redress and the defendant's accountability for the wrong. Given how important the element of accountability is to survivors and how elusive anything like repair of harm will be, this aspect of the compensation is especially significant. That is why discussions of individual reparations often emphasize the need for compensation to be proportionate to the gravity of the wrong. The Australian Royal Commission noted for example how "monetary payments can provide acknowledgment and recognition of the abuse" on the part of the institution.[93] As de Greiff puts it, because redress payments are part of an effort to achieve justice and not mere "mechanisms to distribute indemnities," the "magnitude of the reparation needs to be commensurate with the gravity of the violations" as well as with the impact on the survivor.[94] And so even though redress will often be largely symbolic, a trivial payment could never serve as a mechanism of reparative justice because it could not express the gravity of the wrong. As the Australian Royal Commission pointed out, a "'token' amount would not provide any sense of justice to many survivors."[95] While in cases of historic injustice like the ones that we examined, the wrongs are so grave that it will never be possible to achieve anything like true proportionality, attending to the expressive role of damages in providing a "sense of justice" can help to ensure that they fulfill some of their important symbolic function.

At the same time, the elements of any redress program are, as noted above, deeply connected with each other. And given how important symbolic significance is in cases like these, the meaning of material benefits will be affected not only by these issues related to the quantum of and nature of those benefit but also by a number of other factors. The success of redress programs, in that sense "depends on a complicated judgement about the appropriateness of the whole complex of benefits and of the relationship between them and other justice measures."[96] Recall that compensation functions as a mechanism of justice because of how it connects the survivor's injury and the defendant's wrongdoing. This is what lends it its unique ability to simultaneously vindicate the rights of the survivor and hold the wrongdoer to account. It also makes the question of who pays the damages especially critical.

[93] *Id.* at 224.

[94] de Greiff, *Report of the Special Rapporteur*, *supra* note 2, ¶ 47. The Salvioli Report also stresses that compensation must be "reasonable and proportional." *See* Salvioli, *Report of the Special Rapporteur*, *supra* note 63, ¶ 44(e).

[95] REDRESS AND CIVIL LITIGATION REPORT, *supra* note 9, at 222.

[96] de Greiff, *Report of the Special Rapporteur*, *supra* note 2, ¶ 78.

The fact that the wrongdoer pays the damages to the person they injured is what in ordinary civil cases ensures that compensation functions as "not just a mechanism for the transfer of goods but part of an effort to achieve justice."[97] But the question of who pays becomes more complicated in historic injustice cases because the liability is almost always institutional. And while institutional liability assists claimants by ensuring a viable defendant to pursue, that pragmatic gain has sometimes turned out to be a double-edged sword. The multiplicity of defendants alongside considerations about the ability to pay means that very large institutional defendants such as governments are especially likely to assume the role of key funders. Yet because the compensation carries so much of the symbolic weight in these cases, it also matters to the justice function of redress that all culpable defendants are involved.

The redress program that perhaps strikes the best balance in this regard is Australia's National Redress Scheme for survivors of institutional child sexual abuse. The federal government remains a funder of last resort, thereby protecting claimants. However, institutions that are named by claimants are required to "join the scheme to provide redress to people who experienced child sexual abuse while in the care of their institution."[98] Institutions who refuse to join are publicly named and risk losing access to government grants and their charitable status.[99] This requirement of institutional participation in a government-backed scheme ensures that survivors can access compensation without the strain of civil litigation. At the same time, because it insists on the participation of the relevant institutions, it also incorporates the important relation between the survivor and the institution that is at the heart of the reparative justice function of redress.

While the ideal approach to redress from a justice perspective is to have the culpable parties pay the damages, as Australia's regime largely does, this will not always be possible. In such cases, it is important to find ways to ensure that responsible parties play some significant role, ideally both in the funding arrangements and also in the process itself. A number of redress schemes have tried to balance these issues by simultaneously ensuring secure funding for survivors but also financially engaging other responsible actors. The success here is more mixed. In Canada's Indian Residential Schools Settlement Agreement, the vast majority of the funding came from the federal government, which was one of the responsible parties. But the residential schools

[97] *Id.* ¶ 23.

[98] *See National Redress Scheme*, Australian Government Department of Social Services, https://www.dss.gov.au/national-redress-scheme (Nov. 28, 2024).

[99] *Id. See also National Redress Scheme Grant Connected Policy*, Australian Government Department of Social Services (Feb. 11, 2025), https://www.dss.gov.au/national-redress-scheme/national-redress-scheme-grant-connected-policy.

were actually run by churches, and much of the abuse was carried out by their clergy or employees. Many of the punitive school policies were devised and executed by the church administrators, who also typically received the reports of abuse. All of this meant that some church contribution to redress mattered from the perspective of reparative justice. The settlement agreement was responsive to this, in part by requiring contributions from each of the churches. The Presbyterian, United, and Anglican Churches all fulfilled those commitments, and indeed some went beyond them. However, the Catholic Church reneged, saying it had raised only a fraction of the amount it had committed.[100] When this came to light, survivors expressed outrage and betrayal, particularly in light of the fact that the Catholic Church had run the vast majority of the schools, and it was, at the time, the only one of the parties that had refused to apologize.[101]

The Magdalene Laundries is an even more extreme example. Following decades of survivor advocacy, government reports, and a recommendation by the United Nations Committee Against Torture, Ireland established a compensation fund to provide redress to survivors. The government and the public expected that the religious orders that had run the laundries would contribute.[102] However, they flatly refused to contribute to the fund despite the wealth they had garnered.[103] Their continued professions of regret and desire for healing were greeted with indignation and outrage. One commentator captured the core problem, noting that this refusal meant that the redress scheme offered "[c]ompensation, yet still no justice."[104] As this illustrates, a primary wrongdoer's refusal to contribute can erode the symbolic value of compensation and undermine its justice function, even though the material value remains unchanged.

The importance of a financial contribution from a primary wrongdoer is also apparent in the episode of the "comfort women" case that involved the poorly received Asian Women's Fund. As discussed earlier, that 1995 fund was described as a "quasi-public, quasi-private initiative designed to meet the

[100] *See* Gloria Galloway & Sean Fine, *Other Churches Escape Residential-School Settlement Obligations in Wake of Catholic Deal*, The Globe and Mail (Apr. 27, 2016).

[101] *See* Stephanie Taylor, *Canada Agreed to "Forever Discharge" Catholic Entities from Raising $25M for Residential School Survivors*, CBC News (Aug. 20, 2022).

[102] *See Nuns Say They Will Contribute Nothing to Magdalene Laundry Survivors' Compensation*, National Secular Society (July 16, 2013), https://www.secularism.org.uk/news/2013/07/nuns-say-they-will-contribute-nothing-to-magdalene-laundry-survivors-compensation; *Four Religious Orders in Ireland Refuse to Pay Survivors of Catholic-Run Magdalene* Laundries, CBC News (July 16, 2013).

[103] *See* Sue Lloyd Roberts, *Demanding Justice for Women and Children Abused by Irish Nuns*, BBC News (Sept. 24, 2014); Norma Costello, *Survivors Remember Ireland's Magdalene Laundries*, Al Jazeera (Mar. 6, 2016).

[104] Marelise van der Merwe, *Compensation, Yet Still No Justice for Magdalenes*, Daily Maverick (July 7, 2015).

nation's moral—but not legal—obligation to victim- survivors."[105] However, the money came from private donations, not the government. Upon learning of this, survivors expressed anger and betrayal, and many refused to accept money from the fund, which was dissolved in 2007.[106] As one survivor put it, "[w]hy should I accept money from private Japanese people? They were also victims during the war."[107] The fact that the money did not come from the culpable party led even financially needy survivors to reject it.[108] It is also telling that the episode of the "Asian Women's Fund" effort is widely viewed as undermining, rather than furthering, the effort to resolve this difficult issue.

As these examples illustrate, because the payment of damages serves as a mechanism of justice linking the survivor and the wrongdoer, the source of the money may well matter as much as the amount. Indeed, as our examples and others show, sometimes the way that money is offered can even undermine the point of offering it in the first place. Beyond this, the way that material reparations are offered can also enhance the value of the financial payments themselves. We noted above how, under certain circumstances, the issuing of public apologies may help to serve this function. The Australian redress scheme also made provision for a "direct personal response" from the responsible institution, should the survivor so desire. Such direct personalized apologies can be very meaningful for survivors who are willing to engage with the culpable institutions, and there are numerous examples of such personal responses to survivors among our examples. As the Independent Assessment Process (IAP) for Canada's residential schools developed, the government began to incorporate "direct personal responses" into the hearings themselves in appropriate cases. At the conclusion of the hearing, the representative apologized directly to the claimant on behalf of the government, something described by many claimants as especially significant.[109] And as noted in the Dublin Honours Magdalene Days, survivors found it very meaningful when both the Irish president and the minister of justice directly apologized to them, even though there had already been an official apology.

Because the symbolic significance of compensation looms so large in these cases, tailoring the remedy to be as responsive as possible to the nature of the wrong is another way to enhance the significance of material redress. An example is found in Canada's Band Reparations Settlement, discussed above, which is an

[105] Kim Puja, *The Failure of the Asian Women's Fund*, in DENYING THE COMFORT WOMEN: THE JAPANESE STATE'S ASSAULT ON HISTORICAL TRUTH 93, 96 (Nishino Rumiko et al. eds., 2018).

[106] *See* Norimitsu Onishi, *Japan's 'Atonement' to Former Sex Slaves Stirs Anger*, THE NEW YORK TIMES (Apr. 25, 2007).

[107] *Id.*

[108] *See* Sang-Hun, *Japan and South Korea Settle Dispute*, *supra* note 32; Onishi, *supra* note 106.

[109] INDEPENDENT ASSESSMENT PROCESS OVERSIGHT COMMITTEE, INDEPENDENT ASSESSMENT PROCESS FINAL REPORT 70 (2021).

effort to respond to the wrong of trying to destroy Indigenous languages and culture. It does so by funding projects proposed by Indigenous bands to reinvigorate those languages and culture. Georgetown University's decision to extend preferential admissions treatment to the descendants of those who it sold as slaves is another interesting example, although one with complications. At first blush, this benefit looks promising because giving descendants access to the institution built on the slavery of their ancestors has an aptness that has the potential to be symbolically significant. But Georgetown initially provided no funding to descendants, an omission that was striking because their wrong was a financial transaction that greatly benefited the university.[110] This troubling omission led the students to vote to provide funding themselves.[111] Then, as discussed earlier, in 2021 the Jesuits made a $100 million commitment to the Descendants Truth & Reconciliation Foundation to support the lifelong education of descendants, anti-racism advocacy, and elderly descendants.[112] Georgetown has also indicated that it plans to raise more money for this effort.[113]

Some of the efforts to redress the destruction of Black homes and neighborhoods also serve as interesting efforts to tailor benefits to the particular wrong. Cases like the Tulsa Massacre and Rosewood are illustrations of the much wider impact of historic racial violence on Black communities, which is one reason why California's Reparations Task Force recommended affordable housing preferences and favorable loan arrangements for displaced African Americans.[114] The fact that these are referred to as "right to return" policies calls attention to the nature of the wrong.[115] The City of Evanston's housing grant program discussed earlier is another example of a benefit tailored to the wrong. That "Restorative Housing Program" is designed to acknowledge "the harm caused

[110] *See* Adrienne Green, *Why Georgetown's Offer Falls Short*, The Atlantic (Sept. 1, 2016); Haley Samsel, *Their Ancestors Were Slaves Sold by Georgetown. Now They're Going to School There*, USA Today (June 9, 2017); Erika Gonzalez, *Slaves' Descendants Demand Reparations from Georgetown U*, NBC Washington (Oct. 31, 2018).

[111] *See* V.P. Franklin, *Georgetown Students Demonstrate How Reparations Can Be Made to African-American Students*, ACLU (May 22, 2020), https://www.aclu.org/news/racial-justice/georgetown-students-demonstrate-how-reparations-can-be-made-to-african-american-students.

[112] *See* Iman Milner, *Georgetown University and the Jesuits Have Made a $27 Million Pledge to the Descendants of Enslaves People Sold to Fund the School*, National African-American Reparations Commission (Sept. 19, 2023), https://reparationscomm.org/reparations-news/georgetown-university-27m-reparations/; *Georgetown Continues Support as Jesuits, Descendants of Enslaved Form Foundation*, Georgetown University (Mar. 15, 2021), https://www.georgetown.edu/news/georgetown-continues-support-as-jesuits-descendants-of-enslaved-form-foundation/.

[113] *See* Susan Svrluga, *Jesuits, Georgetown Give $27M to Fund for Descendants of Enslaved People*, The Washington Post (Sept. 13, 2023).

[114] *See Chapter 22: Policies Addressing Housing Segregation & Unjust Property Takings, in* Task Force to Study and Develop Reparation Proposals for African Americans, The California Reparations Report 681 (2023).

[115] *See Chapter 22: Policies Addressing Housing Segregation & Unjust Property Takings*, *supra* note 114; *Sydney* Johnson, *Thousands of SF Homes Destroyed Decades Ago During "Redevelopment" Could Be Rebuilt for Lower-Income Residents*, KQED (Sept. 13, 2023).

to African-American/Black Evanston residents due to discriminatory housing policies and practices and inaction on the part of the City."[116] Washington State's Covenant Homeownership program is another tailored form of reparations for the impact of racially restricted covenants. It provides interest-free down payment loans for those affected and their descendants.[117] Like the above examples, these efforts illustrate how developing a thoughtful connection between the wrong and the remedy can contribute to the symbolic significance of redress and can therefore enhance its justice impact.

The Choice of Mechanism

The cases that we have looked at also show how greater attentiveness to the demands of reparative justice can assist in better shaping not only various elements of material redress but also the mechanism itself. This is particularly relevant because so many redress programs are large, as illustrated in examples from the Holocaust reparations cases to residential schools and institutional abuse cases to programs such as those for survivors of eugenics and wartime violence. Large scale redress programs like these are common alternatives to civil litigation and, as we have seen, they may arise out of settlement or through a political process. Having discussed some of the substantive elements of such programs, let us now briefly look at what we can learn about the mechanism itself.

It is useful to begin by noting the wide array of forms that monetary redress takes. We saw this in examples that included single set payments in cases like *Mutua* and eugenics redress programs, complex pension arrangements like those in some of the slave labor and Holocaust cases, and highly differentiated awards based on very individualized assessments such as those in the Canadian residential schools process and the Australian redress schemes. Looking more closely at these examples in light of some of the reparative justice considerations discussed above suggests some lessons for the choice of mechanism.

In the case of broad systemic injuries where the harms are very similar, a set payment accompanied by appropriate other measures may well be the most desirable approach. Such systems are relatively easy, efficient, inexpensive to administer, and impose comparatively minimal burdens on claimants. In theory, at least this means that a greater proportion of the available funds will be directed

[116] *Evanston Local Reparations*, City of Evanston, https://www.cityofevanston.org/government/city-council/reparations (last visited June 22, 2025).

[117] *See Covenant Homeownership Program*, Washington State Housing Finance Commission, https://wshfc.org/covenant/ (last visited June 22, 2025). The program is facing a legal challenge. *See* Fair v. Walker, Fair for All, https://www.fairforall.org/fair-v-walker/ (last visited June 22, 2025).

to survivors rather than to administration of the system or to legal counsel. Because of these advantages, the set payment or a variation is a common choice in historic redress cases. The Japanese internment cases, most eugenics cases, *Mutua*, the Common Experience Payment in the residential schools context, the Magdalene Laundries lump sum program, and the Rosewood redress program are but a few among many examples. And this approach can be apt, particularly where there is a systemic or legalized wrong and the plaintiffs suffered very similar injuries. The Common Experience Payment in the residential schools case and the Magdalene Laundries lump sum redress program, for example, both relied on a fairly straightforward set of entitlement categories based on the amount of time survivors spent in the institution. In both cases, the wrong was being forced into the institution itself and so the survivors experienced very similar wrongs, with the main distinguishing factor being the amount of time they were forced to stay in the oppressive institution. Factors such as these can make a relatively undifferentiated scheme responsive to the wrong. Similarly, in the Rosewood example, where all of the property was destroyed, the redress scheme specified a fixed amount of $150,000 for living survivors alongside a fund to be distributed to those who could show they had owned property in Rosewood.[118] Fixed payments were also used in many of the eugenics cases discussed above, including in North Carolina, Virginia, Alberta, and California.[119] As cases like these suggest, similar set payments may be responsive to the nature of the wrong done if the nature of the injury is relatively similar across the affected population.

But while relatively simple set payments may often be a desirable mechanism for redress, many historic wrongs are highly personalized. In such cases, responsiveness to reparative justice suggests that the redress should be also more personalized. We have already noted that if the remedy is to be meaningful for the survivor, it is important that it reflect the gravity of both the harm and the wrong. Where the harms at issue are extremely variable, a set remedy cannot accomplish this. Set payments may even threaten to trivialize the harm because they lack the personhood validating quality that is so important to redress, particularly with highly personal injuries such as sexual violations, severe physical abuse, and torture. This is why differentiated assessments are more common in the programs to redress institutional abuse such as those in Ireland and Australia and in the residential schools abuse cases.

However, while recognizing that highly individualized injuries generally require more individualized remedies in order to serve their justice function, mechanisms

[118] *See generally* C. Jeanne Bassett, *House Bill 591: Florida Compensates Rosewood Victims and Their Families for a Seventy-One-Year-Old Injury*, 22 FLA ST. U. L. REV. 503 (1994).

[119] *See e.g.* Richard Craver, *N.C. Eugenics Victims Projected to Get Final State Compensation Payment Soon*, WINSTON-SALEM JOURNAL (Jan. 17, 2018); *Virginia Eugenics Victims Compensated for Sterilisation*, *supra* note 58.

that are highly individualized also pose challenges. Survivors generally say that it is important that more serious injuries are compensated accordingly.[120] Yet the more fine-grained the system, the more it will require the recounting of painful personal details. Highly calibrated systems also generate more complexity. The distinctive inquisitorial adjudication approach of the IAP for residential schools survivors was highly individualized to both gravity of wrong and its impact on the individual. The process sought to give court level damages and to meet the need to test credibility and eligibility within a claimant-centered model. But survivors still had to give difficult testimony, and while the fine-grained categories did ensure remedies tailored to individual circumstances, they also created a system that was difficult to navigate. Health support workers and legal counsel sought to address this, but as we saw reliance on legal counsel raised another set of issues. So while some individualization is necessary if survivors of such variable injuries are to have a sense of vindication, the IAP illustrates that too much individualization also creates challenges for survivors. A less-calibrated system may well have moved more swiftly and put more of the resources into the hands of the survivors.

In this regard, the Australia Redress Scheme provides an interesting alternative. The scheme is perceived by survivors as relatively successful, as discussed above. Because the defendant institution usually pays the damages, it does incorporate the unique link between claimant and wrongdoer that is so critical to reparative justice. And while the scheme does not aim at IAP-style "court level damages," the awards of up to $150,000 do seem significant enough to serve the acknowledgment function and make a tangible difference in the claimants' lives. And especially relevant here, the Australian scheme arguably strikes a better balance from a process point of view. This is because while it is sensitive to the gravity of the harm, it adopts a more streamlined approach that focuses on the type of abuse and uses relatively simple categories. The decision rules are also fairly straight-forward, specifying, for example, that with multiple kinds of abuse, the decision-maker will apply the highest monetary payment.[121] Although complexities undoubtedly remain, this system appears to strike a good balance between the need to differentiate when the abuse itself is extremely varied and the need for simplicity, transparency, and efficient use of resources.

Conclusion

This final chapter focused on the role of individual redress, especially in monetary form, because that is where many of the most difficult issues arise. It is

[120] Redress and Civil Litigation Report, *supra* note 9, at 234–35.
[121] Australian Government, National Redress Guide 5.1 (2025).

also the place where there are important lessons to be learned. I will close our discussion with one overarching thought about the importance of ceremony. As we have noted throughout this chapter and beyond, material reparation—whether by monetary redress or by restitution—is deeply symbolic for survivors. We have traced in particular the justice significance of damages payments, something that is often missed in the discussions of reparations or redress payments. This reminds us that at the end of the day, the survivors are looking for a form of vindication and reintegration, as so many of them have said, into the fold of those whose lives matter. On the other side of the reparative justice relationship, institutions looking to atone for the wrongs of their forebearers are seeking a form of redemption. Because, as we have also noted, these issues are at bottom about establishing relationships of respect and right relations, the ceremony of redress in whatever form it takes is an especially important opportunity.

The importance of such ceremony is apparent across many examples. We noted this, for instance, in the 2008 Canadian residential schools apology with its symbolic integration of Indigenous peoples, language, and culture into the very core of Canada's institutions of government. In that same year, Australia also apologized for the Stolen Generations at an event at Australia Parliament House. Like the Canadian apology, the Australian one also included survivors who played an active role in the event, responding as well as presenting a glass "coolamon" as a symbol of a "new covenant" with "dignity, hope and respect" as the guiding principles. The public packed both the Great Hall and the lawns outside Parliament House.[122] Recall as well how the "Dublin Honours Magdalene" event showed what a profound difference more public facing elements could have. Another Australian example is a powerful illustration of the same point. In the country's first national Walk for Reconciliation with the Indigenous peoples, 250,000 people walked across Sydney Bridge. It remains the largest demonstration of public support for a cause in the country's history.[123] Similarly, the ceremonies of return of the Benin Bronzes, from Edinburgh to Berlin and beyond, all engaged the dispossessed communities and stressed that return was part of confronting a troubling past and building new respectful relations going forward. The 2022 ceremony of return in Berlin, for example, was led by the German foreign minister and the Nigerian ambassador and highlighted the role

[122] *See Apology to Australia's Indigenous Peoples*, PARLIAMENT OF AUSTRALIA, https://www.aph.gov.au/Visit_Parliament/Art/Icons/Apology_to_Australias_Indigenous_Peoples (last visited June 22, 2025).

[123] *"Justice and Equality for All"—2000: Walk for Reconciliation Across Sydney Harbour Bridge*, DIGITAL-CLASSROOM, https://digital-classroom.nma.gov.au/defining-moments/walk-reconciliation (last visited June 22, 2025).

of restitution in accomplishing both "historical justice and renewed cooperation."[124] As we confront these difficult problems, keeping these core ambitions in mind and recognizing the weight of symbolism and the importance of respect will take us a considerable distance toward resolution.

Any discussion about how to do a better job of making amends for such vast historic wrongs is bound to be all too brief. Nonetheless, as examples proliferate, there are useful lessons to be learned about how we can do better. The most important point, as noted throughout, is to listen to the survivors. Sometimes the adversarial nature of the litigation backdrop that lurks behind these cases or the fear of liability prevents the engagement that could be so important. At the same time, we have seen how working with survivors can lead to transformative effects, both for the survivors and for the larger society and that is ultimately what these difficult cases aim at.

[124] Sania Bounaas, *Return of Benin Bronzes Sparks Renewed Diplomatic Engagement*, Berlin Global (Apr. 15, 2025), https://www.berlinglobal.org/index.php?return-of-benin-bronzes-sparks-renewed-diplomatic-engagement#:~:text = The%20restitution%20ceremony%2C%20hosted%20by,center%20for%20international%20cultural%20diplomacy.

Index

For the benefit of digital users, indexed terms that span two pages (e.g., 52–53) may, on occasion, appear on only one of those pages.

www.ingramcontent.com/pod-product-compliance
Ingram Content Group UK Ltd.
Pitfield, Milton Keynes, MK11 3LW, UK
UKHW011915140726
473290UK00009B/72/J

9 780190 927264